SPSS® for Windows™
Professional Statistics™
Release 5

Marija J. Norušis / SPSS Inc.

SPSS Inc.
444 N. Michigan Avenue
Chicago, Illinois 60611
Tel: (312) 329-3500
Fax: (312) 329-3668

SPSS Federal Systems (U.S.)
SPSS Latin America
SPSS Benelux BV
SPSS UK Ltd., New Delhi
SPSS UK Ltd.
SPSS GmbH Software
SPSS Scandinavia AB
SPSS Asia Pacific Pte. Ltd.
SPSS Japan Inc.
SPSS Australasia Pty. Ltd.

For more information about SPSS® software products, please write or call

Marketing Department
SPSS Inc.
444 North Michigan Avenue
Chicago, IL 60611
Tel: (312) 329-3500
Fax: (312) 329-3668

SPSS® for Windows™: Professional Statistics™, Release 5

ISBN 0-923967-50-8

Library of Congress Catalog Card Number: 91-068311

Preface

SPSS® for Windows™ Release 5 is a powerful software package for microcomputer data management and analysis. The Professional Statistics option is an add-on enhancement that provides additional statistical analysis techniques. The procedures in Professional Statistics must be used with the SPSS for Windows Base system and are completely integrated into that system.

The Professional Statistics option includes procedures for discriminant analysis, factor analysis, cluster analysis, proximity and distance measures, reliability analysis, and multidimensional scaling. The algorithms are identical to those used in SPSS software on mainframe computers, and the statistical results will be as precise as those computed on a mainframe.

SPSS for Windows with the Professional Statistics option will enable you to perform many analyses on your PC that were once possible only on much larger machines. We hope that this statistical power will make SPSS for Windows an even more useful tool in your work.

Installation

To install Professional Statistics, follow the instructions for adding and removing features in the Installation Instructions chapter of the *SPSS for Windows Base System User's Guide*. (Hint: Double-click on the SPSS Setup icon in the SPSS program group.)

Compatibility

SPSS Inc. warrants that SPSS for Windows with the Professional Statistics option is designed for personal computers in the IBM PC and IBM PS/2 lines with at least 4MB of random access memory and 20MB of hard disk space, running Windows 3.0 or later. These products also function on closely IBM-compatible hardware.

Serial Numbers

Your serial number is your identification number with SPSS Inc. You will need this serial number when you call SPSS Inc. for information regarding support, payment, a defective diskette, or an upgraded system.

The serial number can be found on the diskette labeled Setup that came with your Base system. Before using the system, please copy this number to the registration card.

Registration Card

STOP! Before continuing on, *fill out and send us your registration card*. Until we receive your registration card, you have an unregistered system. Even if you have previously sent a card to us, please fill out and return the card enclosed in your Professional Statistics package. Registering your system entitles you to:

- Technical support on our customer hotline
- Favored customer status
- New product announcements

Of course, unregistered customers receive none of the above, *so don't put it off—send your registration card now!*

Replacement Policy

Call Customer Service at 1-800-521-1337 to report a defective diskette. You must provide us with the serial number of your system. (The normal installation procedure will detect any damaged diskettes.) SPSS will ship replacement diskettes the same day we receive notification from you.

Training Seminars

SPSS Inc. provides both public and onsite training seminars for SPSS for Windows. All seminars feature hands-on workshops. SPSS for Windows seminars will be offered in major U.S. and European cities on a regular basis. For more information on these seminars, call the SPSS Inc. Training Department toll-free at 1-800-543-6607.

Technical Support

The services of SPSS Technical Support are available to registered customers of SPSS for Windows. Customers may call Technical Support for assistance in using SPSS products or for installation help for one of the warranted hardware environments.

To reach Technical Support, call 1-312-329-3410. Be prepared to identify yourself, your organization, and the serial number of your system.

If you are a Value Plus or Customer EXPress customer, use the priority 800 number you received with your materials. For information on subscribing to the Value Plus or Customer EXPress plan, call SPSS Software Sales at 1-800-543-2185 or 1-312-329-3300.

Additional Publications

Additional copies of all SPSS product manuals may be purchased separately. To order additional manuals, just fill out the Publications insert included with your system and send it to SPSS Publications Sales, 444 N. Michigan Avenue, Chicago IL, 60611.

Note: In Europe, additional copies of publications can be purchased by site-licensed customers only. Please contact your local office at the address listed at the end of this preface for more information.

Lend Us Your Thoughts

Your comments are important. So send us a letter and let us know about your experiences with SPSS products. We especially like to hear about new and interesting applications using the SPSS for Windows system. Write to SPSS Inc. Marketing Department, Attn: Micro Software Products Manager, 444 N. Michigan Avenue, Chicago IL, 60611.

About This Manual

This manual is divided into two sections. The first section provides a guide to the various statistical techniques available with the Professional Statistics option and how to obtain the appropriate statistical analyses with the dialog box interface. The second section of this manual is a syntax reference guide that provides complete command syntax for all the commands included in the Professional Statistics option. Most features of the system can be accessed through the dialog box interface, but some functionality can only be accessed through command syntax.

This manual contains two indexes: a subject index and a syntax index. The subject index covers both sections of the manual. The syntax index applies only to the syntax reference section.

Contacting SPSS Inc.

If you would like to be on our mailing list, write to us at one of the addresses below. We will send you a copy of our newsletter and let you know about SPSS Inc. activities in your area.

SPSS Inc.
444 North Michigan Ave.
Chicago, IL 60611
Tel: (312) 329-3500
Fax: (312) 329-3668

SPSS Federal Systems
12030 Sunrise Valley Dr.
Suite 300
Reston, VA 22091
Tel: (703) 391-6020
Fax (703) 391-6002

SPSS Latin America
444 North Michigan Ave.
Chicago, IL 60611
Tel: (312) 329-3556
Fax: (312) 329-3668

SPSS Benelux BV
P.O. Box 115
4200 AC Gorinchem
The Netherlands
Tel: +31.1830.36711
Fax: +31.1830.35839

SPSS UK Ltd.
SPSS House
5 London Street
Chertsey
Surrey KT16 8AP
United Kingdom
Tel: +44.932.566262
Fax: +44.932.567020

SPSS UK Ltd., New Delhi
c/o Ashok Business Centre
Ashok Hotel
50B Chanakayapuri
New Delhi 110 021
India
Tel: +91.11.600121 x1029
Fax: +91.11.6873216

SPSS GmbH Software
Steinsdorfstrasse 19
D-8000 Munich 22
Germany
Tel:+49.89.2283008
Fax: +49.89.2285413

SPSS Scandinavia AB
Sjöängsvägen 21
S-191 72 Sollentuna
Sweden
Tel: +46.8.7549450
Fax: +46.8.7548816

SPSS Asia Pacific Pte. Ltd.
10 Anson Road, #34-07
International Plaza
Singapore 0207
Singapore
Tel: +65.221.2577
Fax: +65.221.9920

SPSS Japan Inc.
Gyoen Sky Bldg.
2-1-11, Shinjuku
Shinjuku-ku
Tokyo 160
Japan
Tel: +81.3.33505261
Fax: +81.3.33505245

SPSS Australasia Pty. Ltd.
121 Walker Street
North Sydney, NSW 2060
Australia
Tel: +61.2.954.5660
Fax: +61.2.954.5616

Contents

2 Factor Analysis 47

3 Cluster Analysis 83

1 Discriminant Analysis

Gazing into crystal balls is not the exclusive domain of soothsayers. Judges, college admissions counselors, bankers, and many other professionals must foretell outcomes such as parole violation, success in college, and creditworthiness.

An intuitive strategy is to compare the characteristics of a potential student or credit applicant to those of cases whose success or failure is already known. Based on similarities and differences, a prediction can be made. Often this is done subjectively, using only the experience and wisdom of the decision maker. However, as problems grow more complex and the consequences of bad decisions become more severe, a more objective procedure for predicting outcomes is often desirable.

Before considering statistical techniques, let's summarize the problem. Based on a collection of variables, such as yearly income, age, marital status, and total worth, we wish to distinguish among several mutually exclusive groups, such as good credit risks and bad credit risks. The available data are the values of the variables for cases whose group membership is known, that is, cases who have proven to be good or bad credit risks. We also wish to identify the variables that are important for distinguishing among the groups and to develop a procedure for predicting group membership for new cases whose group membership is undetermined.

Discriminant analysis, first introduced by Sir Ronald Fisher, is the statistical technique most commonly used to investigate this set of problems. The concept underlying discriminant analysis is fairly simple. Linear combinations of the independent, sometimes called predictor, variables are formed and serve as the basis for classifying cases into one of the groups.

For the linear discriminant function to be "optimal," that is, to provide a classification rule that minimizes the probability of misclassification, certain assumptions about the data must be met. Each group must be a sample from a multivariate normal population, and the population covariance matrices must all be equal. The section "When Assumptions Are Violated" on p. 36 discusses tests for violations of the assumptions and the performance of linear discriminant analysis when assumptions are violated.

The sections "Selecting Cases for the Analysis" on p. 3 through "Sum of Unexplained Variance" on p. 27 cover the basics of discriminant analysis and the SPSS output using a two-group example. Extending this type of analysis to include more than two groups is discussed beginning in "Three-Group Discriminant Analysis" on p. 27.

1

Investigating Respiratory Distress Syndrome

Respiratory distress syndrome (RDS) is one of the leading causes of death in premature infants. Although intensive research has failed to uncover its causes, a variety of physiological disturbances, such as insufficient oxygen intake and high blood acidity, are characteristic of RDS. These are usually treated by administering oxygen and buffers to decrease acidity. However, a substantial proportion of RDS infants fail to survive.

P. K. J. van Vliet and J. M. Gupta (1973) studied 50 infants with a diagnosis of RDS based on clinical signs and symptoms and confirmed by chest x-ray. For each case they report the infant's outcome—whether the infant died or survived—as well as values for eight variables that might be predictors of outcome. Table 1.1 gives the SPSS names and descriptions of these variables.

Table 1.1 Possible predictors of survival

Variable	Description
survival	Infant's outcome. Coded 1 if infant died, 2 if infant survived.
sex	Infant's sex. Coded 0 for females, 1 for males.
apgar	Score on the Apgar test, which measures infant's responsiveness. Scores range from 0 to 10.
age	The gestational age of the infant measured in weeks. Values of 36 to 38 are obtained for full-term infants.
time	Time that it took the infant to begin breathing spontaneously, measured in minutes.
weight	Birth weight measured in kilograms.
ph	The acidity level of the blood, measured on a scale from 0 to 14.
treatmnt	Type of buffer administered (buffer neutralizes acidity). Coded 1 for THAM, 0 for sodium carbonate.
resp	Indicates whether respiratory therapy was initiated. Coded 0 for no, 1 for yes.

Some dichotomous variables such as *sex* are included among the predictor variables. Although, as previously indicated, the linear discriminant function requires that the predictor variables have a multivariate normal distribution, the function has been shown to perform fairly well in a variety of other situations.

In this example, we will use discriminant analysis to determine whether the variables listed in Table 1.1 distinguish between infants who recover from RDS and those who do not. If high-risk infants can be identified early, special monitoring and treatment procedures may be instituted for them. It is also of interest to determine which variables contribute most to the separation of infants who survive from those who do not.

Selecting Cases for the Analysis

The first step in discriminant analysis is to select cases to be included in the computations. A case is excluded from the analysis if it contains missing information for the variable that defines the groups or for any of the predictor variables.

If many cases have missing values for at least one variable, the actual analysis will be based on a small subset of cases. This may be troublesome for two reasons. First, estimates based on small samples are usually quite variable. Second, if the cases with missing values differ from those without missing values, the resulting estimates may be too biased. For example, if highly educated people are more likely to provide information on the variables used in the analysis, selecting cases with complete data will result in a sample that is highly educated. Results obtained from such a sample might differ from those that would be obtained if people at all educational levels were included. Therefore, it is usually a good strategy to examine cases with missing values to see whether there is evidence that missing values are associated with some particular characteristics of the cases. If there are many missing values for some variables, you should consider eliminating those variables from the analysis.

Figure 1.1 shows the SPSS output produced after all the data have been processed. The first line of the output indicates how many cases are eligible for inclusion. The second line indicates the number of cases excluded from analysis because of missing values for the predictor variables or the variable that defines the groups. In this example, two cases with missing values are excluded from the analysis. If cases are weighted, SPSS displays the sum of the weights in each group and the actual number of cases.

Figure 1.1   Case summary

```
     50 (Unweighted) cases were processed.
      2 of these were excluded from the analysis.
          2 had at least one missing discriminating variable.
     48 (Unweighted) cases will be used in the analysis.


Number of cases by group

                 Number of cases
    SURVIVAL  Unweighted     Weighted  Label
        1            26         26.0   DIE
        2            22         22.0   SURVIVE

     Total           48         48.0
```

Analyzing Group Differences

Although the variables are interrelated and we will need to employ statistical techniques that incorporate these dependencies, it is often helpful to begin analyzing the differences between groups by examining univariate statistics.

Figure 1.2 contains the means for the eight independent variables for infants who died (group 1) and who survived (group 2), along with the corresponding standard deviations. The last row of each table, labeled *Total*, contains the means and standard deviations calculated when all cases are combined into a single sample.

Figure 1.2   Group means and standard deviations

Group means

SURVIVAL	TREATMNT	TIME	WEIGHT	APGAR
1	.38462	2.88462	1.70950	5.50000
2	.59091	2.31818	2.36091	6.31818
Total	.47917	2.62500	2.00806	5.87500

SURVIVAL	SEX	AGE	PH	RESP
1	.65385	32.38462	7.17962	.65385
2	.68182	34.63636	7.34636	.27273
Total	.66667	33.41667	7.25604	.47917

Group standard deviations

SURVIVAL	TREATMNT	TIME	WEIGHT	APGAR
1	.49614	3.48513	.51944	2.77489
2	.50324	3.70503	.62760	2.69720
Total	.50485	3.56027	.65353	2.74152

SURVIVAL	SEX	AGE	PH	RESP
1	.48516	3.11226	.08502	.48516
2	.47673	2.71759	.60478	.45584
Total	.47639	3.12051	.41751	.50485

From Figure 1.2 you can see that 38% of the infants who died were treated with THAM, 65% were male, and 65% received respiratory therapy. (When a variable is coded 0 or 1, the mean of the variable is the proportion of cases with a value of 1.) Infants who died took longer to breathe spontaneously, weighed less, and had lower Apgar scores than infants who survived.

Figure 1.3 shows significance tests for the equality of group means for each variable. The F values and their significance, shown in the third and fourth columns, are the same as those calculated from a one-way analysis of variance with survival as the grouping variable. For example, the F value in Figure 1.4, which is an analysis-of-variance table for *weight* from the SPSS One-Way ANOVA procedure, is 15.49, the same as shown for *weight* in Figure 1.3. (When there are two groups, the F value is just the square of the t value from the two-sample t test.) The significance level is 0.0003. If the observed significance level is small (less than 0.05), the hypothesis that all group means are equal is rejected.

Figure 1.3   Tests for univariate equality of group means

```
Wilks' lambda (U-statistic) and univariate F-ratio
with 1 and 46 degrees of freedom
```

Variable	Wilks' Lambda	F	Significance
TREATMNT	.95766	2.0335	.1606
TIME	.99358	.2971	.5883
WEIGHT	.74810	15.4894	.0003
APGAR	.97742	1.0628	.3080
SEX	.99913	.0402	.8419
AGE	.86798	6.9967	.0111
PH	.95956	1.9388	.1705
RESP	.85551	7.7693	.0077

Figure 1.4   One-way analysis-of-variance table for weight

```
    Variable  WEIGHT    BIRTHWEIGHT IN KILOGRAMS
 By Variable  SURVIVAL  INFANT SURVIVAL
```

Analysis of variance

Source	D.F.	Sum of Squares	Mean Squares	F Ratio	F Prob.
Between groups	1	5.0566	5.0566	15.4894	.0003
WITHIN GROUPS	46	15.0171	.3265		
TOTAL	47	20.0737			

Wilks' Lambda

Another statistic displayed in Figure 1.3 is **Wilks' lambda**, sometimes called the U statistic (see "Other Discriminant Function Statistics" on p. 15). When variables are considered individually, lambda is the ratio of the within-groups sum of squares to the total sum of squares. For example, Figure 1.4 shows the sums of squares for variable *weight*. The ratio of the within-groups sum of squares (15.02) to the total sum of squares (20.07) is 0.748, the value of Wilks' lambda for *weight* in Figure 1.3.

A lambda of 1 occurs when all observed group means are equal. Values close to 0 occur when within-groups variability is small compared to the total variability; that is, when most of the total variability is attributable to differences between the means of the groups. Thus, large values of lambda indicate that group means do not appear to be different, while small values indicate that group means do appear to be different. From Figure 1.3, *weight*, *age*, and *resp* are the variables whose means are most different for survivors and nonsurvivors.

Correlations

Since interdependencies among the variables affect most multivariate analyses, it is worth examining the correlation matrix of the predictor variables. Figure 1.5 is the **pooled within-groups correlation matrix**. *Weight* and *age* have the largest correlation coefficient, 0.84. This is to be expected, since weight increases with gestational age. The section "Function-Variable Correlations" on p. 19 discusses some of the possible consequences of including highly correlated variables in the analysis.

A pooled within-groups correlation matrix is obtained by averaging the separate correlation matrices for all groups and then computing the correlation matrix. A **total correlation matrix** is obtained when all cases are treated as if they are from a single sample.

Figure 1.5   Pooled within-groups correlation matrix

```
Pooled within-groups correlation matrix

                 TREATMNT      TIME    WEIGHT     APGAR       SEX       AGE        PH      RESP

TREATMNT          1.00000
TIME               .01841   1.00000
WEIGHT             .09091   -.21244   1.00000
APGAR             -.03394   -.50152    .22161   1.00000
SEX               -.03637   -.12982    .19500   -.02098   1.00000
AGE                .05749   -.20066    .84040    .36329   -.00129   1.00000
PH                -.08307    .09102    .12436   -.07197   -.03156    .00205   1.00000
RESP              -.00774   -.06994   -.02394    .16123    .26732   -.06828    .03770   1.00000
```

The total and pooled within-groups correlation matrices can be quite different. For example, Figure 1.6 shows a plot of two hypothetical variables for three groups. When each group is considered individually, the correlation coefficient is 0. Averaging, or pooling, these individual estimates also results in a coefficient of 0. However, the correlation coefficient computed for all cases combined (total) is 0.97, since groups with larger X values also have larger Y values.

Figure 1.6   Hypothetical variable plot for three groups

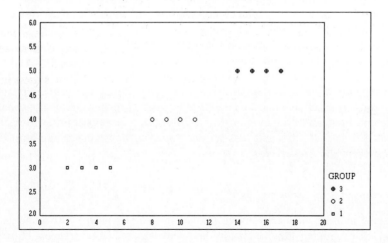

Estimating the Coefficients

Descriptive statistics and univariate tests of significance provide basic information about the distributions of the variables in the groups and help identify some differences among the groups. However, in discriminant analysis and other multivariate statistical procedures, the emphasis is on analyzing the variables together, not one at a time. By considering the variables simultaneously, we are able to incorporate important information about their relationships.

In discriminant analysis, a linear combination of the independent variables is formed and serves as the basis for assigning cases to groups. Thus, information contained in multiple independent variables is summarized in a single index. For example, by finding a weighted average of variables such as *age*, *weight*, and *apgar*, you can obtain a score that distinguishes infants who survive from those who do not. In discriminant analysis, the weights are estimated so that they result in the "best" separation between the groups.

The linear discriminant equation

$$D = B_0 + B_1 X_1 + B_2 X_2 + ... + B_p X_p$$

Equation 1.1

is similar to the multiple linear regression equation. The X's are the values of the independent variables and the B's are coefficients estimated from the data. If a linear discriminant function is to distinguish infants who die from those who survive, the two groups must differ in their D values.

Therefore, the B's are chosen so that the values of the discriminant function differ as much as possible between the groups, or that for the discriminant scores the ratio

$$\frac{\text{between-groups sum of squares}}{\text{within-groups sum of squares}}$$

Equation 1.2

is a maximum. Any other linear combination of the variables will have a smaller ratio. The actual mechanics of computing the coefficients, especially if there are more than two groups, is somewhat involved (see Morrison, 1967; Tatsuoka, 1971).

The coefficients for the eight variables listed in Table 1.1 are shown in Figure 1.7. Small and large values are sometimes displayed in scientific notation. For example, the number 0.0003678 might be displayed as 0.368E-03.

Figure 1.7   Unstandardized discriminant function coefficients

```
Unstandardized canonical discriminant function coefficients

                    Func   1


TREATMNT            .4311545
TIME                .0367127
WEIGHT             2.0440349
APGAR               .1264302
SEX          6.99834313E-03
AGE                -.2180711
PH                  .4078705
RESP              -1.2445389
(Constant)         -.2309344
```

Calculating the Discriminant Score

Based on the coefficients in Figure 1.7, it is possible to calculate the discriminant score for each case. For example, Figure 1.8 contains the value of each variable for the first five cases in the data file. The discriminant score for case 1 is obtained by multiplying

Figure 1.8   Values of the variables for the first five cases

```
    TREATMNT TIME WEIGHT APGAR SEX AGE    PH RESP SURVIVAL   SCORE

1       1     2.0  1.050    5   0   28 7.09   0     1        -.166
2       1     2.0  1.175    4   0   28 7.11   1     1       -1.269
3       1      .5  1.230    7   0   29 7.24   9     1          .
4       1     4.0  1.310    4   1   29 7.13   1     1       -1.123
5       1      .5  1.500    8   1   32 7.23   1     1        -.973
```

the unstandardized coefficients by the values of the variables, summing these products, and adding the constant. For case 1, the discriminant score is

$$D_1 = 0.431\,(1) + 0.0367\,(2) + 2.044\,(1.05) + 0.126\,(5) + 0.007\,(0)$$
$$- 0.218\,(28) + 0.408\,(7.09) - 1.244\,(0) - 0.231 = -0.16$$

Equation 1.3

Figure 1.9 contains basic descriptive statistics for the discriminant scores (*dis1_1*) in the two groups. The mean score for all cases combined is essentially 0 and the pooled within-in-groups variance is 1. This is always true for discriminant scores calculated by SPSS.

Figure 1.9   Descriptive statistics

```
                      - - Analysis of Variance - -

Dependent Variable    DIS1_1     Function 1 for analysis 1
      By levels of    SURVIVAL   INFANT SURVIVAL


      Value  Label                  Mean    Std Dev   Sum of Sq   Cases

          1  DIE                -.7125152   .9055960 20.5026022      26
          2  SURVIVE             .8420634  1.1018901 25.4973978      22
                               ------------------------------------------
Within Groups Total            -5.181E-16  1.0000000 46.0000000      48
```

Bayes' Rule

Using the discriminant score, it is possible to obtain a rule for classifying cases into one of the two groups. The technique used by SPSS is based on Bayes' rule. The probability that a case with a discriminant score of D belongs to group i is estimated by

$$P(G_i|D) = \frac{P(D|G_i)P(G_i)}{\sum\limits_{i=1}^{g} P(D|G_i)P(G_i)}$$

Equation 1.4

The next three sections describe the various components of this equation and their relationships.

Prior Probability

The **prior probability**, represented by $P(G_i)$, is an estimate of the likelihood that a case belongs to a particular group when no information about it is available. For example, if 30% of infants with RDS die, the probability that an infant with RDS will die is 0.3.

The prior probability can be estimated in several ways. If the sample is considered representative of the population, the observed proportions of cases in each group can serve as estimates of the prior probabilities. In this example, 26 out of 48 cases for whom all information is available, or 54%, belong to group 1 (nonsurvivors), and 22 (46%) belong to group 2 (survivors). The prior probability of belonging to group 1, then, is 0.54, and the prior probability of belonging to group 2 is 0.46.

Often samples are chosen so that they include a fixed number of observations per group. For example, if deaths from RDS were rare, say occurring once per 100 RDS births, even reasonably large samples of RDS births would result in a small number of cases in the nonsurvivor group. Therefore, an investigator might include the same number of survivors and nonsurvivors in the study. In such situations, the prior probability of group membership can be estimated from other sources, such as hospital discharge records.

When all groups are equally likely, or when no information about the probability of group membership is known, equal prior probabilities for all groups may be selected. Since each case must belong to one of the groups, the prior probabilities must sum to 1.

Although prior probabilities convey some information about the likelihood of group membership, they ignore the attributes of the particular case. For example, an infant who is known to be very sick based on various criteria is assigned the same probability of dying as is an infant known to be healthier.

Conditional Probability

To take advantage of the additional information available for a case in developing a classification scheme, we need to assess the likelihood of the additional information under different circumstances. For example, if the discriminant function scores are normally distributed for each of two groups and the parameters of the distributions can be estimated, it is possible to calculate the probability of obtaining a particular discriminant function value of D if the case is a member of group 1 or group 2.

This probability is called the **conditional probability** of D given the group and is denoted by $P(D| G_i)$. To calculate this probability, the case is assumed to belong to a particular group and the probability of the observed score given membership in the group is estimated.

Posterior Probability

The conditional probability of D given the group gives an idea of how likely the score is for members of a particular group. However, when group membership is unknown, what is really needed is an estimate of how likely membership in the various groups is, given the available information. This is called the **posterior probability** and is denoted by $P(G_i| D)$. It can be estimated from $P(D| G_i)$ and $P(G_i)$ using Bayes' rule. A case is classified, based on its discriminant score D, in the group for which the posterior probability is the largest. That is, it is assigned to the most likely group based on its discriminant score. (See Tatsuoka, 1971, for further information.)

Classification Output

Figure 1.10 is an excerpt from the SPSS output that lists classification information for each case for a group of cases whose membership is known. The first column, labeled *Case Seqnum*, is the sequence number of the case in the file. The next column, *Mis Val*, contains the number of variables with missing values for that case. Cases with missing values are not used in estimating the coefficients and are not included in the output shown in Figure 1.10 (note the absence of cases 3 and 28). However, those two cases with missing values could have been classified and included in the table by substituting group means for missing values. The third column (*Sel*) indicates whether a case has been excluded from the computations using a selection variable.

Figure 1.10   Classification output

Case Seqnum	Mis Val	Sel	Actual Group	Highest Probability Group	P(D/G)	P(G/D)	2nd Highest Group	P(G/D)	Discriminant Scores...
1			1	1	.5821	.5873	2	.4127	-.1622
2			1	1	.5776	.8884	2	.1116	-1.2695
4			1	1	.6814	.8637	2	.1363	-1.1230
5			1	1	.7962	.8334	2	.1666	-.9708
6			1	1	.9080	.7367	2	.2633	-.5970
7			1 **	2	.4623	.5164	1	.4836	.1070
8			1	1	.8433	.7112	2	.2888	-.5149
9			1	1	.6581	.8695	2	.1305	-1.1551
10			1	1	.4577	.5134	2	.4866	.0302
11			1	1	.6087	.6017	2	.3983	-.2006
12			1	1	.1722	.9655	2	.0345	-2.0775
13			1	1	.1140	.9750	2	.0250	-2.2930
14			1	1	.3430	.9360	2	.0640	-1.6607
15			1	1	.7983	.6923	2	.3077	-.4569
16			1	1	.7008	.6482	2	.3518	-.3283
17			1	1	.2090	.9593	2	.0407	-1.9687
18			1	1	.1128	.9752	2	.0248	-2.2982
19			1	1	.4383	.9178	2	.0822	-1.4875
20			1 **	2	.9418	.7493	1	.2507	.7690
21			1	1	.7384	.6658	2	.3342	-.3786
22			1 **	2	.5161	.5495	1	.4505	.1927
23			1	1	.5399	.8967	2	.1033	-1.3255
24			1	1	.4409	.5026	2	.4974	.0582
25			1 **	2	.8126	.8288	1	.1712	1.0791
26			1	1	.7050	.6502	2	.3498	-.3339
27			1	1	.5804	.5864	2	.4136	-.1597
29			2 **	1	.4595	.5146	2	.4854	.0272
30			2	2	.8552	.7160	1	.2840	.6596
31			2	2	.6172	.6062	1	.3938	.3423
32			2	2	.6928	.6443	1	.3557	.4469
33			2	2	.8887	.8063	1	.1937	.9820
34			2	2	.6169	.8793	1	.1207	1.3423
35			2	2	.6823	.8635	1	.1365	1.2514
36			2	2	.7755	.6824	1	.3176	.5568
37			2	2	.6368	.8746	1	.1254	1.3143
38			2	2	.0874	.9795	1	.0205	2.5512
39			2	2	.1236	.9735	1	.0265	2.3821
40			2	2	.0181	.9925	1	.0075	3.2050
41			2	2	.9033	.7349	1	.2651	.7206
42			2 **	1	.5613	.8920	2	.1080	-1.2934
43			2 **	1	.5270	.5560	2	.4440	-.0799
44			2 **	1	.3851	.9281	2	.0719	-1.5810
45			2	2	.5574	.5735	1	.4265	.2553
46			2	2	.7718	.8401	1	.1599	1.1321
47			2	2	.6792	.6377	1	.3623	.4286
48			2	2	.9649	.7819	1	.2181	.8861
49			2	2	.5742	.8891	1	.1109	1.4040
50			2	2	.4533	.9148	1	.0852	1.5920

For cases included in the computation of the discriminant function, actual group membership is known and can be compared to that predicted using the discriminant function. The group to which a case actually belongs is listed in the column labeled *Actual Group*. The most likely group for a case based on the discriminant analysis (the group with the largest posterior probability) is listed in the column labeled *Highest Group*. Cases that are misclassified using the discriminant function are flagged with asterisks next to the actual group number.

The next value listed is the probability of a case's discriminant score, or one more extreme, if the case is a member of the most-likely group.

The larger posterior probabilities of membership in the two groups $P(G \mid D)$ follow in Figure 1.10. When there are only two groups, both probabilities are given, since one is the highest and the other the second highest. The probabilities 0.5873 and 0.4127 sum to 1, since a case must be a member of one of the two groups.

Classification Summary

You can obtain the number of misclassified cases by counting the number of cases with asterisks in Figure 1.10. In this example, 8 cases out of 48 are classified incorrectly.

More detailed information on the results of the classification phase is available from the output in Figure 1.11, sometimes called the **confusion matrix**. For each group, this output shows the numbers of correct and incorrect classifications. In this example only the cases with complete information for all predictor variables are included in the classification results table. Correctly classified cases appear on the diagonal of the table, since the predicted and actual groups are the same. For example, of 26 cases in group 1, 22 were predicted correctly to be members of group 1 (84.6%), while 4 (15.4%) were assigned incorrectly to group 2. Similarly, 18 out of 22 (81.8%) of the group 2 cases were identified correctly, and 4 (18.2%) were misclassified. The overall percentage of cases classified correctly is 83.3% (40 out of 48).

Figure 1.11   Classification results

```
Classification results -

                         No. of     Predicted Group Membership
         Actual Group     Cases          1            2
    --------------------  ------     --------     --------

    Group       1           26          22            4
    DIE                                84.6%        15.4%

    Group       2           22           4           18
    SURVIVE                            18.2%        81.8%

Percent of "grouped" cases correctly classified:  83.33%
```

Histograms of Discriminant Scores

To see how much the two groups overlap and to examine the distribution of the discriminant scores, it is often useful to plot the discriminant function scores for the groups. Figure 1.12 shows histograms of the scores for each group separately. Four symbols (either 1's or 2's) represent one case. (The number of cases represented by a symbol depends on the number of cases used in an analysis.) The row of 1's and 2's underneath the plot denote the group to which scores are assigned.

The average score for a group is called the group **centroid** and is indicated on each plot as well as in Figure 1.13. These values are the same as the means in Figure 1.9. On the average, infants who died have smaller discriminant function scores than infants who survived. The average value for group 1 infants who died is –0.71, whereas the average value for those who survived is 0.84.

Figure 1.12   Histograms of discriminant scores

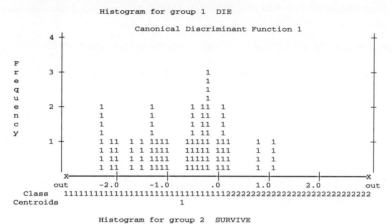

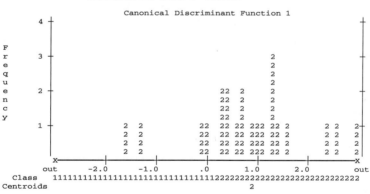

Figure 1.13   Discriminant functions evaluated at group means

```
Canonical discriminant functions evaluated at group means (group centroids)

    Group      Func    1

      1       -.71252
      2        .84206
```

In Figure 1.12 we note that three group 1 cases clearly fall into the group 2 classification region, whereas four group 1 cases are misclassified. Of the two cases that have values around 0.1, one (case 7) has a classification probability for group 1 of 0.48, while the other (case 24) has a value of 0.503. Thus case 7 is misclassified, although on the plot it appears to be correctly classified because the boundary between the two territories falls within an interval attributed to group 1.

The combined distribution of the scores for the two groups is shown in Figure 1.14. Again, four symbols represent a case, and you can see the amount of overlap between the two groups. For example, the interval with midpoint –1.3 has three cases, two from group 1 and one from group 2.

Figure 1.14   All-groups stacked histogram: canonical discriminant function

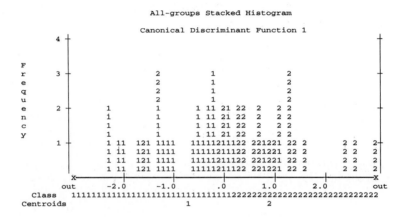

Estimating Misclassification Rates

A model usually fits the sample from which it is derived better than it will fit another sample from the same population. Thus, the percentage of cases classified correctly by the discriminant function is an inflated estimate of the true performance in the population, just as R^2 is an overly optimistic estimate of a model's fit in regression.

There are several ways to obtain a better estimate of the true misclassification rate. If the sample is large enough to be randomly split into two parts, you can use one to derive the discriminant function and the other to test it. Since the same cases are not used for both estimating the function and testing it, the observed error rate in the "test" sample should better reflect the function's effectiveness. However, this method requires large sample sizes and does not make good use of all of the available information.

Another technique for obtaining an improved estimate of the misclassification rate is the **jackknife method**, sometimes called the leaving-one-out method. It involves leaving out each of the cases in turn, calculating the function based on the remaining $n - 1$ cases, and then classifying the left-out case. Again, since the case which is being classified is not included in the calculation of the function, the observed (or apparent) mis-classification rate is a less biased estimate of the true one.

When one of the groups is much smaller than the other, a highly correct classification rate can occur even when most of the "minority" group cases are misclassified. The smaller group—adopters of a new product, diseased individuals, or parole violators—are, however, often of particular interest, and their correct classification is of paramount importance. The desired result is not to minimize the overall misclassification rate but to identify most cases of the smaller group. For example, by judging everyone to be dis-ease-free in a cancer-screening program, the error rate will be very small, since few peo-ple actually have the disease. However, the results are useless, since the goal is to identify the diseased individuals.

The result of different classification rules for identifying "minority" cases can be ex-amined by ranking all cases on the value of their discriminant score and determining how many "minority" cases are in the various deciles. If most of the cases of interest are at the extremes of the distribution, a good rule for identifying them can be obtained at the expense of increasing the number of misclassified cases from the larger group. If the intent of the discriminant analysis is to identify persons to receive promotional materials for a new product, or undergo further screening procedures, this is a fairly reasonable tactic. Unequal costs for misclassification can also be incorporated into the classifica-tion rule by adjusting the prior probabilities to reflect them. For further discussion, see Lachenbruch (1975).

The Expected Misclassification Rate

The percentage of cases classified correctly is often taken as an index of the effective-ness of the discriminant function. When evaluating this measure it is important to com-pare the observed misclassification rate to that expected by chance alone. For example, if there are two groups with equal prior probabilities, assigning cases to groups based on the outcome of a flip of a fair coin—that is, heads allocated to group 1 and tails allocated to group 2—results in an expected misclassification rate of 50%. A discriminant func-tion with an observed misclassification rate of 50% is performing no better than chance. In fact, if the rate is based on the sample used for deriving the function, it is probably doing worse.

As the number of groups with equal prior probabilities increases, the percentage of cases that can be classified correctly by chance alone decreases. If there are 10 groups, only 10% of the cases would be expected to be classified correctly by chance. Observed misclassification rates should always be viewed in light of results expected by chance.

Other Discriminant Function Statistics

The percentage of cases classified correctly is one indicator of the effectiveness of the discriminant function. Another indicator of effectiveness of the function is the actual discriminant scores in the groups. A "good" discriminant function is one that has much between-groups variability when compared to within-groups variability. In fact, the coefficients of the discriminant function are chosen so that the ratio of the between-groups sum of squares to the within-groups sum of squares is as large as possible. Any other linear combination of the predictor variables will have a smaller ratio.

Figure 1.15 is an analysis-of-variance table from the SPSS Means procedure using the discriminant scores as the dependent variable and the group variable as the independent or classification variable. Figure 1.16 shows a variety of statistics based on the analysis-of-variance table. For example, the **eigenvalue** in Figure 1.16 is simply the ratio of the between-groups to within-groups sums of squares. Thus, from Figure 1.15 it is

$$\text{eigenvalue} = \frac{\text{between-groups ss}}{\text{within-groups ss}} = \frac{28.8}{46.0} = 0.626 \qquad \textbf{Equation 1.5}$$

Large eigenvalues are associated with "good" functions. The next two entries in Figure 1.16, percentage of variance and cumulative percentage, are always 100 for the two-group situation. (See "Additional Statistics" on p. 32 for further explanation.)

Figure 1.15   Analysis- of-variance table for discriminant scores

Source	Sum of Squares	d.f.	Mean Square	F	Sig.
Between Groups	28.7992	1	28.7992	28.7992	.0000
Within Groups	46.0000	46	1.0000		

Eta = .6205   Eta Squared = .3850

Figure 1.16   Canonical discriminant functions

Canonical Discriminant Functions

Fcn	Eigenvalue	Pct of Variance	Cum Pct	Canonical Corr	After Fcn	Wilks' Lambda	Chisquare	df	Sig
				:	0	.614980	20.419	8	.0089
1*	.6261	100.00	100.00	.6205 :					

* Marks the 1 canonical discriminant functions remaining in the analysis.

The **canonical correlation** is a measure of the degree of association between the discriminant scores and the groups. It is equivalent to eta from the one-way analysis of variance, in which the discriminant score is the dependent variable and group is the independent variable. Remember eta^2 is the ratio of the between-groups sum of squares to the total sum of squares and represents the proportion of the total variance attributable to differences among the groups. Thus, from Figure 1.15, eta is

$$\text{eta} = \sqrt{\frac{28.8}{74.8}} = 0.6205$$

Equation 1.6

In the two-group situation, the canonical correlation is simply the usual Pearson correlation coefficient between the discriminant score and the group variable, which is coded 0 and 1.

For the two-group case, Wilks' lambda is the ratio of the within-groups sum of squares to the total sum of squares. It is the proportion of the total variance in the discriminant scores not explained by differences among groups ($\text{lambda} + \text{eta}^2 = 1$). From Figure 1.15, lambda is

$$\lambda = \frac{46}{74.8} = 0.615$$

Equation 1.7

As indicated in "Additional Statistics" on p. 32, small values of lambda are associated with functions that have much variability between groups and little variability within groups. A lambda of 1 occurs when the mean of the discriminant scores is the same in all groups and there is no between-groups variability.

A test of the null hypothesis that in the populations from which the samples are drawn there is no difference between the group means can be based on Wilks' lambda. Lambda is transformed to a variable which has approximately a chi-square distribution. Figure 1.16 shows that a lambda of 0.615 is transformed to a chi-square value of 20.42 with 8 degrees of freedom. The observed significance level is 0.0089. Thus, it appears unlikely that infants who die from RDS and those who survive have the same means on the discriminant function.

It is important to remember that even though Wilks' lambda may be statistically significant, it provides little information about the effectiveness of the discriminant function in classification. It only provides a test of the null hypothesis that the population means are equal. Small differences may be statistically significant but still not permit good discrimination among the groups. If the means and covariance matrices are equal, of course, discrimination is not possible.

Interpreting the Discriminant Function Coefficients

Table 1.2 contains the standardized and unstandardized discriminant function coefficients for the RDS example. The **unstandardized coefficients** are the multipliers of the variables when they are expressed in the original units. As in multiple regression, the

standardized coefficients are used when the variables are standardized to a mean of 0 and a standard deviation of 1.

Table 1.2 Standardized and unstandardized discriminant function coefficients

Variable	Unstandardized	Standardized
treatmnt	0.43115	0.21531
time	0.03671	0.13170
weight	2.04404	1.16789
apgar	0.12643	0.34638
sex	0.00700	0.00337
age	–0.21807	–0.64084
ph	0.40787	0.16862
resp	–1.24454	–0.58743
(constant)	–0.23093	

The interpretation of the coefficients is also similar to that in multiple regression. Since the variables are correlated, it is not possible to assess the importance of an individual variable. The value of the coefficient for a particular variable depends on the other variables included in the function.

It is sometimes tempting to interpret the magnitudes of the coefficients as indicators of the relative importance of variables. Variables with large coefficients are thought to contribute more to the overall discriminant function. However, the magnitude of the unstandardized coefficients is not a good index of relative importance when the variables differ in the units in which they are measured. For example, the gestational age is measured in weeks and ranges from 28 to 39 weeks, while the pH level ranges from 6.85 to 7.37. When the absolute values of the unstandardized coefficients are ranked from largest to smallest, age (–0.22) has a rank of 5. However, when the coefficients are standardized to adjust for the unequal means and standard deviations of the independent variables, the coefficient for age (–0.64) is the second largest.

The actual signs of the coefficients are arbitrary. The negative coefficients for age and respiratory therapy could just as well be positive if the signs of the other coefficients were reversed.

By looking at the groups of variables which have coefficients of different signs, we can determine which variable values result in large and small function values. For example, since respiratory therapy is usually initiated for infants who are in considerable distress, it is a bad omen for survival. Values of 1 for the *resp* variable will decrease the function value. Infants who weigh more usually have better-developed lungs and are more likely to survive. Thus, larger weights increase the function. Large function values are associated with survival, while small function values are associated with death.

Function-Variable Correlations

Another way to assess the contribution of a variable to the discriminant function is to examine the correlations between the values of the function and the values of the variables. The computation of the coefficients is straightforward. For each case the value of the discriminant function is computed, and the Pearson correlation coefficients between it and the original variables are obtained.

Separate correlation matrices can be calculated for each group and the results combined to obtain a pooled within-groups correlation matrix like that in Figure 1.17. Or all of the cases can be considered together and a total correlation matrix calculated. The total correlation coefficients are larger than the corresponding within-groups correlations. However, the relative magnitudes will be similar. Variables with high total correlations will also have high pooled within-groups correlations.

Figure 1.17   Pooled within-groups correlations

```
Structure matrix:

Pooled within-groups correlations between discriminating variables
                                   and canonical discriminant functions
(Variables ordered by size of correlation within function)

             Func   1

WEIGHT         .73338
RESP          -.51940
AGE            .49290
TREATMNT       .26572
PH             .25946
APGAR          .19210
TIME          -.10157
SEX            .03738
```

Figure 1.17 indicates that variable *weight* has the highest correlation with the discriminant function. *Resp* has the second largest correlation in absolute value. The negative sign indicates that small function values are associated with the presence of respiratory therapy (coded 1) and larger values are associated with the absence of respiratory therapy. These results are similar to those obtained from the standardized coefficients.

However, if you compare Table 1.2 and Figure 1.17, you will notice that *age*, which has a negative standardized coefficient, is positively correlated with the discriminant function. Similarly, *time*, which has a positive standardized coefficient, has a negative correlation with the discriminant score. This occurs because *weight* and *age*, as expected, are highly correlated. The correlation coefficient is 0.84 from Figure 1.5. Thus, the contribution of *age* and *weight* is shared and the individual coefficients are not meaningful. You should exercise care when attempting to interpret the coefficients, since correlations between variables affect the magnitudes and signs of the coefficients.

Fisher's Classification Function Coefficients

In Table 1.2, the linear discriminant function coefficients are those that maximize the ratio of between-groups to within-groups sums of squares. These coefficients are sometimes called the canonical discriminant function coefficients, since they are identical to those obtained from canonical correlation analysis when maximally correlated linear combinations of the group membership variables and predictor variables are formed (see Tatsuoka, 1971).

Another set of coefficients, sometimes called **Fisher's linear discriminant function coefficients** or classification coefficients, can be used directly for classification. A set of coefficients is obtained for each group and a case is assigned to the group for which it has the largest discriminant score. The classification results are identical for both methods if all canonical discriminant functions are used (see Kshirsagar & Arseven, 1975; Green, 1979).

Relationship to Multiple Regression Analysis

Two-group linear discriminant analysis is closely related to multiple linear regression analysis. If the binary grouping variable is considered the dependent variable and the predictor variables are the independent variables, the multiple regression coefficients in Table 1.3 are obtained. Comparison of these coefficients to the discriminant function coefficients shows that the two sets of coefficients are proportional. The discriminant coefficients can be obtained by multiplying the regression coefficients by 4.04. The exact constant of proportionality varies from data set to data set, but the two sets of coefficients are always proportional. This is true only for two-group discriminant analysis.

Table 1.3   Regression and discriminant coefficients

Variable	B Regression	B Discriminant	Ratio
resp	−0.3082	−1.2445	4.04
time	0.0091	0.0367	4.04
ph	0.1010	0.4079	4.04
treatmnt	0.1068	0.4311	4.04
sex	0.0017	0.0070	4.04
age	−0.0540	−0.2180	4.04
apgar	0.0313	0.1264	4.04
weight	0.5062	2.0440	4.04

Variable Selection Methods

In many situations discriminant analysis, like multiple regression analysis, is used as an exploratory tool. In order to arrive at a good model, a variety of potentially useful variables are included in the data set. It is not known in advance which of these variables are important for group separation and which are, more or less, extraneous. One of the desired end-products of the analysis is identification of the "good" predictor variables. All of the caveats for variable selection procedures in multiple regression discussed in

Chapter 19 of the *SPSS Base System User's Guide* apply to discriminant analysis as well. If you have not read that chapter, you are advised to do so before continuing with this chapter.

A commonly used algorithm for variable selection—**stepwise selection**—is available in the SPSS Discriminant Analysis procedure. The principles are the same as in multiple regression. What differs are the actual criteria for variable selection. In the following example, only minimization of Wilks' lambda will be considered. Other criteria are discussed in "Other Criteria for Variable Selection" on p. 26 through "Sum of Unexplained Variance" on p. 27.

A Stepwise Selection Example

Stepwise variable selection algorithms combine the features of forward selection and backward elimination. Remember that in a stepwise method the first variable included in the analysis has the largest acceptable value for the selection criterion. After the first variable is entered, the value of the criterion is reevaluated for all variables not in the model, and the variable with the largest acceptable criterion value is entered next. At this point, the variable entered first is reevaluated to determine whether it meets the removal criterion. If it does, it is removed from the model.

The next step is to examine the variables not in the equation for entry, followed by examination of the variables in the equation for removal. Variables are removed until none remain that meet the removal criterion. Variable selection terminates when no more variables meet entry or removal criteria.

Variable Selection Criteria

Figure 1.18 is output from the beginning of a stepwise variable selection job, listing the criteria in effect. As mentioned previously, several criteria are available for variable selection. This example uses minimization of Wilks' lambda. Thus, at each step the variable that results in the smallest Wilks' lambda for the discriminant function is selected for entry.

Figure 1.18   Stepwise variable selection

```
Stepwise variable selection
     Selection rule:  minimize Wilks' lambda
     Maximum number of steps..................     16
     Minimum tolerance level.................. .00100
     Minimum F to enter......................   3.84
     Maximum F to remove.....................   2.71
```

Each entry or removal of a variable is considered a step. The maximum number of steps permitted in an analysis is twice the number of independent variables.

As in multiple regression, if there are independent variables that are linear combinations of other independent variables, a unique solution is not possible. To prevent computational difficulties, the tolerance of a variable is checked before it is entered into a model. The **tolerance** is a measure of the degree of linear association between the independent variables. For the ith independent variable, it is $1 - R_i^2$, where R_i^2 is the squared multiple correlation coefficient when the ith independent variable is considered the dependent variable and the regression equation between it and the other independent variables is calculated. Small values for the tolerance indicate that the ith independent variable is almost a linear combination of the other independent variables. Variables with small tolerances (less than 0.001) are not permitted to enter the analysis. Also, if entry of a variable would cause the tolerance of a variable already in the model to drop to an unacceptable level (less than 0.001), the variable is not entered. The smallest acceptable tolerance for a particular analysis is shown in Figure 1.18.

The significance of the change in Wilks' lambda when a variable is entered or removed from the model can be based on an F statistic. Either the actual value of F or its significance level can be used as the criterion for variable entry and removal. These two criteria are not necessarily equivalent, since a fixed F value has different significance levels depending on the number of variables in the model at any step. The actual significance levels associated with the F-to-enter and F-to-remove statistics are not those usually obtained from the F distribution, since many variables are examined and the largest and smallest F values selected. The true significance level is difficult to compute, since it depends on many factors, including the correlations between the independent variables.

The First Step

Before the stepwise selection algorithm begins, at step 0, basic information about the variables is displayed, as shown in Figure 1.19. The tolerance and minimum tolerance are 1, since there are no variables in the model. (The tolerance is based only on the independent variables in the model. The minimum tolerance, which is the smallest tolerance for any variable in the equation if the variable under consideration is entered, is also based only on the variables in the equation.) The F-to-enter in Figure 1.19 is equal to the F test for equality of group means in Figure 1.3. The univariate Wilks' lambda is also the same.

Figure 1.19   Output at step 0

```
--------------- Variables not in the Analysis after Step 0 ---------------

                        Minimum
Variable   Tolerance   Tolerance   F to Enter   Wilks' Lambda

TREATMNT   1.0000000   1.0000000     2.0335       .9576649
TIME       1.0000000   1.0000000      .2971       .9935822
WEIGHT     1.0000000   1.0000000    15.4894       .7480967
APGAR      1.0000000   1.0000000     1.0628       .9774175
SEX        1.0000000   1.0000000      .0402       .9991259
AGE        1.0000000   1.0000000     6.9967       .8679783
PH         1.0000000   1.0000000     1.9388       .9595576
RESP       1.0000000   1.0000000     7.7693       .8555062
```

The *weight* variable has the smallest Wilks' lambda and correspondingly the largest *F*-to-enter, so it is the first variable entered into the equation. When *weight* is entered, as shown in Figure 1.20, the Wilks' lambda and corresponding *F* are the same as in Figure 1.3 and Figure 1.19. The degrees of freedom for the Wilks' lambda displayed in Figure 1.20 are for its untransformed (not converted to an *F*) distribution.

After each step, SPSS displays a table showing the variables in the model (see Figure 1.21). When only one variable is in the model, this table contains no new information. The *F*-to-remove corresponds to that in Figure 1.20, since it represents the change in Wilks' lambda if *weight* is removed. The last column usually contains the value of Wilks' lambda if the variable is removed. However, since removal of *weight* results in a model with no variables, no value is displayed at the first step.

Figure 1.20   Summary statistics for step 1

```
At step 1, WEIGHT was included in the analysis.

                                  Degrees of Freedom  Signif.   Between Groups
Wilks' Lambda        .74810          1    1      46.0
Equivalent F       15.48938               1      46.0    .0003
```

Figure 1.21   Variables in the analysis after step 1

```
--------------- Variables in the Analysis after Step 1 ---------------

Variable  Tolerance  F to Remove   Wilks' Lambda

WEIGHT    1.0000000     15.4894
```

Optionally, you can request a test of differences between pairs of groups after each step. When there are only two groups, the *F* value displayed is the same as that for Wilks' lambda for the overall model, as shown in Figure 1.21 and Figure 1.22.

Figure 1.22   F values and significance at step 1

```
F statistics and significances between pairs of groups after step 1
Each F statistic has 1 and 46 degrees of freedom.

                     Group        1
                       DIE
      Group

        2   SURVIVE          15.4894
                              .0003
```

Statistics for Variables Not in the Model

Also displayed at each step is a set of summary statistics for variables not yet in the model. From Figure 1.23, *resp* is the variable which results in the smallest Wilks' lambda for the model if it is entered next. Note that the Wilks' lambda calculated is for the variables *weight* and *resp* jointly. Its *F* test is a multivariate significance test for group differences.

Figure 1.23   Variables not in the analysis after step 1

```
--------------- Variables not in the Analysis after Step 1 ---------------

                        Minimum
Variable  Tolerance   Tolerance   F to Enter     Wilks' Lambda

TREATMNT   .9917361    .9917361      .8421          .7343549
TIME       .9548707    .9548707      .0649          .7470194
APGAR      .9508910    .9508910      .0194          .7477743
SEX        .9619762    .9619762      .2444          .7440551
AGE        .2937327    .2937327     1.0931          .7303548
PH         .9845349    .9845349      .6061          .7381551
RESP       .9994270    .9994270     5.3111          .6691243
```

The F value for the change in Wilks' lambda when a variable is added to a model which contains p independent variables is

$$F_{\text{change}} = (\frac{n - g - p}{g - 1}) \left(\frac{(1 - \lambda_{p+1}/\lambda_p)}{\lambda_{p+1}/\lambda_p} \right)$$

Equation 1.8

where n is the total number of cases, g is the number of groups, λ_p is Wilks' lambda before adding the variable, and λ_{p+1} is Wilks' lambda after inclusion.

If variable *resp* is entered into the model containing variable *weight*, Wilks' lambda is 0.669. The lambda for *weight* alone is 0.748 (see Figure 1.20). The F value for the change, called F-to-enter, is from Equation 1.8:

$$F = (\frac{48 - 2 - 1}{2 - 1}) (\frac{(1 - 0.669/0.748)}{0.669/0.748}) = 5.31$$

Equation 1.9

This is the value for *resp* in Figure 1.23.

The Second Step

Figure 1.24 shows the output when *resp* is entered into the model. Wilks' lambda for the model is the same as Wilks' lambda for *resp* in Figure 1.23. If *weight* is removed from the current model, leaving only *resp*, the resulting Wilks' lambda is 0.855, the entry for *weight* in the second part of Figure 1.24. The F value associated with the change in lambda, F-to-remove, is 12.5, which is also displayed in Figure 1.24.

$$F\text{-to-remove} = \frac{(48 - 2 - 1)\,(1 - 0.669/0.855)}{(1)\,(0.669/0.855)} = 12.5$$

Equation 1.10

Figure 1.24   Variable for respiratory therapy included in analysis at step 2

```
At step 2, RESP was included in the analysis.

                                  Degrees of Freedom  Signif.   Between Groups
Wilks' Lambda          .66912      2    1      46.0
Equivalent F         11.12604           2      45.0   .0001


---------------- Variables in the Analysis after Step 2 ----------------


Variable   Tolerance   F to Remove   Wilks' Lambda

WEIGHT      .9994270     12.5346        .8555062
RESP        .9994270      5.3111        .7480967


---------------- Variables not in the Analysis after Step 2 ----------------

                           Minimum
Variable   Tolerance   Tolerance   F to Enter    Wilks' Lambda

TREATMNT   .9917051    .9911962      .7159         .6584111
TIME       .9492383    .9492383      .0053         .6690435
APGAR      .9231403    .9231403      .2559         .6652554
SEX        .8879566    .8879566      .0199         .6688221
AGE        .2914116    .2914116     1.3783         .6488012
PH         .9828797    .9828797      .6676         .6591230
```

After *weight* and *resp* have both been included in the model, all *F*-to-remove values are greater than 2.71, so no variables are removed. All variables not in the model after step 2 have *F*-to-enter values less than 3.84, so none are eligible for inclusion and variable selection stops (see Figure 1.24).

Summary Tables

After the last step, SPSS displays a summary table (see Figure 1.25). For each step, this table lists the action taken (entry or removal) and the resulting Wilks' lambda and its significance level. Table 1.4 shows the percentage of cases classified correctly at each

Figure 1.25   Summary table

```
                           Summary Table

          Action       Vars   Wilks'
Step  Entered Removed    in    Lambda   Sig.   Label

  1   WEIGHT            1     .74810   .0003   BIRTHWEIGHT IN KILOGRAMS
  2   RESP             2     .66912   .0001   RESPIRATORY LEVEL
```

step of the analysis. The model with variables *weight* and *resp* classifies 75% of the cases correctly, while the complete model with eight variables classifies 83% of the cases correctly. Including additional variables does not always improve classification. In fact, sometimes the percentage of cases classified correctly actually decreases if poor predictors are included in the model.

Table 1.4 Cases correctly classified by step

Variables included	Percentage classified correctly
weight	68.00
weight, resp	75.00
All eight variables	83.33

Other Criteria for Variable Selection

In previous sections, variables were included in the model based on Wilks' lambda. At each step, the variable that resulted in the smallest Wilks' lambda was selected. Other criteria besides Wilks' lambda are sometimes used for variable selection.

Rao's V

Rao's V, also known as the **Lawley-Hotelling trace**, is defined as

$$V = (n-g) \sum_{i=1}^{p} \sum_{j=1}^{p} w_{ij}^{*} \sum_{k=1}^{g} (\bar{X}_{ik} - \bar{X}_i)(\bar{X}_{jk} - \bar{X}_j)$$

Equation 1.11

where p is the number of variables in the model, g is the number of groups, n_k is the sample size in the kth group, $\bar{X}_{ik}$ is the mean of the ith variable for the kth group, $\bar{X}_i$ is the mean of the ith variable for all groups combined, and w_{ij}^{*} is an element of the inverse of the within-groups covariance matrix. The larger the differences between group means, the larger the Rao's V.

One way to evaluate the contribution of a variable is to see how much it increases Rao's V when it is added to the model. The sampling distribution of V is approximately a chi-square with $p(g-1)$ degrees of freedom. A test of the significance of the change in Rao's V when a variable is included can also be based on the chi-square distribution. It is possible for a variable to actually decrease Rao's V when it is added to a model.

Mahalanobis Distance

Mahalanobis distance, D^2, is a generalized measure of the distance between two groups. The distance between groups a and b is defined as

$$D_{ab}^{2} = (n-g) \sum_{i=1}^{p} \sum_{j=1}^{p} w_{ij}^{*} (\bar{X}_{ia} - \bar{X}_{ib})(\bar{X}_{ja} - \bar{X}_{jb})$$

Equation 1.12

where p is the number of variables in the model, $\overline{X}_{ia}$ is the mean for the ith variable in group a, and w_{ij}^* is an element from the inverse of the within-groups covariance matrix.

When Mahalanobis distance is the criterion for variable selection, the Mahalanobis distances between all pairs of groups are calculated first. The variable that has the largest D^2 for the two groups that are closest (have the smallest D^2 initially) is selected for inclusion.

Between-Groups F

A test of the null hypothesis that the two sets of population means are equal can be based on Mahalanobis distance. The corresponding F statistic is

$$F = \frac{(n-1-p)\, n_1 n_2}{p\,(n-2)\,(n_1+n_2)} D_{ab}^2 \qquad \text{Equation 1.13}$$

This F value can also be used for variable selection. At each step the variable chosen for inclusion is the one with the largest F value. Since the Mahalanobis distance is weighted by the sample sizes when the between-groups F is used as the criterion for stepwise selection, the results from the two methods may differ.

Sum of Unexplained Variance

As mentioned previously, two-group discriminant analysis is analogous to multiple regression in which the dependent variable is either 0 or 1, depending on the group to which a case belongs. In fact, the Mahalanobis distance and R^2 are proportional. Thus

$$R^2 = cD^2 \qquad \text{Equation 1.14}$$

For each pair of groups, a and b, the unexplained variation from the regression is $1 - R_{ab}^2$, where R_{ab}^2 is the square of the multiple correlation coefficient when a variable coded as 0 or 1 (depending on whether the case is a member of a or b) is considered the dependent variable.

The sum of the unexplained variation for all pairs of groups can also be used as a criterion for variable selection. The variable chosen for inclusion is the one that minimizes the sum of the unexplained variation.

Three-Group Discriminant Analysis

The previous example used discriminant analysis to distinguish between members of two groups. This section presents a three-group discriminant example. The basics are the same as in two-group discriminant analysis, although there are several additional considerations.

One of the early applications of discriminant analysis in business was for credit-granting decisions. Many different models for extending credit based on a variety of predictor variables have been proposed. Churchill (1979) describes the case of the Consumer Finance Company, which must screen credit applicants. It has available for analysis 30 cases known to be poor, equivocal, and good credit risks. For each case, the annual income (in thousands of dollars), the number of credit cards, the number of children, and the age of the head of household are known. The task is to use discriminant analysis to derive a classification scheme for new cases based on the available data.

The Number of Functions

With two groups, it is possible to derive one discriminant function that maximizes the ratio of between- to within-groups sums of squares. When there are three groups, two discriminant functions can be calculated (assuming there are two or more predictors). The first function, as in the two-group case, has the largest ratio of between-groups to within-groups sums of squares. The second function is uncorrelated with the first and has the next largest ratio. In general, if there are k groups, $k - 1$ discriminant functions can be computed. They are all uncorrelated with each other and maximize the ratio of between-groups to within-groups sums of squares, subject to the constraint of being uncorrelated.

Figure 1.26 contains the two sets of unstandardized discriminant function coefficients for the credit risk example. Based on these coefficients it is possible to compute two scores for each case, one for each function. Consider, for example, the first case in the file with an annual income of $9,200, 2 credit cards, 3 children, and a 27-year-old head of household. For function 1, the discriminant score is

$$D_{11} = -14.47 + 0.33\,(9.2) + 0.13\,(2) + 0.24\,(27) + 0.15\,(3) = -4.2 \qquad \textbf{Equation 1.15}$$

The discriminant score for function 2 is obtained the same way, using the coefficients for the second function. Figure 1.27 shows the discriminant scores and other classification information for the first 15 cases. The score for function 1 is shown on the first row for a case; the second discriminant score is shown on the second row.

Figure 1.26   Unstandardized canonical discriminant function coefficients

```
Unstandardized canonical discriminant function coefficients

                    Func   1         Func   2


INCOME              .3257077         -.2251991
CREDIT              .1344126  -5.56481758E-03
AGEHEAD             .2444825          .1497008
CHILDREN            .1497964          .1778159
(Constant)        -14.4681087        -2.5402976
```

Figure 1.27   Classification output

Case Number	Mis Val	Sel	Actual Group	Highest Probability Group	P(D/G)	P(G/D)	2nd Highest Group	P(G/D)	Discrim Scores
1			1	1	.8229	.9993	2	.0007	-4.1524
									-.0479
2			1	1	.2100	.9999	2	.0001	-4.7122
									-1.3738
3			1	1	.7864	.9885	2	.0115	-3.3119
									.5959
4			1	1	.8673	.9718	2	.0282	-2.9966
									-.0155
5			1	1	.7610	.9646	2	.0354	-2.9464
									.3933
6			1	1	.8797	.9865	2	.0135	-3.2056
									-.4530
7			1	1	.7589	.9995	2	.0005	-4.2685
									-.1243
8			1	1	.5684	.9812	2	.0188	-3.1762
									.9402
9			1	1	.8191	.9980	2	.0020	-3.7851
									-.6398
10			1	1	.7160	.9336	2	.0664	-2.7267
									.0973
11			2	2	.9923	.9938	1	.0060	-.3287
									-.0043
12			2	2	.7764	.9922	1	.0076	-.3718
									-.5939
13			2	2	.6003	.9938	3	.0059	.5383
									.6958
14			2	2	.2482	.6334	1	.3666	-1.7833
									.8513
15			2	2	.5867	.9856	3	.0143	.7262
									-.0908

Classification

When there is one discriminant function, classification of cases into groups is based on the values for the single function. When there are several groups, a case's values on all functions must be considered simultaneously.

Figure 1.28 contains group means for the two functions. Group 1 has negative means for both functions, group 2 has a negative mean for function 1 and a positive mean for function 2, while group 3 has a positive mean for function 1 and a slightly negative mean for function 2.

Figure 1.28   Canonical discriminant function—group means

```
Canonical discriminant functions evaluated at group means (group centroids)

   Group      Func   1     Func   2

     1       -3.52816      -.06276
     2        -.28634       .11238
     3        3.81449      -.04962
```

Figure 1.29 shows the **territorial map** for the three groups on the two functions. The mean for each group is indicated by an asterisk (*). The numbered boundaries mark off the combination of function values that result in the classification of the cases into the

three groups. All cases with values that fall into the region bordered by the 3's are classified into the third group, those that fall into the region bordered by 2's are assigned to
the second group, and so on.

Figure 1.29   Territorial map

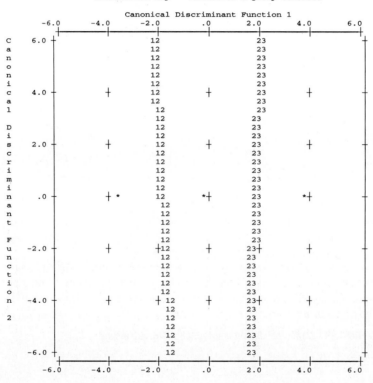

```
Symbols used in territorial map

Symbol  Group  Label
------  -----  --------------------

  1        1   POOR RISK
  2        2   EQUIVOCAL RISK
  3        3   GOOD RISK
  *            Group centroids


            Territorial Map  * indicates a group centroid

                  Canonical Discriminant Function 1
            -6.0      -4.0      -2.0       .0       2.0       4.0       6.0
         +---------+---------+---------+---------+---------+---------+
 C    6.0 +                          12                23                +
 a                                   12                23
 n                                   12                23
 o                                   12                23
 n                                   12                23
 i                                   12                23
 c    4.0 +         +                12       +        23       +        +
 a                                   12                23
 l                                   12                23
                                     12                23
 D                                   12                23
 i                                   12                23
 s    2.0 +         +                12       +        23       +        +
 c                                   12                23
 r                                   12                23
 i                                   12                23
 m                                   12                23
 i                                   12                23
 n     .0 +         + *              12      *+        23      *+        +
 a                                   12                23
 n                                   12                23
 t                                   12                23
                                     12                23
 F                                   12                23
 u   -2.0 +         +               +12       +       23+       +        +
 n                                   12                23
 c                                   12                23
 t                                   12                23
 i                                   12                23
 o                                   12                23
 n   -4.0 +         +             + 12        +       23+       +        +
                                     12                23
 2                                   12                23
                                     12                23
                                     12                23
                                     12                23
     -6.0 +                          12                23                +
         +---------+---------+---------+---------+---------+---------+
            -6.0      -4.0      -2.0       .0       2.0       4.0       6.0
```

Figure 1.30 is a plot of the values of the two discriminant scores for each case. From Figure 1.29 and Figure 1.30 you can see approximately how many cases are misclassified. For example, the case at the (1.6,1.6) coordinates is a good credit risk but falls into the equivocal risk region.

Figure 1.30   All-groups scatterplot

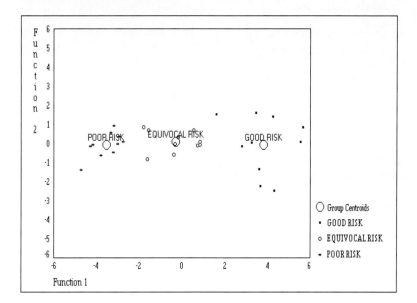

Figure 1.31 is the summary of the classification results. The diagonal elements are the number of cases classified correctly into the groups. For example, all poor and equivocal risks are classified correctly (10 out of 10 in each group). One of the good risks is misclassified as an equivocal risk. The overall percentage of cases classified correctly is the sum of the number of cases classified correctly in each group divided by the total number of cases. In this example, 29 out of 30 cases (96.7%) are classified correctly.

Figure 1.31   Classification table

```
Classification results -

                        No. of   Predicted Group Membership
      Actual Group       Cases      1         2         3
--------------------    ------   --------  --------  --------

Group      1              10        10         0         0
POOR RISK                        100.0%      .0%       .0%

Group      2              10         0        10         0
EQUIVOCAL RISK                     .0%     100.0%      .0%

Group      3              10         0         1         9
GOOD RISK                          .0%      10.0%     90.0%

Percent of "grouped" cases correctly classified:  96.67%


Classification processing summary

        30 cases were processed.
         0 cases were excluded for missing or out-of-range group codes.
         0 cases had at least one missing discriminating variable.
        30 cases were used for printed output.
```

Additional Statistics

When more than one discriminant function is derived, several statistics other than those discussed in "Other Discriminant Function Statistics" on p. 15 are of interest. Consider Figure 1.32. For each function, the eigenvalue is the ratio of between-groups to within-groups sums of squares. From Figure 1.33 (the analysis-of-variance tables for the two functions), the eigenvalue for function 1 is 10.03 ($270.8/27$). For function 2, it is 0.007 ($0.19/27$).

Figure 1.32   Additional statistics

```
                Canonical Discriminant Functions

            Pct of   Cum  Canonical After  Wilks'
 Fcn Eigenvalue Variance Pct   Corr     Fcn  Lambda  Chisquare  df  Sig

                                     :    0 .090030    61.394    8  .0000
 1*   10.0297   99.93  99.93  .9536 :    1 .993001      .179    3  .9809
 2      .0070     .07 100.00  .0837 :
```

The canonical correlation for a function is the square root of the between-groups to total sums of squares. When squared, it is the proportion of total variability explained by differences between groups. For example, for function 1 the canonical correlation is

$$\sqrt{\frac{270.8}{297.8}} = 0.954$$

Equation 1.16

Figure 1.33   One-way analysis of variance for the two functions

```
- - - - - - - - - - - - - - - - O N E W A Y - - - - - - - - - - - - - - - - - - - -

        Variable   DIS1_1      Function 1 for analysis 1
      By Variable  RISK

                                Analysis of variance

                              Sum of          Mean         F       F
             Source      D.F.  Squares        Squares      Ratio   Prob.

Between groups            2    270.8023       135.4011     135.4011  .0000
WITHIN GROUPS            27     27.0000         1.0000
TOTAL                   29    297.8023

- - - - - - - - - - - - - - - - O N E W A Y - - - - - - - - - - - - - - - - - - - -

        Variable   DIS2_1      Function 2 for analysis 1
      By Variable  RISK

                                Analysis of variance

                              Sum of          Mean         F       F
             Source      D.F.  Squares        Squares      Ratio   Prob.

Between groups            2      .1903          .0951       .0951    .9095
WITHIN GROUPS            27    27.0000         1.0000
TOTAL                   29    27.1903
```

When two or more functions are derived, it may be of interest to compare their merits. One frequently encountered criterion is the percentage of the total between-groups variability attributable to each function. Remember from the two-group example that the canonical discriminant functions are derived so that the pooled within-groups variance is 1. (This is seen in Figure 1.33 by the value of 1 for the within-groups mean square.) Thus, each function differs only in the between-groups sum of squares.

The first function always has the largest between-groups variability. The remaining functions have successively less between-groups variability. From Figure 1.32, function 1 accounts for 99.93% of the total between-groups variability:

$$\frac{\text{between-groups SS for function 1}}{\text{between-groups SS for function 1} + \text{between-groups SS for function 2}} = 0.9993$$

Equation 1.17

Function 2 accounts for the remaining 0.07% of the between-groups variability. These values are listed in the column labeled *Pct of Variance* in Figure 1.32. The next column, *Cum Pct*, is simply the sum of the percentage of variance of that function and the preceding ones.

Testing the Significance of the Discriminant Functions

When there are no differences among the populations from which the samples are selected, the discriminant functions reflect only sampling variability. A test of the null hypothesis that, in the population, the means of all discriminant functions in all groups are really equal and 0 can be based on Wilks' lambda. Since several functions must be considered simultaneously, Wilks' lambda is not just the ratio of the between-groups to within-groups sums of squares but is the product of the univariate Wilks' lambda for each function. For example, the Wilks' lambda for both functions considered simultaneously is, from Figure 1.33:

$$\Lambda = (\frac{27}{297.8}) (\frac{27}{27.19}) = 0.09 \hspace{4em} \text{Equation 1.18}$$

The significance level of the observed Wilks' lambda can be based on a chi-square transformation of the statistic. The value of lambda and its associated chi-square value, the degrees of freedom, and the significance level are shown in the second half of Figure 1.32 in the first row. Since the observed significance level is less than 0.00005, the null hypothesis that the means of both functions are equal in the three populations can be rejected.

When more than one function is derived, you can successively test the means of the functions by first testing all means simultaneously and then excluding one function at a time, testing the means of the remaining functions at each step. Using such successive tests, it is possible to find that a subset of discriminant functions accounts for all differences and that additional functions do not reflect true population differences, only random variation.

As shown in Figure 1.32, SPSS displays Wilks' lambda and the associated statistics as functions are removed successively. The column labeled *After Fcn* contains the number of the last function removed. The 0 indicates that no functions are removed, while a value of 2 indicates that the first two functions have been removed. For this example, the Wilks' lambda associated with function 2 after function 1 has been removed is 0.993. Since it is the last remaining function, the Wilks' lambda obtained is just the univariate value from Figure 1.33. The significance level associated with the second function is 0.981, indicating that it does not contribute substantially to group differences. This can also be seen in Figure 1.29, since only the first function determines the classification boundaries. All three groups have similar values for function 2.

Figure 1.34 is a classification map that illustrates the situation in which both functions contribute to group separation. In other words, a case's values on both functions are important for classification. For example, a case with a value of –2 for the first discriminant function will be classified into group 2 if the second function is negative and into group 1 if the second function is positive.

Figure 1.34   Territorial map

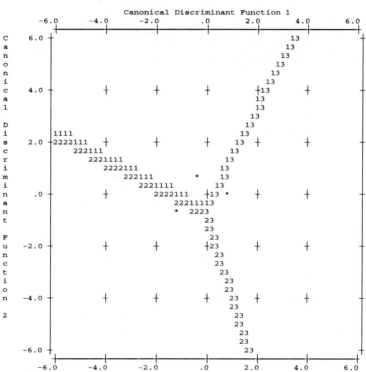

```
Symbols used in territorial map

Symbol  Group  Label
------  -----  --------------------

  1       1    DIE
  2       2    DIE LATER
  3       3    SURVIVE
  *            Group centroids


              Territorial Map   * indicates a group centroid

                 Canonical Discriminant Function 1
            -6.0       -4.0       -2.0       .0        2.0        4.0        6.0
           +---------+---------+---------+---------+---------+---------+
     C   6.0 +                                              13
     a                                                      13
     n                                                      13
     o                                                      13
     n                                                      13
     i                                                      13
     c   4.0 +         +         +         +       +13        +         +
     a                                                      13
     l                                                      13
                                                           13
     D                                                      13
     i       1111                                          13
     s   2.0 +2222111   +         +         +      13 +        +
     c       222111                                13
     r        2221111                              13
     i         2222111                            13
     m           222111           *               13
     i            2221111                         13
     n   .0  +        +         2222111    +13 *    +         +
     a                          22211113
     n                         *   2223
     t                             23
                                   23
     F                             23
     u  -2.0 +        +         +   +23      +         +
     n                             23
     c                             23
     t                             23
     i                             23
     o                             23
     n  -4.0 +        +         +   23       +         +
                                   23
     2                             23
                                   23
                                   23
                                   23
        -6.0 +                     23
           +---------+---------+---------+---------+---------+---------+
            -6.0       -4.0       -2.0       .0        2.0        4.0        6.0
```

The Variables

To assess the contribution of each variable to the discriminant functions, you can compute standardized coefficients. From Figure 1.35, income and age of the head of household appear to be the variables with the largest standardized coefficients.

Figure 1.35   Standardized canonical discriminant functions

```
Standardized canonical discriminant function coefficients

              Func  1     Func  2

INCOME         .89487     -.61872
CREDIT         .31363     -.01298
AGEHEAD        .84508      .51746
CHILDREN       .22936      .27226
```

Another way to examine the contributions of the variables is to examine the correlation coefficients between the variables and the functions, as shown in Figure 1.36. To help you interpret the functions, variables with large coefficients for a particular function are grouped together. These groupings are indicated with asterisks.

Figure 1.36   Correlations between variables and functions

```
Structure matrix:

Pooled within-groups correlations between discriminating variables
                               and canonical discriminant functions
(Variables ordered by size of correlation within function)

              Func  1     Func  2

CREDIT         .22728*     .19774

INCOME         .48482     -.84832*
AGEHEAD        .58577      .72023*
CHILDREN      -.00069      .38568*
```

When Assumptions Are Violated

As previously indicated, the linear discriminant function minimizes the probability of misclassification if in each group the variables are from multivariate normal distributions and the covariance matrices for all groups are equal. A variety of tests for multivariate normality are available (see Andrews et al., 1973). A simple tactic is to examine first the distributions of each of the variables individually. If the variables are jointly distributed as a multivariate normal, it follows that each is individually distributed normally. Therefore, if any of the variables have markedly non-normal distributions, there is reason to suspect that the multivariate normality assumption is violated. However, if all variables are normally distributed, the joint distribution is not necessarily multivariate normal.

There are several ways to test equality of the group covariance matrices. SPSS displays **Box's *M* test**, which is based on the determinants of the group covariance matrices. As shown in Figure 1.37, the significance probability is based on an *F* transformation. A small probability might lead us to reject the null hypothesis that the covariance matrices are equal. However, when sample sizes in the groups are large, the significance probability may be small even if the group covariance matrices are not too dissimilar. The test is also sensitive to departures from multivariate normality. That is, it tends to call matrices unequal if the normality assumption is violated.

Figure 1.37   Test of equality of group covariance matrices

```
Test of Equality of Group Covariance Matrices Using Box's M
   The ranks and natural logarithms of determinants printed are those
   of the group covariance matrices.

      Group Label                 Rank    Log Determinant
        1 DIE                       2        -2.756618
        2 SURVIVE                   2        -2.506420
      Pooled within-groups
      covariance matrix            2        -2.621559

      Box's M   Approximate F   Degrees of freedom   Significance
       .95855       .30431        3,   9467802.9         .8223
```

If the covariance matrices are unequal but the joint distribution of the variables is multivariate normal, the optimum classification rule is the quadratic discriminant function. However, if the covariance matrices are not too dissimilar, the linear discriminant function performs quite well, especially if the sample sizes are small (Wahl & Kronmal, 1977). Simulation studies suggest that with small sample sizes the quadratic rule can perform quite poorly. Since SPSS uses the discriminant function values to classify cases, not the original variables, it is not possible to obtain the optimum quadratic rule. (When covariance matrices are assumed identical, classification based on the original variables and all canonical functions are equivalent.) However, results obtained using the functions and their covariance matrices might not be too different from those obtained using covariance matrices for the original variables (Tatsuoka, 1971). For two groups, SPSS logistic regression (available in the Advanced Statistics option), which does not require multivariate normality, can also be considered.

In situations where the independent variables are all binary (yes–no, male–female) or a mixture of continuous and discrete variables, the linear discriminant function is not optimal. A variety of nonparametric procedures as well as special procedures for binary variables are available (see Hand, 1981; Goldstein & Dillon, 1978). In the case of dichotomous variables, most evidence suggests that the linear discriminant function often performs reasonably well (Gilbert, 1968; Moore, 1973). The SPSS logistic regression procedure can also be used to classify cases into one of two groups. It requires much more limited assumptions about the distributions of the data. (See Chapter 1 of *SPSS Advanced Statistics*.)

How to Obtain a Discriminant Analysis

The Discriminant Analysis procedure provides six methods for obtaining discriminant functions: forced entry and five stepwise procedures. You can use the discriminant functions to classify cases, and you can assess the accuracy of these classifications by examining classification tables, plots, and other statistical output.

The minimum specifications are:

- One or more numeric independent variables.
- One numeric grouping variable.
- Value range for the grouping variable.

To obtain a discriminant analysis and optionally save predicted group memberships or discriminant scores, from the menus choose:

Statistics
  Classify ▶
    Discriminant...

This opens the Discriminant Analysis dialog box, as shown in Figure 1.38.

Figure 1.38   Discriminant Analysis dialog box

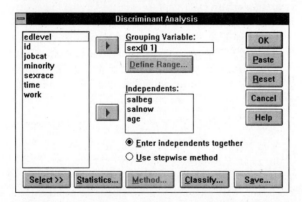

The numeric variables in your data file appear in the source list. Select a grouping variable to split your data file into two or more groups, and select one or more independent or predictor variables. After defining the categories of your grouping variable (see "Discriminant Analysis Define Range," below), click on OK. The default discriminant analysis includes standardized canonical discriminant function coefficients; the structure matrix of discriminant functions and all independent variables (whether they were entered into the equation or not); and group means on the discriminant functions. Cases with missing values on any of the independent variables are excluded during the analysis phase (computation of coefficients and basic statistics). A predictor variable must have a tolerance value of at least 0.001 to be entered into the analysis, regardless of entry method.

You can choose one of the following alternatives for selecting predictor variables:

○ **Enter independents together.** Forced-entry method. This is the default setting. All independent variables that satisfy tolerance criteria are entered simultaneously.

○ **Use stepwise method.** Stepwise method of variable entry. The default stepwise analysis minimizes the overall Wilks' lambda.

Discriminant Analysis Define Range

To define the range of categories for your grouping variable, highlight your variable and click on Define Range... in the Discriminant Analysis dialog box. This opens the Discriminant Analysis Define Range dialog box, as shown in Figure 1.39.

Figure 1.39   Discriminant Analysis Define Range dialog box

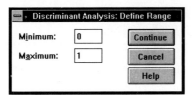

Enter values for minimum and maximum that correspond to the lowest and highest categories of the variable. Both values must be integers and the minimum value must be less than the maximum value. For example, if you specify a minimum value of 0 and a maximum value of 2, only cases with the values 0, 1, or 2 are used. Cases with values outside the bounds or with missing values (ungrouped cases) are excluded during the analysis. The analysis terminates if there are fewer than two non-empty groups.

Selecting a Subset for Analysis

Optionally, you can limit the analysis to a subset of cases having a particular value for a variable. Click on Select>> in the Discriminant Analysis dialog box. This expands the Discriminant Analysis dialog box, as shown in Figure 1.40.

Figure 1.40   Expanded Discriminant Analysis dialog box

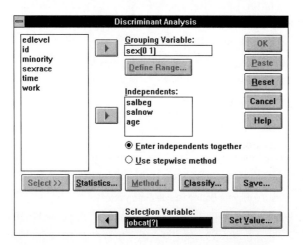

Choose a selection variable and click on Set Value... This opens the Discriminant Analysis Set Value dialog box, as shown in Figure 1.41.

Figure 1.41   Discriminant Analysis Set Value dialog box

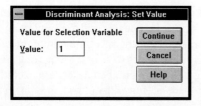

Enter a value for the case-selection variable. Only cases with the specified value are used during the analysis (selected and unselected cases are used in classification). If no cases have the selection value, the analysis terminates. You cannot use a grouping variable or independent variable as a case-selection variable.

Discriminant Analysis Statistics

To obtain optional descriptive statistics, function coefficients, or matrices, click on Statistics... in the Discriminant Analysis dialog box. This opens the Discriminant Analysis Statistics dialog box, as shown in Figure 1.42.

Figure 1.42   Discriminant Analysis Statistics dialog box

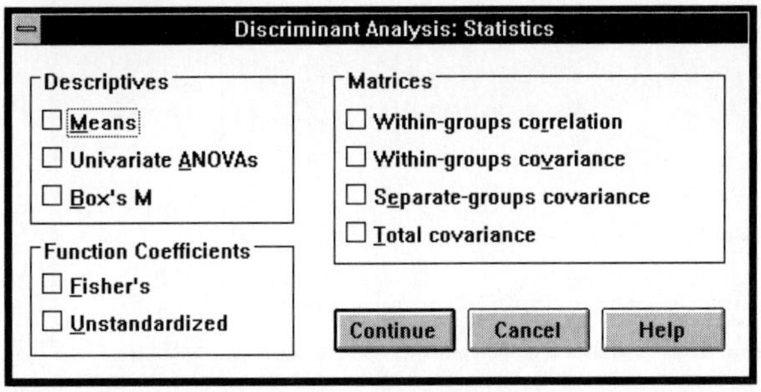

Descriptives. You can choose one or more of the following descriptive statistics:

❑ **Means.** Total and group means and standard deviations for independent variables.

❑ **Univariate ANOVAs.** One-way analysis-of-variance tests for equality of group means for each independent variable.

❑ **Box's M.** Box's *M* test of the equality of group covariance matrices.

Function Coefficients. You can choose one or both of the following:

❑ **Fisher's.** Classification function coefficients.

❑ **Unstandardized.** Unstandardized discriminant function coefficients.

Matrices. You can display one or more of the following matrices:

❑ **Within-groups correlation.** Pooled within-groups correlation matrix.

❑ **Within-groups covariance.** Pooled within-groups covariance matrix.

❑ **Separate-groups covariance.** Separate covariance matrices for each group.

❑ **Total covariance.** Covariance matrix from all cases if they were from a single sample.

Discriminant Analysis Stepwise Method

To select optional methods for stepwise analysis and to control variable entry and removal criteria and the display of summary statistics, click on Method... in the Discriminant Analysis dialog box. This opens the Discriminant Analysis Stepwise Method dialog box, as shown in Figure 1.43.

Figure 1.43   Discriminant Analysis Stepwise Method dialog box

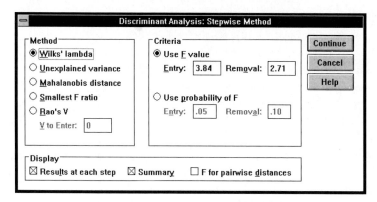

Method. You can choose one of the following methods:

○ **Wilks' lambda.** At each step, the variable that minimizes the overall Wilks' lambda is entered. This is the default.

○ **Unexplained variance.** At each step, the variable that minimizes the sum of the unexplained variation between groups is entered.

○ **Mahalanobis distance.** At each step, the variable that maximizes Mahalanobis distance between the two closest groups is entered.

○ **Smallest F ratio.** At each step, the variable that maximizes the smallest F ratio for pairs of groups is entered.

○ **Rao's V.** At each step, the variable that maximizes the increase in Rao's V is entered.

  ❑ **V to Enter.** By default, the minimum Rao's V that a variable must have to enter the analysis (VIN) is 0. To override this setting, enter a new value for V.

Criteria. You can choose one of the following entry criteria:

○ **Use F value.** Use F-to-enter and F-to-remove values as entry and removal criteria. This is the default setting. The default entry value is 3.84, the default removal value is 2.71. To override these settings, enter new values. The entry value must be greater than the removal value, and both values must be greater than 0.

○ **Use probability of F.** Use probability of F-to-enter and probability of F-to-remove as the entry and removal criteria. The default entry value is 0.05, the default removal value is 0.10. To override these settings, enter new values. The entry value must be less than the removal value, and both must be greater than 0 and less than or equal to 1.

Display. You can choose one or more of the following:

❏ **Results at each step.** Step-by-step output is displayed by default for stepwise methods. Statistics displayed include Wilks' lambda, equivalent F, degrees of freedom, and significance of F for each step. Tolerance, F-to-remove, and the value of the statistic used for variable selection are reported for each variable in the equation. Tolerance, minimum tolerance, F-to-enter, and the value of the statistic used for variable selection are reported for each variable not in the equation. To suppress step-by-step output, deselect this option.

❏ **Summary.** Summary table. Displayed by default for stepwise methods. For each step the output indicates entry or removal and gives the resulting value of the statistic used for variable selection and its significance. To suppress summary tables, deselect this option.

❏ **F for pairwise distances.** Displays a matrix of pairwise F ratios for each pair of groups. The F's are for significance tests for Mahalanobis distances between groups.

Discriminant Analysis Classification

To control the computation of prior probabilities, obtain summary classification output, or control the classification of cases with missing values, click on Classify... in the Discriminant Analysis dialog box. This opens the Discriminant Analysis Classification dialog box, as shown in Figure 1.44.

Figure 1.44   Discriminant Analysis Classification dialog box

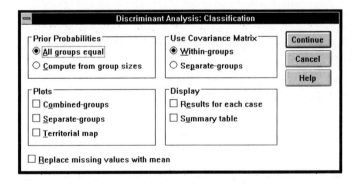

Prior Probabilities. You can choose one of the following alternatives:

○ **All groups equal.** Prior probabilities of group membership are assumed to be equal. This is the default.

○ **Compute from group sizes.** Prior probabilities are based on the sample proportion of cases in each group (after cases with missing values for any predictor are deleted).

Plots. You can choose one or more of the following plots:

❏ **Combined-groups.** All-groups scatterplot of the first two discriminant function values. If there is only one function, a histogram is displayed instead.

❏ **Separate-groups.** Separate-groups scatterplots of the first two discriminant function values. If there is only one function, histograms are displayed instead.

❏ **Territorial map.** Map shows group centroids and boundaries used for classification of the groups. Map is not displayed if there is only one discriminant function.

Use Covariance Matrix. You can choose one of the following alternatives:

○ **Within-groups.** The pooled within-groups covariance matrix is used to classify cases. This is the default.

○ **Separate-groups.** Separate-groups covariance matrices are used for classification. Since classification is based on the discriminant functions and not on the original variables, this option is not always equivalent to quadratic discrimination.

Display. You can choose one or both of the following display options:

❏ **Results for each case.** Codes for actual group and predicted group, posterior probabilities, and discriminant scores are displayed for each case.

❏ **Summary table.** Classification table summarizing actual and predicted group membership. If you use a selection variable, two tables are produced—one for selected cases and one for unselected cases.

Cases with missing or out-of-range values for the grouping variable (ungrouped cases) are classified. Cases with missing values for any independent variable are always excluded during the analysis and, by default, during classification. The following option is available:

❏ **Replace missing values with mean.** During classification, means are substituted for missing values for predictor variables, and cases with missing values are classified.

Discriminant Analysis Save New Variables

To save classification information or discriminant scores for each case, click on Save... in the Discriminant Analysis dialog box. This opens the Discriminant Analysis Save New Variables dialog box, as shown in Figure 1.45.

Figure 1.45   Discriminant Analysis Save New Variables dialog box

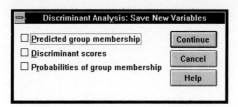

A table in the output shows the name of each new variable and its contents. You can choose one or more of the following:

❑ **Predicted group membership.** The group with largest posterior probability.

❑ **Discriminant scores.** One score is saved for each discriminant function derived.

❑ **Probabilities of group membership.** Creates as many variables as there are groups. The first variable contains the posterior probability of membership in the first group, the second new variable contains the probability of membership in the second group, etc.

Additional Features Available with Command Syntax

You can customize your discriminant analysis if you paste your selections to a syntax window and edit the resulting DISCRIMINANT command syntax (see Chapter 5 in the *SPSS Base System User's Guide*). Additional features include:

• Matrix facility to write a correlation matrix or to read a matrix of correlations that can be used in place of raw data (with the MATRIX subcommand).

• Multiple analyses using different variables or methods (with the ANALYSIS and METHOD subcommands).

• User-specified tolerance level (with the TOLERANCE subcommand).

• User-specified rootnames for new variables (with the SAVE subcommand).

• User-specified prior probabilities (with the PRIORS subcommand).

• Orthogonal rotation of pattern and structure matrices (with the ROTATE subcommand).

• The option to limit classification to a subset of discriminant functions (with the FUNCTIONS subcommand) or to unselected or unclassified cases (with the CLASSIFY subcommand).

See the Syntax Reference section of this manual for command syntax rules and for complete DISCRIMINANT command syntax.

2 Factor Analysis

What *are* creativity, love, and altruism? Unlike variables such as weight, blood pressure, and temperature, they cannot be measured on a scale, sphygmomanometer, or thermometer, in units of pounds, millimeters of mercury, or degrees Fahrenheit. Instead, they can be thought of as unifying constructs or labels that characterize responses to related groups of variables. For example, answers of "strongly agree" to items such as "sends me flowers," "listens to my problems," "reads my manuscripts," "laughs at my jokes," and "gazes deeply into my soul" may lead you to conclude that love is present. Thus, love is not a single measurable entity but a construct which is derived from measurement of other, directly observable variables. Identification of such underlying dimensions—factors—greatly simplifies the description and understanding of complex phenomena like social interaction. For example, postulating the existence of something called "love" explains the observed correlations between the responses to numerous and varied situations.

Factor analysis is a statistical technique used to identify a relatively small number of factors that can be used to represent relationships among sets of many interrelated variables. For example, variables such as scores on a battery of aptitude tests may be expressed as a linear combination of factors that represent verbal skills, mathematical aptitude, and perceptual speed. Variables such as consumer ratings of products in a survey can be expressed as a function of factors such as product quality and utility. Factor analysis helps identify these underlying, not-directly-observable constructs.

A huge number of variables can be used to describe a community—degree of industrialization, commercial activity, population, mobility, average family income, extent of home ownership, birth rate, and so forth. However, descriptions of what is meant by the term *community* might be greatly simplified if it were possible to identify underlying dimensions, or factors, of communities. This was attempted by Jonassen and Peres (1960), who examined 82 community variables from 88 counties in Ohio. This chapter uses a subset of their variables (shown in Table 2.1) to illustrate the basics of factor analysis.

Table 2.1 Community variables

popstabl	Population stability.
newscirc	Weekly per capita local newspaper circulation.
femempld	Percentage of females 14 years or older in labor force.
farmers	Percentage of farmers and farm managers in labor force.
retailng	Per capita retail sales in dollars.
commercl	Total per capita commercial activity in dollars.
industzn	Industrialization index.
health	Health index.
chldnegl	Total per capita expenditures on county Aid to Dependent Children.
commeffc	Index of the extent to which a community fosters a high standard of living.
dwelgnew	Percentage of dwelling units built recently.
migrnpop	Index of the extent of migration into and out of the community.
unemploy	Unemployment index.
mentalil	Extent of mental illness.

The Factor Analysis Model

The basic assumption of factor analysis is that underlying dimensions, or factors, can be used to explain complex phenomena. Observed correlations between variables result from their sharing these factors. For example, correlations between test scores might be attributable to such shared factors as general intelligence, abstract reasoning skill, and reading comprehension. The correlations between the community variables might be due to factors like amount of urbanization, the socioeconomic level, or welfare, of the community, and the population stability. The goal of factor analysis is to identify the not-directly-observable factors based on a set of observable variables.

The mathematical model for factor analysis appears somewhat similar to a multiple regression equation. Each variable is expressed as a linear combination of factors which are not actually observed. For example, the industrialization index might be expressed as

$$\text{industzn} = a\,(\text{urbanism}) + b\,(\text{welfare}) + c\,(\text{influx}) + U_{\text{industzn}} \qquad \textbf{Equation 2.1}$$

This equation differs from the usual multiple regression equation in that *urbanism*, *welfare*, and *influx* are not single independent variables. Instead, they are labels for groups of variables that characterize these concepts. These groups of variables constitute the factors. Usually, the factors useful for characterizing a set of variables are not known in advance but are determined by factor analysis.

Urbanism, welfare, and *influx* are called **common factors**, since all variables are expressed as functions of them. The U in Equation 2.1 is called a **unique factor**, since it represents that part of the industrialization index that cannot be explained by the common factors. It is unique to the industrialization index variable.

In general, the model for the ith standardized variable is written as

$$X_i = A_{i1}F_1 + A_{i2}F_2 + ... + A_{ik}F_k + U_i \qquad \text{Equation 2.2}$$

where the F's are the common factors, the U is the unique factor, and the A's are the coefficients used to combine the k factors. The unique factors are assumed to be uncorrelated with each other and with the common factors.

The factors are inferred from the observed variables and can be estimated as linear combinations of the variables. For example, the estimated urbanism factor is expressed as

$$\text{urbanism} = C_1 \,(\text{popstabl}) + C_2 \,(\text{newscirc}) + ... + C_{14} \,(\text{mentalil}) \qquad \text{Equation 2.3}$$

where the C's are coefficients. While it is possible that all of the variables contribute to the urbanism factor, we hope that only a subset of variables characterizes urbanism, as indicated by their large coefficients. The general expression for the estimate of the jth factor, F_j, is

$$F_j = \sum_{i=1}^{p} W_{ji}X_i = W_{j1}X_1 + W_{j2}X_2 + ... + W_{jp}X_p \qquad \text{Equation 2.4}$$

The W_i's are known as factor score coefficients, and p is the number of variables.

Ingredients of a Good Factor Analysis Solution

Before examining the mechanics of a factor analysis solution, let's consider the characteristics of a successful factor analysis. One goal is to represent relationships among sets of variables parsimoniously. That is, we would like to explain the observed correlations using as few factors as possible. If many factors are needed, little simplification or summarization occurs. We would also like the factors to be meaningful. A good factor solution is both simple and interpretable. When factors can be interpreted, new insights are possible. For example, if liquor preferences can be explained by such factors as sweetness and regional tastes (Stoetzel, 1960), marketing strategies can reflect this.

Steps in a Factor Analysis

Factor analysis usually proceeds in four steps.

1. In the first step, the correlation matrix for all variables is computed, as shown in Figure 2.1. Variables that do not appear to be related to other variables can be identified from the matrix and associated statistics. The appropriateness of the factor model can also be evaluated. At this step, you should also decide what to do with cases that have missing values for some of the variables.

2. In the second step, factor extraction—the number of factors necessary to represent the data and the method for calculating them—must be determined. At this step, you also ascertain how well the chosen model fits the data.

3. The third step, rotation, focuses on transforming the factors to make them more interpretable.

4. At the fourth step, scores for each factor can be computed for each case. These scores can then be used in a variety of other analyses.

Examining the Correlation Matrix

The correlation matrix for the 14 community variables is shown in Figure 2.1. Since one of the goals of factor analysis is to obtain factors that help explain these correlations, the variables must be related to each other for the factor model to be appropriate. If the correlations between variables are small, it is unlikely that they share common factors. Figure 2.1 shows that almost half the coefficients are greater than 0.3 in absolute value. All variables, except the extent of mental illness, have a large correlation with at least one of the other variables in the set.

Bartlett's test of sphericity can be used to test the hypothesis that the correlation matrix is an **identity matrix**; that is, all diagonal terms are 1 and all off-diagonal terms are 0. The test requires that the data be a sample from a multivariate normal population. From Figure 2.2, the value of the test statistic for sphericity (based on a chi-square transformation of the determinant of the correlation matrix) is large and the associated significance level is small, so it appears unlikely that the population correlation matrix is an identity. If the hypothesis that the population correlation matrix is an identity cannot be rejected because the observed significance level is large, you should reconsider the use of the factor model.

Figure 2.1   Correlation matrix of 14 community variables

	POPSTABL	NEWSCIRC	FEMEMPLD	FARMERS	RETAILNG	COMMERCL	INDUSTZN
POPSTABL	1.00000						
NEWSCIRC	-.17500	1.00000					
FEMEMPLD	-.27600	.61600	1.00000				
FARMERS	.36900	-.62500	-.63700	1.00000			
RETAILNG	-.12700	.62400	.73600	-.51900	1.00000		
COMMERCL	-.06900	.65200	.58900	-.30600	.72700	1.00000	
INDUSTZN	-.10600	.71200	.74200	-.54500	.78500	.91100	1.00000
HEALTH	-.14900	-.03000	.24100	-.06800	.10000	.12300	.12900
CHLDNEGL	-.03900	-.17100	-.58900	.25700	-.55700	-.35700	-.42400
COMMEFFC	-.00500	.10000	.47100	-.21300	.45200	.28700	.35700
DWELGNEW	-.67000	.18800	.41300	-.57900	.16500	.03000	.20300
MIGRNPOP	-.47600	-.08600	.06400	-.19800	.00700	-.06800	-.02400
UNEMPLOY	.13700	-.37300	-.68900	.45000	-.65000	-.42400	-.52800
MENTALIL	.23700	.04600	-.23700	.12100	-.19000	-.05500	-.09500

	HEALTH	CHLDNEGL	COMMEFFC	DWELGNEW	MIGRNPOP	UNEMPLOY	MENTALIL
HEALTH	1.00000						
CHLDNEGL	-.40700	1.00000					
COMMEFFC	.73200	-.66000	1.00000				
DWELGNEW	.29000	-.13800	.31100	1.00000			
MIGRNPOP	.08300	.14800	.06700	.50500	1.00000		
UNEMPLOY	-.34800	.73300	-.60100	-.26600	.18100	1.00000	
MENTALIL	-.27900	.24700	-.32400	-.26600	-.30700	.21700	1.00000

Figure 2.2   Test statistic for sphericity

KAISER-MEYER-OLKIN MEASURE OF SAMPLING ADEQUACY =   .76968

BARTLETT TEST OF SPHERICITY = 946.15313, SIGNIFICANCE =   .00000

Another indicator of the strength of the relationship among variables is the partial correlation coefficient. If variables share common factors, the partial correlation coefficients between pairs of variables should be small when the linear effects of the other variables are eliminated. The partial correlations are then estimates of the correlations between the unique factors and should be close to 0 when the factor analysis assumptions are met. (Recall that the unique factors are assumed to be uncorrelated with each other.)

The negative of the partial correlation coefficient is called the **anti-image correlation**. The matrix of anti-image correlations is shown in Figure 2.3. If the proportion of large coefficients is high, you should reconsider the use of the factor model.

Figure 2.3   Anti-image correlation matrix

```
ANTI-IMAGE CORRELATION MATRIX:
```

	POPSTABL	NEWSCIRC	FEMEMPLD	FARMERS	RETAILNG	COMMERCL	INDUSTZN
POPSTABL	.58174						
NEWSCIRC	.01578	.82801					
FEMEMPLD	.10076	-.24223	.90896				
FARMERS	.03198	.43797	-.00260	.73927			
RETAILNG	.14998	-.14295	-.12037	.16426	.86110		
COMMERCL	.20138	-.27622	.20714	-.49344	-.19535	.68094	

	POPSTABL	NEWSCIRC	FEMEMPLD	FARMERS	RETAILNG	COMMERCL	INDUSTZN
INDUSTZN	-.23815	.08231	-.32790	.41648	-.04602	-.85499	.75581
HEALTH	.26114	-.02839	-.02332	.05845	.38421	-.16150	.08627
CHLDNEGL	.10875	-.24685	.27281	-.03446	.13062	.07043	-.07979
COMMEFFC	-.39878	.05772	.03017	-.16386	-.33700	.09427	-.06742
DWELGNEW	.55010	.04505	-.09493	.33479	.26678	.13831	-.13726
MIGRNPOP	.20693	.22883	-.06689	.11784	-.15886	-.07421	.06501
UNEMPLOY	-.17774	-.05946	.18631	-.12699	.19591	-.01262	-.02503
MENTALIL	-.08437	-.10058	.07770	.03053	.07842	-.02921	-.00056

	HEALTH	CHLDNEGL	COMMEFFC	DWELGNEW	MIGRNPOP	UNEMPLOY	MENTALIL
HEALTH	.59124						
CHLDNEGL	.02899	.87023					
COMMEFFC	-.70853	.19554	.68836				
DWELGNEW	.07480	-.04008	-.30434	.70473			
MIGRNPOP	.07460	-.10809	-.14292	-.24074	.61759		
UNEMPLOY	-.02904	-.33523	.19240	.02181	-.38208	.87230	
MENTALIL	.06821	-.04163	.04728	-.02505	.20487	-.02708	.88390

```
MEASURES OF SAMPLING ADEQUACY (MSA) ARE PRINTED ON THE DIAGONAL.
```

The **Kaiser-Meyer-Olkin measure** of sampling adequacy is an index for comparing the magnitudes of the observed correlation coefficients to the magnitudes of the partial correlation coefficients. It is computed as

$$KMO = \frac{\sum\sum_{i \neq j} r_{ij}^2}{\sum\sum_{i \neq j} r_{ij}^2 + \sum\sum_{i \neq j} a_{ij}^2}$$

Equation 2.5

where r_{ij} is the simple correlation coefficient between variables i and j, and a_{ij} is the partial correlation coefficient between variables i and j. If the sum of the squared partial correlation coefficients between all pairs of variables is small when compared to the sum of the squared correlation coefficients, the KMO measure is close to 1. Small values for the KMO measure indicate that a factor analysis of the variables may not be a good idea, since correlations between pairs of variables cannot be explained by the other variables. Kaiser (1974) characterizes measures in the 0.90's as *marvelous*, in the 0.80's as *meri-*

torious, in the 0.70's as *middling*, in the 0.60's as *mediocre*, in the 0.50's as *miserable*, and below 0.5 as *unacceptable*. The value of the overall KMO statistic for this example is shown in Figure 2.2. Since the KMO measure is close to 0.8, we can comfortably proceed with the factor analysis.

A measure of sampling adequacy can be computed for each individual variable in a similar manner. Instead of including all pairs of variables in the summations, only coefficients involving that variable are included. For the ith variable, the measure of sampling adequacy is

$$MSA_i = \frac{\sum_{j \neq i} r_{ij}^2}{\sum_{j \neq i} r_{ij}^2 + \sum_{j \neq i} a_{ij}^2}$$

Equation 2.6

These measures of sampling adequacy are displayed on the diagonals of Figure 2.3. Again, reasonably large values are needed for a good factor analysis. Thus, you might consider eliminating variables with small values for the measure of sampling adequacy.

The squared multiple correlation coefficient between a variable and all other variables is another indication of the strength of the linear association among the variables. These values are shown in the column labeled *Communality* in Figure 2.9. The extent-of-mental-illness variable has a small multiple R^2, suggesting that it should be eliminated from the set of variables being analyzed. However, it will be kept in the analysis for illustrative purposes.

Factor Extraction

The goal of **factor extraction** is to determine the factors. In this example, we will obtain estimates of the initial factors from principal components analysis. Other methods for factor extraction are described in "Methods for Factor Extraction" on p. 60. In **principal components analysis**, linear combinations of the observed variables are formed. The first principal component is the combination that accounts for the largest amount of variance in the sample. The second principal component accounts for the next largest amount of variance and is uncorrelated with the first. Successive components explain progressively smaller portions of the total sample variance, and all are uncorrelated with each other.

It is possible to compute as many principal components as there are variables. If all principal components are used, each variable can be exactly represented by them, but nothing has been gained, since there are as many factors (principal components) as variables. When all factors are included in the solution, all of the variance of each variable is accounted for, and there is no need for a unique factor in the model. The proportion of variance accounted for by the common factors, or the **communality** of a variable, is 1 for all the variables, as shown in Figure 2.4. In general, principal components analysis is a separate technique from factor analysis. That is, it can be used whenever uncorrelated linear combinations of the observed variables are desired. All it does is transform a set of correlated variables to a set of uncorrelated variables (principal components).

Figure 2.4   Initial statistics

```
EXTRACTION   1   FOR ANALYSIS   1, PRINCIPAL-COMPONENTS ANALYSIS (PC)


INITIAL STATISTICS:


VARIABLE      COMMUNALITY  *  FACTOR    EIGENVALUE   PCT OF VAR   CUM PCT
                           *
POPSTABL       1.00000     *    1        5.70658       40.8        40.8
NEWSCIRC       1.00000     *    2        2.35543       16.8        57.6
FEMEMPLD       1.00000     *    3        2.00926       14.4        71.9
FARMERS        1.00000     *    4         .89745        6.4        78.3
RETAILNG       1.00000     *    5         .75847        5.4        83.8
COMMERCL       1.00000     *    6         .53520        3.8        87.6
INDUSTZN       1.00000     *    7         .50886        3.6        91.2
HEALTH         1.00000     *    8         .27607        2.0        93.2
CHLDNEGL       1.00000     *    9         .24511        1.8        94.9
COMMEFFC       1.00000     *   10         .20505        1.5        96.4
DWELGNEW       1.00000     *   11         .19123        1.4        97.8
MIGRNPOP       1.00000     *   12         .16982        1.2        99.0
UNEMPLOY       1.00000     *   13         .10202         .7        99.7
MENTALIL       1.00000     *   14         .03946         .3       100.0
```

To help us decide how many factors we need to represent the data, it is helpful to examine the percentage of total variance explained by each. The total variance is the sum of the variance of each variable. For simplicity, all variables and factors are expressed in standardized form, with a mean of 0 and a standard deviation of 1. Since there are 14 variables and each is standardized to have a variance of 1, the total variance is 14 in this example.

Figure 2.4 contains the initial statistics for each factor. The total variance explained by each factor is listed in the column labeled *Eigenvalue*. The next column contains the percentage of the total variance attributable to each factor. For example, the linear combination formed by factor 2 has a variance of 2.35, which is 16.8% of the total variance of 14. The last column, the cumulative percentage, indicates the percentage of variance attributable to that factor and those that precede it in the table. Note that the factors are arranged in descending order of variance explained. Note also that although variable names and factors are displayed on the same line, there is no correspondence between the lines in the two halves of the table. The first two columns provide information about the individual variables, while the last four columns describe the factors.

Figure 2.4 shows that almost 72% of the total variance is attributable to the first three factors. The remaining eleven factors together account for only 28.1% of the variance. Thus, a model with three factors may be adequate to represent the data.

Several procedures have been proposed for determining the number of factors to use in a model. One criterion suggests that only factors that account for variances greater than 1 (eigenvalue greater than 1) should be included. Factors with a variance less than 1 are no better than a single variable, since each variable has a variance of 1. Although this is the default criterion in the SPSS Factor Analysis procedure, it is not always a good solution (see Tucker, Koopman, & Linn, 1969).

Figure 2.5 is a plot of the total variance associated with each factor. The plot shows a distinct break between the steep slope of the large factors and the gradual trailing off of the rest of the factors. This gradual trailing off is called the **scree** (Cattell, 1966) because it resembles the rubble that forms at the foot of a mountain. Experimental evidence indicates that the scree begins at the kth factor, where k is the true number of factors. From the scree plot, it again appears that a three-factor model should be sufficient for the community example.

Figure 2.5   Scree plot

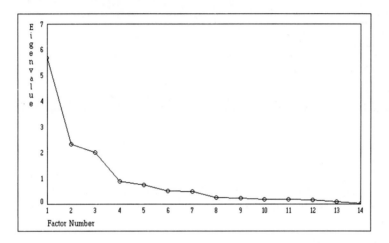

The Three Factors

Figure 2.6 displays the coefficients that relate the variables to the three factors. The figure shows that the industrialization index can be expressed as

$$industzn = 0.844F_1 + 0.300F_2 + 0.238F_3$$

Equation 2.7

Similarly, the health index is

$$health = 0.383F_1 - 0.327F_2 - 0.635F_3$$

Equation 2.8

Each row of Figure 2.6 contains the coefficients used to express a standardized variable in terms of the factors. These coefficients are called **factor loadings**, since they indicate how much weight is assigned to each factor. Factors with large coefficients (in absolute value) for a variable are closely related to the variable. For example, factor 1 is the factor with the largest loading for the industrialization index. The matrix of factor loadings is called the **factor pattern matrix**.

Figure 2.6   Factor matrix

```
FACTOR MATRIX:

                    FACTOR  1        FACTOR  2        FACTOR  3

POPSTABL            -.30247           .68597          -.36451
NEWSCIRC             .67238           .28096           .49779
FEMEMPLD             .89461           .01131           .08063
FARMERS             -.68659           .20002          -.40450
RETAILNG             .85141           .24264           .09351
COMMERCL             .72503           .39394           .19896
INDUSTZN             .84436           .29956           .23775
HEALTH               .38347          -.32718          -.63474
CHLDNEGL            -.67430          -.12139           .52896
COMMEFFC             .63205          -.15540          -.64221
DWELGNEW             .45886          -.73940           .18706
MIGRNPOP             .07894          -.74371           .24335
UNEMPLOY            -.78714          -.09777           .30110
MENTALIL            -.30025           .45463           .27134
```

When the estimated factors are uncorrelated with each other (orthogonal), the factor loadings are also the correlations between the factors and the variables. Thus, the correlation between the health index and factor 1 is 0.383. Similarly, there is a slightly smaller correlation between the health index and factor 2 (–0.327). The matrix of correlations between variables and factors is called the **factor structure matrix**. When the factors are orthogonal, the factor structure matrix and the factor pattern matrix are equivalent. As shown in Figure 2.6, such a matrix is called the *Factor Matrix* in SPSS output.

More on the Factor Matrix

There is yet another interpretation of the factor matrix in Figure 2.6. Whether the factors are orthogonal or not, the factor loadings are the standardized regression coefficients in the multiple regression equation with the original variable as the dependent variable and the factors as the independent variables. If the factors are uncorrelated, the values of the coefficients are not dependent on each other. They represent the unique contribution of each factor and are the correlations between the factors and the variable.

To judge how well the three-factor model describes the original variables, we can compute the proportion of the variance of each variable explained by the three-factor model. Since the factors are uncorrelated, the total proportion of variance explained is simply the sum of the variance proportions explained by each factor.

Consider, for example, the health index. Factor 1 accounts for 14.7% of the variance for this variable. This is obtained by squaring the correlation coefficient for factor 1 and *health* (0.383). Similarly, factor 3 explains 40.3% (-0.635^2) of the variance. The total percentage of variance in the health index accounted for by this three-factor model is therefore 65.7% (14.7% + 10.7% + 40.3%). The proportion of variance explained by the common factors is called the communality of the variable.

The communalities for the variables are shown in Figure 2.7, together with the percentage of variance accounted for by each of the retained factors. This table is called *Final Statistics,* since it shows the communalities and factor statistics after the desired number of factors has been extracted. When factors are estimated using the method of principal components, the factor statistics are the same in the tables for initial statistics and final statistics. However, the communalities are different, since all of the variances of the variables are not explained when only a subset of factors is retained.

Figure 2.7   Communality of variables

```
FINAL STATISTICS:

VARIABLE      COMMUNALITY  *  FACTOR   EIGENVALUE   PCT OF VAR   CUM PCT
                           *
POPSTABL         .69491    *    1        5.70658       40.8        40.8
NEWSCIRC         .77882    *    2        2.35543       16.8        57.6
FEMEMPLD         .80696    *    3        2.00926       14.4        71.9
FARMERS          .67503    *
RETAILNG         .79253    *
COMMERCL         .72044    *
INDUSTZN         .85921    *
HEALTH           .65699    *
CHLDNEGL         .74921    *
COMMEFFC         .83607    *
DWELGNEW         .79226    *
MIGRNPOP         .61855    *
UNEMPLOY         .71981    *
MENTALIL         .37047    *
```

Communalities can range from 0 to 1, with 0 indicating that the common factors explain none of the variance and 1 indicating that all the variance is explained by the common factors. The variance that is not explained by the common factors is attributed to the unique factor and is called the **uniqueness** of the variable.

The Reproduced Correlation Matrix

One of the basic assumptions of factor analysis is that the observed correlation between variables is due to the sharing of common factors. Therefore, the estimated correlations between the factors and the variables can be used to estimate the correlations between the variables. In general, if factors are orthogonal, the estimated correlation coefficient for variables i and j is

$$r_{ij} = \sum_{f=1}^{k} r_{fi}r_{fj} = r_{1i}r_{1j} + r_{2i}r_{2j} + \dots + r_{ki}r_{kj}$$ **Equation 2.9**

where k is the number of common factors and r_{fi} is the correlation between the fth factor and the ith variable.

From Figure 2.6 and Equation 2.9, the estimated correlation coefficient for *health* and *commeffc*, based on the three-factor model, is

$$r_{8,\,10} = (0.38)\,(0.63) + (-0.33)\,(-0.16) + (-0.63)\,(-0.64) = 0.70$$ **Equation 2.10**

Figure 2.1 shows that the observed correlation coefficient between *health* and *commeffc* is 0.73, so the difference between the observed correlation coefficient and that estimated from the model is about -0.03. This difference is called a **residual**. The estimated correlation coefficients and the residuals are shown in Figure 2.8. The residuals are listed

Figure 2.8   Estimated correlations and residuals

Reproduced Correlation Matrix:

	POPSTABL	NEWSCIRC	FEMEMPLD	FARMERS	RETAILNG
POPSTABL	.69491*	.01709	.01623	−.12332	−.00183
NEWSCIRC	−.19209	.77882*	−.02883	−.01820	−.06320
FEMEMPLD	−.29223	.64483	.80696*	.00758	−.03597
FARMERS	.49232	−.60680	−.64458	.67503*	.05486
RETAILNG	−.12517	.68720	.77197	−.57386	.79253*
COMMERCL	−.02159	.69721	.66912	−.49948	.73149
INDUSTZN	−.13656	.77024	.77793	−.61598	.81382
HEALTH	−.10906	−.15005	.28818	−.07198	.18775
CHLDNEGL	−.07212	−.22418	−.56196	.22473	−.55410
COMMEFFC	−.06368	.06163	.51190	−.20527	.44037
DWELGNEW	−.71418	.19390	.41722	−.53861	.22876
MIGRNPOP	−.62274	−.03474	.08183	−.30139	−.09049
UNEMPLOY	.06126	−.40684	−.68101	.39909	−.66575
MENTALIL	.30378	.06093	−.24158	.18733	−.11995

	COMMERCL	INDUSTZN	HEALTH	CHLDNEGL	COMMEFFC
POPSTABL	−.04741	.03056	−.03994	.03312	.05868
NEWSCIRC	−.04521	−.05824	.12005	.05318	.03837
FEMEMPLD	−.08012	−.03593	−.04718	−.02704	−.04090
FARMERS	.19348	.07098	.00398	.03227	−.00773
RETAILNG	−.00449	−.02882	−.08775	−.00290	.01163
COMMERCL	.72044*	.13350	.10014	.07447	.01773
INDUSTZN	.77750	.85921*	.05413	.05596	.02256
HEALTH	.02286	.07487	.65699*	.14761	.03114
CHLDNEGL	−.43147	−.47996	−.55461	.74921*	.08703
COMMEFFC	.26927	.33444	.70086	−.74703	.83607*
DWELGNEW	.07863	.21042	.29914	−.12070	.28479
MIGRNPOP	−.18732	−.09828	.11913	.16577	.00918
UNEMPLOY	−.54931	−.62233	−.46098	.70191	−.67569
MENTALIL	.01539	−.05282	−.43612	.29080	−.43468

	DWELGNEW	MIGRNPOP	UNEMPLOY	MENTALIL
POPSTABL	.04418	.14674	.07574	−.06678
NEWSCIRC	−.00590	−.05126	.03384	−.01493
FEMEMPLD	−.00422	−.01783	−.00799	.00458
FARMERS	−.04039	.10339	.05091	−.06633
RETAILNG	−.06376	.09749	.01575	−.07005
COMMERCL	−.04863	.11932	.12531	−.07039
INDUSTZN	−.00742	.07428	.09433	−.04218
HEALTH	−.00914	−.03613	.11298	.15712
CHLDNEGL	−.01730	−.01777	.03109	−.04380
COMMEFFC	.02621	.05782	.07469	.11068
DWELGNEW	.79226*	−.12664	−.03343	.15717
MIGRNPOP	.63164	.61855*	.09715	−.01121
UNEMPLOY	−.23257	.08385	.71981*	−.05659
MENTALIL	−.42317	−.29579	.27359	.37047*

The lower left triangle contains the reproduced correlation matrix; the diagonal, reproduced communalities; and the upper right triangle residuals between the observed correlations and the reproduced correlations.

There are 42 (46.0%) residuals (above diagonal) with absolute values > 0.05.

above the diagonal and the estimated correlation coefficients are below the diagonal. The values with asterisks (on the diagonal) are reproduced communalities.

Below the matrix is a message indicating how many residuals are greater than 0.05 in absolute value. In the community data example, less than half (46%) are greater than 0.05 in absolute value. The magnitudes of the residuals indicate how well the fitted model reproduces the observed correlations. If the residuals are large, the model does not fit the data well and should probably be reconsidered.

Some Additional Considerations

If a method other than principal components analysis is used to extract the initial factors, there are differences in parts of the factor output. For example, consider Figure 2.9, which contains the initial statistics obtained when the maximum-likelihood algorithm is used.

Figure 2.9   Maximum-likelihood extractions

```
INITIAL STATISTICS:


VARIABLE      COMMUNALITY  *   FACTOR   EIGENVALUE   PCT OF VAR   CUM PCT
                           *
POPSTABL        .62385     *     1        5.70658       40.8       40.8
NEWSCIRC        .71096     *     2        2.35543       16.8       57.6
FEMEMPLD        .77447     *     3        2.00926       14.4       71.9
FARMERS         .74519     *     4         .89745        6.4       78.3
RETAILNG        .79259     *     5         .75847        5.4       83.8
COMMERCL        .90987     *     6         .53520        3.8       87.6
INDUSTZN        .92914     *     7         .50886        3.6       91.2
HEALTH          .66536     *     8         .27607        2.0       93.2
CHLDNEGL        .67987     *     9         .24511        1.8       94.9
COMMEFFC        .79852     *    10         .20505        1.5       96.4
DWELGNEW        .72576     *    11         .19123        1.4       97.8
MIGRNPOP        .50560     *    12         .16982        1.2       99.0
UNEMPLOY        .72549     *    13         .10202         .7       99.7
MENTALIL        .23825     *    14         .03946         .3      100.0
```

Regardless of the algorithm used, by default the number of factors to be retained is determined by the principal components solution because it is easily obtainable. Thus, most of the output in Figure 2.9 is identical to that displayed in Figure 2.4. The only exception is the communalities column. In the principal components solution, all initial communalities are listed as 1's. In all other solutions, the initial estimate of the communality of a variable is the multiple R^2 from the regression equation that predicts that variable from all other variables. These initial communalities are used in the estimation algorithm.

When a method other than principal components analysis is used to estimate the final factor matrix, the percentage of variance explained by each final factor is usually different. Figure 2.10 contains the final statistics from a maximum-likelihood solution. The final three factors extracted explain only 63% of the total variance, as compared to 72% for the first three principal components. The first factor accounts for 35.5% of the total variance, as compared to 40.8% for the first principal component.

Figure 2.10   Maximum-likelihood final statistics

```
Final Statistics:

Variable     Communality  *  Factor   SS Loadings  Pct of Var   Cum Pct
                          *
POPSTABL        .52806    *    1        4.96465       35.5        35.5
NEWSCIRC        .57439    *    2        2.17833       15.6        51.0
FEMEMPLD        .75057    *    3        1.67661       12.0        63.0
FARMERS         .56808    *
RETAILNG        .72089    *
COMMERCL        .87128    *
INDUSTZN        .96817    *
HEALTH          .33382    *
CHLDNEGL        .78341    *
COMMEFFC        .62762    *
DWELGNEW        .87445    *
MIGRNPOP        .35074    *
UNEMPLOY        .70833    *
MENTALIL        .15977    *
```

The proportion of the total variance explained by each factor can be calculated from the factor matrix. The proportion of the total variance explained by factor 1 is calculated by summing the proportions of variance of each variable attributable to factor 1. Figure 2.11, the factor matrix for the maximum-likelihood solution, shows that factor 1 accounts for $(-0.16)^2$ of the *popstabl* variance, 0.72^2 of the *newscirc* variance, 0.81^2 of the *femempld* variance, and so on for the other variables. The total variance attributable to factor 1 is therefore

$$
\begin{aligned}
\text{Total variance for factor 1} = & \ (-0.16)^2 + 0.72^2 + 0.81^2 + (-0.59)^2 \\
& + 0.83^2 + 0.89^2 + 0.97^2 + 0.20^2 \\
& + (-0.52)^2 + 0.44^2 + 0.27^2 + (-0.00)^2 \\
& + (-0.62)^2 + (-0.15)^2 = 4.96
\end{aligned}
$$

Equation 2.11

This is the value displayed in the column labeled *SS loadings* for factor 1 in Figure 2.10.

Methods for Factor Extraction

Several different methods can be used to obtain estimates of the common factors. These methods differ in the criterion used to define "good fit." **Principal-axis factoring** proceeds much as principal components analysis, except that the diagonals of the correlation matrix are replaced by estimates of the communalities. At the first step, squared multiple correlation coefficients can be used as initial estimates of the communalities. Based on these, the requisite number of factors is extracted. The communalities are re-

Figure 2.11   Maximum-likelihood factor matrix

```
FACTOR MATRIX:


                  FACTOR  1       FACTOR  2       FACTOR  3

    POPSTABL       -.16474        -.62235         -.33705
    NEWSCIRC        .71934        -.04703          .23394
    FEMEMPLD        .80703         .27934         -.14573
    FARMERS        -.58607        -.43787         -.18130
    RETAILNG        .83267         .00538         -.16588
    COMMERCL        .88945        -.27142          .08063
    INDUSTZN        .97436        -.10452          .08869
    HEALTH          .19912         .35743         -.40795
    CHLDNEGL       -.51856        -.17816          .69481
    COMMEFFC        .44351         .33795         -.56277
    DWELGNEW        .27494         .86373          .22983
    MIGRNPOP       -.00353         .49141          .33052
    UNEMPLOY       -.62354        -.25283          .50558
    MENTALIL       -.14756        -.33056          .16948
```

estimated from the factor loadings, and factors are again extracted with the new communality estimates replacing the old. This continues until negligible change occurs in the communality estimates.

The **unweighted least-squares method** produces, for a fixed number of factors, a factor pattern matrix that minimizes the sum of the squared differences between the observed and reproduced correlation matrices (ignoring the diagonals). The **generalized least-squares method** minimizes the same criterion; however, correlations are weighted inversely by the uniqueness of the variables. That is, correlations involving variables with high uniqueness are given less weight than correlations involving variables with low uniqueness.

The **maximum-likelihood method** produces parameter estimates that are the most likely to have produced the observed correlation matrix if the sample is from a multivariate normal distribution. Again, the correlations are weighted by the inverse of the uniqueness of the variables, and an iterative algorithm is employed.

The **alpha method** considers the variables in a particular analysis to be a sample from the universe of potential variables. It maximizes the alpha reliability of the factors. This differs from the previously described methods, which consider the cases to be a sample from some population and the variables to be fixed. With alpha factor extraction, the eigenvalues can no longer be obtained as the sum of the squared factor loadings and the communalities for each variable are not the sum of the squared loadings on the individual factors.

In **image factoring**, the common part of a variable is defined as its linear regression on remaining variables, rather than a function of hypothetical factors. This common part is called a **partial image**. The residual about the regression, which represents the unique part of a variable, is called a **partial anti-image**. See Harman (1967) and Kim and Mueller (1978) for discussions of the different factor estimation algorithms.

Goodness of Fit of the Factor Model

When factors are extracted using generalized least squares or maximum-likelihood estimation, and it is assumed that the sample is from a multivariate normal population, it is possible to obtain goodness-of-fit tests for the adequacy of a k-factor model. For large sample sizes, the goodness-of-fit statistic tends to be distributed as a chi-squared variate. In most applications, the number of common factors is not known, and the number of factors is increased until a reasonably good fit is obtained—that is, until the observed significance level is no longer small. The statistics obtained in this fashion are not independent and the true significance level is not the same as the observed significance level at each step.

The value of the chi-square goodness-of-fit statistic is directly proportional to the sample size. The degrees of freedom are a function of only the number of common factors and the number of variables. (For the chi-square statistic to have positive degrees of freedom, the number of common factors cannot exceed the largest integer satisfying $m < 0.5\,(2p + 1 - \sqrt{8p + 1})$, where m is the number of common factors to be extracted and p is the number of variables). For large sample sizes, the goodness-of-fit test may cause rather small discrepancies in fit to be deemed statistically significant, resulting in a larger number of factors being extracted than is really necessary.

Table 2.2 contains the goodness-of-fit statistics for maximum-likelihood extraction for different numbers of common factors. Using this criterion, at least six common factors are needed to adequately represent the community data.

Table 2.2   Goodness-of-fit statistics

Number of factors	Chi-square statistic	Iterations required	Significance
3	184.8846	13	0.0000
4	94.1803	8	0.0000
5	61.0836	11	0.0010
6	27.3431	15	0.1985

Summary of the Extraction Phase

In the factor extraction phase, the number of common factors needed to adequately describe the data is determined. This decision is based on eigenvalues and the percentage of the total variance accounted for by different numbers of factors. A plot of the eigenvalues (the scree plot) is also helpful in determining the number of factors.

The Rotation Phase

Although the factor matrix obtained in the extraction phase indicates the relationship between the factors and the individual variables, it is usually difficult to identify meaningful factors based on this matrix. Often the variables and factors do not appear correlated in any interpretable pattern. Most factors are correlated with many variables. Since one of the goals of factor analysis is to identify factors that are substantively meaningful (in the sense that they summarize sets of closely related variables), the **rotation** phase of factor analysis attempts to transform the initial matrix into one that is easier to interpret.

Consider Figure 2.12, which is a factor matrix for four hypothetical variables. From the factor loadings, it is difficult to interpret any of the factors, since the variables and factors are intertwined. That is, all factor loadings are quite high, and both factors explain all of the variables.

Figure 2.12   Hypothetical factor matrix

```
FACTOR MATRIX:


                   FACTOR   1      FACTOR   2

X1                  .50000          .50000
X2                  .50000         -.40000
X3                  .70000          .70000
X4                 -.60000          .60000
```

In the factor matrix in Figure 2.13, variables *x1* and *x3* are highly related to factor 1, while *x2* and *x4* load highly on factor 2. By looking at what variables *x2* and *x4* have in common (such as a measurement of job satisfaction, or a characterization of personality), we may be able to identify factor 2. Similar steps can be taken to identify factor 1. The goal of rotation is to transform complicated matrices like the one in Figure 2.12 into simpler ones like the matrix in Figure 2.13.

Figure 2.13   Rotated hypothetical factor matrix

```
ROTATED FACTOR MATRIX:


                   FACTOR   1      FACTOR   2

X1                  .70684         -.01938
X2                  .05324         -.63809
X3                  .98958         -.02713
X4                  .02325          .84821
```

Consider Figure 2.14, which is a plot of variables *x1* to *x4* using the factor loadings in Figure 2.12 as the coordinates, and Figure 2.15, which is the corresponding plot for factor loadings in Figure 2.13. Note that Figure 2.14 would look exactly like Figure 2.15 if the dotted lines were rotated to be the reference axes. When the axes are maintained at right angles, the rotation is called **orthogonal**. If the axes are not maintained at right angles, the rotation is called **oblique**. Oblique rotation is discussed on p. 70.

Figure 2.14   Prior to rotation

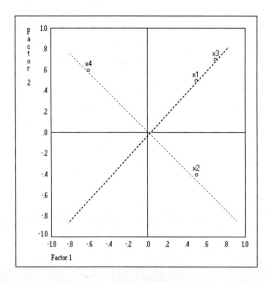

Figure 2.15   Orthogonal rotation

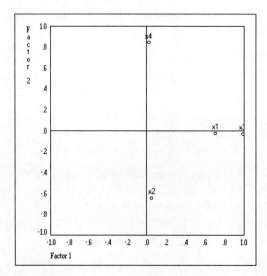

The purpose of rotation is to achieve a **simple structure**. This means that we would like each factor to have nonzero loadings for only some of the variables. This helps us interpret the factors. We would also like each variable to have nonzero loadings for only a few factors, preferably one. This permits the factors to be differentiated from each other. If several factors have high loadings on the same variables, it is difficult to ascertain how the factors differ.

Rotation does not affect the goodness of fit of a factor solution. That is, although the factor matrix changes, the communalities and the percentage of total variance explained do not change. The percentage of variance accounted for by each of the factors *does* change, however. Rotation redistributes the explained variance for the individual factors. Different rotation methods may actually result in the identification of somewhat different factors.

A variety of algorithms are used for orthogonal rotation to a simple structure. The most commonly used method is the **varimax method**, which attempts to minimize the number of variables that have high loadings on a factor. This should enhance the interpretability of the factors.

The **quartimax method** emphasizes simple interpretation of variables, since the solution minimizes the number of factors needed to explain a variable. A quartimax rotation often results in a general factor with high-to-moderate loadings on most variables. This is one of the main shortcomings of the quartimax method.

The **equamax method** is a combination of the varimax method, which simplifies the factors, and the quartimax method, which simplifies variables.

Consider Figure 2.16 through Figure 2.19, which show the factor matrices for the community data before rotation and again after a varimax, quartimax, and equamax orthogonal rotation procedure.

Figure 2.16   Unrotated factor matrix

```
FACTOR MATRIX:


               FACTOR   1     FACTOR   2     FACTOR   3

POPSTABL        -.30247        .68597        -.36451
NEWSCIRC         .67238        .28096         .49779
FEMEMPLD         .89461        .01131         .08063
FARMERS         -.68659        .20002        -.40450
RETAILNG         .85141        .24264         .09351
COMMERCL         .72503        .39394         .19896
INDUSTZN         .84436        .29956         .23775
HEALTH           .38347       -.32718        -.63474
CHLDNEGL        -.67430       -.12139         .52896
COMMEFFC         .63205       -.15540        -.64221
DWELGNEW         .45886       -.73940         .18706
MIGRNPOP         .07894       -.74371         .24335
UNEMPLOY        -.78714       -.09777         .30110
MENTALIL        -.30025        .45463         .27134
```

Figure 2.17   Varimax-rotated factor matrix

```
VARIMAX CONVERGED IN    6 ITERATIONS.


ROTATED FACTOR MATRIX:


              FACTOR  1      FACTOR  2      FACTOR  3

POPSTABL      -.13553         .00916        -.82247
NEWSCIRC       .86634        -.14256         .08920
FEMEMPLD       .78248         .37620         .23055
FARMERS       -.65736        -.04537        -.49077
RETAILNG       .83993         .29454         .01705
COMMERCL       .83432         .11068        -.11000
INDUSTZN       .91325         .15773         .01730
HEALTH        -.05806         .79424         .15101
CHLDNEGL      -.39791        -.75492         .14486
COMMEFFC       .21186         .88794         .05241
DWELGNEW       .17484         .22931         .84208
MIGRNPOP      -.12119        -.00660         .77706
UNEMPLOY      -.57378        -.62483         .01311
MENTALIL       .03133        -.47460        -.37979
```

Figure 2.18   Equamax-rotated factor matrix

```
EQUAMAX CONVERGED IN    6 ITERATIONS.


ROTATED FACTOR MATRIX:


              FACTOR  1      FACTOR  2      FACTOR  3

POPSTABL      -.12961         .01218        -.82338
NEWSCIRC       .86917        -.12003         .09470
FEMEMPLD       .77037         .39514         .23949
FARMERS       -.65223        -.05898        -.49613
RETAILNG       .83157         .31678         .02580
COMMERCL       .83185         .13387        -.10273
INDUSTZN       .90854         .18199         .02554
HEALTH        -.08047         .79116         .15682
CHLDNEGL      -.37857        -.76645         .13585
COMMEFFC       .18756         .89284         .06103
DWELGNEW       .16236         .22710         .84518
MIGRNPOP      -.12675        -.01613         .77603
UNEMPLOY      -.55688        -.64006         .00379
MENTALIL       .04688        -.47050        -.38327
```

Figure 2.19   Quartimax-rotated factor matrix

```
QUARTIMAX CONVERGED IN    5 ITERATIONS.


ROTATED FACTOR MATRIX:


              FACTOR  1      FACTOR  2      FACTOR  3

POPSTABL      -.14884         .00769        -.82018
NEWSCIRC       .85549        -.20254         .07706
FEMEMPLD       .81105         .32272         .21214
FARMERS       -.66736        -.00515        -.47920
RETAILNG       .85885         .23432        -.00105
COMMERCL       .83802         .04963        -.12529
INDUSTZN       .92229         .09267         .00000
HEALTH         .00097         .79832         .14028
CHLDNEGL      -.44778        -.72272         .16242
COMMEFFC       .27508         .87127         .03590
DWELGNEW       .20527         .22763         .83565
MIGRNPOP      -.10781         .01249         .77896
UNEMPLOY      -.61627        -.58226         .03168
MENTALIL      -.00897        -.48069        -.37326
```

The unrotated factor matrix is difficult to interpret. Many variables have moderate-size correlations with several factors. After rotation, the number of large and small factor loadings increases. Variables are more highly correlated with single factors. Interpretation of the factors also appears possible. For example, the first factor shows positive correlation with newspaper circulation, percentage of females in the labor force, sales, commercial activity, and the industrialization index. It also shows a strong negative correlation with the number of farmers. Thus factor 1 might be interpreted as measuring something like "urbanism." The second factor is positively correlated with health and a high standard of living and negatively correlated with Aid to Dependent Children, unemployment, and mental illness. This factor describes the affluence or welfare of a community. The last factor is associated with the instability or influx of a community. Thus, communities may be fairly well characterized by three factors—urbanism, welfare, and influx.

Factor Loading Plots

A convenient means of examining the success of an orthogonal rotation is to plot the variables using the factor loadings as coordinates. When the factor solution involves more than two dimensions, SPSS produces a three-dimensional plot of the first three factors, as shown in Figure 2.20. The coordinates correspond to the factor loadings in Figure 2.17 for the varimax-rotated solution.

Figure 2.20   Varimax-rotated solution

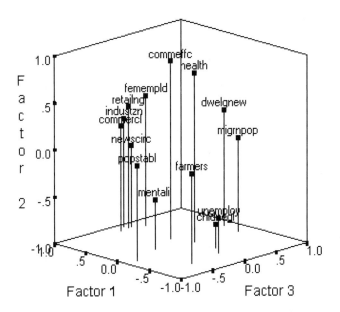

Let's look more closely at the effect of the rotation on factors 1 and 2. In Figure 2.21, the variables are plotted using factors 1 and 2 after varimax rotation of the two factors. In Figure 2.22, the variables are plotted using factors 1 and 2 before rotation. (You can obtain a two-dimensional plot for a solution that involves three or more dimensions if you edit the default three-dimensional plot in the Chart Editor. Select Edit in the Chart Carousel, Scatter... from the Gallery menu, and then select Simple from the Scatterplots dialog box. Click on New. After you select the factors you want to plot—factors 1 and 2 are plotted by default—click on OK to obtain the two-dimensional plot.)

If a rotation has achieved a simple structure, clusters of variables should occur near the ends of the axes and at their intersection. Variables at the end of an axis are those that have high loadings on only that factor. Variables near the origin of the plot (0,0) have small loadings on both factors. Variables that are not near the axes are explained by both factors. If a simple structure has been achieved, there should be few if any variables with large loadings on more than one factor.

Figure 2.21   Varimax-rotated solution for factors 1 and 2

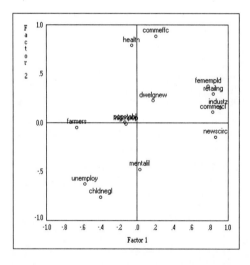

Figure 2.22   Unrotated solution for factors 1 and 2

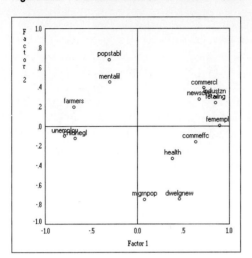

Interpreting the Factors

To identify the factors, it is necessary to group the variables that have large loadings for the same factors. Plots of the loadings are one way of determining the clusters of variables. Another convenient strategy is to sort the factor pattern matrix so that variables with high loadings on the same factor appear together, as shown in Figure 2.23. Small factor loadings can be omitted from such a table. In Figure 2.24, no loadings less than 0.5 in absolute value are displayed. Note that the mental illness variable, as expected, does not correlate highly with any of the factors.

Figure 2.23   Sorted loadings

ROTATED FACTOR MATRIX:

	FACTOR 1	FACTOR 2	FACTOR 3
INDUSTZN	.91325	.15773	.01730
NEWSCIRC	.86634	-.14256	.08920
RETAILNG	.83993	.29454	.01705
COMMERCL	.83432	.11068	-.11000
FEMEMPLD	.78248	.37620	.23055
FARMERS	-.65736	-.04537	-.49077
COMMEFFC	.21186	.88794	.05241
HEALTH	-.05806	.79424	.15101
CHLDNEGL	-.39791	-.75492	.14486
UNEMPLOY	-.57378	-.62483	.01311
MENTALIL	.03133	-.47460	-.37979
DWELGNEW	.17484	.22931	.84208
POPSTABL	-.13553	.00916	-.82247
MIGRNPOP	-.12119	-.00660	.77706

Figure 2.24   Sorted and blanked loadings

```
ROTATED FACTOR MATRIX:


                    FACTOR  1      FACTOR  2      FACTOR  3

INDUSTZN              .91325
NEWSCIRC             .86634
RETAILNG             .83993
COMMERCL             .83432
FEMEMPLD             .78248
FARMERS            -.65736

COMMEFFC                             .88794
HEALTH                               .79424
CHLDNEGL                            -.75492
UNEMPLOY            -.57378         -.62483
MENTALIL

DWELGNEW                                            .84208
POPSTABL                                           -.82247
MIGRNPOP                                            .77706
```

Oblique Rotation

Orthogonal rotation results in factors that are uncorrelated. Although this is an appealing property, sometimes allowing for correlations among factors simplifies the factor pattern matrix. Consider Figure 2.25, which is a plot of the factor loadings for six variables. Note that if the axes (the dotted lines) went through the points, a simpler factor pattern matrix would result than with an orthogonal rotation. Factor pattern matrices for both rotations are shown in Figure 2.26.

Figure 2.25   Plot of factor loadings

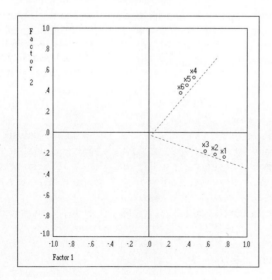

Figure 2.26   Rotated varimax and oblique factor loadings

```
ROTATED FACTOR MATRIX varimax:

              FACTOR  1      FACTOR  2

X1              .78312         .16345
X2              .68524         .14301
X3              .58734         .12259
X4              .14301         .68523
X5              .12258         .58735
X6              .10216         .48945


PATTERN MATRIX oblique:

              FACTOR  1      FACTOR  2

X1              .80000         .00000
X2              .70001         .00000
X3              .60000         .00000
X4              .00000         .70000
X5              .00000         .60000
X6              .00000         .50000
```

There are several reasons why oblique rotation is useful. It is unlikely that influences in nature are uncorrelated. And even if they are uncorrelated in the population, they need not be so in the sample. Thus, oblique rotations have often been found to yield substantively meaningful factors.

Factor Pattern and Structure Matrices

Oblique rotation preserves the communalities of the variables, as does orthogonal rotation. When oblique rotation is used, however, the factor loadings and factor variable correlations are no longer identical. The factor loadings are still partial regression coefficients, but since the factors are correlated, they are no longer equal to the simple factor variable correlations. (Remember that the regression coefficients depend on the interrelationships of the independent variables when these are correlated.) Therefore, separate factor loading and factor structure matrices are displayed as part of the output.

Algorithm for Oblique Rotation

The method for oblique rotation available in the SPSS Factor Analysis procedure is called **oblimin**. A parameter called **delta** (δ) controls the extent of obliqueness. When δ is 0, the factors are most oblique. For negative values of δ, the factors become less oblique as δ becomes more negative. Harman (1967) recommends that δ be either 0 or negative.

The factor loadings for the community data after an oblique rotation are shown in the factor pattern matrix in Figure 2.27. The loadings are no longer constrained to a range of -1 to $+1$. The correlations between the factors and variables are shown in Figure 2.28, the factor structure matrix.

Figure 2.27   Factor pattern matrix

```
PATTERN MATRIX:


              FACTOR   1      FACTOR   2      FACTOR   3

  INDUSTZN      .91577         .02882         -.04731
  NEWSCIRC      .90594        -.06987          .26053
  COMMERCL      .84325         .15024         -.01504
  RETAILNG      .82253         .03760         -.19782
  FEMEMPLD      .74906        -.17274         -.27862
  FARMERS      -.65969         .46636         -.06041


  POPSTABL     -.12570         .82380         -.06787
  DWELGNEW      .13426        -.82258         -.17248
  MIGRNPOP     -.13720        -.78724          .03070


  COMMEFFC      .09940         .02770         -.88775
  HEALTH       -.16689        -.08909         -.81993
  CHLDNEGL     -.31128        -.22218          .73693
  UNEMPLOY     -.50651        -.08531          .57387
  MENTALIL      .10140         .34462          .47495
```

Figure 2.28   Factor structure matrix

```
STRUCTURE MATRIX:


              FACTOR   1      FACTOR   2      FACTOR   3

  INDUSTZN      .92553        -.04717         -.27457
  RETAILNG      .86963        -.05222         -.40031
  NEWSCIRC      .84545        -.10235          .02205
  COMMERCL      .83566         .08423         -.20712
  FEMEMPLD      .83252        -.26822         -.49178
  FARMERS      -.67979         .50798          .17096


  DWELGNEW      .24017        -.85671         -.32064
  POPSTABL     -.17101         .82390          .07829
  MIGRNPOP     -.08527        -.77258         -.04400


  COMMEFFC      .32149        -.10314         -.90901
  HEALTH        .04692        -.19032         -.79016
  CHLDNEGL     -.48053        -.09623          .78468
  UNEMPLOY     -.64496         .03280          .68993
  MENTALIL     -.04466         .40290          .49721
```

The correlation matrix for the factors is shown in Figure 2.29. Note that there are small correlations between all three factors. In the case of an orthogonal rotation, the factor correlation matrix is an identity matrix. That is, there are 1's on the diagonal and 0's elsewhere.

Figure 2.29   Factor correlation matrix

```
FACTOR CORRELATION MATRIX:


              FACTOR   1      FACTOR   2      FACTOR   3

  FACTOR   1    1.00000
  FACTOR   2    -.07580        1.00000
  FACTOR   3    -.25253         .13890         1.00000
```

The oblique rotation resulted in the same grouping of variables as did the orthogonal rotation. The interpretation of the factors does not change based on oblique rotation.

Factor Scores

Since one of the goals of factor analysis is to reduce a large number of variables to a smaller number of factors, it is often desirable to estimate factor scores for each case. The factor scores can be used in subsequent analyses to represent the values of the factors. Plots of factor scores for pairs of factors are useful for detecting unusual observations.

Recall from "The Factor Analysis Model" on p. 48 that a factor can be estimated as a linear combination of the original variables. That is, for case k, the score for the jth factor is estimated as

$$\hat{F}_{jk} = \sum_{i=1}^{p} W_{ji} X_{ik}$$

Equation 2.12

where X_{ik} is the standardized value of the ith variable for case k and W_{ji} is the factor score coefficient for the jth factor and the ith variable. Except for principal components analysis, exact factor scores cannot be obtained. Estimates are obtained instead.

There are several methods for estimating factor score coefficients. Each has different properties and results in different scores (see Tucker, 1971; Harman, 1967). The three methods available in the SPSS Factor Analysis procedure (Anderson-Rubin, regression, and Bartlett) all result in scores with a mean of 0. The Anderson-Rubin method always produces uncorrelated scores with a standard deviation of 1, even when the original factors are estimated to be correlated. The regression factor scores (the default) have a variance equal to the squared multiple correlation between the estimated factor scores and the true factor values. (These are shown on the diagonal in Figure 2.31.) Regression-method factor scores can be correlated even when factors are assumed to be orthogonal. If principal components extraction is used, for an orthogonal solution all three methods result in the same factor scores, which are no longer estimated but are exact.

Figure 2.30 contains the factor score coefficients used to calculate regression-method factor scores for the community data. The correlation matrix for the estimated scores is shown in Figure 2.31.

Figure 2.30   Factor coefficient matrix

```
FACTOR SCORE COEFFICIENT MATRIX:


                  FACTOR  1        FACTOR  2        FACTOR  3

POPSTABL           -.00150          .03191          -.15843
NEWSCIRC            .05487         -.06095           .03524
FEMEMPLD            .01729          .14014           .05328
FARMERS            -.01797          .00113          -.11462
RETAILNG            .03728          .09460          -.03577
COMMERCL            .20579         -.11667          -.10723
INDUSTZN            .77285         -.27024           .00882
HEALTH             -.02786          .09971          -.00161
CHLDNEGL            .08404         -.44657           .16521
COMMEFFC           -.05030          .23211          -.03623
DWELGNEW           -.05117          .07034           .68792
MIGRNPOP            .00029         -.03198           .09778
UNEMPLOY            .03856         -.26435           .05378
MENTALIL            .01264         -.04224          -.01691
```

Figure 2.31   Covariance matrix for estimated regression factor scores

```
COVARIANCE MATRIX FOR ESTIMATED REGRESSION FACTOR SCORES:


                  FACTOR  1      FACTOR  2      FACTOR  3

FACTOR  1          .96763
FACTOR  2          .03294        .87641
FACTOR  3          .00042        .02544         .89452
```

To see how factor scores are calculated, consider Table 2.3, which contains standardized values for the original 14 variables for five counties, and factor score values for the three factors. For each factor, the factor scores are obtained by multiplying the standardized values by the corresponding factor score coefficients. Thus, for Adams county the value for factor 1 is

$$
\begin{aligned}
\text{Value for factor } 1 = {} & (-0.00150)\,(-0.36) + (0.05487)\,(-0.93) \\
& + (0.01729)\,(-1.06) + \ldots + (0.01264)\,(-0.76) \qquad \textbf{Equation 2.13} \\
& = -1.328
\end{aligned}
$$

Table 2.3 Standardized values and factor scores

Variable	County				
	Adams	Butler	Crawford	Cuyahoga	Hamilton
popstabl	−0.36	−1.49	2.44	−0.13	−0.30
newscirc	−0.93	0.39	−0.26	2.04	1.17
femempld	−1.06	0.41	0.24	1.30	1.03
farmers	2.20	−0.67	0.01	−0.93	−0.90
retailng	−1.41	0.49	0.58	1.15	1.07
commercl	−0.89	−0.30	−0.07	1.58	2.02
industzn	−1.14	−0.11	0.03	1.53	1.85
health	−0.25	−0.56	−1.32	−0.36	−1.17
chldnegl	−1.26	0.79	−0.61	0.63	0.99
commeffc	−0.20	0.78	−0.87	−0.78	−1.66
dwelgnew	−0.52	0.52	−1.09	−0.01	−0.22
migrnpop	−0.98	0.16	−0.60	0.63	1.13
unemploy	−0.75	−0.36	−0.44	1.56	0.76
mentalil	−0.76	−0.77	−0.46	−0.14	0.61

Factor	Scores				
Factor 1	−1.328	−0.089	0.083	1.862	2.233
Factor 2	0.897	0.027	0.197	−1.362	−1.79
Factor 3	−0.830	0.831	−1.290	0.342	0.226

How to Obtain a Factor Analysis

The Factor Analysis procedure provides a variety of factor extraction and rotation techniques. You can obtain related plots and descriptive statistics and save factor scores.

The minimum specification is two or more numeric variables.

To obtain a factor analysis, from the menus choose:

Statistics
  Data Reduction ▶
    Factor...

This opens the Factor Analysis dialog box, as shown in Figure 2.32.

Figure 2.32   Factor Analysis dialog box

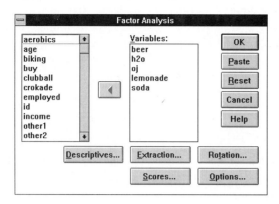

The numeric variables in your data file appear in the source list. Select two or more variables and click on OK to obtain the default analysis using unrotated principal components. By default, the output displays initial statistics, factor pattern matrix, and final statistics.

Factor Analysis Descriptives

To obtain optional descriptive statistics, click on Descriptives... in the Factor Analysis dialog box. This opens the Factor Analysis Descriptives dialog box, as shown in Figure 2.33.

Figure 2.33   Factor Analysis Descriptives dialog box

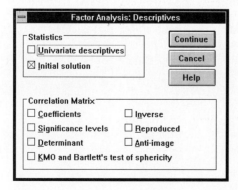

Statistics. You can choose one or both of the following:

❏ **Univariate descriptives.** Displays the number of valid observations, the mean, and the standard deviation for each variable.

❏ **Initial solution.** Displays initial communalities, eigenvalues, and percentage of variance explained. This is the default.

Correlation Matrix. You can choose one or more of the following:

❏ **Coefficients.** Correlation matrix for variables in the analysis.

❏ **Significance levels.** One-tailed significance levels of correlations.

❏ **Determinant.** Determinant of the correlation matrix.

❏ **KMO and Bartlett's test of sphericity.** The Kaiser-Meyer-Olkin measure of sampling adequacy and Bartlett's test of sphericity.

❏ **Inverse.** The inverse of the correlation matrix.

❏ **Reproduced.** Matrix of reproduced correlations and their residuals. Correlation coefficients are shown below the diagonal; residuals appear above the diagonal.

❏ **Anti-image.** Anti-image covariance and correlation matrices. The measure of sampling adequacy for a variable is displayed on the diagonal of the anti-image correlation matrix.

Factor Analysis Extraction

To choose an extraction method other than the default, obtain a scree plot, or control how many factors are extracted, click on Extraction... in the Factor Analysis dialog box. This opens the Factor Analysis Extraction dialog box, as shown in Figure 2.34.

Figure 2.34   Factor Analysis Extraction dialog box

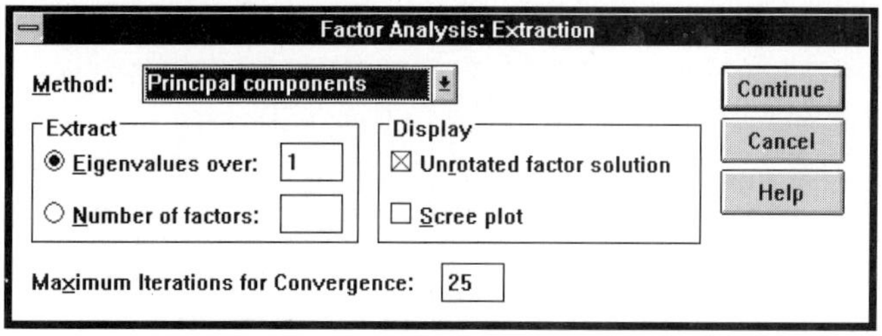

⬇ **Method.** You can choose one of the following extraction methods:

Principal components. Principal components factor extraction. This is the default method.

Unweighted least squares. Unweighted least-squares factor extraction.

Generalized least squares. Generalized least-squares factor extraction.

Maximum likelihood. Maximum-likelihood factor extraction.

Principal-axis factoring. Principal-axis factoring method of factor extraction.

Alpha factoring. Alpha factoring method of factor extraction.

Image factoring. Image factoring method of factor extraction.

Extract. You can choose one of the following extraction criteria:

○ **Eigenvalues over n.** By default, factors with eigenvalues greater than 1 are extracted. To use a different eigenvalue as the cutoff value for factor extraction, enter a number between 0 and the total number of variables in your analysis.

○ **Number of factors.** Extracts a user-specified number of factors, regardless of their eigenvalues. Enter a positive integer.

Display. You can choose one or both of the following display options:

❏ **Unrotated factor solution.** Unrotated factor loadings (factor pattern matrix), communalities, and eigenvalues for the factor solution. Displayed by default.

❏ **Scree plot.** Plot of eigenvalues in descending order. The plot shows rotated factors if rotation is requested (see "Factor Analysis Rotation," below).

The following option is also available:

Maximum Iterations for Convergence. By default, a maximum of 25 iterations is performed for factor extraction. To specify a different maximum, enter a positive integer. The convergence criterion for extraction is 0.001.

Factor Analysis Rotation

To specify a rotation method or obtain factor loading plots, click on Rotation... in the Factor Analysis dialog box. This opens the Factor Analysis Rotation dialog box, as shown in Figure 2.35.

Figure 2.35   Factor Analysis Rotation dialog box

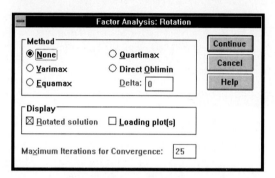

Method. Rotation is not performed if only one factor is extracted. Kaiser normalization is used with any rotation method. You can choose one of the following rotation methods:

○ **None.** Factors are not rotated. This is the default setting.

○ **Varimax.** Varimax method. An orthogonal rotation.

○ **Equamax.** Equamax method. An orthogonal rotation.

○ **Quartimax.** Quartimax method. An orthogonal rotation.

○ **Direct Oblimin.** Oblimin method. An oblique rotation.

   Delta. To override the default delta of 0, enter a number less than or equal to 0.8.

Display. You can choose one or both of the following display option:

❑ **Rotated solution.** Displayed by default when rotation is requested. For orthogonal rotations, the rotated pattern matrix and factor transformation matrix are displayed. For oblimin rotation, the pattern, structure, and factor correlation matrices are displayed. To suppress rotated factor solution output, deselect this item.

❑ **Loading plot(s).** Three-dimensional factor loading plot of the first three factors. For a two-factor solution, a two-dimensional plot is shown. The plot is not displayed if only one factor is extracted. Plots display rotated solutions if rotation is requested.

The following option is available if you request rotation:

Maximum Iterations for Convergence. By default, a maximum of 25 iterations is performed for factor rotation. To specify a different maximum, enter a positive integer.

Factor Analysis Factor Scores

To save factor scores for use in other analyses, click on Scores... in the Factor Analysis dialog box. This opens the Factor Analysis Factor Scores dialog box, as shown in Figure 2.36.

Figure 2.36   Factor Analysis Factor Scores dialog box

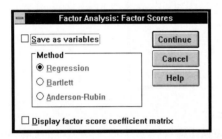

To save factor scores, select Save as variables and then select a factor score method:

❏ **Save as variables.** Saves factor scores as variables. One variable is created for each factor in the solution. A table in the output shows the name of each new variable and a variable label indicating the method used to calculate factor scores.

Method. Method selection controls computation of factor scores. You can choose one of the following methods:

○ **Regression.** Regression method. This is the default method.

○ **Bartlett.** Bartlett method.

○ **Anderson-Rubin.** Anderson-Rubin method.

The following option is also available:

❏ **Display factor score coefficient matrix.** Displays the factor score coefficient matrix. The factor score covariance matrix is also displayed.

Factor Analysis Options

To change the treatment of missing values or sort the display of factor matrices, click on Options... in the Factor Analysis dialog box. This opens the Factor Analysis Options dialog box, as shown in Figure 2.37.

Figure 2.37   Factor Analysis Options dialog box

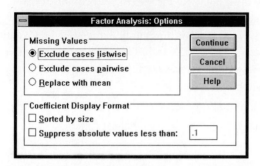

Missing Values. You can choose one of the following alternatives:

○ **Exclude cases listwise.** Only cases with valid values for all variables are used in the analysis. This is the default.

○ **Exclude cases pairwise.** Excludes cases with missing values on a correlation-by-correlation basis. In computing a correlation, SPSS uses all cases having valid values for both variables (even if those cases have missing values on other variables).

○ **Replace with mean.** Replaces missing values with the variable mean, and uses all cases in the factor analysis.

Coefficient Display Format. You can choose one or both of the following coefficient display formats:

❑ **Sorted by size.** Sorts factor loading and structure matrices so that variables with high loadings on the same factor appear together.

❑ **Suppress absolute values less than n.** Suppresses coefficients with absolute values less than a specified value. The default value is 0.1. To override the default, enter a number between 0 and 1.

You can combine these two features, sorting the display and omitting low coefficient values. For example, Figure 2.24 is a sorted matrix that suppresses coefficients with absolute values less than 0.5.

Additional Features Available with Command Syntax

You can customize your factor analysis if you paste your selections to a syntax window and edit the resulting FACTOR command syntax (see Chapter 5 in the *SPSS Base System User's Guide*). Additional features include:

- Matrix facility to write a correlation or factor loading matrix, or to read a matrix that can be used in place of raw data (with the MATRIX subcommand).

- The ability to analyze different sets of variables with a single command (with the ANALYSIS subcommand), and perform multiple extractions and rotations within a single analysis (with the EXTRACTION and ROTATION subcommands).

- The ability to save a subset of factor scores or supply rootnames for factor score variables (with the SAVE subcommand).

- Additional extraction and rotation criteria (with the CRITERIA subcommand).

- User-specified diagonal values for the principal-axis method (with the DIAGONAL subcommand).

See the Syntax Reference section of this manual for command syntax rules and for complete FACTOR command syntax.

3 Cluster Analysis

Despite the old adage that opposites attract, it appears instead that likes attract. Birds of a feather and many other animate and inanimate objects that share similar characteristics tend to cluster together. You can form groups of similar objects using a statistical procedure called a **cluster analysis**.

In biology, cluster analysis is used to classify animals and plants. This is called numerical taxonomy. In medicine, cluster analysis is used to identify diseases and their stages. For example, by examining patients who are diagnosed as depressed, you might find that there are several distinct subgroups of patients with different types of depression. In marketing, cluster analysis is used to identify people with similar buying habits. By examining their characteristics, you may be able to target future marketing strategies more efficiently. See Romesburg (1984) for more examples of the use of cluster analysis.

Although both cluster analysis and discriminant analysis classify objects, or cases, into categories, discriminant analysis requires you to know group membership for the cases used to derive the classification rule. For example, if you are interested in distinguishing among several disease groups, cases with known diagnoses must be available. Then, based on cases whose group membership is known, discriminant analysis derives a rule for allocating undiagnosed patients. In cluster analysis, group membership for all cases is unknown. In fact, even the number of groups is often unknown. The goal of cluster analysis is to identify homogeneous groups or clusters.

In this chapter the fundamentals of cluster analysis are illustrated using a subset of data presented in a Consumer Reports (1983) survey of beer. Each of 20 beers is characterized in terms of cost per 12 ounces, alcohol content, sodium content, and the number of calories per 12-ounce serving. From these variables it is possible to identify several distinct subgroups of beer.

Basic Steps

As in other statistical procedures, a number of decisions must be made before you embark on the actual analysis. Which variables will serve as the basis for cluster forma-

83

tion? How will the distance between cases be measured? What criteria will be used for combining cases into clusters?

Selecting the variables to include in an analysis is always crucial. If important variables are excluded, poor or misleading findings may result. For example, in a regression analysis of salary, if variables such as education and experience are not included, the results may be questionable. In cluster analysis, the initial choice of variables determines the characteristics that can be used to identify subgroups. If you are interested in clustering schools within a city and do not include variables like the number of students or the number of teachers, size is automatically excluded as a criterion for establishing clusters. By excluding all measures of taste or quality from the beer data, only physical characteristics and price will determine which beers are deemed similar.

How Alike Are the Cases?

The concepts of distance and similarity are basic to many statistical techniques. **Distance** is a measure of how far apart two objects are, and **similarity** measures closeness. Distance measures are small and similarity measures are large for cases that are similar. In cluster analysis, these concepts are especially important, since cases are grouped on the basis of their "nearness." There are many different definitions of distance and similarity. Selection of a distance measure should be based both on the properties of the measure and on the algorithm for cluster formation. See "More on Calculating Distances and Similarities" on p. 96 for further discussion of distance measures.

To see how a simple distance measure is computed, consider Table 3.1, which shows the values for calories and cost for two of the beers. There is a 13-calorie and a 5-cent difference between the two beers. This information can be combined into a single index or distance measure in many different ways. A commonly used index is the **squared Euclidean distance**, which is the sum of the squared differences over all of the variables. In this example, the squared Euclidean distance is $13^2 + 5^2$, or 194.

Table 3.1 Values for calories and cost for two beers

	Calories	Cost
Budweiser	144	43
Lowenbrau	157	48

The squared Euclidean distance has the disadvantage that it depends on the units of measurement for the variables. For example, if the cost were given in pennies per ounce instead of pennies per 12 ounces, the computed distance would change. Another disadvantage is that when variables are measured on different scales, as in this example, variables that are measured in larger numbers will contribute more to the computed distance than variables that are recorded in smaller numbers. For example, the 13-calorie difference contributes much more to the distance score than the 5-cent difference in cost does.

One means of circumventing this problem is to express all variables in standardized form. That is, transform all variables to have a mean of 0 and a standard deviation of 1. This is not always the best strategy, however, since the variability of a particular measure can provide useful information (see Sneath & Sokal, 1973). (See Chapter 9 in the *SPSS Base System User's Guide* for further discussion.)

Table 3.2 shows the Z scores for calories and cost for Budweiser and Lowenbrau beers based on the means and standard deviations for all 20 beers. The squared Euclidean distance based on the standardized variables is $(0.38 - 0.81)^2 + (-0.46 - (-0.11))^2$, or 0.307. The differences in calories and cost are now weighted equally.

Table 3.2 Z scores for calories and cost for two beers

	Calories	Cost
Budweiser	0.38	–0.46
Lowenbrau	0.81	–0.11

Forming Clusters

Just as there are many methods for calculating distances between objects, there are many methods for combining objects into clusters. A commonly used method for forming clusters is agglomerative hierarchical cluster analysis. In **agglomerative hierarchical clustering**, clusters are formed by grouping cases into bigger and bigger clusters until all cases are members of a single cluster. For a discussion of nonhierarchical clustering methods, see Everitt (1980).

Agglomerative Clustering

Before discussing the rules for forming clusters, let's consider what happens at each step of agglomerative hierarchical cluster analysis. Before the analysis begins, all cases are considered separate clusters: there are as many clusters as there are cases. At the first step, two of the cases are combined into a single cluster. At the second step, either a third case is added to the cluster already containing two cases, or two other cases are merged into a new cluster. At every step, either individual cases are added to existing clusters or two existing clusters are combined. Once a cluster is formed, it cannot be split; it can only be combined with other clusters. Thus, the agglomerative hierarchical clustering method does not allow cases to separate from clusters to which they have been assigned. For example, if two beers are deemed members of the same cluster at the first step, they will always be members of the same cluster, although they may be combined with additional cases at a later step.

Criteria for Combining Clusters

There are many criteria for deciding which cases or clusters should be combined at each step. All of these criteria are based on a matrix of either distances or similarities between pairs of cases. One of the simplest methods is **single linkage**, sometimes called **nearest neighbor**. The first two cases combined are those that have the smallest distance (or largest similarity) between them. The distance between the new cluster and individual cases is then computed as the minimum distance between an individual case and a case in the cluster. The distances between cases that have not been joined do not change. At every step, the distance between two clusters is the distance between their two closest points.

Another commonly used method is called **complete linkage**, or the **furthest neighbor** technique. In this method, the distance between two clusters is calculated as the distance between their two furthest points. Other methods for combining clusters are described in "Methods for Combining Clusters" on p. 97.

Performing a Cluster Analysis

Before considering other distance measures and methods of combining clusters, consider Figure 3.1, which shows the original and standardized values for calories, sodium content, alcohol content, and cost for the 20 beers, and Figure 3.2, which displays the squared Euclidean distance coefficients for all possible pairs of the 20 beers, based on the standardized values.

Figure 3.1   Original and standardized values for the 20 beers

ID	BEER	CALORIES	SODIUM	ALCOHOL	COST	ZCALORIE	ZSODIUM	ZALCOHOL	ZCOST
1	BUDWEISER	144	15	4.7	.43	.38	.01	.34	-.46
2	SCHLITZ	151	19	4.9	.43	.61	.62	.61	-.46
3	LOWENBRAU	157	15	4.9	.48	.81	.01	.61	-.11
4	KRONENBOURG	170	7	5.2	.73	1.24	-1.21	1.00	1.62
5	HEINEKEN	152	11	5.0	.77	.65	-.60	.74	1.90
6	OLD MILWAUKEE	145	23	4.6	.28	.42	1.22	.21	-1.51
7	AUGSBERGER	175	24	5.5	.40	1.41	1.38	1.40	-.67
8	STROHS BOHEMIAN STYLE	149	27	4.7	.42	.55	1.83	.34	-.53
9	MILLER LITE	99	10	4.3	.43	-1.10	-.75	-.18	-.46
10	BUDWEISER LIGHT	113	8	3.7	.44	-.64	-1.06	-.97	-.39
11	COORS	140	18	4.6	.44	.46	.25	.21	-.39
12	COORS LIGHT	102	15	4.1	.46	-1.00	.01	-.45	-.25
13	MICHELOB LIGHT	135	11	4.2	.50	.09	-.60	-.32	.02
14	BECKS	150	19	4.7	.76	.58	.62	.34	1.83
15	KIRIN	149	6	5.0	.79	.55	-1.36	.74	2.04
16	PABST EXTRA LIGHT	68	15	2.3	.38	-2.82	.01	-2.82	-.81
17	HAMMS	136	19	4.4	.43	.12	.62	-.05	-.46
18	HEILEMANS OLD STYLE	144	24	4.9	.43	.38	1.38	.61	-.46
19	OLYMPIA GOLD LIGHT	72	6	2.9	.46	-2.00	-1.36	-2.03	-.25
20	SCHLITZ LIGHT	97	7	4.2	.47	-1.17	-1.21	-.32	-.18

Figure 3.2   The squared Euclidean distance coefficient matrix

Squared Euclidean Dissimilarity Coefficient Matrix

Case	BUDWEISE	SCHLITZ	LOWENBRA	KRONENBO	HEINEKEN
SCHLITZ	.4922				
LOWENBRA	.3749	.5297			
KRONENBO	7.0040	8.2298	4.8424		
HEINEKEN	6.1889	7.0897	4.4835	.8700	
OLD MILW	2.5848	1.6534	3.7263	17.0154	15.2734
AUGSBERG	4.0720	1.8735	3.1573	12.1251	11.5371
STROHS B	3.3568	1.5561	3.6380	14.8000	12.0038
MILLER L	3.0662	5.4473	4.9962	11.4721	9.5339
BUDWEISE	3.9181	6.8702	5.8179	11.5391	10.0663
COORS	.2474	.3160	.7568	8.4698	6.8353
COORS LI	2.5940	4.1442	4.4322	12.1519	9.1534
MICHELOB	1.1281	2.8432	1.7663	5.9995	4.9519
BECKS	5.6782	5.3399	4.2859	4.2382	1.6427
KIRIN	8.3245	10.1947	6.6075	.7483	.6064
PABST EX	16.4081	19.7255	20.8463	33.3380	28.0650
HAMMS	.5952	.6788	1.4051	10.0509	7.9746
HEILEMAN	1.9394	.6307	2.1757	11.9216	9.5828
OLYMPIA	13.1887	17.6915	16.7104	23.2048	19.8574
SCHLITZ	4.4010	7.4360	6.2635	10.8241	9.1372

Case	OLD MILW	AUGSBERG	STROHS B	MILLER L	BUDWEISE
AUGSBERG	3.1061				
STROHS B	1.3526	2.0742			
MILLER L	7.4577	13.3723	9.6850		
BUDWEISE	8.9551	15.7993	11.5019	.9349	
COORS	1.8432	3.6498	1.9953	3.4745	4.5082
COORS LI	5.4981	11.2604	6.4385	.6999	1.5600
MICHELOB	6.0530	9.0610	6.8673	1.6931	1.3437
BECKS	11.5628	8.6397	7.0724	10.2578	10.9762
KIRIN	19.5528	16.0118	16.9620	10.2201	10.3631
PABST EX	17.6016	32.1339	20.5466	8.6771	6.9127
HAMMS	1.6159	4.3782	1.8230	3.3828	4.2251
HEILEMAN	1.2688	1.7169	.3092	7.3607	9.4595
OLYMPIA	19.0673	30.9530	22.3479	4.6046	3.0565
SCHLITZ	10.4511	16.4825	12.7426	.3069	.7793

Case	COORS	COORS LI	MICHELOB	BECKS	KIRIN
COORS LI	2.2375				
MICHELOB	1.6100	1.6536			
BECKS	5.1046	7.8646	5.4275		
KIRIN	9.6179	10.9556	5.9694	4.1024	
PABST EX	15.2083	7.1851	12.2231	24.6793	29.7992
HAMMS	.1147	1.8315	1.7851	5.6395	10.9812
HEILEMAN	1.0094	4.9491	5.0762	5.9553	13.7962
OLYMPIA	13.4011	5.3477	7.9175	20.5149	19.3851
SCHLITZ	5.1340	1.5271	1.9902	10.8954	9.0403

Case	PABST EX	HAMMS	HEILEMAN	OLYMPIA
HAMMS	13.1806			
HEILEMAN	20.0105	1.0802		
OLYMPIA	2.8209	12.3170	20.1156	
SCHLITZ	9.0418	5.1327	10.0114	3.6382

The first entry in Figure 3.2 is the distance between the first two cases, Budweiser and Schlitz (case 1 and case 2 in Figure 3.1). Cases form the rows and columns of the distance matrix. The rows and columns are labeled with the first eight characters of the values for the variable *beer*. The distance between Budweiser and Schlitz can be calculated from the standardized values in Figure 3.1 as

$$D^2 = (0.38 - 0.61)^2 + (0.01 - 0.62)^2$$
$$+ (0.34 - 0.61)^2 + (-0.46 - (-0.46))^2 = 0.49$$

Equation 3.1

Since the distance between pairs of cases is symmetric (that is, the distance between Budweiser and Schlitz is the same as the distance between Schlitz and Budweiser), SPSS displays only the lower half of the distance matrix in the output. Redundant values are excluded from the matrix.

Icicle Plots

Once the distance matrix has been calculated, the actual formation of clusters can commence. Figure 3.3 summarizes a cluster analysis that uses the complete linkage method. This type of figure is sometimes called a **vertical icicle plot** because it resembles a row of icicles hanging from eaves.

The columns in Figure 3.3 correspond to the objects being clustered (in this instance, the 20 beers). They are identified by a sequential number corresponding to their order or location in the file and by their labels. (If labels are not defined, then only the case number is used.) Thus, the first column in the figure represents the last beer in the file, beer 19, Olympia Gold Light, and the last column represents the first beer in the file, Budweiser. Rows represent steps in the cluster analysis; the figure is read from bottom to top. Row 19 represents step 1 in the analysis and row 1 represents the last step, where all cases form a single cluster. (In step 0 of the cluster analysis, not pictured in the figure, each case is a separate cluster.)

As previously described, initially each case is considered an individual cluster. Since there are twenty beers in this example, there are 20 clusters. At the first step of the analysis (row 19 in the figure), the two closest cases are combined into a single cluster, resulting in 19 clusters. (The step number corresponds to the number of clusters in the solution.) Each case is represented by a solid dark bar and cases are separated by a blank space. The two cases that have been merged into a single cluster, Coors and Hamms, do not have a space separating them and are represented by consecutive solid bars. Row 18 in Figure 3.3 corresponds to the solution at the next step, when 18 clusters are present. At this step, Miller Lite and Schlitz Light are merged into a single cluster. At this point there are 18 clusters, 16 consisting of individual beers and 2 consisting of pairs of beers. At each subsequent step an additional cluster is formed either by joining a case to an existing multicase cluster, by joining two separate cases into a single cluster, or by joining two multicase clusters.

For example, row 5 in Figure 3.3 corresponds to a solution that has five clusters. Beers 19 and 16, the very light beers, form one cluster. Beers 13, 12, 10, 20, and 9 form the next cluster. These beers—Michelob Light, Coors Light, Budweiser Light, Schlitz

Figure 3.3   Vertical icicle plot for the 20 beers

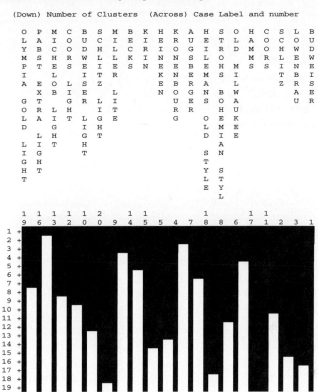

```
Vertical Icicle Plot using Complete Linkage

(Down) Number of Clusters   (Across) Case Label and number

     O   P   M   C   B   S   M   B   K   H   K   A   H   S   O   H   C   S   L   B
     L   A   I   O   U   C   I   E   I   E   R   U   E   T   L   A   O   C   O   U
     Y   B   C   O   D   H   L   C   R   I   O   G   I   R   D   M   O   H   W   D
     M   S   H   R   W   L   L   K   I   N   N   S   L   O       M   R   L   E   W
     P   T   E   S   E   I   E   S   N   E   E   B   E   H   M   S   S   I   N   E
     I       L       I   T   R       K   N   E   M   S   I               T   B   I
     A   E   O   L   S   Z           E   B   R   A       L               Z   R   S
         X   B   I   E       L       N   O   G   N   B   W                   A   E
     G   T       G   R   L   I           U   E   S   O   A                   U   R
     O   R   L   H       I   T           R   R       H   U
     L   A   I   T   L   G   E           G       O   E   K
     D       G       I   H                       L   M   E
         L   H       G   T                       D   I   E
     L   I   T       H                           S   I
     I   G           T                           S   I
     G   H                                       T
     H   T                                       Y   S
     T                                           L   T
                                                 E   Y
                                                     L
```

```
      1  1  1  1  1  2     1  1           1        1  1
      9  6  3  2  0  0  9  4  5  5  4  7  8  8  6  7  1  2  3  1
   1 +
   2 +
   3 +
   4 +
   5 +
   6 +
   7 +
   8 +
   9 +
  10 +
  11 +
  12 +
  13 +
  14 +
  15 +
  16 +
  17 +
  18 +
  19 +
```

Light, and Miller Light—are all light beers, but not as light as the two in the first cluster. The third cluster consists of Becks, Kirin, Heineken, and Kronenbourg; these are all imported beers. Although no variable in this example explicitly indicates whether beers are domestic or imported, the cost variable (see Figure 3.2) causes the imported beers to cluster together, since they are quite a bit more expensive than the domestic ones. A fourth cluster consists of Augsberger, Heilemans Old Style, Strohs Bohemian Style, and Old Milwaukee; Figure 3.4, produced with the SPSS Tables option, shows that all of these beers are distinguished by high sodium content. The last cluster consists of five beers, Hamms, Coors, Schlitz, Lowenbrau, and Budweiser. These beers share the distinction of being average; they are neither particularly high nor particularly low on the variables measured. Note from Figure 3.4 that, based on the standard deviations, beers in the same cluster, when compared to all beers, are more homogeneous on the variables measured.

Figure 3.4   Cluster characteristics

	CALORIES PER 12 FLUID OUNCES		COST PER 12 FLUID OUNCES		ALCOHOL BY VOLUME (IN %)		SODIUM PER 12 FLUID OUNCES IN MG	
	Mean	Standard Deviation	Mean	Standard Deviation	Mean	Standard Deviation	Mean	Standard Deviation
CLUSMEM5								
AVERAGE	146	8	.44	.02	4.7	.2	17	2
EXPENSIVE	155	10	.76	.03	5.0	.2	11	6
HIGH NA	153	15	.38	.07	4.9	.4	25	2
LIGHT	109	16	.46	.03	4.1	.2	10	3
VERY LIGHT	70	3	.42	.06	2.6	.4	11	6
TOTAL	132	30	.50	.14	4.4	.8	15	7

Cluster formation continues until all cases are merged into a single cluster, as in row 1 in Figure 3.3. Thus, all steps of the cluster analysis are displayed. If we were clustering people instead of beers, the last row would represent individuals and earlier rows would perhaps represent individuals merged into families, families merged into neighborhoods, and so forth. Often there is no single, meaningful cluster solution, but many, depending on what characteristic is of interest.

The Agglomeration Schedule

The results of the cluster analysis are summarized in the **agglomeration schedule** in Figure 3.5, which identifies the cases or clusters being combined at each stage. The first row of the schedule represents stage 1, the 19-cluster solution. At this stage beers 11 and 17 are combined, as indicated in the *Cluster 1* and *Cluster 2* columns under the heading *Clusters Combined* (in this column, *cluster* can refer to either an individual case or a multicase cluster). The squared Euclidean distance between these two beers is displayed in the column labeled *Coefficient*. (This coefficient is identical to the distance measure for cases 11 and 17—Coors and Hamms—in Figure 3.2.) The column entitled *Stage Cluster 1st Appears* indicates at which stage a multicase cluster is first formed. For example, looking at the row for stage 5, the 4 in the *Cluster 1* column indicates that case 1 was first involved in a merge in the previous step, stage 4. Reading across the row for stage 4, you can see that case 1 was involved in a merge with case 3. The last column, labeled *Next Stage*, indicates the next stage at which another case or cluster is combined with this one. Looking at stage 5, we see that the new cluster (cases 1, 2, and 3), numbered cluster 1, is next involved in a merge at stage 10, where it combines with cases 11 and 17. (The cluster number is always the same as the number of its earliest case; thus, the cluster formed by cases 1, 2, and 3 is called cluster 1, and the cluster formed by cases 11 and 17 is called cluster 11.)

Figure 3.5   Agglomeration schedule using complete linkage

Agglomeration Schedule using Complete Linkage

Stage	Clusters Cluster 1	Combined Cluster 2	Coefficient	Stage Cluster 1st Appears Cluster 1	 Cluster 2	Next Stage
1	11	17	.114695	0	0	10
2	9	20	.306903	0	0	8
3	8	18	.309227	0	0	9
4	1	3	.374859	0	0	5
5	1	2	.529696	4	0	10
6	5	15	.606378	0	0	7
7	4	5	.870016	0	6	15
8	9	10	.934909	2	0	11
9	6	8	1.352618	0	3	14
10	1	11	1.405148	5	1	16
11	9	12	1.559987	8	0	12
12	9	13	1.990205	11	0	17
13	16	19	2.820897	0	0	19
14	6	7	3.106108	9	0	16
15	4	14	4.238165	7	0	17
16	1	6	4.378198	10	14	18
17	4	9	12.151937	15	12	18
18	1	4	19.552841	16	17	19
19	1	16	33.338039	18	13	0

The information in Figure 3.5 that is not available in the icicle plot is the value of the distance between the two most dissimilar points of the clusters being combined at each stage, or the coefficient. By examining these values, you can get an idea of how unlike the clusters being combined are. Small coefficients indicate that fairly homogeneous clusters are being merged. Large coefficients indicate that clusters containing quite dissimilar members are being combined. The actual value depends on the clustering method and the distance measure used.

These coefficients can also be used for guidance in deciding how many clusters are needed to represent the data. You usually want to stop agglomeration as soon as the increase between two adjacent steps becomes large. For example, in Figure 3.5 there is a fairly large increase in the value of the distance measure from a four-cluster to a three-cluster solution (stages 16 and 17).

The Dendrogram

Another way of visually representing the steps in a hierarchical clustering solution is with a display called a **dendrogram**. The dendrogram identifies the clusters being combined and the values of the coefficients at each step. The dendrogram produced by SPSS does not plot actual distances but rescales them to numbers between 0 and 25. Thus, the ratio of the distances between steps is preserved, but the scale displayed at the top of the figure does not correspond to actual distance values.

To understand how a dendrogram is constructed, consider a simple four-beer example. Figure 3.6 contains the icicle plot for clustering Kirin, Becks, Old Milwaukee, and Budweiser. From the icicle plot, you can see that at the first step Budweiser and Old Milwaukee are combined, at the second step Becks and Kirin are merged, and at the last step all four beers are merged into a single cluster.

Figure 3.6   Vertical icicle plot for the four-beer example

```
Vertical Icicle Plot using Complete Linkage

  (Down) Number of Clusters   (Across) Case Label and number

        K   B   O   B
        I   E   L   U
        R   C   D   D
        I   K       W
        N   S   M   E
                I   I
                L   S
                W   E
                A   R
                U
                K
                E
                E


        4  3  2  1
    1 +
    2 +
    3 +
```

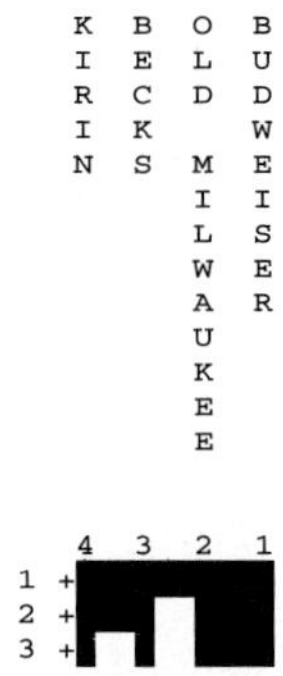

The distances at which the beers are combined are shown in the agglomeration schedule in Figure 3.7. From this schedule, we see that the distance between Budweiser and Old Milwaukee (cases 1 and 2) is 2.017 when they are combined. Similarly, when Becks and Kirin (cases 3 and 4) are combined, their distance is 6.323. Since the method of complete linkage is used, the distance coefficient displayed for the last stage is the largest distance between a member of the Budweiser–Milwaukee cluster and a member of the Becks–Kirin cluster. This distance is 16.789.

Figure 3.7   Agglomeration schedule for the four-beer example

Agglomeration Schedule using Complete Linkage

Stage	Clusters Combined Cluster 1	Cluster 2	Coefficient	Stage Cluster 1st Appears Cluster 1	Cluster 2	Next Stage
1	1	2	2.017019	0	0	3
2	3	4	6.323440	0	0	3
3	1	3	16.789230	1	2	0

The information in Figure 3.7 is displayed in the dendrogram in Figure 3.8, which is read from left to right. Vertical lines denote joined clusters. The position of the line on the scale indicates the distance at which clusters were joined. Since the distances are re-scaled to fall in the range of 1 to 25, the largest distance, 16.8, corresponds to the value of 25. The smallest distance, 2.017, corresponds to the value 1. The second distance, 6.32, corresponds to a value of about 8. Note that the ratio of the rescaled distances is, after the first, the same as the ratios of the original distances.

The first two clusters that are joined are Budweiser and Old Milwaukee. They are connected by a line that is one unit from the origin, since this is the rescaled distance between these points. When Becks and Kirin are joined, the line that connects them is 8 units from the origin. Similarly, when these two clusters are merged into a single cluster, the line that connects them is 25 units from the origin. Thus, the dendrogram indicates not only which clusters are joined but also the distance at which they are joined.

Figure 3.8   Dendrogram for the four-beer example

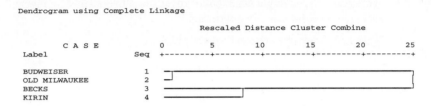

Figure 3.9 contains the dendrogram for the complete 20-beer example. Since many of the distances at the beginning stages are similar in magnitude, you cannot tell the sequence in which some of the early clusters are formed. However, at the last three stages the distances at which clusters are being combined are fairly large. Looking at the dendrogram, it appears that the five-cluster solution (very light beers, light beers, imported beers, high-sodium beers, and "average" beers) may be appropriate, since it is easily interpretable and occurs before the distances at which clusters are combined become too large.

Figure 3.9   Dendrogram using complete linkage for the 20 beers

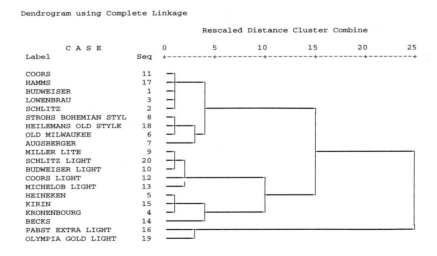

Some Additional Displays and Modifications

The agglomeration schedule, icicle plot, and dendrogram illustrate the results produced by a hierarchical clustering solution. Several variations of these plots may also be useful. For example, when there are many cases, the initial steps of the cluster analysis may not be of particular interest. You might want to display solutions for only certain numbers of clusters. Or you might want to see the results at every kth step. Figure 3.10 shows the icicle plot of results at every fifth step.

Figure 3.10   Icicle plot with results at every fifth step

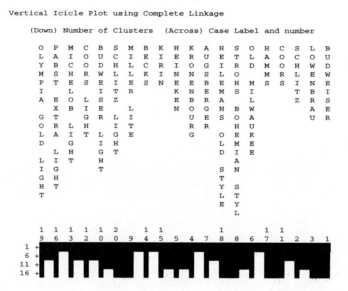

When there are many cases, all of them may not fit across the top of a single page. In this situation it may be useful to turn the icicle plot on its side. This is called a **horizontal icicle plot**. Figure 3.11 contains the horizontal icicle plot corresponding to Figure 3.3.

Figure 3.11   Horizontal icicle plot

```
Horizontal Icicle Plot Using Complete Linkage

                              Number of Clusters

                                      1111111111
                 C A S E      1234567890123456789
         Label            Seq  +++++++++++++++++++
```

```
OLYMPIA GOLD LIGHT    19
PABST EXTRA LIGHT     16
MICHELOB LIGHT        13
COORS LIGHT           12
BUDWEISER LIGHT       10
SCHLITZ LIGHT         20
MILLER LITE            9
BECKS                 14
KIRIN                 15
HEINEKEN               5
KRONENBOURG            4
AUGSBERGER             7
HEILEMANS OLD STYLE   18
STROHS BOHEMIAN STYL   8
OLD MILWAUKEE          6
HAMMS                 17
COORS                 11
SCHLITZ                2
LOWENBRAU              3
BUDWEISER              1
```

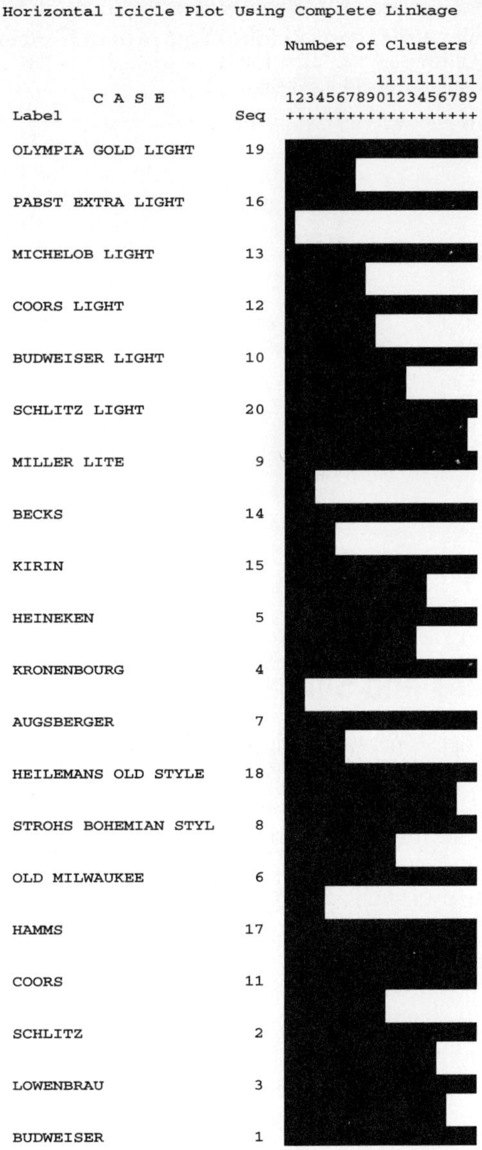

Although the composition of clusters at any stage can be discerned from the icicle plots, it is often helpful to display the information in tabular form. Figure 3.12 contains the cluster memberships for the cases at different stages of the solution. From Figure 3.12, you can easily tell to which clusters cases belong in the two- to five-cluster solutions.

Figure 3.12   Cluster membership at different stages

Cluster Membership of Cases using Complete Linkage

		\multicolumn{4}{c}{Number of Clusters}			
Label	Case	5	4	3	2
BUDWEISER	1	1	1	1	1
SCHLITZ	2	1	1	1	1
LOWENBRAU	3	1	1	1	1
KRONENBOURG	4	2	2	2	1
HEINEKEN	5	2	2	2	1
OLD MILWAUKEE	6	3	1	1	1
AUGSBERGER	7	3	1	1	1
STROHS BOHEMIAN STYL	8	3	1	1	1
MILLER LITE	9	4	3	2	1
BUDWEISER LIGHT	10	4	3	2	1
COORS	11	1	1	1	1
COORS LIGHT	12	4	3	2	1
MICHELOB LIGHT	13	4	3	2	1
BECKS	14	2	2	2	1
KIRIN	15	2	2	2	1
PABST EXTRA LIGHT	16	5	4	3	2
HAMMS	17	1	1	1	1
HEILEMANS OLD STYLE	18	3	1	1	1
OLYMPIA GOLD LIGHT	19	5	4	3	2
SCHLITZ LIGHT	20	4	3	2	1

More on Calculating Distances and Similarities

There are many methods for estimating the distance or similarity between two cases. But even before these measures are computed, you must decide whether the variables need to be rescaled. When the variables have different scales, such as cents and calories, and they are not standardized, any distance measure will reflect primarily the contributions of variables measured in the large units. For example, the beer data variables were standardized prior to cluster analysis to have a mean of 0 and a standard deviation of 1. Besides standardization to Z scores, variables can be standardized by dividing them by just the standard deviation, the range, the mean, or the maximum. See Romesburg (1984) or Anderberg (1973) for further discussion.

Based on the transformed data, it is possible to calculate many different types of distance and similarity measures. Different distance and similarity measures weight data characteristics differently. The choice among the measures should be based on which differences or similarities in the data are important for a particular application. For example, if one is clustering animal bones, what may matter is not the actual differences in bone size but relationships among the dimensions, since we know that even animals of the same species differ in size. Bones with the same relationship between length and diameter should be judged as similar, regardless of their absolute magnitudes. See Romesburg (1984) for further discussion.

The most commonly used distance measure, the squared Euclidean distance, has been discussed previously. Sometimes its square root, the **Euclidean distance**, is also used. A distance measure that is based on the absolute values of differences is the **city-block distance**, or **Manhattan distance**. For two cases it is just the sum of the absolute differences of the values for all variables. Since the differences are not squared, large differences are not weighted as heavily as in the squared Euclidean distances. The **Chebychev distance** defines the distance between two cases as the maximum absolute difference in the values over all variables. Thus, it ignores much of the available information.

When variables are binary, special distance and similarity measures are required. Many are based on the familiar measures of association for contingency tables. See Chapter 5 for further discussion of distance and similarity measures.

Methods for Combining Clusters

Many methods can be used to decide which cases or clusters should be combined at each step. In general, clustering methods fall into three groups: linkage methods, error sums of squares or variance methods, and centroid methods. All are based on either a matrix of distances or a matrix of similarities between pairs of cases. The methods differ in how they estimate distances between clusters at successive steps. Since the merging of clusters at each step depends on the distance measure, different distance measures can result in different cluster solutions for the same clustering method. See Milligan (1980) for comparisons of the performance of some of the different clustering methods.

One of the simplest methods for joining clusters is single linkage, sometimes called nearest neighbor. The first two cases combined are those with the smallest distance, or greatest similarity, between them. The distance between the new cluster and individual cases is then computed as the minimum distance between an individual case and a case in the cluster. The distances between cases that have not been joined do not change. At every step the distance between two clusters is taken to be the distance between their two closest points.

Another commonly used method is called complete linkage, or the furthest neighbor technique. In this method the distance between two clusters is calculated as the distance between their two furthest points.

The **average linkage between groups method**, often called **UPGMA** (unweighted pair-group method using arithmetic averages), defines the distance between two clusters as the average of the distances between all pairs of cases in which one member of the pair is from each of the clusters. For example, if cases 1 and 2 form cluster A and cases 3, 4, and 5 form cluster B, the distance between clusters A and B is taken to be the average of the distances between the following pairs of cases: (1,3) (1,4) (1,5) (2,3) (2,4) (2,5). This differs from the other linkage methods in that it uses information about all pairs of distances, not just the nearest or the furthest. For this reason it is usually preferred to the single and complete linkage methods for cluster analysis.

The UPGMA method considers only distances between pairs of cases in different clusters. A variant of it, the **average linkage within groups method**, combines clusters so that the average distance between all cases in the resulting cluster is as small as possible. Thus, the distance between two clusters is taken to be the average of the distances between all possible pairs of cases in the resulting cluster.

Another frequently used method for cluster formation is **Ward's method**. For each cluster the means for all variables are calculated. Then for each case the squared Euclidean distance to the cluster means is calculated. These distances are summed for all of the cases. At each step, the two clusters that merge are those that result in the smallest increase in the overall sum of the squared within-cluster distances.

The **centroid method** calculates the distance between two clusters as the distance between their means for all of the variables. One disadvantage of the centroid method is that the distance at which clusters are combined can actually decrease from one step to the next. Since clusters merged at later stages are more dissimilar than those merged at early stages, this is an undesirable property.

In the centroid method, the centroid of a merged cluster is a weighted combination of the centroids of the two individual clusters, where the weights are proportional to the sizes of the clusters. In the **median method**, the two clusters being combined are weighted equally in the computation of the centroid, regardless of the number of cases in each. This allows small groups to have equal effect on the characterization of larger clusters into which they are merged.

When similarity measures are used, the criteria for combining is reversed. That is, clusters with large similarity-based measures are merged.

Clustering Variables

In the previous example, the units used for cluster analysis were individual cases (the different brands of beer). Cluster analysis can also be used to find homogeneous groups of variables. For example, consider the 14 community variables described in Chapter 2. We could use cluster analysis to group the 88 counties included in the study and then examine the resulting clusters to establish what characteristics they share. Another approach is to cluster the 14 variables used to describe the communities. In this case, the unit used for analysis is the variable. The distance or similarity measures are computed for all pairs of variables.

Figure 3.13 shows the results of clustering the community variables using the absolute value of the correlation coefficient as a measure of similarity. The absolute value of the coefficient is used, since it is a measure of the strength of the relationship. The sign indicates only the direction. If you want clusters for positively correlated variables only, the sign of the coefficient should be maintained.

Figure 3.13   Cluster analysis of the community variables

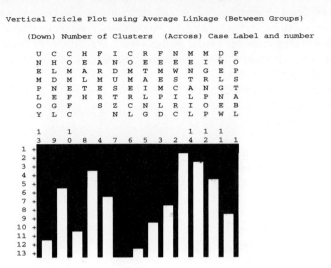

```
Vertical Icicle Plot using Average Linkage (Between Groups)

   (Down) Number of Clusters   (Across) Case Label and number

       U   C   C   H   F   I   C   R   F   N   M   M   D   P
       N   H   O   E   A   N   O   E   E   E   E   E   I   O
       E   L   M   A   R   D   M   T   M   W   N   G   E   P
       M   D   M   L   M   U   M   A   E   S   T   R   L   S
       P   N   E   T   E   S   E   I   M   C   A   N   G   T
       L   E   F   H   R   T   R   L   P   I   L   P   N   A
       O   G   F       S   Z   C   N   L   R   I   O   E   B
       Y   L   C           N   L   G   D   C   L   P   W   L

       1       1                           1   1   1
       3   9   0   8   4   7   6   5   3   2   4   2   1   1
   1 +
   2 +
   3 +
   4 +
   5 +
   6 +
   7 +
   8 +
   9 +
  10 +
  11 +
  12 +
  13 +
```

The clustering procedure is the same whether variables or cases are clustered. It starts out with as many clusters as there are variables. At each successive step, variables or clusters of variables are merged, as shown in the icicle plot in Figure 3.13.

Consider the four-cluster solution (in row 4). The *unemploy, chldnegl, commeffc,* and *health* variables form one cluster; the *farmers, industzn, commercl, retailng, femempld,* and *newscirc* variables form the second cluster; *mentalil* is a cluster by itself; and the fourth cluster is *migrnpop, dwelgnew,* and *popstabl.*

If you've read Chapter 2, this solution should appear familiar. The groupings of the variables are exactly those established by the factor analysis. The first cluster is the *welfare* factor, the second the *urbanism,* and the fourth *influx.* In both cases the extent of mental illness does not appear to be related to the remainder of the variables.

This is not a chance occurrence. Although factor analysis has an underlying theoretical model and cluster analysis is much more ad hoc, both identify related groups of variables. However, factor analysis allows variables to be either positively or negatively related to a factor. Cluster analysis can be restricted to search only for positive associations between variables. Thus, if the absolute values of the correlation coefficients are not taken, variables that correlate negatively with a factor do not appear in the same cluster with variables that correlate positively. For example, the *farmers* variable would not appear with the other urbanism variables. Factor analysis and cluster analysis need not always arrive at the same variable groupings, but it is comforting when they do.

How to Obtain a Hierarchical Cluster Analysis

The Hierarchical Cluster Analysis procedure groups similar cases or variables for moderate-size data files. You can obtain optional statistics and plots or save cluster memberships. To obtain a casewise cluster analysis when the number of cases exceeds several hundred, use k-means clustering, described in Chapter 4.

The minimum specifications are:

- For casewise clustering, one or more numeric variables.
- For clustering of variables, three or more numeric variables.

To obtain a hierarchical cluster analysis, from the menus choose:

Statistics
  Classify ▶
    Hierarchical Cluster...

This opens the Hierarchical Cluster Analysis dialog box, as shown in Figure 3.14.

Figure 3.14   Hierarchical Cluster Analysis dialog box

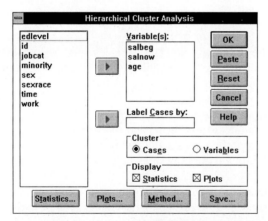

The variables in your data file appear in the source list. For casewise clustering, select one or more numeric variables for analysis and click on OK to get the default casewise cluster analysis using Euclidean distances and between-groups average linkage. An agglomeration schedule and vertical icicle plot, and the case count, are displayed by default. Cases with missing values on any clustering variable are excluded from the analysis.

Alternately, you can cluster variables. Select three or more numeric variables and select Variables for Cluster. Click on OK to get the default cluster analysis for variables using Euclidean distances and between-groups average linkage. Variables with missing cases are excluded from the analysis.

By default, cases are identified in output by case number. Optionally, you can use the values of a string variable to identify cases. Select a string variable for Label Cases by. For example, selecting *beer* as the case-labeling variable produced the beer-name labels in Figure 3.3. This option is not available for clustering of variables.

Cluster. You can choose one of the following alternatives:

○ **Cases**. Produces a casewise cluster analysis. This is the default. Distances are computed between cases.

○ **Variables**. Variables are clustered. Distances are computed between variables.

Display. You can choose one or both of the following display options:

❏ **Statistics**. Displays statistics. This is the default. To suppress statistical output, deselect this item. (See "Hierarchical Cluster Analysis Statistics," below, for optional statistics.)

❏ **Plots**. Displays plots. This is the default. To suppress plots, deselect this item. (See "Hierarchical Cluster Analysis Plots," below, for optional plots.)

Hierarchical Cluster Analysis Statistics

To display a distance matrix or cluster memberships, click on Statistics... in the Hierarchical Cluster Analysis dialog box. This opens the Hierarchical Cluster Analysis Statistics dialog box, as shown in Figure 3.15.

Figure 3.15   Hierarchical Cluster Analysis Statistics dialog box

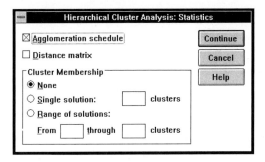

At least one statistical display must be selected. To suppress all statistical output, deselect Statistics for Display in the Hierarchical Cluster Analysis dialog box.

You can choose one or both of the following:

❑ **Agglomeration schedule**. Displays the order or stage at which cases or clusters were combined and their distance coefficient. Displayed by default. To suppress the agglomeration schedule, deselect this item.

❑ **Distance matrix**. Matrix of distances between the items. The type of matrix produced (similarities or dissimilarities) depends upon the measure selected. With a large number of items, this specification produces a large volume of output.

Cluster Membership. You can choose one of the following alternatives:

○ **None**. Suppresses cluster membership output. This is the default.

○ **Single solution**. Displays cluster memberships for a single-cluster solution with a specified number of clusters. Enter an integer greater than 1. For example, to display cluster memberships for a three-cluster solution, enter 3.

○ **Range of solutions**. Displays cluster memberships for a range of cluster solutions. Enter values corresponding to the lowest and highest cluster solutions. For example, Figure 3.12 was produced by specifying 2 for the lowest solution and 5 for the highest solution. Both values must be integers greater than 1, and the first value must be less than the second value.

Hierarchical Cluster Analysis Plots

To display a dendrogram or to control the format of icicle plots, click on Plots... in the Hierarchical Cluster Analysis dialog box. This opens the Hierarchical Cluster Analysis Plots dialog box, as shown in Figure 3.16.

Figure 3.16   Hierarchical Cluster Analysis Plots dialog box

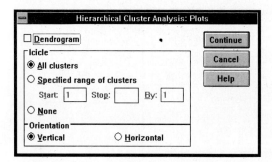

At least one plot must be selected. To suppress all plots, deselect Plots... for display in the Hierarchical Cluster Analysis dialog box.

You can choose the following option:

❏ **Dendrogram**. Shows the clusters being combined and values of distance coefficients at each step. The dendrogram is scaled by joining the distances of the clusters. Actual distances are rescaled to a range of 1 to 25.

Icicle. You can choose one of the following alternatives for icicle plots:

○ **All clusters**. Displays icicle plot for all cluster solutions. This is the default.

○ **Specified range of clusters**. Limits icicle plot to a range of cluster solutions. By default, the icicle plot shows all cluster solutions. To specify a range other than the default, enter positive integers for Start and Stop that correspond to the lowest and highest cluster solution. Enter a positive integer for By for the increment value. The Start and By values must be less than or equal to the Stop value. For example, if you enter Start, Stop, and By values of 2, 8, and 2, the icicle plot displays solutions for 2, 4, 6, and 8 clusters.

○ **None**. Suppresses icicle plot output.

Orientation. You can choose one of the following alternatives:

○ **Vertical**. Displays icicle plot in vertical format. This is the default setting.

○ **Horizontal**. Displays icicle plot in horizontal format. Select horizontal format when there are too many items to fit across the top of a page.

Hierarchical Cluster Analysis Method

To select an alternate clustering method or distance measure, click on Method... in the Hierarchical Cluster Analysis dialog box. This opens the Hierarchical Cluster Analysis Method dialog box, as shown in Figure 3.17.

Figure 3.17   Hierarchical Cluster Analysis Method dialog box

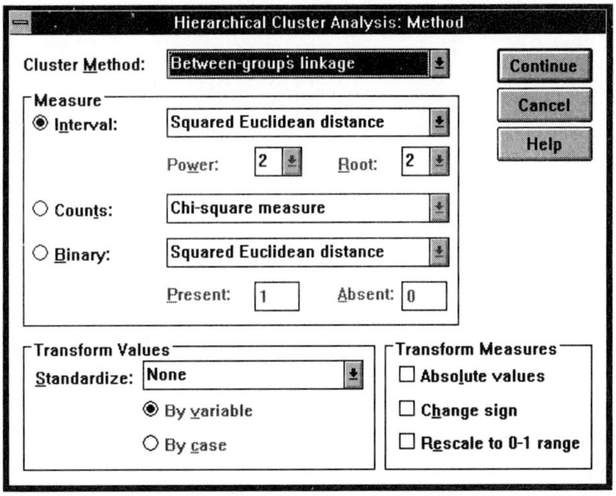

⬇ **Cluster Method**. Method selection controls the method used to determine which cases or clusters are combined at each step. You can choose one of the following alternatives:

Between-groups linkage. Average linkage between groups (UPGMA). This is the default method.

Within-groups linkage. Average linkage within groups.

Nearest neighbor. Also known as single linkage.

Furthest neighbor. Also known as complete linkage.

Centroid clustering. Calculates the distance between two clusters as the distance between their means for all variables.

Median clustering. Clusters combined are weighted equally in the computation of the centroid, regardless of the number of cases. (See "Methods for Combining Clusters" on p. 97 for further discussion.)

Ward's method. Combines clusters with the smallest increase in the overall sum of the squared within-cluster distances. (See "Methods for Combining Clusters" on p. 97 for further discussion.)

Measure. Measure selection controls the computation of the similarities or dissimilarities matrix. There are three types of measures available—interval, frequency-count, and binary. You can choose one of the following alternatives:

◯ **Interval**. Dissimilarity and similarity measures for interval data. This is the default. You can choose one of the following alternatives:

⬇ **Euclidean distance**. The distance between two items, X and Y, is the square root of the sum of the squared differences between the values for the items:

$$\text{Distance } (X, Y) \; = \; \sqrt{\sum_i (X_i - Y_i)^2}$$

Squared Euclidean distance. This is the default for interval data. The distance between two items is the sum of the squared differences between the values for the items:

$$\text{Distance } (X, Y) \; = \; \sum_i (X_i - Y_i)^2$$

Cosine. This is a similarity measure. Cosines of vectors of values:

$$\text{Similarity } (X, Y) \; = \; \left(\sum_i X_i Y_i\right) / \sqrt{\left(\sum X_i^2\right)\left(\sum Y_i^2\right)}$$

Pearson correlation. This is a similarity measure. Correlations between vectors of values:

$$\text{Similarity } (X, Y) \;=\; \frac{\sum\limits_{i} Z_{Xi} Z_{Yi}}{N - 1}$$

where Z_{Xi} is the (standardized) Z score value of X for the ith item, and N is the number of items.

Chebychev. Chebychev distance metric. The distance between two items is the maximum absolute difference between the values for the items:

$$\text{Distance } (X, Y) \;=\; MAX_i |X_i - Y_i|$$

Block. City-block, or Manhattan, distance. The distance between two items is the sum of the absolute differences between the values for the items:

$$\text{Distance } (X, Y) \;=\; \sum_i |X_i - Y_i|$$

Minkowski. Distance in an absolute Minkowski power metric. The distance between two items is the pth root of the sum of the absolute differences to the pth power between the values for the items:

$$\text{Distance } (X, Y) \;=\; \left(\sum_i |X_i - Y_i|^p \right)^{\frac{1}{p}}$$

Customized. Distance in an absolute power metric. The distance between two items is the rth root of the sum of the absolute differences to the pth power between the values for the items:

$$\text{Distance } (X, Y) \;=\; \left(\sum_i |X_i - Y_i|^p \right)^{\frac{1}{r}}$$

⬇ **Power and Root**. For the Minkowski and customized measures, you can override the default power value of 2. Optionally, you can choose 1, 3, or 4. For customized measures, you can also override the default root value. Choose 1, 3, or 4. For both methods, the default values yield Euclidean distances. Appropriate selection of p and r yields squared Euclidean, Minkowski, city-block, and many other distance metrics.

○ **Counts**. Dissimilarities for frequency-count data. You can choose one of the following alternatives:

⬇ **Chi-square measure**. This is the default for counts. Based on the chi-square test of equality for two sets of frequencies. The magnitude of this measure depends on the total frequencies of the two items whose distance is computed. Expected values are from the model of independence of items X and Y.

$$\text{Distance } (X, Y) = \sqrt{\sum_i \frac{(X_i - E(X_i))^2}{E(X_i)} + \sum_i \frac{(Y_i - E(Y_i))^2}{E(Y_i)}}$$

Phi-square measure. This is the chi-square dissimilarity measure normalized by the square root of the combined frequency. Therefore, its value does not depend on the total frequencies of the two items whose distance is computed.

$$\text{Distance } (X, Y) = \sqrt{\frac{\sum_i \dfrac{(X_i - E(X_i))^2}{E(X_i)} + \sum_i \dfrac{(Y_i - E(Y_i))^2}{E(Y_i)}}{N}}$$

○ **Binary**. Dissimilarity measures for binary data. SPSS constructs a 2×2 contingency table for each pair of items. It uses this table to compute a distance measure for the pair. SPSS computes all binary measures from the values of the four cells in the table (a, b, c, and d). These values are tallies across variables (when the items are cases) or tallies across cases (when the items are variables).

		Item 2	
		Present	Absent
Item 1	Present	a	b
	Absent	c	d

You can choose one of the following binary measures:

⬇ **Euclidean distance**. Binary Euclidean distance. It has a minimum value of 0 and no upper limit.

$$\text{Distance } (X, Y) = \sqrt{b + c}$$

Squared Euclidean distance. Binary squared Euclidean distance. This is the default for binary data. It has a minimum of 0 and no upper limit.

$$\text{Distance } (X, Y) = b + c$$

Size difference. It has a minimum value of 0 and no upper limit.

$$\text{Distance } (X, Y) = \frac{(b - c)^2}{(a + b + c + d)^2}$$

Pattern difference. It has a range of 0 to 1.

$$\text{Distance } (X, Y) = \frac{bc}{(a+b+c+d)^2}$$

Variance. It has a minimum value of 0 and no upper limit.

$$\text{Distance } (X, Y) = \frac{b+c}{4(a+b+c+d)}$$

Shape. Binary shape difference. It has no upper or lower limit.

$$\text{Distance } (X, Y) = \frac{(a+b+c+d)(b+c) - (b-c)^2}{(a+b+c+d)^2}$$

Lance and Williams. Binary Lance-and-Williams nonmetric dissimilarity measure (also known as the Bray-Curtis nonmetric coefficient). This measure has a range of 0 to 1.

$$\text{Distance } (X, Y) = \frac{b+c}{2a+b+c}$$

Present and Absent. By default, if you select a binary measure, the data value 1 indicates presence of a characteristic and 0 indicates absence (other values are ignored). Optionally, you can specify different integer values for Present and Absent.

Transform Values. You can standardize data values for either cases or variables to equalize the effect of variables measured on different scales.

⬇ **Standardize**. To control standardization of item values prior to computation of distances, you can choose one of the following alternatives. Standardization is available for counts and interval data only.

None. Does not standardize. This is the default.

Z Scores. Standardizes values to Z scores, with a mean of 0 and a standard deviation of 1. SPSS subtracts the mean from each value for the item being standardized and then divides by the standard deviation of the values. If a standard deviation is 0, all values are set to 0.

Range –1 to 1. Standardizes values to unit range. Each value for the item being standardized is divided by the range of the values. If the range is 0, all values are left unchanged.

Range 0 to 1. Standardizes values to a range of 0 to 1. SPSS subtracts the minimum value from each item being standardized and then divides by the range. If a range is 0, all values for the item are set to 0.50.

Maximum magnitude of 1. Standardizes values to a maximum magnitude of 1. SPSS divides each value for the item being standardized by the maximum of the values. If the maximum of a set of values is 0, SPSS divides by the absolute magnitude of the smallest value and adds 1.

Mean of 1. Standardizes values to unit mean. SPSS divides each value for the item being standardized by the mean of the values. If a mean is 0, SPSS adds 1 to all values for the case or variable to produce a mean of 1.

Standard deviation of 1. Standardizes values to unit standard deviation. SPSS divides each value for the variable or case being standardized by the standard deviation of the values. SPSS does not change the values if their standard deviation is 0.

If you request standardization, you can choose one of the following alternatives:

○ **By variable**. Standardizes the values for each variable. This is the default.

○ **By case**. Standardizes the values within each case.

Transform Measures. You can choose one or more of the following transformations. If you specify more than one transformation, values are transformed in the order shown below.

❑ **Absolute values**. Takes absolute values of distances. Select this item when the sign indicates the direction of the relations (as with correlation coefficients), but only the magnitude of the relations is of interest.

❑ **Change sign**. Transforms similarities into dissimilarities, or vice versa. For example, you can select this item to reverse the ordering of proximities.

❑ **Rescale to 0–1 range**. Rescales distance values to a range of 0 to 1. Standardizes the values by first subtracting the value of the smallest distance and then dividing by the range. You would not usually rescale measures that are already standardized on meaningful scales (for example, correlations and cosines).

Hierarchical Cluster Analysis Save New Variables

To save cluster membership, click on Save... in the Hierarchical Cluster Analysis dialog box. This opens the Hierarchical Cluster Analysis Save New Variables dialog box, as shown in Figure 3.18.

Figure 3.18   Hierarchical Cluster Analysis Save New Variables dialog box

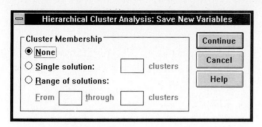

Cluster Membership. Saving cluster memberships is available for casewise clustering. Names of cluster membership variables and the clustering method are shown in the output. You can choose one of the following alternatives:

❍ **None**. Does not save cluster memberships. This is the default setting.

❍ **Single solution**. Saves cluster memberships for a single cluster solution with a specified number of clusters. Enter an integer greater than 1. For example, to save cluster memberships for a four-cluster solution, enter 4.

❍ **Range of solutions**. Saves cluster memberships for a range of cluster solutions. Enter values corresponding to the lowest and highest cluster solutions. For example, to save memberships for solutions having 3, 4, and 5 clusters, enter 3 for the lowest solution and 5 for the highest solution. Both values must be integers greater than 1 and the first value must be less than the second value.

Additional Features Available with Command Syntax

You can customize your cluster analysis if you paste your selections to a syntax window and edit the resulting PROXIMITIES and CLUSTER command syntax (see Chapter 5 in the *SPSS Base System User's Guide*). Additional features include:

• Matrix facility to write distance matrices or to read existing matrices that can be used in place of raw data (with the MATRIX subcommand).

• Additional distance measures created by the PROXIMITIES procedure.

• User-specified rootnames for cluster membership variables (with the SAVE subcommand).

• Multiple analyses using different clustering methods (with the METHOD subcommand).

• Additional power and root values for customized distances (with the MEASURE subcommand).

See the Syntax Reference section of this manual for command syntax rules and for complete PROXIMITIES and CLUSTER command syntax.

4 Cluster Analysis for Large Files

Chapter 3 discusses the basics of cluster analysis and describes a commonly used method for cluster formation—agglomerative hierarchical clustering. This is but one of many methods available for cluster formation. For a particular problem, selection of a method to use depends not only on the characteristics of the various methods but also on the data set to be analyzed. For example, when the number of cases is large, algorithms that require many computations or storage of all cases in memory may pose difficulties in terms of either the time required to perform the computations or available memory.

This chapter describes the K-Means Cluster Analysis procedure, which can be used to cluster large numbers of cases (200 or more) efficiently without requiring substantial computer resources. Unlike the Hierarchical Cluster Analysis procedure, which results in a series of solutions corresponding to different numbers of clusters, the K-Means Cluster Analysis procedure produces only one solution for the number of clusters requested. The number of clusters must be specified by the user.

The Method

The algorithm used for determining cluster membership in the K-Means Cluster Analysis procedure is based on **nearest centroid sorting** (Anderberg, 1973). That is, a case is assigned to the cluster with the smallest distance between the case and the center of the cluster (centroid). The actual mechanics of the procedure depend on the information available. If the cluster centers are known, they can be specified, and case assignment is based on them. Otherwise, cluster centers are iteratively estimated from the data.

Since k-means cluster analysis requires a user-specified number of clusters, you may want to use hierarchical cluster analysis on a random sample or subset of cases to help determine the number of clusters before using k-means cluster analysis on all cases. Hierarchical cluster analysis can also be used to determine the **initial cluster centers** for k-means cluster analysis.

Classification When Cluster Centers Are Known

Consider again the beer data described in Chapter 3. Using hierarchical cluster analysis, we identified five interpretable clusters for twenty beers. If there are additional beers that we want to classify into one of these five clusters, we can use the K-Means Cluster Analysis procedure as a quick and efficient means of doing so. Each of the new beers is assigned to the cluster to whose center it is closest. For each cluster, the center is simply the mean of the four variables for cases in the cluster; these values, standardized, are shown in Figure 4.1. (The unstandardized values are shown in Figure 3.1 in Chapter 3.)

Figure 4.1   Standardized means for the five clusters

```
               - - Description of Subpopulations - -

Summaries of      ZCALORIE
By levels of      CLUSMEM5


Variable       Value  Label                      Mean

CLUSMEM5          1   AVERAGE                    .4362
CLUSMEM5          2   EXPENSIVE                  .7551
CLUSMEM5          3   HIGH NA                    .6890
CLUSMEM5          4   LIGHT                     -.7667
CLUSMEM5          5   VERY LIGHT               -2.0621

Summaries of      ZCOST
By levels of      CLUSMEM5


Variable       Value  Label                      Mean

CLUSMEM5          1   AVERAGE                   -.3790
CLUSMEM5          2   EXPENSIVE                 1.8498
CLUSMEM5          3   HIGH NA                   -.7928
CLUSMEM5          4   LIGHT                     -.2538
CLUSMEM5          5   VERY LIGHT                -.5320

               - - Description of Subpopulations - -

Summaries of      ZALCOHOL
By levels of      CLUSMEM5


Variable       Value  Label                      Mean

CLUSMEM5          1   AVERAGE                    .3421
CLUSMEM5          2   EXPENSIVE                  .7039
CLUSMEM5          3   HIGH NA                    .6382
CLUSMEM5          4   LIGHT                     -.4474
CLUSMEM5          5   VERY LIGHT               -2.4211

Summaries of      ZSODIUM
By levels of      CLUSMEM5


Variable       Value  Label                      Mean

CLUSMEM5          1   AVERAGE                    .3419
CLUSMEM5          2   EXPENSIVE                 -.6383
CLUSMEM5          3   HIGH NA                   1.4514
CLUSMEM5          4   LIGHT                     -.7219
CLUSMEM5          5   VERY LIGHT                -.6763
```

The 15 cases in the new data set are standardized using the means and standard deviations from the original data set (see Chapter 3). The original and standardized values are shown in Figure 4.2.

Figure 4.2   Original and standardized values for the 15 new beers

BEER	CALORIES	SODIUM	ALCOHOL	COST	ZCALORIE	ZSODIUM	ZALCOHOL	ZCOST
MILLER HIGH LIFE	149	17	4.7	42.0	.55	.31	.34	-.53
MICHELOB	162	10	5.0	50.0	.98	-.75	.74	.02
LABATTS	147	17	5.0	53.0	.48	.31	.74	.23
MOLSON	154	17	5.1	56.0	.71	.31	.87	.44
HENRY WEINHARD	149	7	4.7	61.0	.55	-1.21	.34	.79
ANCHOR STEAM	154	17	4.7	120	.71	.31	.34	4.89
SCHMIDTS	147	7	4.7	30.0	.48	-1.21	.34	-1.37
PABST BLUE RIBBON	152	8	4.9	38.0	.65	-1.06	.61	-.81
OLYMPIA	153	27	4.6	44.0	.68	1.83	.21	-.39
DOS EQUIS	145	14	4.5	70.0	.42	-.14	.08	1.42
SCOTCH BUY (SAFEWAY)	145	18	4.5	27.0	.42	.46	.08	-1.58
BLATZ	144	13	4.6	30.0	.38	-.30	.21	-1.37
ROLLING ROCK	144	8	4.7	36.0	.38	-1.06	.34	-.95
TUBORG	155	13	5.0	43.0	.75	-.30	.74	-.46
ST PAULI GIRL	144	21	4.7	77.0	.38	.92	.34	1.90

To classify the cases, the Euclidean distance (see Chapter 3) from each new case to each of the cluster centers is calculated. The cluster centers are simply the means from Figure 4.1. To use these values as initial centers in the K-Means Cluster Analysis procedure, enter them using the Data Editor and save them as an SPSS data file. Figure 4.3 shows the cluster centers file *c:\spss5\qcls.sav* used in this example. The file contains the variable *cluster_* indicating cluster number and values for each clustering variable (*zcalorie, zcost, zalcohol, zsodium*) for each cluster.

Figure 4.3   Initial cluster centers file

c:\spss5\qcls.sav

	cluster_	zcalorie	zcost	zalcohol	zsodium
1	1	.436	-.379	.342	.342
2	2	.755	1.850	.704	-.639
3	3	.689	-.793	.638	1.450
4	4	-.767	-.254	-.447	-.722
5	5	-2.060	-.532	-2.420	-.676

Figure 4.4 shows these centers as they appear in output from the K-Means Cluster Analysis procedure.

Figure 4.4   Initial cluster centers

```
Initial Cluster Centers.  (From subcommand FILE)

Cluster       ZCALORIE      ZCOST        ZALCOHOL      ZSODIUM

    1           .4360       -.3790         .3420         .3420
    2           .7550       1.8500         .7040        -.6390
    3           .6890       -.7930         .6380        1.4500
    4          -.7670       -.2540        -.4470        -.7220
    5         -2.0600       -.5320       -2.4200        -.6760
```

The first new beer to be classified is Miller High Life. From Figure 4.2, its standardized value for calories is 0.55, for cost is −0.53, for alcohol is 0.34, and for sodium is 0.31. Its Euclidean distance to cluster 1 is

$$\sqrt{(0.55 - 0.44)^2 + (-0.53 - (-0.38))^2 + (0.34 - 0.34)^2 + (0.31 - 0.34)^2} = 0.19$$

Equation 4.1

Distances to the other cluster centers are computed in the same way. The distance to cluster 2 is 2.6, to cluster 3 is 1.21, to cluster 4 is 1.87, and to cluster 5 is 3.92. Since the distance is smallest to cluster 1, Miller High Life is assigned to cluster 1.

Figure 4.5 shows the clusters to which the new beers are assigned, as well as the Euclidean distance from the case to the center of its assigned cluster. As shown in Figure 4.6, ten beers are assigned to cluster 1, four beers to cluster 2, and one beer to cluster 3. No beers are assigned to the last two clusters.

Figure 4.5   Case listing of cluster membership

```
Case listing of Cluster membership.

BEER                    Cluster      Distance

MILLER HIGH LIFE           1           .192
MICHELOB                   1          1.345
LABATTS                    1           .730
MOLSON                     1          1.014
HENRY WEINHARD             2          1.274
ANCHOR STEAM               2          3.208
SCHMIDTS                   1          1.839
PABST BLUE RIBBON          1          1.502
OLYMPIA                    3           .699
DOS EQUIS                  2           .969
SCOTCH BUY (SAFEWAY)       1          1.231
BLATZ                      1          1.184
ROLLING ROCK               1          1.511
TUBORG                     1           .817
ST PAULI GIRL              2          1.643
```

Figure 4.6   Number of cases in each cluster

```
Number of Cases in each Cluster.

   Cluster        unweighted cases     weighted cases

      1                   10.0                 10.0
      2                    4.0                  4.0
      3                    1.0                  1.0
      4                     .0                   .0
      5                     .0                   .0

Missing                     0
Total                      15.0                 15.0
```

Once the beers have been assigned to clusters, it is possible to calculate the actual centers of the resulting clusters, which are simply the average values of the variables for cases in the cluster. These values, called the *final cluster centers*, are shown in Figure 4.7. Since no cases were assigned to the last two clusters, system-missing values are displayed. From this table, we can see that the clusters do not differ much in average calories, since all three have similar standardized values. Cluster 2 has the beers with the highest cost, while cluster 3 contains the high-sodium beers.

Figure 4.7   Final cluster centers

```
Final Cluster Centers.

   Cluster     ZCALORIE      ZCOST        ZALCOHOL      ZSODIUM

      1          .5783       -.6363         .5000       -.3267
      2          .5155      2.2497         .2763       -.0304
      3          .6808       -.3929         .2105      1.8313
      4            .            .             .            .
      5            .            .             .            .
```

Once clusters have been formed, you can assess how "well separated" they are by calculating the distances between their centers. Hopefully, the clusters will have centers that are far apart, with cases within a cluster hovering fairly closely to the cluster's center.

Euclidean distances between pairs of final cluster centers are displayed in Figure 4.8. For example, the distance between clusters 1 and 2 is

$$\sqrt{(0.58-0.52)^2 + (-0.64-2.25)^2 + (0.50-0.28)^2 + (-0.33-(-0.03))^2} = 2.91$$

Equation 4.2

Similarly, the distance between clusters 1 and 3 is 2.19, while the distance between clusters 2 and 3 is 3.24.

Figure 4.8   Euclidean distances between final cluster centers

```
Distances between Final Cluster centers.

  Cluster         1              2              3              4

     1          .0000
     2         2.9104          .0000
     3         2.1933         3.2374          .0000
     4            .              .              .            .0000
     5            .              .              .              .
```

The table of final cluster centers (Figure 4.7) contains the average values of the variables for each cluster but provides no idea of the variability. One way of assessing the between-cluster to within-cluster variability is to compute a one-way analysis of variance for each of the variables and examine the ratio of the between-cluster to within-cluster mean squares.

Figure 4.9 contains the mean squares for examining differences between the clusters. The between-clusters mean square is labeled *Cluster MS*, and the within-cluster mean square is labeled *Error MS*. Their ratio is displayed in the column labeled *F*. Large ratios and small observed significance levels are associated with variables that differ between the clusters. However, the *F* tests should be used only for descriptive purposes, since the clusters have been chosen to maximize the differences among cases in different clusters. The observed significance levels are not corrected for this and thus cannot be interpreted as tests of the hypothesis that the cluster means are equal.

Figure 4.9   Cluster mean squares

```
Analysis of Variance.

  Variable      Cluster MS    DF        Error MS      DF            F      Prob

  ZCALORIE         .0124       2          .0334      12.0        .3712     .698
  ZCOST         12.0558       2         1.2003      12.0      10.0438     .003
  ZALCOHOL         .0952       2          .0586      12.0       1.6256     .237
  ZSODIUM         2.1316       2          .5242      12.0       4.0665     .045
```

As expected from Figure 4.7, the calories variable (*zcalorie*) does not differ between the clusters. The *F* value is small and the associated significance level is large. Beers in the three clusters also have fairly similar alcohol content (*zalcohol*). However, they do seem to be different in sodium (*zsodium*) and cost (*zcost*).

Classification When Cluster Centers Are Unknown

In the previous example, the cluster centers for classifying cases were already known. The initial cluster solution and the center values were obtained from the hierarchical cluster solution. In many situations the center values for the clusters are not known in advance. Instead, they too must be estimated from the data. Several different methods for estimating cluster centers are available. Most of them involve examining the data several times.

Good cluster centers separate the cases well. One strategy is to choose cases that have large distances between them and use their values as initial estimates of the cluster centers. The number of cases selected is the number of clusters specified.

The algorithm for this strategy proceeds as follows. The first k cases in the data file, where k is the number of clusters requested, are selected as temporary centers. As subsequent cases are processed, a case replaces a center if its smallest distance to a center is greater than the distance between the two closest centers. The center that is closer to the case is replaced. A case also replaces a center if the smallest distance from the case to a center is larger than the smallest distance between that center and all other centers. Again, it replaces the center closest to it.

To illustrate the basics of the k-means cluster analysis when centers are estimated from the data, let's consider the beer data again, this time using k-means clustering to cluster all 35 beers into five clusters.

Selecting Initial Cluster Centers

The first step of cluster formation, as previously described, is making a first guess at cluster centers. Figure 4.10 contains the values of five centers selected by the program, the *initial cluster centers*. Each center corresponds to a beer. The first center is Schlitz Light, the second, Kronenbourg, the third, Pabst Extra Light, the fourth, Anchor Steam, and the fifth, Heileman's Old Style. These are, in terms of the variables under consideration, well-separated beers. Schlitz Light is a low-calorie beer; Kronenbourg is a low-sodium beer; Pabst Extra Light is a very light beer; Anchor Steam is a very expensive beer; and Heileman's Old Style is an average beer, though somewhat higher in sodium than most of the beers.

Figure 4.10   Initial cluster centers for all 35 beers

```
Initial Cluster Centers.

Cluster      ZCAL        ZSOD        ZALC        ZCST

   1        -1.7496     -1.2461      -.6255      -.1907
   2         1.2365     -1.2461     1.0330      1.1973
   3        -2.9358       .0558    -3.7765      -.6711
   4          .5820       .3813      .2038      3.7064
   5          .1730      1.5204      .5354      -.4042
```

After the initial cluster centers have been selected, cluster centers are updated in an iterative process. All cases are grouped into the cluster with the closest center. Then, average values for the variables are computed from the cases that have been assigned to each cluster and the cases that were the initial cluster centers. This process of assigning cases and recomputing cluster centers is repeated until no further changes occur in cluster centers or until the maximum number of iterations has been reached. The resulting centers are used to classify the cases. The changes in cluster centers at each iteration are displayed in Figure 4.11

Figure 4.11   Iteration history

```
Convergence achieved due to no or small distance change.
The maximum distance by which any center has changed is .0542
Current iteration is   3

Minimum distance between initial centers is 3.1717

Iteration        Change in Cluster Centers
                 1         2         3         4         5
        1      .6183    1.0854     .6096     .0000    1.0722
        2      .1031     .1206     .2032     .0000     .0536
        3      .0172     .0134     .0677     .0000     .0027
```

The results of assigning cases based on the cluster centers when iteration stops is shown in Figure 4.12. Beer names, cluster assignment, and distances to the cluster centers used for classification are shown for the first ten beers. The number of cases in each cluster is shown in Figure 4.13.

Figure 4.12   Case listing of cluster membership

```
Case listing of Cluster membership.

BEER                      Cluster       Distance

  MILLER HIGH LIFE          5            .172
  BUDWEISER                 5            .470
  SCHLITZ                   5            .361
  LOWENBRAU                 5            .660
  MICHELOB                  2           1.218
  LABATTS                   5            .751
  MOLSON                    5            .989
  HENRY WEINHARD            2            .981
  KRONENBOURG               2           1.219
  HEINEKEN                  2            .455
  .
  .
  .
```

Figure 4.13   Number of cases in each cluster

```
Number of Cases in each Cluster.

  Cluster     unweighted cases     weighted cases

       1             5.0                5.0
       2             8.0                8.0
       3             2.0                2.0
       4             1.0                1.0
       5            19.0               19.0

Missing              0
Valid cases         35.0               35.0
```

Once the cases have been classified, average values of the variables are again computed. These are termed **final cluster centers** and are shown in Figure 4.14. The resulting five clusters are quite similar to those obtained with hierarchical cluster analysis in Chapter 3 using a subset of the beers. Cluster 1 contains the light beers, cluster 3 contains the very light beers, and cluster 5 contains the average beers. Anchor Steam, which was not included in the previous analysis, constitutes a separate cluster (cluster 4).

Figure 4.14   Final cluster centers

Final Cluster Centers.

Cluster	ZCAL	ZSOD	ZALC	ZCST
1	-1.2505	-.7253	-.7913	-.2440
2	.5258	-.4527	.4525	1.0572
3	-2.8540	-.6765	-3.2790	-.4576
4	.5820	.3813	.2038	3.7064
5	.3775	.4327	.3521	-.5278

Euclidean distances between the final cluster centers are shown in Figure 4.15. Based on this, you can assess how different the final clusters are. The largest distance is between the very light beers and Anchor Steam. From Figure 4.16, it appears that for all of the variables, variability within a cluster is less than the variability between the clusters.

Figure 4.15   Euclidean distances between final cluster centers

Distances between Final Cluster Centers.

Cluster	1	2	3	4
1	.0000			
2	2.5436	.0000		
3	2.9678	5.2623	.0000	
4	4.6020	2.7890	6.5110	.0000
5	2.3193	1.8243	4.9862	4.2420

Figure 4.16   Cluster mean squares

Analysis of Variance.

Variable	Cluster MS	DF	Error MS	DF	F	Prob
ZCAL	7.3419	4	.1544	30.0	47.5448	.000
ZSOD	2.2219	4	.8371	30.0	2.6543	.052
ZALC	7.1675	4	.1777	30.0	40.3421	.000
ZCST	7.1720	4	.1771	30.0	40.5044	.000

How to Obtain a K-Means Cluster Analysis

The K-Means Cluster Analysis procedure can cluster many cases without requiring substantial time or computer memory. You can save cluster memberships, distance information, and final cluster centers. For moderate-size data files, hierarchical cluster analysis, described in Chapter 3, is also available.

The minimum specification is one or more numeric variables.

To get a *k*-means cluster analysis, from the menus choose:

Statistics
  Classify ▶
    K-Means Cluster...

This opens the K-Means Cluster Analysis dialog box, as shown in Figure 4.17.

Figure 4.17   K-Means Cluster Analysis dialog box

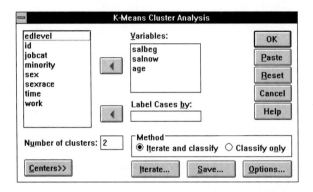

The variables in your data file appear in the source list. Select one or more numeric variables and click on OK to get the default *k*-means cluster analysis, which displays initial and final cluster centers, and the number of cases in each cluster. By default, initial centers are estimated from the sample.

By default, cases are identified in the output by case number. Optionally, you can use values of a variable to label cases. Select a variable for Label Cases by. For example, *beer* was used as the case-labeling variable in Figure 4.5.

Two clusters are formed by default. Optionally, you can obtain a solution with more clusters. Enter an integer value for Number of clusters. The number of clusters must not be greater than the number of cases.

Method. Method selection controls operation of the clustering algorithm. You can choose one of the following alternatives:

○ **Iterate and classify**. Updates initial cluster centers in an iterative process. Updated centers are used to classify cases. This is the default.

○ **Classify only**. Uses initial cluster centers to classify cases. Cluster centers are not updated.

Cluster Centers

You can supply your own initial cluster centers or save final centers for subsequent analyses. Click on Centers>> in the K-Means Cluster Analysis dialog box. This expands the main dialog box, as shown in Figure 4.18.

Figure 4.18   Expanded K-Means Cluster Analysis dialog box

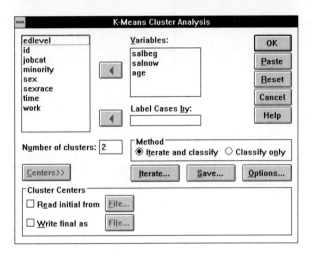

Cluster Centers. You can choose one or both of the following:

❏ **Read initial from.** Read initial cluster centers from an SPSS data file. The current file selection (if any) is shown.

❏ **Write final as.** Save final cluster centers to an SPSS data file. You can use these final cluster centers as initial centers for a different sample of cases. The current file selection (if any) is shown.

K-Means Cluster Analysis Read from File

To name an SPSS data file containing initial cluster centers, choose Read initial from for Cluster Centers in the expanded K-Means Cluster Analysis dialog box and click on File... to open the K-Means Cluster Analysis Read from File dialog box, as shown in Figure 4.19.

Figure 4.19   K-Means Cluster Analysis Read from File dialog box

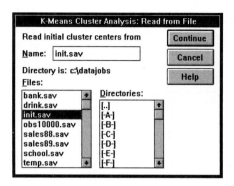

Name. Enter a filename and extension. By default, SPSS supplies the wildcard *.sav. To read the file from a different directory, you can enter the directory path before the file-name, as in c:\mydata\clus.sav.

You can also select a file and directory using the Files and Directories lists.

Files. All files in the directory that match the wildcard search appear in the Files list.

Directories. To change directories, select the name of the directory in the Directories list. To move up a directory level, select [..].

The file you select must be an SPSS data file containing:

- A numeric variable cluster_ that contains cluster numbers.
- One row for each cluster.
- Initial values for each clustering variable.

These values can be entered with the Data Editor, as shown in Figure 4.3. You can also use final centers saved in a prior k-means cluster analysis (see "K-Means Cluster Analysis Write to File," below).

K-Means Cluster Analysis Write to File

To name an SPSS file to contain final cluster centers, choose Write final as for Cluster Centers in the expanded K-Means Cluster Analysis dialog box and click on File... to open the K-Means Cluster Analysis Write to File dialog box, as shown in Figure 4.20.

Figure 4.20   K-Means Cluster Analysis Write to File dialog box

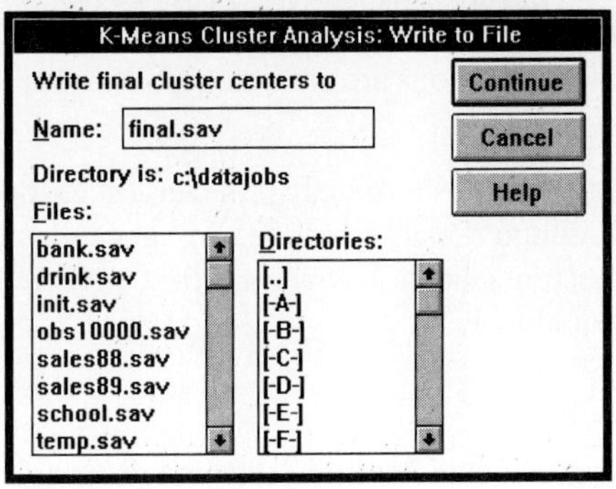

By default, the file is saved in the current directory. Do not use the same name for files containing initial and final centers.

Name. Enter a filename and extension. By default, SPSS supplies the wildcard *.sav. To save the file in a different directory, you can enter the directory path before the filename, as in c:\mydata\clus.sav.

You can also select a file and directory using the Files and Directories lists.

Files. All files in the current directory appear in the Files list. If you select a file from the list, SPSS asks you if you want to replace the existing file.

Directories. To change directories, select the name of the directory in the Directories list. To move up a directory level, select [..].

K-Means Cluster Analysis Iterate

To modify criteria used in updating initial cluster centers, select Iterate and classify for Method in the K-Means Cluster Analysis dialog box and click on Iterate... to open the K-Means Cluster Analysis Iterate dialog box, as shown in Figure 4.21.

Figure 4.21   K-Means Cluster Analysis Iterate dialog box

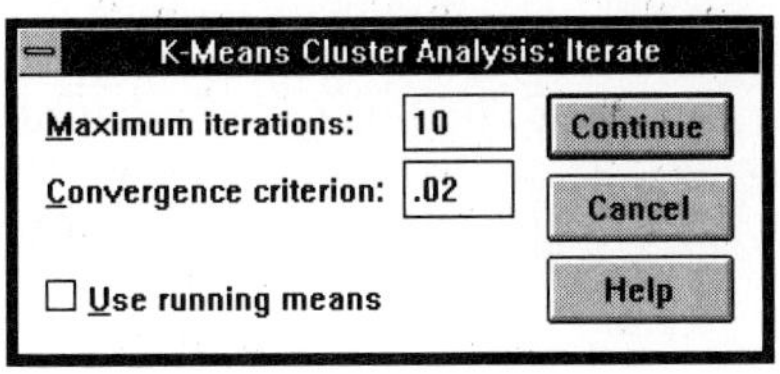

Maximum Iterations. Maximum number of iterations for updating of cluster centers. In each iteration, cases are assigned in turn to the nearest cluster center and cluster means are updated. The default maximum number of iterations is 10. To override this value, enter a positive integer. If 2 or more iterations are performed, SPSS displays an iteration history.

Convergence Criterion. By default, iterations terminate if the largest change in any cluster center is less than 2% of the minimum distance between initial centers (or if the maximum number of iterations has been reached). To override the convergence value, enter a positive number less than or equal to 1.

The following option is also available:

❏ **Use running means.** By default, during an iteration, cluster centers are recalculated after all cases are assigned to a cluster. Select this option to compute new cluster centers each time a case is assigned to a cluster. When running means are used, the order of cases in the data file can affect the cluster centers.

K-Means Cluster Analysis Save New Variables

To save cluster memberships or distances, click on Save... in the K-Means Cluster Analysis dialog box. This opens the K-Means Cluster Save New Variables dialog box, as shown in Figure 4.22.

Figure 4.22   K-Means Cluster Save New Variables dialog box

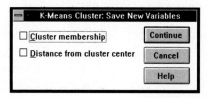

A table in the output shows the names and contents of new variables. You can choose one or both of the following:

❏ **Cluster membership.** Save the final cluster to which each case is assigned. Values range from 1 to the total number of clusters.

❏ **Distance from cluster center**. Save the Euclidean distance between each case and the cluster center used to classify the case.

K-Means Cluster Analysis Options

To obtain optional statistics or modify the handling of missing values, click on Options... in the K-Means Cluster Analysis dialog box. This opens the K-Means Cluster Analysis Options dialog box, as shown in Figure 4.23.

Figure 4.23   K-Means Cluster Analysis Options dialog box

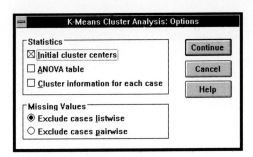

Statistics. SPSS always displays final cluster centers and the number of cases in each cluster. You can choose one or more of the following additional statistics:

❏ **Initial cluster centers.** Displayed by default. To suppress the display of initial centers, deselect this item.

❏ **ANOVA table.** Univariate F tests for each clustering variable. The F tests are only descriptive. You should not interpret the resulting probabilities as a test of the hypothesis of no differences among clusters. The ANOVA table is not displayed if all cases are assigned to a single cluster.

❏ **Cluster information for each case.** Displays for each case the final cluster assignment and Euclidean distance between the case and the cluster center used to classify the case. This option also displays Euclidean distances between final cluster centers.

Missing Values. You can choose one of the following alternatives:

○ **Exclude cases listwise.** Excludes cases with missing values for any clustering variable from the analysis. This is the default.

○ **Exclude cases pairwise.** Assigns cases to clusters based on distances computed from all variables with nonmissing values.

Additional Features Available with Command Syntax

You can customize your *k*-means cluster analysis if you paste your selections to a syntax window and edit the resulting QUICK CLUSTER command syntax (see Chapter 5 in the *SPSS Base System User's Guide*). Additional features include:

- User-specified names for new cluster membership and distance variables (with the SAVE subcommand).

- The ability to use the first few cases in your data file as initial centers (with the CRITERIA subcommand). This option can reduce processing time.

See the Syntax Reference section of this manual for command syntax rules and for complete QUICK CLUSTER command syntax.

5 Distance and Proximity Measures

Many statistical procedures such as cluster analysis, factor analysis, and multidimensional scaling have as their starting point a matrix of **distances** or **proximities** between pairs of cases or variables. Based on these measures, clusters are formed, factors extracted, and structures and dimensions identified.

There are many different measures that can be used to quantify similarity or dissimilarity. The Pearson correlation coefficient is one of the most frequently used measures of similarity between two variables; large absolute values of the correlation coefficient indicate that two variables are similar. In general, measures of similarity are constructed so that large values indicate much similarity and small values indicate little similarity.

Unlike similarity measures, which estimate the amount of closeness between two objects, dissimilarity measures estimate the distance or unlikeness of two objects. A large dissimilarity value tells you that two objects are far apart. The larger the measure, the more distant or unlike the two objects are. The squared Euclidean distance, discussed in the cluster analysis chapter, is one of the most commonly used dissimilarity measures when data are interval or ratio.

Selecting a Measure

In order to decide which similarity or dissimilarity measure to use, you must consider the characteristics of your data. Special measures are available for interval data, frequency counts, and binary data. You must also decide whether you want to standardize the original data in some fashion and whether you want to standardize the resulting distance measure in some way.

Standardizing the Data

Suppose you want to look at the distances between pairs of automobiles. For each make of car, you have recorded expected mileage per gallon, engine displacement, curb weight, number of cylinders, and horsepower. These variables are measured on scales that have very different ranges. The number of cylinders probably won't exceed twelve, while the curb weight may well exceed 5000 pounds. If you compute a distance measure based on the differences of the values of all of the variables, the variables with large values will overwhelm the variables with smaller values. For example, a difference of 4 cylinders will be nothing compared to a difference of 100 pounds.

One way to overcome this difficulty is to standardize the variables in some fashion. For example, you can transform each variable into a standardized variable with a mean of 0 and a standard deviation of 1. The contributions of all the variables to the distance measure will then be more comparable. SPSS offers several methods for standardization which are described in "How to Obtain a Distance Matrix" on p. 130.

Measures for Interval Data

Chapter 3 gives an example of using and computing the squared Euclidean distance between two cases for cluster analysis. Often its square root, the Euclidean distance, is also used.

A distance measure based on the absolute values of differences, instead of their squares, is the **city-block distance**, or **Manhattan distance**. It is simply the sum of the absolute differences of the values for all variables for two cases. Since the differences are not squared, large differences are not weighted as heavily as in the squared Euclidean distances.

The **Chebychev distance** defines the distance between two cases as the maximum absolute difference in the values over all variables. Thus, it ignores much of the available information.

SPSS can calculate a variety of other measures, as described in "How to Obtain a Distance Matrix" on p. 130.

Measures for Frequency Data

When the variables are frequency counts, measures of dissimilarity based on the chi-square statistic can be computed. For example, suppose you want to see how dissimilar authors are in their use of articles. For each author you count the number of times "a," "the," and "an" occur in 600-word passages. For two authors you obtain the results shown in Table 5.1.

Table 5.1 Frequency of use of articles by two authors

	"a"	"the"	"an"
Author 1	41	23	10
Author 2	32	10	28

You can calculate a dissimilarity measure based on the chi-square test of independence (see Chapter 11 of the *SPSS Base System User's Guide*). In this example, the chi-square value is 14.66 and the chi-square-based dissimilarity measure, which is the square root of chi-square, is 3.83.

Since the value of the chi-square statistic depends on sample size, there is a variant of the chi-square dissimilarity measure that attempts to take sample size into account so that the values of the measure don't depend as much on the actual observed frequencies. The **phi-square measure** attempts to normalize the chi-square dissimilarity measure by dividing it by the square root of the sum of the frequencies in the table. In this example, the sum of the frequencies is 144 and the value of phi-square is 0.32 ($3.83/\sqrt{144}$).

Measures for Binary Data

There are numerous similarity coefficients for sets of binary variables. They differ in the importance they attach to the different cells of a 2×2 table.

Consider Table 5.2, which shows the values of seven binary variables for two cases. By default, the value 1 is assumed to indicate presence of a characteristic, while 0 indicates its absence.

Table 5.2 Binary variables for two cases

	V1	V2	V3	V4	V5	V6	V7
Case 1	0	0	0	0	1	1	1
Case 2	1	1	0	0	1	1	0

These data are summarized in Table 5.3. The first cell of the table tells you that for two variables (V5 and V6 in Table 5.2), both cases have values of present. Similarly, for two other variables (V3 and V4), both cases have values of absent. For the remaining three variables, the cases have different values.

Table 5.3 2 x 2 summary table for binary variables

		Case 1	
		Present	Absent
Case 2	Present	2	2
	Absent	1	2

The importance attached to the various cells of the table depends on the nature of the variables. For example, if both cases responded "no" to the question "Have you ever won at least a million dollars in the state lottery," that doesn't convey much information about similarity. On the other hand, a positive answer to the same question may indicate remarkable similarity between the two cases. However, if the question is "Do you own a television set," matches on the negative may be more informative than matches on the positive. In such situations we may want to weight the positive–positive cell and the negative–negative cell differently.

Similarity measures for binary variables differ in their treatment of the four cells of the table. Some measures exclude the negative–negative cell altogether. Some measures weight matches more than mismatches, and others weight mismatches more than matches. Selection of an appropriate measure must depend on the nature of the variables and the information they convey.

Consider the values of several coefficients for the data in Table 5.2. The **simple matching measure** is defined as the number of matches divided by the total number of variables. In this example, we have four matches out of seven variables (V3, V4, V5, and V6), so the simple matching coefficient is 4/7 or 0.5714. Positive matches and negative matches are weighted equally.

The **Russell and Rao similarity measure** is computed by dividing the number in the positive–positive cell by the total number of entries. For the data in Table 5.3, its value is 2/7 or 0.28. Note that this measure excludes negative–negative matches from the numerator but not from the denominator.

The **Jaccard measure** excludes the negative–negative cell from both the numerator and the denominator. For the data in Table 5.3, the Jaccard value is 2/5, or 0.4.

The **Dice measure** excludes negative–negative matches from both the numerator and the denominator and assigns a double weight to the positive–positive cell. In this example, the numerator is twice the number of matches, or 4, and the denominator is twice the number of positive–positive matches plus the number of nonmatches, or 7, so the value of the Dice coefficient is 0.5714.

Other Types of Binary Coefficients

Binary similarity coefficients that measure how well one variable predicts the other can also be computed. One of these is the symmetric Goodman and Kruskal's lambda, discussed in Chapter 11 of the *SPSS Base System User's Guide*. Yule's Y and Yule's Q can also be used. Measures based on conditional probabilities are also available. SPSS can calculate a wide variety of binary coefficients.

To learn more about distance matrices and their uses, consult Anderberg (1973) and Romesburg (1984).

How to Obtain a Distance Matrix

The Distances procedure computes similarities and dissimilarities for cases or variables. Measures are available for interval, frequency-count, and binary data.

The minimum specifications are:

• For casewise distances, one or more numeric variables.

• For distances between variables, two or more numeric variables.

To obtain a distance matrix, from the menus choose:

Statistics
  Correlate ▶
    Distances...

This opens the Distances dialog box, as shown in Figure 5.1.

Figure 5.1   Distances dialog box

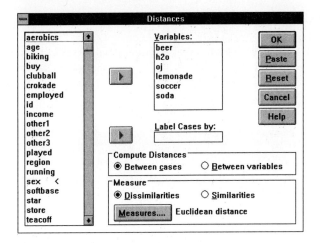

The variables in your data file appear in the source list. To compute distances between cases, select one or more numeric variables and click on OK to get the default casewise Euclidean distance matrix. The distance measure and number of cases are shown in the output. Cases with missing values for any variable are excluded from the matrix.

Alternately, you can compute distances between variables. Select two or more numeric variables and select Between variables for Compute Distances. Click on OK to get the default Euclidean distance matrix.

By default, cases are identified in the output by case number. Optionally, you can use the values of a string variable to identify cases. Select a string variable for Label Cases by. Case labeling is not available if you request distances between variables.

Compute Distances. You can choose one of the following alternatives:

○ **Between cases.** A distance is computed for each pair of cases. This is the default.

○ **Between variables.** A distance is computed for each pair of variables.

Measure. Measure selection controls whether a dissimilarities or similarities matrix is computed. The default measure (Euclidean distance for dissimilarity measures and Pearson correlation for similarity measures) is displayed. To select a different measure, click on Measures... to open the Dissimilarity or Similarity Measures dialog box, as described below.

You can choose one of the following alternatives:

○ **Dissimilarities**. Computes a dissimilarities matrix. This is the default.

○ **Similarities**. Computes a similarities matrix.

Distances Dissimilarity Measures

To choose a dissimilarity measure other than the default, select Dissimilarities in the Distances dialog box and click on Measures.... This opens the Distances Dissimilarity Measures dialog box, as shown in Figure 5.2.

Figure 5.2   Distances Dissimilarity Measures dialog box

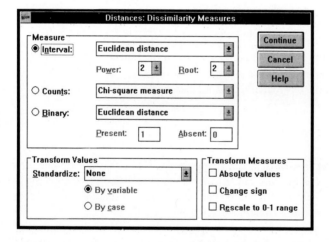

Measure. Measure selection controls the computation of dissimilarities. There are three types of measures available—interval, frequency-count, and binary. You can choose one of the following alternatives:

○ **Interval**. Dissimilarity measures for interval data. This is the default for dissimilarities. You can choose one of the following alternatives:

   ⬇ **Euclidean distance**. This is the default for interval data. The distance between two items, X and Y, is the square root of the sum of the squared differences between the values for the items:

$$\text{Distance }(X, Y) \ = \ \sqrt{\sum_i (X_i - Y_i)^2}$$

Squared Euclidean distance. The distance between two items is the sum of the squared differences between the values for the items:

$$\text{Distance }(X, Y) \ = \ \sum_i (X_i - Y_i)^2$$

Chebychev. Chebychev distance metric. The distance between two items is the maximum absolute difference between the values for the items:

$$\text{Distance }(X, Y) \ = \ MAX_i |X_i - Y_i|$$

Block. City-block, or Manhattan, distance. The distance between two items is the sum of the absolute differences between the values for the items:

$$\text{Distance }(X, Y) \ = \ \sum_i |X_i - Y_i|$$

Minkowski. Distance in an absolute Minkowski power metric. The distance between two items is the pth root of the sum of the absolute differences to the pth power between the values for the items:

$$\text{Distance }(X, Y) \ = \ \left(\sum_i |X_i - Y_i|^p\right)^{\frac{1}{p}}$$

Customized. Distance in an absolute power metric. The distance between two items is the rth root of the sum of the absolute differences to the pth power between the values for the items:

$$\text{Distance }(X, Y) \ = \ \left(\sum_i |X_i - Y_i|^p\right)^{\frac{1}{r}}$$

- ⬇ **Power and Root.** For the Minkowski and customized measures, you can override the default power value of 2. Optionally, you can choose 1, 3, or 4. For customized measures, you can also override the default root value. Choose 1, 3, or 4. For both methods, the default values yield Euclidean distances. Appropriate selection of p and r yields squared Euclidean, Minkowski, city-block, and many other distance metrics.

○ **Counts.** Dissimilarity measures for frequency-count data. You can choose one of the following alternatives:

- ⬇ **Chi-square measure.** Based on the chi-square test of equality for two sets of frequencies. This is the default for counts. The magnitude of this measure depends on the total frequencies of the two items whose distance is computed. Expected values are from the model of independence of items X and Y. (See "Measures for Frequency Data" on p. 128.)

$$\text{Distance } (X, Y) \; = \; \sqrt{ \sum_i \frac{(X_i - E(X_i))^2}{E(X_i)} + \sum_i \frac{(Y_i - E(Y_i))^2}{E(Y_i)} }$$

Phi-square measure. This is the chi-square dissimilarity measure normalized by the square root of the combined frequency. Therefore, its value does not depend on the total frequencies of the two items whose distance is computed.

$$\text{Distance } (X, Y) \; = \; \sqrt{ \frac{\displaystyle\sum_i \frac{(X_i - E(X_i))^2}{E(X_i)} + \sum_i \frac{(Y_i - E(Y_i))^2}{E(Y_i)}}{N} }$$

○ **Binary.** Dissimilarity measures for binary data. SPSS constructs a 2×2 contingency table for each pair of items. It uses this table to compute a distance measure for the pair. SPSS computes all binary measures from the values of the four cells in the table ($a, b, c,$ and d). These values are tallies across variables (when the items are cases) or tallies across cases (when the items are variables). See "Measures for Binary Data" on p. 129.

		Item 2	
		Present	Absent
Item 1	Present	a	b
	Absent	c	d

You can choose one of the following binary measures:

⬇ **Euclidean distance.** Binary Euclidean distance. This is the default for binary data. It has a minimum value of 0 and no upper limit.

$$\text{Distance } (X, Y) \; = \; \sqrt{b + c}$$

Squared Euclidean distance. Binary squared Euclidean distance. It has a minimum of 0 and no upper limit.

$$\text{Distance } (X, Y) \; = \; b + c$$

Size difference. It has a minimum value of 0 and no upper limit.

$$\text{Distance } (X, Y) \; = \; \frac{(b - c)^2}{(a + b + c + d)^2}$$

Pattern difference. It has a range of 0 to 1.

$$\text{Distance } (X, Y) = \frac{bc}{(a+b+c+d)^2}$$

Variance. It has a minimum value of 0 and no upper limit.

$$\text{Distance } (X, Y) = \frac{b+c}{4(a+b+c+d)}$$

Shape. Binary shape difference. It has no upper or lower limit.

$$\text{Distance } (X, Y) = \frac{(a+b+c+d)(b+c) - (b-c)^2}{(a+b+c+d)^2}$$

Lance and Williams. Binary Lance-and-Williams nonmetric dissimilarity measure (also known as the Bray-Curtis nonmetric coefficient). This measure has a range of 0 to 1.

$$\text{Distance } (X, Y) = \frac{b+c}{2a+b+c}$$

Present and Absent. By default, if you select a binary measure, the data value 1 indicates presence of a characteristic and 0 indicates absence (other values are ignored). Optionally, you can specify different integer values for **Present** and **Absent**.

Transform Values. You can standardize data values for either cases or variables to equalize the effect of variables measured on different scales.

⬇ **Standardize.** To control standardization of item values prior to computation of dissimilarities, you can choose one of the following alternatives. Standardization is available for interval data and frequency counts only.

None. Does not standardize. This is the default.

Z Scores. Standardizes values to Z scores, with a mean of 0 and a standard deviation of 1. SPSS subtracts the mean from each value for the item being standardized and then divides by the standard deviation of the values. If a standard deviation is 0, all values are set to 0.

Range –1 to 1. Standardizes values to unit range. Each value for the item being standardized is divided by the range of the values. If the range is 0, all values are left unchanged.

Range 0 to 1. Standardizes values to a range of 0 to 1. SPSS subtracts the minimum value from each item being standardized and then divides by the range. If a range is 0, all values for the item are set to 0.50.

Maximum magnitude of 1. Standardizes values to a maximum magnitude of 1. SPSS divides each value for the item being standardized by the maximum of the values. If the maximum of a set of values is 0, SPSS divides by the absolute magnitude of the smallest value and adds 1.

Mean of 1. Standardizes values to unit mean. SPSS divides each value for the item being standardized by the mean of the values. If a mean is 0, SPSS adds 1 to all values for the case or variable to produce a mean of 1.

Standard deviation of 1. Standardizes values to unit standard deviation. SPSS divides each value for the variable or case being standardized by the standard deviation of the values. SPSS does not change the values if their standard deviation is 0.

If you request standardization, you can choose one of the following alternatives:

○ **By variable**. Standardizes the values for each variable. This is the default.

○ **By case**. Standardizes the values within each case.

Transform Measures. You can choose one or more of the following transformations. If you specify more than one transformation, values are transformed in the order shown below.

❑ **Absolute values**. Takes the absolute values of the distances. Select this item when the sign indicates the direction of the relations (as with correlation coefficients), but only the magnitude of the relations is of interest.

❑ **Change sign**. Transforms dissimilarities into similarities. Select this item to reverse the ordering of the distances.

❑ **Rescale to 0–1 range**. Rescales distance values to a range of 0 to 1. Standardizes the values by first subtracting the value of the smallest distance and then dividing by the range. You would not usually rescale measures that are already standardized on meaningful scales.

Distances Similarity Measures

To choose a similarity measure other than the default, select Similarities in the Distances dialog box and click on Measures.... This opens the Distances Similarity Measures dialog box, as shown in Figure 5.3.

Figure 5.3   Distances Similarity Measures dialog box

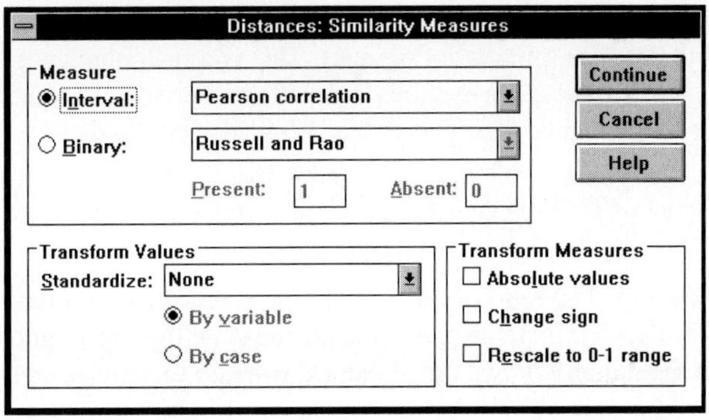

Measure. Measure selection controls computation of the similarities matrix. There are two types of measures available—interval and binary. You can choose one of the following alternatives:

❍ **Interval.** Similarity measures for interval data. This is the default for similarities. You can choose one of the following alternatives:

  ☡ **Pearson correlation.** This is the default for interval data. Correlations between vectors of values:

  $$\text{Similarity } (X, Y) \; = \; \frac{\Sigma_i \, (Z_{Xi} Z_{Yi})}{N - 1}$$

  where Z_{Xi} is the (standardized) Z score value of X for the ith item and N is the number of items.

  Cosine. Cosines of vectors of values:

  $$\text{Similarity } (X, Y) \; = \; \left(\sum_i \, (X_i Y_i) \right) / \left(\sqrt{\sum_i \, (X_i^2) \sum_i \, (Y_i^2)} \right)$$

❍ **Binary.** Similarity measures for binary data. For binary measures, SPSS constructs a 2×2 contingency table for each pair of items (see "Measures for Binary Data" on p.

129). The available measures fall into four categories: matching coefficients, conditional probabilities, predictability measures, and other measures.

For matching coefficients measures, matches are joint presences or joint absences. Conditional probability measures determine the probability that a characteristic is present in one item, given that it is present in the other item. Predictability measures assess the association between items as the predictability of one item, given the other.

You can choose one of the following binary measures:

⬇ **Russell and Rao**. The binary dot product. This is a matching coefficients measure in which joint absences are excluded from the numerator and equal weight is given to matches and nonmatches. This is the default for binary data.

$$\text{Similarity } (X, Y) \ = \ \frac{a}{a + b + c + d}$$

Simple matching. The ratio of the number of matches to the total number of characteristics. This is a matching coefficients measure in which joint absences are included in the numerator and equal weight is given to matches and nonmatches.

$$\text{Similarity } (X, Y) \ = \ \frac{a + d}{a + b + c + d}$$

Jaccard. Also known as the similarity ratio. This is a matching coefficients measure in which joint absences are excluded in both the numerator and the denominator and equal weight is given to matches and nonmatches.

$$\text{Similarity } (X, Y) \ = \ \frac{a}{a + b + c}$$

Dice. Also known as the Czekanowski or Sorensen measure. This is a matching coefficients measure in which joint absences are excluded in both the numerator and the denominator and double weight is given to matches.

$$\text{Similarity } (X, Y) \ = \ \frac{2a}{2a + b + c}$$

Rogers and Tanimoto. This is a matching coefficients measure in which joint absences are included in the numerator and double weight is given to nonmatches.

$$\text{Similarity } (X, Y) \ = \ \frac{a + d}{a + d + 2\,(b + c)}$$

Sokal and Sneath 1. This is a matching coefficients measure in which joint absences are included in the numerator and double weight is given to matches.

$$\text{Similarity } (X, Y) = \frac{2(a+d)}{2(a+d)+b+c}$$

Sokal and Sneath 2. This is a matching coefficients measure in which joint absences are excluded in both the numerator and the denominator and double weight is given to nonmatches.

$$\text{Similarity } (X, Y) = \frac{a}{a+2(b+c)}$$

Sokal and Sneath 3. This is a matching coefficients measure in which all matches are excluded from the denominator, and joint absences are included in the numerator. Equal weight is given to matches and nonmatches. This measure has a minimum value of 0, no upper limit, and is undefined when there are no nonmatches ($b = 0$ and $c = 0$). SPSS assigns an artificial upper limit of 9999.999 when it is undefined or exceeds this value.

$$\text{Similarity } (X, Y) = \frac{a+d}{b+c}$$

Kulczynski 1. This is a matching coefficients measure in which all matches are excluded from the denominator, and joint absences are excluded in the numerator. Equal weight is given to matches and nonmatches. This measure has a minimum value of 0, no upper limit, and is undefined when there is perfect agreement ($b = 0$ and $c = 0$). SPSS assigns an artificial upper limit of 9999.999 when it is undefined or exceeds this value.

$$\text{Similarity } (X, Y) = \frac{a}{b+c}$$

Kulczynski 2. The average conditional probability that a characteristic is present in one item, given that the characteristic is present in the other item. The measure is an average over both items acting as predictors. It has a range of 0 to 1.

$$\text{Similarity } (X, Y) = \frac{a/(a+b) + a/(a+c)}{2}$$

Sokal and Sneath 4. The conditional probability that a characteristic of one item is in the same state (presence or absence) as the characteristic of the other item. The measure is an average over both items acting as predictors. It has a range of 0 to 1.

$$\text{Similarity } (X, Y) = \frac{a/(a+b) + a/(a+c) + d/(b+d) + d/(c+d)}{4}$$

Hamann. The probability that a characteristic has the same state in both items (present in both or absent from both) minus the probability that a characteristic has different states in the two items (present in one and absent from the other). This measure has a range of −1 to 1 and is monotonically related to the simple matching, Sokal and Sneath 1, and Rogers and Tanimoto measures.

$$\text{Similarity } (X, Y) \ = \ \frac{(a+d) - (b+c)}{a+b+c+d}$$

Lambda. Goodman and Kruskal's lambda. Assesses the predictability of the state of a characteristic of one item (presence or absence) given the state of the other. Specifically, lambda measures the proportional reduction in error using one item to predict the other when the directions of prediction are of equal importance. Lambda has a range of 0 to 1.

$$\text{Similarity } (X, Y) \ = \ \frac{max\,(a, b) + max\,(c, d) + max\,(a, c) + max\,(b, d)}{2\,(a+b+c+d)}$$
$$- \ (\frac{max\,(a+c, b+d) + max\,(a+b, c+d)}{2\,(a+b+c+d)})$$

Anderberg's D. Measures the predictability of the state of a characteristic of one item (presence or absence) given the state of the other. Measures the actual reduction in the error probability when one item is used to predict the other. The range of D is 0 to 1.

$$\text{Similarity } (X, Y) \ = \ \frac{max\,(a, b) + max\,(c, d) + max\,(a, c) + max\,(b, d)}{2\,(a+b+c+d)}$$
$$+ \ \frac{max\,(a+c, b+d) + max\,(a+b, c+d)}{2\,(a+b+c+d)}$$

Yule's Y. Yule's Y coefficient of colligation. This is a function of the cross-ratio for a 2×2 table. It has a range of −1 to 1.

$$\text{Similarity } (X, Y) \ = \ \frac{\sqrt{ad} - \sqrt{bc}}{\sqrt{ad} + \sqrt{bc}}$$

Yule's Q. This is the 2×2 version of the Goodman and Kruskal ordinal measure *gamma*. Like Yule's Y, Q is a function of the cross-ratio for a 2×2 table and has a range of −1 to 1.

$$\text{Similarity } (X, Y) \ = \ \frac{ad - bc}{ad + bc}$$

Ochiai. The binary form of the cosine. It has a range of 0 to 1.

$$\text{Similarity } (X, Y) \ = \ \sqrt{\left(\frac{a}{a + b}\right) \left(\frac{a}{a + c}\right)}$$

Sokal and Sneath 5. It has a range of 0 to 1.

$$\text{Similarity } (X, Y) \ = \ \frac{ad}{\sqrt{(a + b) \ (a + c) \ (b + d) \ (c + d)}}$$

Phi 4-point correlation. The binary form of the Pearson correlation coefficient. It has a range of 0 to 1.

$$\text{Similarity } (X, Y) \ = \ \frac{ad - bc}{\sqrt{(a + b) \ (a + c) \ (b + d) \ (c + d)}}$$

Dispersion. This measure has a range of −1 to 1.

$$\text{Similarity } (X, Y) \ = \ \frac{ad - bc}{(a + b + c + d)^2}$$

Present and Absent. By default, if you select a binary measure, the data value 1 indicates presence of a characteristic and 0 indicates absence (other values are ignored). Optionally, you can specify different integer values for Present and Absent.

Transform Values. You can standardize data values for either cases or variables to equalize the effect of variables measured on different scales by transforming the values of variables.

⬇ **Standardize**. To control standardization of item values prior to computation of similarities, you can choose one of the following alternatives. Standardization is available for interval data only.

None. Does not standardize. This is the default.

Z Scores. Standardizes values to Z scores, with a mean of 0 and a standard deviation of 1. SPSS subtracts the mean from each value for the item being standardized and then divides by the standard deviation of the values. If a standard deviation is 0, all values are set to 0.

Range –1 to 1. Standardizes values to unit range. Each value for the item being standardized is divided by the range of the values. If the range is 0, all values are left unchanged.

Range 0 to 1. Standardizes values to a range of 0 to 1. From each value for the item being standardized, SPSS subtracts the minimum value and then divides by the range. If a range is 0, all values for the item are set to 0.50.

Maximum magnitude of 1. Standardizes values to a maximum magnitude of 1. SPSS divides each value for the item being standardized by the maximum of the values. If the maximum of a set of values is 0, SPSS divides by the absolute magnitude of the smallest value and adds 1.

Mean of 1. Standardizes values to unit mean. SPSS divides each value for the item being standardized by the mean of the values. If a mean is 0, SPSS adds 1 to all values for the case or variable to produce a mean of 1.

Standard deviation of 1. Standardizes values to unit standard deviation. SPSS divides each value for the variable or case being standardized by the standard deviation of the values. SPSS does not change the values if their standard deviation is 0.

If you request standardization, you can choose one of the following alternatives:

○ **By variable**. Standardizes the values for each variable. This is the default.

○ **By case**. Standardizes the values within each case.

Transform Measures. You can choose one or more of the following transformations. If you specify more than one transformation, values are transformed in the order shown below.

❑ **Absolute values**. Takes absolute values of the similarities. Select this item when the sign indicates the direction of the relations (as with correlation coefficients), but only the magnitude of the relations is of interest.

❑ **Change sign**. Transforms similarities into dissimilarities. Select this item to reverse the ordering of the similarities.

❑ **Rescale to 0–1 range**. Rescales similarity values to a range of 0 to 1. Standardizes the values by first subtracting the value of the smallest distance and then dividing by the range. You would not usually rescale measures that are already standardized on meaningful scales, as are correlations and cosines.

Additional Features Available with Command Syntax

You can customize your distance matrix if you paste your selections to a syntax window and edit the resulting PROXIMITIES command syntax (see Chapter 5 in the *SPSS Base System User's Guide*). Additional features include:

- Matrix facility to read an existing matrix (for example, to transform its values) or to write a distance matrix (with the MATRIX subcommand).

- Additional power and root values for customized distances (with the MEASURE subcommand).

See the Syntax Reference section of this manual for command syntax rules and for complete PROXIMITIES command syntax.

6 Measuring Scales: Reliability Analysis

From the moment we're born, the world begins to "score" us. One minute after birth, we're rated on the 10-point Apgar scale, followed closely by the five-minute Apgar scale, and then on to countless other scales that will track our intelligence, credit-worthiness, likelihood of hijacking a plane, and so forth. A dubious mark of maturity is when we find ourselves administering these scales.

Constructing a Scale

When we want to measure characteristics such as driving ability, mastery of course materials, or the ability to function independently, we must construct some type of measurement device. Usually we develop a **scale** or test that is composed of a variety of related items. The responses to each of the items can be graded and summed, resulting in a score for each case. A question that frequently arises is, How good is our scale? In order to answer this question, consider some of the characteristics of a scale or test.

When we construct a test to measure how well college students have learned the material in an introductory psychology course, the questions actually included in the test are a small sample from all of the items that may have been selected. Though we have selected a limited number of items for inclusion in a test, we want to draw conclusions about the students' mastery of the entire course contents. In fact, we'd like to think that even if we changed the actual items on the test, there would be a strong relationship between students' scores on the test actually given and the scores they would have received on other tests we could have given. A good test is one that yields stable results. That is, it's reliable.

Reliability and Validity

Everyone knows the endearing qualities of a reliable car. It goes anytime, anywhere, for anybody. It behaves the same way under a wide variety of circumstances. Its performance is repeatable. A **reliable** measuring instrument behaves similarly: the test yields similar results when different people administer it and when alternative forms are used. When conditions for making the measurement change, the results of the test should not.

A test must be reliable to be useful. But it's not enough for a test to be reliable; it must also be **valid**. That is, the instrument must measure what it is intended to measure. A test that requires students to do mirror drawing and memorize nonsense syllables may be quite reliable, but it is a poor indicator of mastery of the concepts of psychology. The test has poor validity.

There are many different ways to assess both reliability and validity. In this chapter, we will be concerned only with measures of reliability.

Describing Test Results

Before embarking on a discussion of measures of reliability, let's take a look at some of the descriptive statistics that are useful for characterizing a scale. We will be analyzing a scale of the physical activities of daily living in the elderly.[1] The goal of the scale is to assess an elderly person's competence in the physical activities of daily living. Three hundred and ninety-five people were rated on the eight items shown in Figure 6.1. For each item, a score of 1 was assigned if the patient was unable to perform the activity, 2 if the patient was able to perform the activity with assistance, and 3 if the patient required no assistance to perform the activity.

Figure 6.1   Physical activity items

```
1.      ITEM1       Can eat
2.      ITEM2       Can dress and undress
3.      ITEM3       Can take care of own appearance
4.      ITEM4       Can walk
5.      ITEM5       Can get in and out of bed
6.      ITEM6       Can take a bath or shower
7.      ITEM7       Can get to bathroom on time
8.      ITEM8       Has been able to do tasks for 6 months
```

When we summarize a scale, we want to look at the characteristics of the individual items, the characteristics of the overall scale, and the relationship between the individual items and the entire scale. Figure 6.2 contains descriptive statistics for the individual items. You see that the average scores for the items range from 2.93 for item 1 to 1.66 for item 8. Item 7 has the largest standard deviation, 0.5190.

1. Thanks to Dr. Michael Counte of Rush–Presbyterian—St. Luke's Medical Center, Chicago, Principal Investigator of the National Institute of Aging Panel Study of Elderly Health Beliefs and Behavior, for making these data available.

Figure 6.2   Univariate descriptive statistics

		Mean	Std dev	Cases
1.	ITEM1	2.9266	.3593	395.0
2.	ITEM2	2.8962	.4116	395.0
3.	ITEM3	2.9165	.3845	395.0
4.	ITEM4	2.8684	.4367	395.0
5.	ITEM5	2.9114	.3964	395.0
6.	ITEM6	2.8506	.4731	395.0
7.	ITEM7	2.7873	.5190	395.0
8.	ITEM8	1.6582	.4749	395.0

The correlation coefficients between the items are shown in Figure 6.3. The only item that appears to have a small correlation with the other items is item 8. Its highest correlation is 0.26, with item 6.

Figure 6.3   Inter-item correlation coefficients

Correlation Matrix

	ITEM1	ITEM2	ITEM3	ITEM4	ITEM5
ITEM1	1.0000				
ITEM2	.7893	1.0000			
ITEM3	.8557	.8913	1.0000		
ITEM4	.7146	.7992	.7505	1.0000	
ITEM5	.8274	.8770	.8173	.8415	1.0000
ITEM6	.6968	.8326	.7684	.8504	.7684
ITEM7	.5557	.5736	.5340	.5144	.5497
ITEM8	.0459	.1427	.0795	.2108	.0949

	ITEM6	ITEM7	ITEM8
ITEM6	1.0000		
ITEM7	.5318	1.0000	
ITEM8	.2580	.1883	1.0000

Additional statistics for the scale as a whole are shown in Figure 6.4 and Figure 6.5. The average score for the scale is 21.82 and the standard deviation is 2.7 (Figure 6.4). The average score on an item (Figure 6.5) is 2.73, with a range of 1.27. Similarly, the average of the item variances is 0.19, with a minimum of 0.13 and a maximum of 0.27.

Figure 6.4   Scale statistics

Statistics for	Mean	Variance	Std Dev	Variables
Scale	21.8152	7.3896	2.7184	8

Figure 6.5   Summary statistics for items

Item Means	Mean	Minimum	Maximum	Range	Max/Min	Variance
	2.7269	1.6582	2.9266	1.2684	1.7649	.1885

Item Variances	Mean	Minimum	Maximum	Range	Max/Min	Variance
	.1891	.1291	.2694	.1403	2.0864	.0022

Inter-item Correlations	Mean	Minimum	Maximum	Range	Max/Min	Variance
	.5843	.0459	.8913	.8454	19.4033	.0790

The correlations between items range from 0.046 to 0.891. The ratio between the largest and smallest correlation is $0.891/0.046$, or 19.4. The average correlation is 0.584.

Relationship Between the Scale and the Items

Now let's take a look at the relationship between the individual items and the composite score (see Figure 6.6).

Figure 6.6   Item-total summary statistics

Item-Total statistics

	Scale Mean if Item Deleted	Scale Variance if Item Deleted	Corrected Item– Total Correlation	Squared Multiple Correlation	Alpha if Item Deleted
ITEM1	18.8886	5.8708	.7981	.7966	.8917
ITEM2	18.9190	5.5061	.8874	.8882	.8820
ITEM3	18.8987	5.7004	.8396	.8603	.8873
ITEM4	18.9468	5.4718	.8453	.8137	.8848
ITEM5	18.9038	5.6202	.8580	.8620	.8852
ITEM6	18.9646	5.3084	.8520	.8029	.8833
ITEM7	19.0278	5.6414	.5998	.3777	.9095
ITEM8	20.1570	6.7316	.1755	.1331	.9435

For each item, the first column of Figure 6.6 shows what the average score for the scale would be if the item were excluded from the scale. For example, we know from Figure 6.4 that the average score for the scale is 21.82. If item 1 were eliminated from the scale, the average score would be 18.89. This is computed by simply subtracting the average score for the item from the scale mean. In this case it's $21.82 - 2.93 = 18.89$. The next column is the scale variance if the item were eliminated. The column labeled *Corrected Item-Total Correlation* is the Pearson correlation coefficient between the score on the individual item and the sum of the scores on the remaining items. For example, the correlation between the score on item 8 and the sum of the scores of items 1 through 7 is only 0.176. This indicates that there is not much of a relationship between the eighth item and the other items. On the other hand, item 2 has a very high correlation, 0.887, with the other items.

Another way to look at the relationship between an individual item and the rest of the scale is to try to predict a person's score on the item based on the scores obtained on the other items. We can do this by calculating a multiple regression equation with the item of interest as the dependent variable and all of the other items as independent variables. The multiple R^2 from this regression equation is displayed for each of the items in the column labeled *Squared Multiple Correlation*. We can see that almost 80% of the observed variability in the responses to item 1 can be explained by the other items. As expected, item 8 is poorly predicted from the other items. Its multiple R^2 is only 0.13.

The Reliability Coefficient

By looking at the statistics shown above, we've learned quite a bit about our scale and the individual items of which it is composed. However, we still haven't come up with an index of how reliable the scale is. There are several different ways to measure reliability (see Lord & Novick, 1968; Nunnally, 1978):

- You can compute an estimate of reliability based on the observed correlations or covariances of the items with each other.

- You can correlate the results from two alternate forms of the same test or split the same test into two parts and look at the correlation between the two parts.

One of the most commonly used reliability coefficients is **Cronbach's alpha**. Alpha (or α) is based on the "internal consistency" of a test. That is, it is based on the average correlation of items within a test, if the items are standardized to a standard deviation of 1; or on the average covariance among items on a scale, if the items are not standardized. We assume that the items on a scale are positively correlated with each other because they are measuring, to a certain extent, a common entity. If items are not positively correlated with each other, we have no reason to believe that they are correlated with other possible items we may have selected. In this case, we do not expect to see a positive relationship between this test and other similar tests.

Interpreting Cronbach's Alpha

Cronbach's α has several interpretations. It can be viewed as the correlation between this test or scale and all other possible tests or scales containing the same number of items, which could be constructed from a hypothetical universe of items that measure the characteristic of interest. In the physical activities scale, for example, the eight questions actually selected for inclusion can be viewed as a sample from a universe of many possible items. The patients could have been asked whether they can walk up a flight of stairs, or get up from a chair, or cook a meal, or whether they can perform a myriad of other activities related to daily living. Cronbach's α tells us how much correlation we expect between our scale and all other possible eight-item scales measuring the same thing.

Another interpretation of Cronbach's α is the squared correlation between the score a person obtains on a particular scale (the observed score) and the score he would have obtained if questioned on *all* of the possible items in the universe (the true score).

Since α can be interpreted as a correlation coefficient, it ranges in value from 0 to 1. (Negative α values can occur when items are not positively correlated among themselves and the reliability model is violated.)

Cronbach's α for the physical activity scale is shown in Figure 6.7. Note that the value, 0.91, is large, indicating that our scale is quite reliable. The other entry in Figure 6.7, labeled *Standardized item alpha,* is the α value that would be obtained if all of the items were standardized to have a variance of 1. Since the items in our scale have fairly comparable variances, there is little difference between the two α's. If items on the scale have widely differing variances, the two α's may differ substantially.

Figure 6.7   Cronbach's alpha

```
Reliability coefficients      8 items

Alpha =    .9089              Standardized item alpha =    .9183
```

Cronbach's α can be computed using the following formula:

$$\alpha = \frac{k\overline{cov}/\overline{var}}{1 + (k-1)\,\overline{cov}/\overline{var}} \qquad \text{Equation 6.1}$$

where k is the number of items in the scale, $\overline{cov}$ is the average covariance between items, and $\overline{var}$ is the average variance of the items. If the items are standardized to have the same variance, the formula can be simplified to

$$\alpha = \frac{k\overline{r}}{1 + (k-1)\,\overline{r}} \qquad \text{Equation 6.2}$$

where $\overline{r}$ is the average correlation between items.

Looking at Equation 6.2, we can see that Cronbach's α depends on both the length of the test (k in the formula) and the correlation of the items on the test. For example, if the average correlation between items is 0.2 on a 10-item scale, α is 0.71. If the number of items is increased to 25, α is 0.86. You can have large reliability coefficients, even when the average inter-item correlation is small, if the number of items on the scale is large enough.

Alpha If Item Deleted

When we are examining individual items, as in Figure 6.6, you may want to know how each of the items affects the reliability of the scale. This can be accomplished by calculating Cronbach's α when each of the items is removed from the scale. These α's are shown in the last column of Figure 6.6. You can see that eliminating item 8 from the physical activity scale causes α to increase from 0.91 (as in Figure 6.7) to 0.94 (Figure 6.6). From the correlation matrix in Figure 6.3 we saw that item 8 is not strongly related to the other items, so we would expect that eliminating it from the scale would increase the overall reliability of the scale. Elimination of any of the other items from the scale causes little change in α.

The Split-Half Reliability Model

Cronbach's α is based on correlations of items on a single scale. It's a measure based on the internal consistency of the items. Other measures of reliability are based on splitting the scale into two parts and looking at the correlation between the two parts. Such measures are called **split-half coefficients**. One of the disadvantages of this method is that the results depend on the allocation of items to halves. The coefficient you get depends on how you split your scale. Sometimes split-half methods are applied to situations in which two tests are administered or the same test is administered twice.

Figure 6.8 contains summary statistics that would be obtained if we split the physical ability scale into two equal parts. The first four items are part 1, while the second four items are part 2. Note that separate descriptive statistics are given for each of the parts, as well as for the entire scale. Reliability statistics for the split model are shown in Figure 6.9.

Figure 6.8   Split-half statistics

```
       # of Cases =          395.0

                                                  # of
   Statistics for      Mean    Variance   Std Dev  Variables
        Part 1       11.6076    2.1527    1.4672        4
        Part 2       10.2076    1.8959    1.3769        4
        Scale        21.8152    7.3896    2.7184        8

   Item Means         Mean    Minimum   Maximum    Range    Max/Min   Variance
        Part 1        2.9019    2.8684    2.9266    .0582    1.0203     .0007
        Part 2        2.5519    1.6582    2.9114   1.2532    1.7557     .3575
        Scale         2.7269    1.6582    2.9266   1.2684    1.7649     .1885

   Item Variances     Mean    Minimum   Maximum    Range    Max/Min   Variance
        Part 1        .1593     .1291     .1907    .0616    1.4774     .0007
        Part 2        .2190     .1571     .2694    .1123    1.7147     .0021
        Scale         .1891     .1291     .2694    .1403    2.0864     .0022

   Inter-item
   Correlations       Mean    Minimum   Maximum    Range    Max/Min   Variance
        Part 1        .8001     .7146     .8913    .1768    1.2474     .0039
        Part 2        .3985     .0949     .7684    .6735    8.0973     .0606
        Scale         .5843     .0459     .8913    .8454   19.4033     .0790
```

Figure 6.9   Split-half reliability

```
   Reliability coefficients     8 items

   Correlation between forms =    .8269    Equal length Spearman-Brown =      .9052


   Guttman split-half =           .9042    Unequal-length Spearman-Brown =    .9052

   Alpha for part 1 =             .9387    Alpha for part 2 =                 .7174

       4 items in part 1              4 items in part 2
```

The correlation between the two halves, labeled on the output as *Correlation between forms*, is 0.8269. This is an estimate of the reliability of the test if it has four items. The equal-length **Spearman-Brown coefficient**, which has a value of 0.9052 in this case, tells us what the reliability of the eight-item test would be if it was made up of two equal parts that have a four-item reliability of 0.8269. (Remember, the reliability of a test increases as the number of items on the test increase, provided that the average correlation between items does not change.) If the number of items on each of the two parts is not equal, the unequal-length Spearman-Brown coefficient can be used to estimate what the reliability of the overall test would be. In this case, since the two parts are of equal length, the two Spearman-Brown coefficients are equal. The **Guttman split-half coefficient** is another estimate of the reliability of the overall test. It does not assume that the two parts are equally reliable or have the same variance. Separate values of Cronbach's α are also shown for each of the two parts of the test.

Other Reliability Models

In the previous models we've considered, we didn't make any assumptions about item means or variances. If we have information about item means and variances, we can incorporate this additional information in the estimation of reliability coefficients. Two commonly used models are the **strictly parallel model** and the **parallel model**. In the strictly parallel model, all items are assumed to have the same means, the same variances for the true (unobservable) scores, and the same error variances over replications. When the assumption of equal means is relaxed, we have what's known as a parallel model.

Additional statistics can be obtained from a strictly parallel or parallel model. Figure 6.10 contains a test of the goodness of fit for the parallel model applied to the physical activity data. (This model is not appropriate for these data. We'll use it, however, to illustrate the output for this type of model.)

Figure 6.10   Goodness of fit for parallel model

```
Test for Goodness of Fit of Model          Parallel

Chi square =      1660.1597      Degrees of freedom =        34
Log of determinant of unconstrained matrix =      -21.648663
Log of determinant of constrained matrix   =      -17.403278
Probability =    .0000
```

As you can see, the chi-square value is very large and we must reject the hypothesis that the parallel model fits. If the parallel model were appropriate we could consider the results, which are shown in Figure 6.11.

Figure 6.11   Maximum-likelihood reliability estimate

```
    Parameter estimates

Estimated common variance =        .1891
         Error variance =        .0842
          True variance =        .1049
Estimated common interitem correlation =      .5549

Estimated reliability of scale   =   .9089
Unbiased estimate of reliability =   .9093
```

The first entry is an estimate of the common variance for an item. It is the sum of the true variance and the error variance, which are displayed below it. An estimate of the common inter-item correlation, based on the model, is also shown. Figure 6.11 also shows two reliability coefficients. The first is a **maximum-likelihood estimate** of the reliability coefficient, while the second is the maximum-likelihood estimate corrected for bias. If either the parallel or the strictly parallel model fits the data, then the best linear combination of the items is simply their sum.

How to Obtain a Reliability Analysis

The Reliability Analysis procedure produces reliability statistics for multiple-item additive scales: scales formed by simply adding a number of component variables. The Reliability Analysis procedure can analyze different items to help you choose the "best" scale. After choosing the items you want, you can compute the scale as the sum of the items. (See the *SPSS Base System User's Guide* for information on computing variables.)

The minimum specification is two or more numeric variables.

To obtain a reliability analysis, from the menus choose:

Statistics
  Scale ▶
    Reliability Analysis...

This opens the Reliability Analysis dialog box, as shown in Figure 6.12.

Figure 6.12   Reliability Analysis dialog box

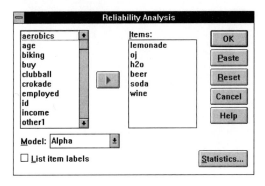

The numeric variables in your data file appear in the source list. Select two or more items (variables) that compose the scale you want to analyze. Cases with missing values on any item are excluded from the analysis. To obtain the default reliability analysis using Cronbach's α, click on OK.

↓ **Model.** You can choose one of the following reliability models:

Alpha. Cronbach's α. This is the default. If your data are dichotomous, α is equivalent to coefficient KR20 (Kuder-Richardson 20). To obtain the standardized alpha, select Alpha and at least one summary statistic from the statistics dialog box (see "Reliability Analysis Statistics," below).

Split-half. Spearman-Brown and Guttman split-half coefficients. A split-half reliability analysis is performed, based on the order of variables in the Items list. The first half of the items (rounding up if the number of items is odd) form the first part, and the remaining items form the second part.

Guttman. Guttman's lower bounds for true reliability.

Parallel. Maximum-likelihood reliability estimate under the assumption that the items have the same variance.

Strict parallel. Maximum-likelihood reliability estimate under the assumptions that the items have the same mean, true score variance, and error variance over replications.

The following option is also available:

❏ **List item labels.** Displays names and variable labels for all items in the output.

Reliability Analysis Statistics

To obtain additional scale and item statistics, click on Statistics... in the Reliability Analysis dialog box. This opens the Reliability Analysis Statistics dialog box, as shown in Figure 6.13.

Figure 6.13   Reliability Analysis Statistics dialog box

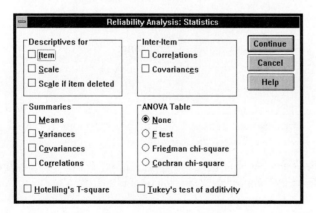

Descriptives for. You can choose one or more of the following:

❏ **Item.** Item means and standard deviations.

❏ **Scale.** Scale mean, variance, and standard deviation.

❏ **Scale if item deleted.** Summary statistics comparing each item to the scale composed of the other items. Statistics include scale mean and variance if the item were deleted from the scale; correlation between the item and the scale composed of other items; and Cronbach's α if the item were deleted from the scale. To obtain the squared multiple correlation with the other items, choose Scale if item deleted and at least one summary statistic.

Summaries. You can choose one or more of the following summary statistics:

❏ **Means.** Summary statistics for item means. The smallest, largest, and average item mean, the range and variance of item means, and the ratio of the largest to the smallest item mean.

❏ **Variances.** Summary statistics for item variances. The smallest, largest, and average item variance, the range and variance of item variances, and the ratio of the largest to the smallest item variances.

❏ **Covariances.** Summary statistics for inter-item covariances. The smallest, largest, and average inter-item covariances, the range and variance of inter-item covariances, and the ratio of the largest to the smallest inter-item covariances.

❏ **Correlations.** Summary statistics for inter-item correlations. The smallest, largest, and average inter-item correlation, the range and variance of inter-item correlations, and the ratio of the largest to the smallest inter-item correlations.

Figure 6.5 was produced by choosing Means, Variances, and Correlations.

Inter-Item. You can choose one or both of the following:

❏ **Correlations.** Inter-item correlation matrix.

❏ **Covariances.** Inter-item covariance matrix.

ANOVA Table. You can choose one of the following:

○ **None.** Suppresses ANOVA table. This is the default.

○ **F test.** Repeated measures analysis-of-variance table.

○ **Friedman chi-square.** Friedman's chi-square and Kendall's coefficient of concordance. This option is appropriate for data that are in the form of ranks. The chi-square test replaces the usual F test in the ANOVA table.

○ **Cochran chi-square.** Cochran's Q. This option is appropriate for data that are dichotomous. The Q statistic replaces the usual F statistic in the ANOVA table.

You can also choose one or both of the following statistics:

❏ **Hotelling's T-square.** Hotelling's T^2. Tests the hypothesis that all item means are equal.

❏ **Tukey's test of additivity.** Estimates the power to which a scale must be raised to achieve additivity. Tests the assumption that there is no multiplicative interaction among the items.

Additional Features Available with Command Syntax

You can customize your reliability analysis if you paste your selections to a syntax window and edit the resulting RELIABILITY command syntax (see Chapter 5 in the *SPSS Base System User's Guide*). Additional features include:

• Analysis of multiple scales or different models for the same scale (with the SCALE and MODEL subcommands).

• Matrix facility to write a correlation matrix or to read a matrix of correlations that can be used in place of raw data for reliability analysis (with the MATRIX subcommand).

• User-specified splits for split-half analyses (with the MODEL subcommand).

See the Syntax Reference section of this manual for command syntax rules and for complete RELIABILITY command syntax.

7 Multidimensional Scaling[1]

What characteristics of an automobile do people consider when they are deciding which car to buy: its economy? Its sportiness? Its reliability? What aspects of a political candidate are important when a voter is making a decision: the candidate's party? The candidate's position on defense issues? What interpersonal characteristics come into play when one member of a work group is talking to another member: the status of the two members? Their knowledge of the task of the work group? Their socioeconomic characteristics?

How do you go about answering such questions? The variables mentioned in the first paragraph are subjective, as are their units of measure and the values of these units. These variables are presumed to exist in the minds of people, and do not have an independent, objective existence.

There are at least two ways of answering the questions posed above; at least two ways to construct objective scales that can be reasonably thought to correspond to a person's internal "scales." One of these ways is to obtain multivariate data and then use factor analysis (see Chapter 2).

The other way is to obtain dissimilarity data and to then use multidimensional scaling to analyze the data. In this chapter we focus on the multidimensional scaling of dissimilarity data as a way to construct objective scales of subjective attributes.

Data, Models, and Analysis of Multidimensional Scaling

What is multidimensional scaling? **Multidimensional scaling** (**MDS**) is designed to analyze distance-like data called **dissimilarity data**, or data that indicate the degree of dissimilarity (or similarity) of two things. For example, MDS could be used with data that indicate the apparent (dis)similarity of a pair of political candidates, or a pair of automobiles. MDS analyzes the dissimilarity data in a way that displays the structure

---

1. This chapter was written by Forrest W. Young and David F. Harris of the Psychometric Laboratory, University of North Carolina.

157

of the distance-like data as a geometrical picture. MDS has its origins in psychometrics, where it was proposed to help understand people's judgments of the similarity of members of a set of objects. MDS has now become a general data analysis technique used in a wide variety of fields.

What are dissimilarities data? MDS pictures the structure of a set of objects from data that approximate the distances between pairs of the objects. The data, which are called similarities, dissimilarities, distances, or proximities, must reflect the amount of (dis)similarity between pairs of objects. In this chapter we use the term dissimilarity generically to refer to both similarities (where large numbers indicate great similarity) and dissimilarities (where large numbers indicate great dissimilarity).

Traditionally, dissimilarity data are subjective data obtained by asking people to judge the dissimilarity of pairs of things, such as automobiles, political candidates, types of wines, etc. But dissimilarity data can also be objective measures, such as the driving time between two cities, or the frequency with which pairs of people in a work group talk to each other. Dissimilarity data can also be calculated from multivariate data, as when we use voting records in the United States Senate to calculate the proportion of agreement in the votes cast by pairs of senators. However, the data must always represent the degree of dissimilarity of pairs of objects or events.

There may be one or more matrices of dissimilarity data. For example, if we have observed the frequency with which pairs of people in a business communicate with each other, then we have a single similarity matrix where the frequency of communication indicates the similarity between the pair of people. On the other hand, if we have judgments from many drivers of the dissimilarity between pairs of automobiles, then we have many dissimilarity matrices, one for each driver.

What is the MDS model? Each object or event is represented by a point in a multidimensional space. The points are arranged in this space so that the distances between pairs of points have the strongest possible relation to the similarities among pairs of objects. That is, two similar objects are represented by two points that are close together, and two dissimilar objects are represented by two points that are far apart. The space is usually a two- or three-dimensional Euclidean space but may have more dimensions. This model is called the Euclidean model. Sometimes, a model that was originally designed to portray individual differences in judgments of dissimilarity is used. This model, which is called the INDSCAL (individual differences scaling) model, uses weights for individuals on the dimensions of the Euclidean space. This model is discussed in greater detail below.

What types of MDS analyses are there? MDS is a generic term that includes many different types of analyses. The type of MDS analysis depends on the number of dissimilarity matrices, the measurement level of the dissimilarity data, and the MDS model used to analyze the data.

We can classify the types of MDS analyses according to how many matrices there are and what model is being used in the analysis. This gives us four kinds of MDS analyses: classical MDS (one matrix, Euclidean model), replicated MDS (several matrices, Euclidean model), weighted MDS (several matrices, weighted Euclidean model—also called the INDSCAL model), and generalized MDS (several matrices, general Euclidean model). For the INDSCAL and generalized models, you need more than one data matrix.

We can also classify types of MDS according to whether the dissimilarities data are measured on an ordinal scale (called **nonmetric MDS**) or an interval or ratio scale (**metric MDS**). The nonmetric/metric distinction can be combined with the classical/replicated/weighted distinction to provide six different types of MDS. We discuss these types in the following sections.

The SPSS Multidimensional Scaling algorithm is capable of many kinds of analyses, not all of which are covered in this chapter. See Young and Lewyckyj (1979) or Young and Hamer (1987) for more information.

Example: Flying Mileages

The purpose of MDS is to construct a map of the locations of objects relative to each other from data that specify how different the objects are. This is similar to the problem faced by a surveyor who, once he has surveyed the distances between a set of places, needs to draw a map showing the relative locations of those places.

Consider a road map, which shows cities and the roads between them. On such a map there is usually a small table of driving mileages between major cities on the map. In our example we start with such a table, except that it is a table of flying mileages rather than driving mileages. With MDS, we can use these data to construct a map showing where the cities are located, relative to each other. We use these data because most of us are familiar with the relative locations of the large cities in the United States. We know what structure to expect, and we will be looking to see if MDS can show us that structure.

In Figure 7.1 we present a matrix of dissimilarity data entered using the SPSS Data Editor. These data are actually the flying mileages between 10 American cities. The cities are the "objects" and the mileages are the "dissimilarities." For example, the distance between Atlanta and Chicago (shown in row 2, column 1) is 587 miles. Chicago and Denver are 920 miles apart, as shown in row 3, column 2. Note that all diagonal values are 0, since they represent the distance between a city and itself. Note also that each column of the matrix contains data for a different variable. The first column contains distances for *atlanta*, the second column contains *chicago* distances, and so forth.

Figure 7.1   Flying mileages between 10 American cities

	atlanta	chicago	denver	houston	losangel	miami	newyork	sanfran	seattle	washdc
1	0	.	.	.	.	.	.	.	.	.
2	587	0	.	.	.	.	.	.	.	.
3	1212	920	0	.	.	.	.	.	.	.
4	701	940	879	0	.	.	.	.	.	.
5	1936	1745	831	1374	0	.	.	.	.	.
6	604	1188	1726	968	2339	0	.	.	.	.
7	748	713	1631	1420	2451	1092	0	.	.	.
8	2139	1858	949	1645	347	2594	2571	0	.	.
9	2182	1737	1021	1891	959	2734	2408	678	0	.
10	543	597	1494	1220	2300	923	205	2442	2329	0

(Newdata)

Figure 7.2 shows the MDS map based on these data; it shows the relative locations of the 10 cities in the United States. The plot has 10 points, one for each city.

Figure 7.2   MDS plot of intercity flying mileage

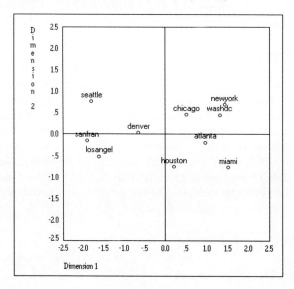

Cities that are similar (have short flying mileages) are represented by points that are close together, and cities that are dissimilar (have long mileages) are represented by points that are far apart. Note that the orientation is arbitrary. For this particular analysis, SPSS has determined the dimensions such that the first dimension is the longest, the second is the next longest, and so forth. By coincidence, north is located at the top (rather than the bottom), and west to the left (instead of right).

The Nature of Data Analyzed in MDS

The SPSS Multidimensional Scaling procedure analyzes dissimilarity data. The data can either be obtained directly in some empirical situation, or computed from multivariate data. In either case, the basic nature of dissimilarity data is exemplified by the flying mileages: the individual elements of the data matrix indicate the degree of dissimilarity between the pairs represented by the rows and columns of the matrix. In the flying mileage example, the dissimilarities are the various flying mileages and the pairs of objects are pairs of cities.

SPSS is very flexible with regard to the kinds of dissimilarity data that can be analyzed. The data can vary in terms of their measurement level, shape, and conditionality. There can be any pattern of missing data. These aspects are discussed briefly in this section. For a more detailed discussion, see Young and Hamer (1987).

The SPSS Multidimensional Scaling procedure can directly analyze multivariate data, but we don't usually recommend that it be used for this purpose. SPSS can calculate dissimilarities from multivariate data, which can then be used by the scaling algorithm.

The Measurement Level of Data

The data can be analyzed in ways that respect the basic nature of any of three commonly identified levels of measurement: ordinal, interval, or ratio. Examples of nominal dissimilarities data are exceedingly rare and are not discussed here. The remaining three levels of measurement (ordinal, interval, and ratio) fall into two categories that define two types of data and two types of analyses. The ordinal level of measurement defines data that are qualitative and analyses that are nonmetric. The interval and ratio levels, on the other hand, define data that are quantitative and analyses that are metric. All three measurement levels, and both metric and nonmetric analyses, will be discussed in this chapter.

The Shape of Data

A less commonly discussed aspect of data is their shape. Data can be square or rectangular. Square data, in turn, can be **symmetric** or **asymmetric**. Thus, we have three basic data shapes: symmetric, asymmetric, and rectangular. SPSS can analyze all three shapes.

In this chapter we only discuss square data, both symmetric and asymmetric. For both types of data the rows and columns refer to the same set of objects. For example, the rows and columns of square data may refer to political candidates or to automobiles. In both examples, the data indicate the degree of dissimilarity of a pair from the set of objects. Thus, if the rows and columns refer to automobiles, the data indicate the degree of dissimilarity of pairs of automobiles.

The difference between symmetric and asymmetric data is whether the degree of dissimilarity between, say, a Ford and a Chevrolet is the same as the dissimilarity between a Chevrolet and a Ford, regardless of the order in which the two objects are considered. If the dissimilarity is the same, then the data are symmetric. Otherwise, they are asymmetric.

The SPSS Multidimensional Scaling procedure can analyze rectangular data, the most common example being multivariate data. Rectangular data elements specify the dissimilarity of all objects in one set to all objects in a second set. But for these data there is no information about the dissimilarity of objects within either set, which is often a problem for MDS. Rectangular data should be analyzed directly with the greatest care, as the results are often not robust.

The Conditionality of Data

In this chapter we discuss two kinds of data conditionality: matrix conditionality and row conditionality. Most dissimilarity data are **matrix conditional**. That is, most dissimilarities are such that the numbers within a matrix are on the same measurement scale. Thus, if we have a matrix where the dissimilarity index is the proportion of times that a pair of senators voted differently out of all their votes during a session of the senate, then all of the proportion indexes are on the same scale and the data are said to be matrix conditional. As a second example, consider judgments of dissimilarity about pairs of wines made by several different experts. Here, the judgments for a given expert are presumed to be on a single scale, but the experts probably each have their own idiosyncratic ways of responding, so the actual meaning of a specific judgment is conditional on which expert made the judgment. Thus, these data are also matrix conditional.

Missing Data

SPSS can analyze data with any pattern of missing values. Of course, the more values that are missing from the data, the lower the probable reliability of the analysis. You should always try to have data with as few missing values as possible. Certain patterns of missing data are not susceptible to robust analysis, as discussed by Young and Hamer (1987).

Multivariate Data

As has been discussed by Young and Hamer (1987), multivariate data can be viewed as rectangular (since the number of observations usually does not equal the number of variables) and column conditional (since the variables are usually measured on different scales). The measurement level of multivariate data often varies from variable to variable, some variables being nominal, others ordinal, and still others interval.

While SPSS can analyze multivariate data directly, it rarely produces useful results. If the multivariate data are quantitative (that is, if all the variables are at the interval or ratio levels of measurement), or if all variables are dichotomous, then SPSS can calculate dissimilarity data from the multivariate data, using Euclidean or binary Euclidean distances. These dissimilarities can then be analyzed by SPSS.

While the SPSS Multidimensional Scaling procedure can be used to analyze a matrix of dissimilarities calculated from a multivariate matrix, there is no real advantage in doing so if you have only one multivariate matrix, since the analysis will be equivalent to a principal components analysis when the default specifications are used, and since the SPSS Factor Analysis procedure (see Chapter 2) can perform the same analysis more efficiently and easily.

The real strength of SPSS with multivariate data is when you have multiple multivariate matrices. In this case you can calculate a separate dissimilarity matrix for each multivariate matrix. These multivariate matrices can then be simultaneously analyzed by SPSS. This feature provides you with three-mode factor analysis, a family of analyses that provide one of the few methods for analyzing multiple-matrix multivariate data in any statistical system.

Classical MDS

Classical MDS (CMDS) is the simplest kind of MDS. The identifying aspect of CMDS is that there is only one dissimilarity matrix. SPSS can analyze many dissimilarity matrices simultaneously, resulting in other kinds of MDS that are not CMDS. They are discussed later in this chapter.

Example: Flying Mileages Revisited

Consider the flying mileage example at the beginning of the chapter. This is an example of classical MDS because there is only one dissimilarity matrix, the matrix of flying mileages shown in Figure 7.1. The data are square symmetric and are at the ratio level of measurement. The only model that can be used for a single matrix of dissimilarities is the Euclidean model, and we know that two dimensions are appropriate.

Figure 7.3 summarizes all options in effect for this particular MDS analysis. Figure 7.4 gives the data matrix, which was requested for this analysis. The mileage values are identical to those shown in Figure 7.1.

Figure 7.3   Analysis options

```
Alscal Procedure Options


Data Options-

Number of Rows (Observations/Matrix).    10
Number of Columns (Variables) .  .  .    10
Number of Matrices  .  .  .  .  .  .     1
Measurement Level .  .  .  .  .  .  .    Ratio
Data Matrix Shape .  .  .  .  .  .  .    Symmetric
Type  .  .  .  .  .  .  .  .  .  .  .    Dissimilarity
Approach to Ties  .  .  .  .  .  .  .    Leave Tied
Conditionality .  .  .  .  .  .  .  .    Matrix
Data Cutoff at .  .  .  .  .  .  .  .      .000000

Maximum Dimensionality  .  .  .  .  .    2
Minimum Dimensionality  .  .  .  .  .    2
Negative Weights  .  .  .  .  .  .  .    Not Permitted


Output Options-

Job Option Header .  .  .  .  .  .  .    Printed
Data Matrices  .  .  .  .  .  .  .  .    Printed
Configurations and Transformations  .    Plotted
Output Dataset .  .  .  .  .  .  .  .    Not Created
Initial Stimulus Coordinates  .  .  .    Computed


Algorithmic Options-

Maximum Iterations  .  .  .  .  .  .     30
Convergence Criterion  .  .  .  .  .       .00100
Minimum S-stress  .  .  .  .  .  .  .      .00100
Missing Data Estimated by  .  .  .  .    Ulbounds
```

Figure 7.4   Matrix of flying mileages

```
     Raw (unscaled) Data for Subject 1

           1          2          3          4          5

 1      .000
 2    587.000      .000
 3   1212.000    920.000      .000
 4    701.000    940.000    879.000      .000
 5   1936.000   1745.000    831.000   1374.000      .000
 6    604.000   1188.000   1726.000    968.000   2339.000
 7    748.000    713.000   1631.000   1420.000   2451.000
 8   2139.000   1858.000    949.000   1645.000    347.000
 9   2182.000   1737.000   1021.000   1891.000    959.000
10    543.000    597.000   1494.000   1220.000   2300.000

           6          7          8          9         10

 6      .000
 7   1092.000      .000
 8   2594.000   2571.000      .000
 9   2734.000   2408.000    678.000      .000
10    923.000    205.000   2442.000   2329.000      .000
```

The iteration history in Figure 7.5 is produced by default. However, if a minimum s-stress of 0.001 is not specified, SPSS produces only one iteration, since the default minimum value for s-stress for further iterations is 0.005 and the s-stress value for the first iteration is only 0.003. **S-stress** is a measure of fit ranging from 1 (worst possible fit) to 0 (perfect fit).

Next, the procedure displays two more measures of fit, Kruskal's stress measure (0.002) and the squared correlation coefficient (r-squared $= 1.000$) between the data and the distances. All three measures of fit, which are discussed and defined below, indicate that the two-dimensional Euclidean model describes these flying mileages perfectly.The stimulus coordinates in Figure 7.6 are the coordinates used to generate the plot in Figure 7.2.

Figure 7.5   Iteration history

```
Iteration history for the 2 dimensional solution(in squared distances)

                  Young's S-stress formula 1 is used.

            Iteration      S-stress      Improvement

                1            .00308
                2            .00280          .00029
                  Iterations stopped because
            S-stress improvement less than  .001000


            Stress and squared correlation (RSQ) in distances

RSQ values are the proportion of variance of the scaled data (disparities)
            In the partition (row, matrix, or entire data) which
            is accounted for by their corresponding distances.
              Stress values are Kruskal's stress formula 1.


                 For  matrix
        Stress  =   .002      RSQ = 1.000
```

Figure 7.6   Stimulus coordinates

```
              Configuration derived in 2 dimensions



                     Stimulus Coordinates

                         Dimension

    Stimulus    Stimulus      1           2
    Number       Name

        1       ATLANTA      .9587      -.1913
        2       CHICAGO      .5095       .4537
        3       DENVER      -.6435       .0330
        4       HOUSTON      .2149      -.7626
        5       LOSANGEL   -1.6041      -.5163
        6       MIAMI       1.5105      -.7732
        7       NEWYORK     1.4293       .6907
        8       SANFRAN    -1.8940      -.1482
        9       SEATTLE    -1.7870       .7676
       10       WASHDC      1.3059       .4466
```

Next, the procedure displays a matrix called *Optimally scaled data (disparities) for subject 1*, as shown in Figure 7.7. For this analysis, in which the data are specified to be at the ratio level of measurement, the values in this matrix of disparities are linearly related to the original flying mileages.

Figure 7.7   Optimally scaled data for subject 1

```
Optimally scaled data (disparities) for subject   1

          1              2            3            4            5

 1       .000
 2       .783          .000
 3      1.616         1.227         .000
 4       .935         1.254        1.172         .000
 5      2.582         2.327        1.108        1.832         .000
 6       .806         1.584        2.302        1.291        3.119
 7       .998          .951        2.175        1.894        3.269
 8      2.853         2.478        1.266        2.194         .463
 9      2.910         2.317        1.362        2.522        1.279
10       .724          .796        1.992        1.627        3.067

          6              7            8            9           10

 6       .000
 7      1.456          .000
 8      3.459         3.429         .000
 9      3.646         3.211         .904         .000
10      1.231          .273        3.257        3.106         .000
```

The perfect fit summarized by the three fit indexes is represented in Figure 7.8. This plot is a scatterplot of the raw data (horizontal axis) versus the distances (vertical axis). The raw data have been standardized, so their units have been changed. The distances are the Euclidean distances between all pairs of points shown in the configuration plot. This plot is an ordinary scatterplot and is interpreted as such. It represents the fit of the distances to the data, which is the fit that is being optimized by the procedure and that is summarized by the fit indexes. In fact, *RSQ* is simply the squared correlation between the data and the distances. Thus, we look at this scatterplot to see how much scatter there is around the perfect-fit line that runs from the lower left to the upper right. In this analysis we see that there is no scatter and no departure from perfect linear fit.

Figure 7.8   Scatterplot of raw data vs. distances

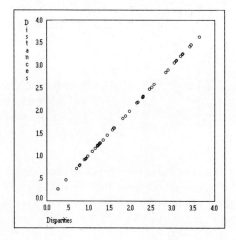

These high-quality results occur because the data have essentially no error, and because we have properly assumed that the data are at the ratio level of measurement. These results also imply that a two-dimensional space is sufficient to explain the flying mileages between cities in the United States. These results, then, assure us that the scaling algorithm is doing what it is supposed to do, since it is recovering structure that we know to be in the data.

The Euclidean Model

In this section we present the **Euclidean model**. First we present the algebra of the model, and then the geometry. Then we return to the algebra of the model, this time presented in matrix algebra instead of scalar algebra. Since the details of the matrix algebra are not crucial to the remainder of the chapter, they can be skipped.

Algebra of the Euclidean Model

Classical MDS employs Euclidean distance to model dissimilarity. That is, the distance d_{ij} between points i and j is defined as

$$d_{ij} = \left[\sum_{a}^{r} (x_{ia} - x_{ja})^2 \right]^{1/2} \qquad \text{Equation 7.1}$$

where x_{ia} specifies the position (coordinate) of point i on dimension a. The x_{ia} and x_{ja} are the stimulus coordinates in Figure 7.6, which are used to plot the derived stimulus configuration in Figure 7.2. The distances d_{ij} are plotted on the vertical axis of the scatterplot in Figure 7.8, versus the corresponding dissimilarities (after normalization) on the horizontal axis.

Note that there are n points in Figure 7.2. In this case $n = 10$, one for each of the n objects (cities). There are also r dimensions (here, $r = 2$). The default value of r is 2, but you can specify a different number of dimensions. The dissimilarity of objects i and j is denoted as s_{ij}, displayed in Figure 7.4 under the heading *Raw (unscaled) data for subject 1*. In this case, the dissimilarities are the actual flying mileages.

The dimensions of the space can be reflected, translated, permuted, and rotated, and they can all be rescaled by the same scaling factor. They cannot, however, be individually rescaled by different scaling factors.

Geometry of the Euclidean Model

Geometrically, the Euclidean distance model presented above is a multidimensional generalization of the two-dimensional Pythagorean theorem, as demonstrated in Figure 7.9.

Figure 7.9   Euclidean distance

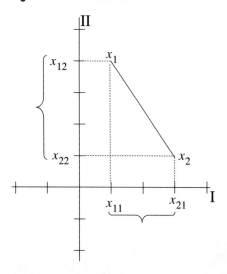

In this figure, the points x_1 and x_2 are shown with dashed lines that project orthogonally onto the two dimensions. The place that these dashed lines project onto the dimensions corresponds to the two coordinates for each point. Thus, the point x_1 has projection x_{11} on dimension 1 and x_{12} on dimension 2, while the point x_2 has projections x_{21} and x_{22} on the two dimensions. By comparing this figure with the previous formula, we see that the formula calculates d_{12} (the length of the hypotenuse of the right triangle) as the square root of the sum of the squared lengths of the two other sides of the triangle, where these squared lengths are $(x_{11} - x_{21})^2$ and $(x_{12} - x_{22})^2$, respectively.

Matrix Algebra of the Euclidean Model

Using matrix algebra, the Euclidean model can be defined as

$$d_{ij} = [(x_i - x_j)(x_i - x_j)']^{1/2}$$

Equation 7.2

where x_i is the ith row of X, consisting of the r coordinates of the ith point on all r dimensions. The dimensions of a Euclidean space can be rotated. This characteristic will be contrasted with other MDS models which are not rotatable.

Normalization. The stimulus coordinates X can be changed in a number of ways that do not change the distances by more than a multiplicative constant (the type of change in scaling of the distances which is permitted by the Euclidean model). Permissible changes in the coordinates include changing the mean of each dimension and multiplying all coordinates by a constant. Since the mean and unit are arbitrary, these are fixed to be the same for all analyses. In particular, the mean of each dimension is made to be 0:

$$\sum_{i}^{n} x_{ia} = 0$$

Equation 7.3

and the dimensions are given an average length equal to the number of points:

$$\sum_{i}^{n}\sum_{a}^{r} x_{ia}^2 = nr$$

Equation 7.4

Note that nothing is done to rotate the space to any specific orientation. However, the first iteration is begun with the configuration oriented so that the first dimension is the longest, the second the next longest, and so forth ("longest" means greatest sum of squared coordinates).

Details of CMDS

In this section we discuss some important details of CMDS, including the distinction between metric and nonmetric CMDS, the measures of goodness of fit displayed by SPSS, and the fundamental CMDS equation.

Metric CMDS

The seminal MDS work was done by Torgerson (1952) and is now known as **metric CMDS**. The flying mileage example presented above is an example. It is *metric* because the flying mileages are assumed to be at the ratio level of measurement. It is *classical* because there is exactly one matrix of dissimilarities. For metric classical MDS, SPSS fits the squared Euclidean distances D^2 to the dissimilarities S so that they are as much like S as possible, in a least-squares sense. (The matrix D^2 has elements that are the squares of the elements of the matrix D.)

The fitting of the squared Euclidean distances to the dissimilarities is represented by the equation

$$l\{S\} = D^2 + E$$

Equation 7.5

where $l\{S\}$ is read "a linear transformation l of the dissimilarities S." The transformation l takes the matrix S as its argument and yields as its value the matrix

$$T = l\{S\}$$

Equation 7.6

If the measurement level is ratio (as in the example), then the linear transformation has a 0 intercept. The intercept can be nonzero when the level is interval. For dissimilarities, the slope of the transformation is positive. If the data are row conditional, the transformations are somewhat more complex, as will be explained below.

Note that the transformations for the interval measurement level are subject to indeterminacies that do not occur at other measurement levels. If warning messages appear, you should try another measurement level.

Note also that, for technical reasons, similarities are not as robust as dissimilarities for the SPSS Multidimensional Scaling procedure, so you should convert similarities to dissimilarities before performing multidimensional scaling. This recommendation holds regardless of other analysis details.

In the preceding equation, E is a matrix of errors (residuals). SPSS minimizes s-stress, a normalized sum of squares of this matrix, as described below. Thus, the s-stress measure is defined on the squared distances in D^2, whereas the stress and R measures are defined on the (unsquared) distances in D. This point has certain implications for information output by the procedure, as will be discussed in the examples below.

Since the distances D (and the squared distances D^2) are a function of the coordinates X, the goal of CMDS is to calculate the coordinates X so that the sum of squares of E is minimized, subject to suitable normalizations. SPSS also calculates the slope (and intercept) of the transformation $l\{S\}$ to minimize E.

Nonmetric CMDS

The first major breakthrough in multidimensional scaling was due to Shepard (1962) and Kruskal (1964) and is known as **nonmetric CMDS**. Nonmetric CMDS refers to analyses in which the measurement level is specified to be ordinal. For nonmetric CMDS, we define

$$m\{S\} = D^2 + E \qquad \text{Equation 7.7}$$

where $m\{S\}$ is "a monotonic transformation m of the dissimilarities S." As with the transformation l, m takes the matrix S as its argument, and yields as its value the matrix

$$T = m\{S\} \qquad \text{Equation 7.8}$$

If S is actually dissimilarities, then $m\{S\}$ preserves rank order, whereas if S is actually similarities, then $m\{S\}$ reverses rank order. Thus, for nonmetric CMDS, SPSS solves for the monotonic (order-preserving) transformation $m\{S\}$ and the coordinates X, which together minimize the sum of squares of the errors E (after normalization).

The matrix of transformed dissimilarities $m\{S\}$ (or the matrix $l\{S\}$) appears in output under the heading *Optimally scaled data (disparities) for subject 1* as shown in Figure 7.7. This terminology refers to the fact that the transformation m (or l) induces a new scaling of the data that is the scaling which optimizes the s-stress index. It also refers to the fact that, historically, this information was originally called "disparities."

The nonmetric minimization problem represents a much more difficult problem to solve than the corresponding metric problem. The nonmetric minimization problem belongs to the general class of problems discussed by Young (1981). These problems require iterative solutions, implying that nonmetric analyses take much more computer time than the metric ones.

Measures of Fit

As shown in Figure 7.5, SPSS produces an iteration history that lists, for each iteration, the s-stress and improvement of the iteration. Note that the fit formula is based on the squared distances contained in the matrix D^2. This is the s-stress index proposed by Takane et al. (1977). The improvement simply represents the amount of improvement in s-stress from one iteration to the next. S-stress indicates the fit of the squared distances D^2 to the transformed data $m\{S\}$ or $l\{S\}$.

In the presentation above, we denoted the result of the monotonic and linear transformations of the data by the matrix T, so that $T = m\{S\}$ or $T = l\{S\}$, depending on measurement level. Then

$$s\text{-stress} = (\frac{\|E\|}{\|T\|})^{1/2}$$

Equation 7.9

where the notation $\|E\|$ indicates the sum of all squared elements of the error (residual) matrix E, and $\|T\|$ indicates the sum of all squared elements of the matrix of transformed data T. Note that

$$\|E\| = \|T - D^2\|$$

Equation 7.10

which means that s-stress is the square root of the ratio of the error sums of squares to the total sums of squares, where the error sums of squares is calculated between the squared distances and the transformed data, and the total sums of squares is calculated on the transformed data. That is, s-stress is the square root of the proportion of the total sums of squares of the transformed data which is error, error being indicated by lack of fit of the squared distances to the transformed data.

Except for the s-stress index, all results (including the two additional measures of fit) are reported in terms of the distances D, not squared distances D^2. Two additional indexes of fit are stress and RSQ. The **stress index** is Kruskal's (1964) stress formula. It is defined in exactly the same fashion as s-stress, except that distances are used instead of squared distances. Note that the SPSS multidimensional scaling algorithm optimizes s-stress, not stress. This has certain implications for information output by the procedure, which will be discussed in the examples below.

RSQ is the squared simple correlation between corresponding elements of T and D. It can be interpreted as the proportion of variance of the transformed data T that is accounted for by the distances D of the MDS model.

The Fundamental CMDS Equation

We can now summarize, in a single equation, the CMDS data analysis problem being solved by the MDS procedure. The fundamental equation is

$$S \overset{\perp}{=} T = D^2 + E \qquad\qquad\qquad \textbf{Equation 7.11}$$

which reads S (the original dissimilarity data) are equal, by transformation (the symbol $\overset{\perp}{=}$ represents the error-free one-to-one transformation), to T (the transformed dissimilarity data), which in turn are equal to the model's squared Euclidean distances D^2 plus error E. SPSS solves for D^2 and for $\overset{\perp}{=}$ so that the sum of the squared elements of E is minimized.

We can think of the transformed data T as an interface between the measurement characteristics of S (which may have a variety of measurement levels, shapes, and conditionalities, and which may have missing values) and those of D^2 (which is always at the ratio level of measurement, is always symmetric and unconditional, and never has missing values). T is in fact identical to S when looked at through the filters imposed by S's various measurement characteristics. That is, T and S have identical ordinal characteristics if the measurement level of S is ordinal. Similarly, T is identical to $D^2 + E$ when viewed through their measurement characteristic's filters.

Example: Ranked Flying Mileages

As an example of nonmetric CMDS, we now return to the flying mileages, but we use their ranks instead of the actual mileages. We still hope that the scaling algorithm can construct a reasonable map of the United States, even though we have degraded the information from mileages to ranks.

In Figure 7.10 we show the new matrix of dissimilarity data for intercity flying mileages. These data differ from the first set of data in that they have been converted into their ranking numbers—that is, an element in this new data matrix specifies the rank position of the corresponding mileage element in the first data matrix. Note that there are 45 elements and that the ranks range from 1 through 45. Thus, the flying mileage between New York and Washington, D.C., is the shortest (rank of 1), while the flying mileage between Miami and Seattle is the longest (45). Since these data are at the ordinal level of measurement, they are suitable for nonmetric CMDS. A nonmetric CMDS of these data produces the plot in Figure 7.11, which is virtually indistinguishable from the plot in Figure 7.2.

Figure 7.10   Ranked distances between cities

	atlanta	chicago	denver	houston	losangel	miami	newyork	sanfran	seattle	washdc
1	0	.	.	.	.	.	.	.	.	.
2	4	0	.	.	.	.	.	.	.	.
3	22	13	0	.	.	.	.	.	.	.
4	8	15	12	0	.	.	.	.	.	.
5	34	31	11	24	0	.	.	.	.	.
6	6	21	29	18	39	0	.	.	.	.
7	10	9	27	25	42	20	0	.	.	.
8	35	32	16	28	2	44	43	0	.	.
9	36	30	19	33	17	45	40	7	0	.
10	3	5	26	23	37	14	1	41	38	0

(Newdata)

Figure 7.11   Plot of nonmetric (ranked) distances

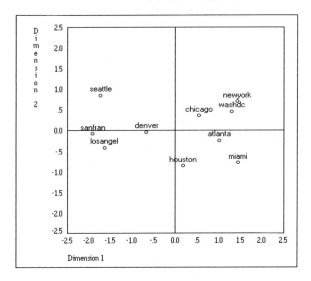

The remaining output for this analysis is shown in Figure 7.12 through Figure 7.17. SPSS displays a warning message, telling us that the number of parameters being estimated (which for these data is 20: $n = 10 \times r = 2$) is dangerously large compared to the number of elements in the data matrix (which is $n(n-1)/2 = 45$). This warning message did not appear for the previous analysis because we had assumed the data were quantitative. In general, we should be cautious when this message appears.

Next, the procedure displays the iteration history for the two-dimensional solution, shown in Figure 7.12. Note that the s-stress index starts at 0.03346, and after eight iterations reduces to 0.00585, where it stops due to the default minimum improvement criterion of 0.001 being reached. This index of fit is not as good as in the metric CMDS of the flying mileages, reflecting the fact that the precision of the data has been reduced because ranks are used instead of actual mileages.

Figure 7.12   Iteration history

```
Iteration history for the 2 dimensional solution(in squared distances)

              Young's S-stress formula 1 is used.

       Iteration      S-stress        Improvement

           1            .03346
           2            .02259            .01086
           3            .01656            .00604
           4            .01270            .00385
           5            .01009            .00261
           6            .00821            .00188
           7            .00684            .00137
           8            .00585            .00100
               Iterations stopped because
       S-stress improvement less than   .001000
```

Next, the procedure gives the two additional measures of fit, stress (0.008) and RSQ (1.000), as shown in Figure 7.13. The stress measure indicates worse fit than in the metric analysis, as would RSQ if more decimal places were displayed. (The RSQ value has been rounded *up* to 1.) Even though the fit has become somewhat worse, the overall conclusion is that the squared distances D^2 of this two-dimensional Euclidean model describe the monotonic transformation of the data $T = m\{S\}$ perfectly.

Figure 7.13   Measures of fit

```
            Stress and squared correlation (RSQ) in distances

RSQ values are the proportion of variance of the scaled data (disparities)
          In the partition (row, matrix, or entire data) which
          is accounted for by their corresponding distances.
          Stress values are Kruskal's stress formula 1.


              For  matrix
        Stress  =    .008      RSQ = 1.000
```

Figure 7.14 shows the stimulus coordinates, which are very similar to the coordinates from the metric analysis in Figure 7.6.

Figure 7.14 Stimulus coordinates

```
                  Configuration derived in 2 dimensions


                         Stimulus Coordinates

                             Dimension

   Stimulus   Stimulus     1         2
   Number      Name

      1       ATLANTA     1.0195    -.2396
      2       CHICAGO      .5557     .3622
      3       DENVER      -.6609    -.0344
      4       HOUSTON      .1816    -.8583
      5       LOSANGEL   -1.6307    -.4110
      6       MIAMI       1.4377    -.7782
      7       NEWYORK     1.4227     .7106
      8       SANFRAN    -1.9047    -.0734
      9       SEATTLE    -1.7195     .8553
     10       WASHDC      1.2986     .4668
```

Four plots are produced for this nonmetric analysis, whereas only two plots were produced for the metric analysis. For both analyses the first two plots are the plot of the derived configuration (Figure 7.11) and the scatterplot of linear fit.

The scatterplot of linear fit, shown in Figure 7.15, plots the monotonically transformed data (disparities) $T = m\{S\}$ horizontally versus the distances D vertically. This plot displays the departures from linearity that are measured by the stress and RSQ indexes. We see that there is very little scatter, although what scatter there is appears for the small distances and disparities. For this nearly perfectly fitting analysis there are some departures from perfect fit for the small transformed data, but very few for the large transformed data. This is a common result and is an artifact of the fit index s-stress, which tends to overfit large data values and underfit small ones because the *squared* distances are being fit to the data. Figure 7.16 is the plot of nonlinear fit. It plots the raw data S horizontally versus the distances D vertically. This plot displays the same departures from fit as in the previous plot, but displays them relative to the raw data instead of the transformed data. Here we see that large ranks are better fit than small ranks.

Figure 7.17 is the plot of transformation. It plots the raw data S horizontally versus the monotonically transformed data $T = m\{S\}$ vertically. The transformed data are called **disparities**. This plot displays the transformation that rescores the ranked flying mileages so that they are as much like the distances, given that the new scores must be in the same order as the original ranks. Since this is a monotonic transformation, the plotted values must never go down as we move from left to right (unless the data are similarities, in which case the transformation line moves monotonically from upper left to lower right). The transformation plot can be placed on top of the nonlinear fit plot and can be interpreted as the monotonic regression line that minimizes error, where error is measured vertically in both plots.

Figure 7.15   Scatterplot of linear fit

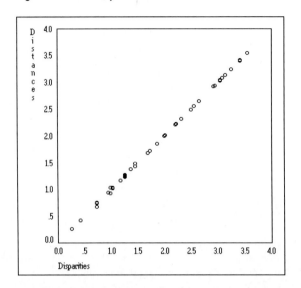

Figure 7.16   Plot of nonlinear fit

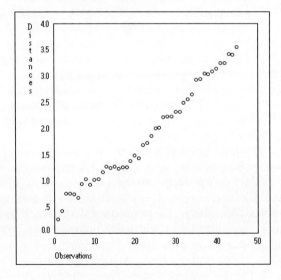

Figure 7.17   Plot of transformation

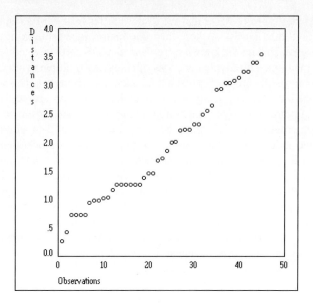

To interpret the transformation plot, we look at its overall shape and smoothness. This particular transformation is quite linear and smooth. The linearity leads us to conclude that the nonmetric analysis of the ranks is essentially the same as the metric analysis of the raw data. This conclusion would be stronger if the nonmetric analysis were of the actual flying mileages. Then, a linear transformation would yield the same results as the metric analysis. The smoothness suggests that we have a reasonably continuous, nondegenerate transformation. In particular, we should be suspicious of transformations that consist of a series of a few horizontal steps. These "step functions" suggest a discontinuous, possibly degenerate transformation.

Our overall conclusion, then, is that the results of the nonmetric analysis of the ranked flying mileages are very concordant with the results of the metric analysis of the flying mileages themselves. Since the transformation is quite linear in the nonmetric analysis, this tells us that the metric analysis, which is more parsimonious, is to be preferred. We can conclude from the two analyses that it is reasonable to assume that the flying mileages are in fact measured at the ratio level of measurement. We can also conclude from the metric analysis that the mileages are nearly error free and are basically two dimensional.

Repeated CMDS

All of the remaining types of MDS that we discuss differ from CMDS in that they are appropriate to data that consist of more than one matrix of dissimilarities. The major ways of analyzing such data are known as replicated MDS and weighted MDS.

It should be mentioned briefly that one way of analyzing multiple matrices of dissimilarity data is to repeatedly apply classical MDS, once to each matrix. This approach implies that you believe that the many matrices of data have no shared structure. The configurations of points underlying each dissimilarity matrix are presumed to be totally unrelated to each other in any fashion. If the several matrices of data are obtained from several individual judges, then this is an individual differences model that permits the greatest freedom in modeling individual differences. There are, in fact, no constraints. However, this individual differences model is the least parsimonious model, there being an entire configuration of points for each individual. If there are n points (cities, in the previous examples) with coordinates on r dimensions, then there are $n \times r$ parameters per individual. If there are m individuals, then there are $m \times n \times r$ parameters. Not only is this very nonparsimonious, but the results are difficult to interpret, since you are faced with the task of having to compare m separate analyses.

Replicated MDS

Historically, the next major development in the multidimensional scaling literature was **replicated MDS** (McGee, 1968). Replicated MDS (RMDS) was the first proposal that extended MDS to permit the analysis of more than one matrix of dissimilarities—a particularly important development, since researchers typically have more than one dissimilarity matrix. This is not the sole defining characteristic of RMDS, however, as the weighted MDS analyses discussed in later portions of this chapter also use several matrices of dissimilarities.

The defining characteristic of RMDS is that it applies the Euclidean distance model to several dissimilarity matrices simultaneously. The basic assumption is that the stimulus configuration X applies with equal validity to every matrix of data. Thus, the implication is that all the data matrices are, except for error, the same; they are replicates of each other, there being no systematic differences other than, perhaps, systematic response bias differences. This is the most parsimonious, and the most constrained, model of individual differences in MDS. Note that the number of parameters is the same as in CMDS; there are a total of $n \times r$ parameters for the n points on r dimensions. Another distance model forms the foundation of weighted MDS. This model relaxes the assumption that all data matrices are replicates of each other. The model is less parsimonious and less constrained than RMDS.

For RMDS, the matrix of squared distances D^2 is still defined by the same Euclidean distance formula that is involved in CMDS. The difference is that the data consist of several dissimilarity matrices S_k, $k = 1, \dots, m$, there being m data matrices in total. The analysis is such that the matrix of squared distances D^2 is calculated so that it is simultaneously like all of the several dissimilarity matrices S_k.

Details of RMDS

In this section we discuss some details of RMDS, including the metric and nonmetric varieties, individual differences in response bias in RMDS, measures of fit in RMDS, and the fundamental RMDS equation.

Metric RMDS

For metric RMDS, the analysis is based on fitting the equation

$$l_k \{S_k\} = D^2 + E_k \qquad\qquad\qquad \text{Equation 7.12}$$

where $l_k \{S_k\}$ is the linear transformation of the kth dissimilarity matrix S_k that best fits the squared Euclidean distances D^2. The data may be similarities or dissimilarities and may be at the ratio or interval levels, just as in metric CMDS. The analysis minimizes the sum of the squared elements, where the sum is taken over all elements in all matrices E_k, subject to normalization of X. The details of the fit index and normalization are discussed later in this chapter.

Nonmetric RMDS

For nonmetric RMDS, SPSS minimizes the several E_k, just as in metric RMDS, except that the equation becomes

$$m_k \{S_k\} = D^2 + E_k \qquad\qquad\qquad \text{Equation 7.13}$$

where $m_k \{S_k\}$ is the monotonic transformation of the dissimilarity matrix S_k that is least-squares fit to the squared distances in D^2. The data and their monotonic transformation are the same as for nonmetric CMDS, except that there are k matrices instead of just one.

Individual Response Bias Differences

It is important to notice that for RMDS each linear or monotonic transformation l_k or m_k is subscripted, letting each data matrix S_k have a unique linear or monotonic relation to the squared Euclidean distances contained in D^2. Since k ranges up to m, there are m separate linear or monotonic transformations, one for each of the m dissimilarity matrices S_k. This implies that RMDS treats all the matrices of the data as being related to each other (through D) by a systematic linear or monotonic transformation (in addition to the random error contained in E_k).

In psychological terms, RMDS accounts for differences in the ways subjects use the response scale (that is, differences in their response bias). Consider, for example, a response scale consisting of the numbers 1 through 9. Even though each subject has the same scale to respond on, they won't necessarily use the scale the same way. It could be that one subject uses only categories 1, 5, and 9, while another uses only the even numbers, and a third uses only the middle three categories of 4, 5, and 6. These differences in response style (bias) are taken into account by the separate transformations for each subject.

Measures of Fit

As discussed above for CMDS, SPSS produces an iteration history that lists, for each iteration, the s-stress and improvement of the iteration. S-stress uses a formula based on the squared distances contained in the matrix D^2. To define the formula, we begin by denoting the matrix of transformed data by the symbol T_k, where $T_k = m_k\{S_k\}$ or $T_k = L_k\{S_k\}$, depending on measurement level. Then

$$\text{s-stress} = \left[\frac{1}{m} \sum_k^m (\|E_k\| / \|T_k\|) \right]^{\frac{1}{2}}$$

Equation 7.14

where the notation $\|E_k\|$ indicates the sum of all squared elements of the error (residual) matrix E_k, and $\|T_k\|$ indicates the sum of all squared elements of the matrix of transformed data T_k. Note that

$$\|E_k\| = \|T_k - D^2\|$$

Equation 7.15

which means that for RMDS, s-stress is the square root of the mean of the ratio of the error sums of squares for a matrix to the total sums of squares for that matrix, where the error sums of squares is calculated between the squared distances and the transformed data for one matrix, and the total sums of squares is calculated on the transformed data for one matrix. That is, s-stress is the square root of the mean, averaged over the several matrices of data, of the proportion of the total sums of squares for one matrix of transformed data which is error, error being indicated by lack of fit of the squared distances to the transformed data.

In addition, stress and RSQ (but not s-stress) are calculated and displayed for each matrix of data. These are exactly the same formulas as for CMDS, calculated separately for each matrix. Then, the average stress and RSQ (again, not s-stress) are calculated and displayed (labeled *Overall Stress and RSQ* in the output). (The average stress is the square root of the mean of the squared stress values, while the average RSQ is the mean of the RSQ values.) The stress indexes for each matrix are Kruskal's stress and can be interpreted as such. The RSQ for a matrix indicates the proportion of variance of the disparities in the matrix which is accounted for by the squared distances. The overall RSQ is an average squared correlation, and it indicates the average proportion of variance accounted for in all of the transformed data.

For row conditional data the stress and RSQ (but not s-stress) values are displayed for each row of each matrix, as are the overall indexes for each matrix. The interpretation of these values corresponds to their interpretation for matrix conditional data.

Note: The final s-stress in the iteration list and the overall stress value do not correspond because the former is defined on squared distances and the latter on distances.

The Fundamental RMDS Equation

We can now summarize, in a single equation, the RMDS data analysis problem being solved by the scaling procedure. The fundamental equation is:

$$S_k \overset{\perp}{=} T_k = D^2 + E \qquad\qquad \text{Equation 7.16}$$

This equation parallels the fundamental CMDS equation and is to be understood in a similar fashion.

Example: Perceived Body-Part Structure

Jacobowitz (see Young, 1974) used RMDS to study the way language develops as children grow to adulthood. In his experiment he asked children and adults to judge the dissimilarity of all pairs of 15 parts of the human body. The judges were five-, seven-, and nine-year-olds, and adults. There were 15 judges at each age. Here we report two separate RMDS analyses, one for the seven-year-olds and the other for the adults. These data, and the RMDS of them, are discussed extensively by Young (1974).

Each of 15 subjects at each of the four age groups was asked to do the following task. The experimenter wrote the 15 body-part terms on a slip of paper, 15 slips in all. The experimenter then selected one of the body-part terms and called it the "standard." He then asked the subject to select the term from the remaining 14 which seemed most similar to the standard. The experimenter then removed this slip and asked the subject to select the most similar term from the remaining 13. This continued until all 14 "comparison" terms were rank ordered by their similarity to the standard. This task was then repeated 15 times per subject, one time with each term as standard.

Table 7.1 shows the variable names and data for one subject. The value 0 indicates the "standard" term, the value 1 indicates the comparison term that was picked first (most similar), the value 2 is the term picked second, and so forth. Note that each row of the data contains the numbers 1 through 14, plus a 0. The numbers 1 through 14 indicate the judged similarity order, and the 0 indicates that a term was not compared to itself (that is, zero dissimilarity). In the complete data set (not shown) there are 225 rows of data, 15 sets (for 15 subjects) of 15 rows each (for 15 terms). Also note that each data matrix is asymmetric,

Table 7.1 Body-part data for one subject

Cheek	Face	Mouth	Head	Ear	Body	Arm	Elbow	Hand	Palm	Finger	Leg	Knee	Foot	Toe
0	1	2	3	4	9	7	10	6	5	8	12	11	13	14
2	0	1	3	4	8	6	10	12	5	11	7	9	13	14
2	1	0	3	4	6	8	12	7	10	5	9	11	13	14
3	1	2	0	4	5	6	7	10	8	9	12	11	13	14
3	2	4	1	0	5	9	10	7	8	6	11	12	13	14
3	2	6	1	8	0	7	10	12	9	14	4	11	5	13
13	11	12	10	14	4	0	1	2	9	3	5	7	6	8
11	12	13	10	14	5	1	0	2	9	3	6	4	7	8
13	8	10	11	14	9	3	5	0	1	2	12	7	4	6
12	11	7	13	14	10	6	4	1	0	2	8	9	3	5
10	11	6	8	7	5	9	14	1	2	0	12	13	4	3
13	9	12	10	14	4	5	11	6	7	8	0	1	2	3
13	12	11	10	14	9	6	2	5	8	7	1	0	3	4
13	11	14	10	12	6	7	9	4	8	5	2	3	0	1
13	12	14	10	11	5	8	9	6	7	3	2	4	1	0

and that the data are **row conditional**, as the values in a row are ranked only relative to other values in the same row, not in other rows.

The RMDS results for adults and seven-year-olds are shown in Figure 7.18 and Figure 7.19. Both figures are based on plots generated by the scaling procedure. (A two-dimensional MDS plot for the adult data is shown in Figure 7.23.)

Figure 7.18   Three-dimensional body-part RMDS for adults

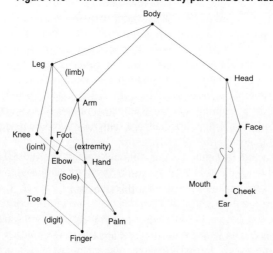

Figure 7.19   Three-dimensional body-part RMDS for seven-year-olds

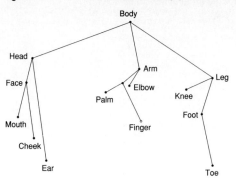

The lines were drawn to interpret the psycholinguistic structure that people have for body-part words. Jacobowitz theorized that the structure would be hierarchical. We can see that it is. (Note that there is nothing in the RMDS that forces the structure to be hierarchical. This structure is imposed on the solution by the data themselves, not by the analysis.) This hierarchical structure corresponds, psycholinguistically, to the phrase "has a." We say that a body "has a" head, which in turn "has a" face, which "has a" mouth.

Jacobowitz further theorized that the structure would become more complex as the children became adults. This theory is also supported, since the adults' hierarchy also involves a classification of corresponding arm and leg terms. In Figure 7.18 we have not only drawn the hierarchy, but we have also shown corresponding arm and leg terms linked by the dashed lines. In addition, the implied classification terms are shown in parentheses, and the term "sole," which was not a stimulus, is shown in the position that we would predict it to be in if the study were repeated with sole as a 16th stimulus.

The structure for adults shown in Figure 7.18 is based on a three-dimensional RMDS. For this analysis, there are 15 matrices of dissimilarity judgments. The judgments are specified as ordinal, asymmetric, and row conditional (conditionality and asymmetry are explained below). The default Euclidean model is used. When the Euclidean model is used with multiple matrices of dissimilarities, the result is RMDS. Three RMDS analyses are requested, the first with three dimensions, the second with two, and the last with one. Plots of results are also requested.

Figure 7.20 shows the iteration history for the three-dimensional solution. The s-stress index starts at 0.24780 and improves only slightly to 0.23624 after six iterations. Iterations stop because the rate of improvement is slow. For this size data, the fit is rather good, but not excellent.

It is not, unfortunately, possible to say exactly what a "good" or "bad" s-stress value is. We do know, however, that the value is a function of many things in addition to the amount of error in the data. For example, s-stress gets larger when the number of stimuli or matrices goes up.

Figure 7.20   Iteration history for the three-dimensional solution

```
Iteration history for the 3 dimensional solution(in squared distances)

              Young's S-stress formula 1 is used.

         Iteration      S-stress      Improvement

             1           .24780
             2           .24221         .00559
             3           .23959         .00262
             4           .23802         .00157
             5           .23697         .00105
             6           .23624         .00073
               Iterations stopped because
          S-stress improvement less than   .001000
```

The next information displayed is a large number of fit indexes. The stress and RSQ indexes are displayed for every row of every matrix (there are $15 \times 15 = 225$ of these). In addition, an averaged stress and RSQ index is calculated for each matrix (subject). Then, an average RSQ (but not stress) index is displayed for each stimulus (body-part term). Finally, the RSQ and stress indexes are averaged over all data. It is useful to look

Figure 7.21   Fit indexes

```
                            Matrix    1
      Stimulus     Stress     RSQ    Stimulus     Stress      RSQ
         1          .072     .974        2          .062      .982
         3          .092     .962        4          .043      .988
         5          .114     .937        6          .112      .876
         7          .077     .959        8          .120      .928
         9          .091     .954       10          .117      .907
        11          .211     .730       12          .114      .917
        13          .090     .958       14          .157      .882
        15          .141     .886

   Averaged (rms) over stimuli
   Stress  =   .115       RSQ =  .923

                            Matrix    2
      Stimulus     Stress     RSQ    Stimulus     Stress      RSQ
         1          .219     .764        2          .359      .403
         3          .033     .995        4          .316      .388
         5          .157     .880        6          .122      .853
         7          .241     .614        8          .210      .783
         9          .270     .602       10          .266      .528
        11          .032     .993       12          .207      .725
        13          .179     .836       14          .167      .867
        15          .159     .854

   Averaged (rms) over stimuli
   Stress  =   .215       RSQ =  .739

                            Matrix    3
      Stimulus     Stress     RSQ    Stimulus     Stress      RSQ
         1          .043     .991        2          .030      .996
         3          .091     .963        4          .020      .997
         5          .115     .936        6          .059      .966
         7          .103     .926        8          .198      .807
         9          .152     .872       10          .036      .991
        11          .149     .859       12          .071      .968
        13          .171     .850       14          .210      .793
        15          .137     .893

   Averaged (rms) over stimuli
   Stress  =   .122       RSQ =  .921
```

over all of the fit measures to see if there are any that are particularly poor. Figure 7.21 shows the output for the first three subjects. For these data, there are no great anomalies, although we do note that subject 2 does not fit as well as subjects 1 and 3. Figure 7.22 shows the stimulus coordinates used to produce the plot of dimensions 1 and 2 in Figure 7.23. Figure 7.18 is based on the coordonates in Figure 7.22.

Figure 7.22   RMDS stimulus coordinates for adults

```
                    Configuration derived in 3 dimensions
                    Stimulus Coordinates

                              Dimension

Stimulus    Stimulus      1          2          3
Number        Name

    1       CHEEK       1.6756     -.8000      .2893
    2       FACE        1.7508     -.0705      .5369
    3       MOUTH       1.4671     -.5392      .8706
    4       HEAD        1.6199      .8363      .5339
    5       EAR         1.3866     -.7665     1.0340
    6       BODY         .6873     1.9263     -.4371
    7       ARM         -.4621      .7918    -1.1974
    8       ELBOW      -1.1132      .0736     -.9565
    9       HAND        -.5005     -.4627    -1.2429
   10       PALM        -.0353     -.9172    -1.5053
   11       FINGER      -.8682    -1.1875     -.3785
   12       LEG        -1.1363     1.1501      .5941
   13       KNEE       -1.5253      .4856      .7355
   14       FOOT       -1.4240     -.0328      .2423
   15       TOE        -1.5222     -.4873      .8812
```

Figure 7.23   Plot of RMDS stimulus coordinates for adults

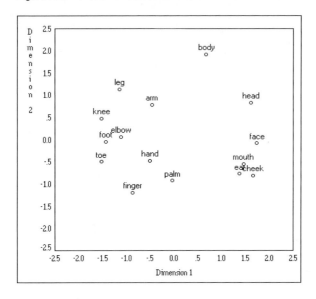

The scatterplot in Figure 7.24 is interpreted just like any other scatterplot, including the scatterplots discussed above for the analyses of the flying mileages and their ranks. The scatter is between the transformed data (horizontal axis, the disparities) and the distances between the points in the configuration (vertical axis). If the scatter is tight, the fit is good; if it is loose, it is bad. The overall RSQ value (0.846) is calculated from this scatterplot and is rather good.

Figure 7.24   Scatterplot of RMDS results for adults

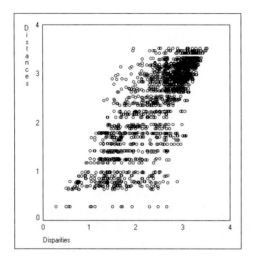

While the initial impression of this particular scatterplot is fairly poor, the density indicated by the plotting symbols reveals that the scatter is much more dense along the diagonal than away from it. Thus, the scatter is not as poor as it initially appears.

SPSS displays the same type of output for the two-dimensional solution and the one-dimensional solution. A notable feature of the three separate analyses is that the two-dimensional solution fits somewhat less well, but not a lot less well (s-stress = 0.27912) than the three-dimensional solution, whereas the one-dimensional solution fits quite a lot less well than the two- and three-dimensional solutions (s-stress = 0.35133). This suggests that the two-dimensional solution may be the best of these, since it is more parsimonious than the three-dimensional but fits nearly as well, and it fits quite a lot better then the one-dimensional solution.

Another notable feature of the three analyses is that the one-dimensional solution is clearly degenerate. The one-dimensional plot of the derived configuration in Figure 7.25 shows that the points are clustering together into two distinct clusters; on the bottom of the plot we have all the head terms and body, whereas all the arm and leg terms are on top (body part labels are not shown in Figure 7.25). The cluster structure shows that the solution is degenerating into a simple geometric pattern, in this case consisting of all points in two places. Also, by looking at the scatterplot in Figure 7.26, we see a strange pattern that should be taken as another warning; there is a large horizontal gap in the scatter. This gap indicates that there are no medium-sized distances; instead, all distances are either large or small. This is another way of seeing the cluster-like nature of this solution.

Figure 7.25   Plot of one-dimensional solution

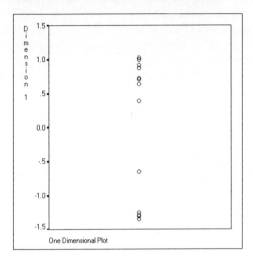

Figure 7.26   Scatterplot of one-dimensional solution

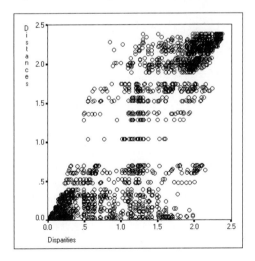

What we conclude from all these clues is that the one-dimensional analysis is actually telling us about the gross (as opposed to fine) structure of the data. The arm and leg terms are seen as being more similar to themselves than they are to the head terms or to the body terms. But the analysis appears to have degenerated into an oversimplified structure, suggesting in this case that we may have too few dimensions.

There are some indications that the two-dimensional solution may be partially degenerate. The two-dimensional plot of the derived configuration in Figure 7.27 looks quite circular, another kind of simple geometric pattern that should be interpreted cautiously and that may indicate that the analysis has degenerated into an oversimplified structure. We can see the hierarchical structure in this plot, so the analysis is, perhaps, only partially degenerate. However, caution is appropriate—this space may also be too low in dimensionality.

Figure 7.27   Plot of two-dimensional solution

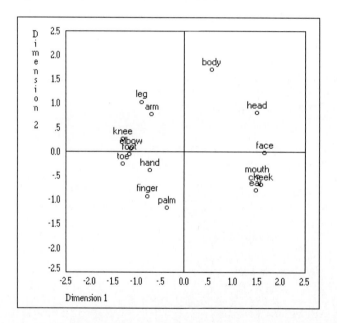

The conclusion that can be drawn from these three analyses is that the three-dimensional solution is the best. It fits reasonably well and shows no signs of degeneracy, whereas the two-dimensional and one-dimensional solutions seem somewhat questionable.

Weighted MDS

The second major breakthrough in multidimensional scaling was due to Carroll and Chang (1970). This development, which is called **weighted MDS (WMDS)**, generalized the Euclidean distance model so that the several dissimilarity matrices S_k could be assumed to differ from each other in systematically nonlinear or nonmonotonic ways. Whereas RMDS accounts only for individual differences in response bias, WMDS can also account for individual differences in the perceptual or cognitive processes that generate the responses. For this reason, WMDS is often called individual differences scaling (INDSCAL).

WMDS is based on the weighted Euclidean model. In this model we still have the stimulus space X that we have had in the (unweighted) Euclidean model, but we also have a new weight space W. We can think of the stimulus space X as representing the information that is shared in common across the individuals about the structure of the stimuli, just as in RMDS. In addition, we can think of the weight space W as representing the information that is unique to each individual about the structure of the stimuli, a notion that we did not have in RMDS.

We now turn to a detailed presentation of WMDS. We discuss the geometry, algebra, and matrix algebra of this model in the next three sections. In the fourth section we discuss a number of WMDS details. Then we present an example. Finally, we discuss two statistics developed for WMDS, and flattened weights.

Geometry of the Weighted Euclidean Model

The weighted Euclidean model assumes that the individuals vary in the importance they attach to the dimensions of the stimulus space X. While one individual may perceive one of the dimensions as being more important than another, another individual may have just the opposite perception. The notion of salience is incorporated into the model by weights w_{ka} for each individual k on each dimension a. These weights vary from 0.0 to 1.0. If the weight is large (near 1.0), then the dimension is relatively important; if it is small (near 0), the dimension is not so important.

Geometrically, the weighted Euclidean model represents individual differences in a special space called the **weight space**. In this space individuals are represented by vectors emanating from the origin of the space. The direction of the vector from the origin represents the relative weighting of each dimension. The length of the vector represents the overall salience of the dimension to the individual.

A schematic diagram of the geometry of the weighted Euclidean model is presented in Figure 7.28. At the top are two hypothetical data matrices concerning four stimuli (potato, spinach, lettuce, and tuna). These matrices are labeled S_2 and S_5, indicating that they are matrices number 2 and 5 of (we assume for this example) five such matrices. (Note that the MDS algorithm would not actually analyze data matrices that have only four rows and columns, since they are too small to support meaningful results.)

Figure 7.28   Geometry of the weighted Euclidean model

Data Matrices

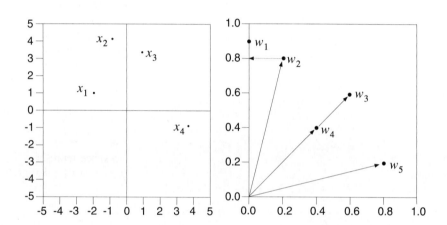

S_2	Potato	Spinach	Lettuce	Tuna
Potato		4	2	3
Spinach	4		1	6
Lettuce	2	1		5
Tuna	3	6	5	

S_5	Potato	Spinach	Lettuce	Tuna
Potato		1	3	6
Spinach	1		2	5
Lettuce	3	2		4
Tuna	6	5	4	

Group Coordinates X

	I	II
x_1	−2	1
x_2	−1	4
x_3	1	3
x_4	4	−1

Matrix Weights W

	I	II	Length
w_1	0	0.9	0.90
w_2	0.2	0.8	0.82
w_3	0.6	0.6	0.85
w_4	0.4	0.4	0.56
w_5	0.8	0.2	0.82

Group Distances D

	Potato	Spinach	Lettuce	Tuna
Potato		3.16	3.61	6.32
Spinach	3.16		2.24	7.07
Lettuce	3.61	2.24		5.00
Tuna	6.32	7.07	5.00	

In the middle of Figure 7.28 are two spaces, each two-dimensional. The left-hand space is the hypothetical group stimulus space X. In it are four points labeled x_1 through x_4. These points correspond to the four stimuli. The right-hand space is a hypothetical weight space W with five vectors labeled w_1 through w_5. These vectors correspond to the five data matrices. Note that the dimensionality of X is always the same as that of W in WMDS.

At the bottom of Figure 7.28 we present numerical information that corresponds to the diagrams in the middle of the figure; on the left is the group-stimulus-coordinates matrix X and in the middle the weights matrix W. The two columns of the matrix X correspond to the two dimensions of the stimulus space. The rows of this matrix specify the positions of each point on each dimension of the stimulus space. The first two columns of the weight matrix W correspond to the two dimensions of the weight space. The values in these columns for each row specify the location of the tips of the weight vectors in the weight space. The third column contains the length of each weight vector in the weight space, which is the square root of the sum of the squares of the other values in the row of the weight matrix. At the bottom-right of the figure is the matrix D of Euclidean distances between the points in the group stimulus space X.

The stimulus space X is the same as that in RMDS and CMDS. For this reason, we use the same notation as used previously. We call the space the **group stimulus space** for the same reasons we called it that for RMDS. The group Euclidean distances D are also the same as the Euclidean distances in the (unweighted) Euclidean model, except that they are for the group stimulus space, and so are called **group distances**. The group space and its distances present information about how the entire group of individuals (or whatever group of things generated the several data matrices) structures the stimuli and carries the same interpretation as that for RMDS, with one major (and one minor) exception to be discussed next. Note, however, that this group information does not represent the structure for any individual, as each individual's structure is modified from the group structure by the individual's weights w_k. Rather, the group space represents the information that is shared in common by all the individuals about the structure of the stimuli.

The stimulus space X has the same characteristics for WMDS as it does for CMDS and RMDS, except for two differences. One very important difference is that for WMDS the stimulus space is not rotatable, as will be proven in the matrix algebra section below. The other difference, which is less important but occasionally confusing, is that the dimensions can be stretched or shrunk by separate scaling factors, whereas the Euclidean model requires that the same scaling factor be used for all dimensions. The two models are the same in that for both models the dimensions can be reflected, permuted, and translated.

The fact that the stimulus space is not rotatable is very important because it implies that the dimensions themselves should be meaningful. We should, if the model describes the data accurately, be able to directly interpret the dimensions of the space, not having to worry about rotations of the dimensions into another orientation for interpretation. It should be kept in mind, however, that the stability of the dimensions depends on two things: the goodness of fit of the analysis and the variation in the weights. First, if there is no variation in the orientation of the weight vectors, then the dimensions can be rotated. Also, if there is little variation in the weight vectors' orientations, the orientation of the dimensions is not as tightly determined as when there is great variation. Secondly, if the model fits the data perfectly, then the dimensions are completely stable (unless there is no variation in the weights). However, the degree of stability decreases as the fit decreases. Thus, for a poorly fitting analysis the orientation of the dimensions is not as well determined as for an analysis that fits very well.

Now we turn to the weights W. Each individual (each matrix of data) is represented by a weight vector, the vectors being labeled w_1 through w_5 for the five individual matrices. Notice that the weight space has vectors only in the positive quadrant. Generally, only positive weights are interpretable. Thus, by default SPSS restricts weights to be non-negative. Notice also that no weights are greater than 1.00. This is because they have been normalized so that their length equals the proportion of variance accounted for in the individual's data by the model (the RSQ value discussed earlier).

In the weighted Euclidean model, individual differences in perception or cognition are represented by differences in the orientation and length of the vectors w_k in the weight space W. Of these two aspects of a vector, variation in orientation of the vectors is most important, since it reflects differences in the importance of the dimensions to the individuals. Two vectors that point in exactly the same direction indicate that the two individuals have the same relative weighting of the dimensions, regardless of the length of the vectors. The different lengths simply indicate that one person's data are better described by the analysis than the other's, the longer vector (and larger weights) representing the person whose data are better fit.

The nature of the individual differences can be seen most readily by comparing the personal stimulus spaces for the several individuals. The personal stimulus space for an individual is what results after applying the (square root of the) weights for an individual to the group space. The weights shrink the dimensions of the group space, with important dimensions being shrunk less than unimportant dimensions (since weights near 1.00 represent important dimensions and will shrink a dimension relatively little). Thus, in the personal space important dimensions are longer than unimportant dimensions. The algebra for this will be shown in the next section.

The idea of an individual's personal space is illustrated in Figure 7.29 for three individuals. Information at the top of the figure is for individual 2, at the middle is for individual 5, and at the bottom is for individual 4.

Figure 7.29   Personal space structures

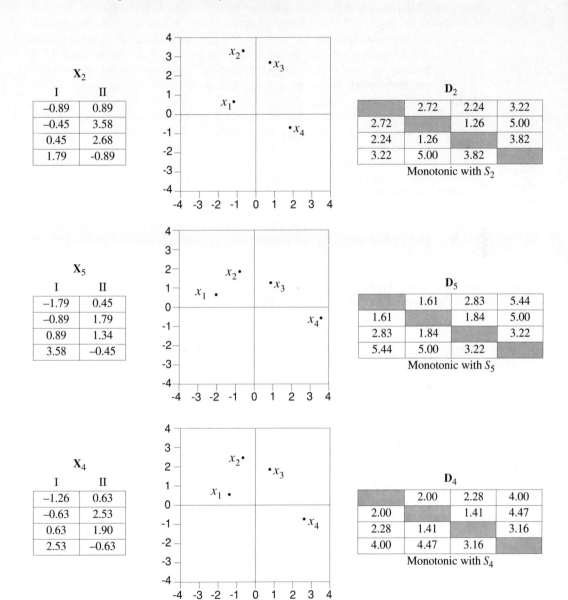

X₂

I	II
−0.89	0.89
−0.45	3.58
0.45	2.68
1.79	-0.89

D₂

	2.72	2.24	3.22
2.72		1.26	5.00
2.24	1.26		3.82
3.22	5.00	3.82	

Monotonic with S_2

X₅

I	II
−1.79	0.45
−0.89	1.79
0.89	1.34
3.58	−0.45

D₅

	1.61	2.83	5.44
1.61		1.84	5.00
2.83	1.84		3.22
5.44	5.00	3.22	

Monotonic with S_5

X₄

I	II
−1.26	0.63
−0.63	2.53
0.63	1.90
2.53	−0.63

D₄

	2.00	2.28	4.00
2.00		1.41	4.47
2.28	1.41		3.16
4.00	4.47	3.16	

Monotonic with S_4

Consider the information for individual 2 at the top of the figure. At top left is this individual's matrix of personal coordinates, labeled X_2. (Note that X_2 is a matrix of coordinates for all the stimuli in the personal space for individual 2, whereas x_2 is a row of coordinates for stimulus 2 in the group stimulus space.) At top middle is the personal space X_2 for this individual (the coordinates are given in the matrix X_2). At top right is the individual's matrix of personal distances, labeled D_2, which are unweighted Euclidean distances between the points in the personal space X_2, and weighted Euclidean distances between the points in the group space X as weighted by the square root of the weights w_2 for this individual.

It is informative to compare the personal space structures for each of these three individuals with their weights. Individual 2 has weights of 0.2 and 0.8, as can be seen at the bottom middle of Figure 7.28. Thus, this individual finds dimension 2 four times as important as dimension 1. This is reflected in the top-middle of Figure 7.29 by the fact that dimension 2 is relatively longer than dimension 1. For this person the personal space is mostly the vertical dimension.

Individual 5 has weights that are opposite to individual 2's—0.8 and 0.2. These weights indicate that individual 5 finds dimension 2 to be one-fourth as important as dimension 1. We see, in the middle of Figure 7.29, that person 5's personal space is much longer along dimension 1 than dimension 2 (the space is mostly horizontal).

Individual 4, on the other hand, finds the two dimensions to be equally important, having weights of 0.4 and 0.4 on both dimensions. Thus, this person's own stimulus structure is the same as the group's, except that it has shrunk due to the relatively small weights.

The last point we want to make about the geometry of WMDS is that one individual's personal distances are not related to another individual's personal distances by any type of simple one-to-one function. In particular, they are not linearly related, nor are they even monotonically related. As can be seen in Figure 7.29, person 2's distances D_2 are not monotonic with the distances for person 5 or person 4. This implies that it is possible to use the weighted Euclidean model to perfectly describe data in several dissimilarity data matrices even though the data are not even monotonically related to each other. In fact, the top two distance matrices in Figure 7.29 (D_2 and D_5) are monotonically related to the two data matrices S_2 and S_5 in Figure 7.28, even though the data matrices are not monotonically related to each other. Thus, the structure in X and W perfectly describes the data from these two people, even though their data are not simply related to each other. This is an important distinction from RMDS, where the model assumes that all data matrices are monotonically (or linearly) related to each other, except for error.

Algebra of the Weighted Euclidean Model

WMDS is based on the following definition of weighted Euclidean distance:

$$d_{ijk} = \left[\sum_a^r w_{ka} (x_{ia} - x_{ja})^2 \right]^{\frac{1}{2}}$$

Equation 7.17

where $0 \leq w_{ka} \leq 1$, $r \geq 2$, and d_{ijk} is the distance between stimuli i and j as perceived by subject k. We discuss the algebraic characteristics of the weighted distance model in the next several sections, first presenting several concepts in scalar algebra, then several more concepts in matrix algebra.

Group Stimulus Space

The x_{ia} are the same stimulus coordinates as those in the CMDS and RMDS situations, with the new restriction that one-dimensional solutions are not permitted. Taken together, the x_{ia} form the $n \times r$ stimulus coordinates matrix X. A row of this matrix is denoted x_i and contains all r of the coordinates for stimulus i. As in the RMDS case, the stimulus space X represents the structure of the stimuli as perceived by the entire group of individuals. Thus, it is called the group stimulus space.

As mentioned above, the WMDS group stimulus space has the same characteristics as the RMDS group stimulus space, except that it is not rotatable and the dimensions can be arbitrarily rescaled by separate constant factors. We discuss the rotation issue in the matrix algebra section that follows. Here we discuss the rescaling issue.

In WMDS we can rescale each dimension a by a unique constant c_a if we rescale the dimensions of the weight space by corresponding constants c_a^{-2}. This can be shown by noting that

$$d_{ijk} = \left[\sum_a^r w_{ka} c_a^{-2} (c_a x_{ia} - c_a x_{ja})^2 \right]^{\frac{1}{2}}$$

$$d_{ijk} = \left[\sum_a^r w_{ka} c_a^{-2} c_a^2 (x_{ia} - x_{ja})^2 \right]^{\frac{1}{2}}$$

Equation 7.18

$$d_{ijk} = \left[\sum_a^r w_{ka} (x_{ia} - x_{ja})^2 \right]^{\frac{1}{2}}$$

which is the basic WMDS equation. This implies that there is an arbitrary normalization of the dimensions that must be defined. This normalization and its implications are discussed below. Note that this arbitrary aspect does not exist in the Euclidean model, since there are no weights that can be rescaled in a way that compensates for rescalings of the stimulus space.

The w_{ka} in the equation above represent the weights that individual k associates with the dimensions a of the stimulus space. As noted above, the weights are collected together into an $m \times r$ matrix W, which has one row for each of the m individuals (data matrices) and one column for each of the r dimensions.

For WMDS, the configuration derived by SPSS is normalized as follows. For all models the coordinates are centered

$$\sum_i^n x_{ia} = 0 \qquad\qquad \text{Equation 7.19}$$

and the length of the stimulus space dimensions are each set equal to the number of points:

$$\sum_i^n x_{ia}^2 = n \qquad\qquad \text{Equation 7.20}$$

The weights are normalized so that

$$\sum_a^r w_{ka}^2 = r_k^2 \qquad\qquad \text{Equation 7.21}$$

where r_k^2 is RSQ, the squared correlation between subject k's squared weighted Euclidean distances D_k^2 and the same subject's dissimilarity data S_k. This normalization has the characteristic that the sum of an individual's squared weights reflects the proportion of the total variance of the individual's transformed data S_k that is accounted for by the model.

Note that there is a subtle difference in normalization of the stimulus space in the weighted and unweighted models. In the weighted model the dimensions of the stimulus space X are each separately normalized to be of equal length n, whereas in the unweighted model the dimensions are jointly normalized to have an average length of n. Thus, in CMDS and RMDS, you interpret the relative length of the stimulus space dimensions as indicating their relative importance, whereas in WMDS you cannot interpret the relative importance of stimulus space dimensions because they are arbitrarily normalized to be equal. The relative importance of WMDS dimensions is found in the average weights on a dimension, rather than in the spread of the stimulus coordinates. This will be seen in the example below.

Personal Spaces

One essential difference between the weighted and unweighted Euclidean models is that in WMDS the coordinates x_{ia} of the group stimulus space X can be weighted by the square root of an individual's weights w_{ka} to obtain the individual's personal stimulus space. The coordinates x_{ika} of stimuli in an individual's personal stimulus space X_k are derived from the group space X and the weights W by the equation:

$$x_{ika} = x_{ia} (w_{ka})^{\frac{1}{2}}$$

Equation 7.22

It can be shown that the distances d_{ijk} for an individual can be re-expressed in terms of the coordinates x_{ika} as the simple Euclidean distances in the personal stimulus space

$$d_{ijk} = \left[\sum_{a}^{r} (x_{ika} - x_{jka})^2 \right]^{\frac{1}{2}}$$

Equation 7.23

Matrix Algebra of the Weighted Euclidean Model

To state the weighted Euclidean model in matrix algebra we must first define a new set of weight matrices W_k. There are m of these weight matrices W_k, one for each of the m individuals. Each W_k is an $r \times r$ diagonal matrix, with the weights for individual k on the diagonal.

Note that the new diagonal weight matrices W_k are not the same as the previously defined rectangular weight matrix W. However, the new diagonal matrices contain the same information as the earlier rectangular matrix; the rows w_k of the earlier W have become the diagonals of the new W_k (note that lowercase w_k is a row of W, whereas uppercase W_k is a diagonal matrix). Furthermore, the diagonal elements w_{kaa} of matrix W_k correspond to the elements w_{ka} of the kth row of the earlier matrix W.

Now that we have introduced the new notation W_k, we can state the weighted Euclidean model in matrix algebra terminology. The model is

$$d_{ijk} = [(x_i - x_j) W_k (x_i - x_j)']^{\frac{1}{2}}$$

Equation 7.24

Personal Spaces

We mentioned above that an essential aspect of the weighted model is the notion of an individual's personal stimulus space. The personal space for individual k is represented by the matrix X_k, which is defined as

$$X_k = XW_k^{\frac{1}{2}}$$

Equation 7.25

giving an alternative expression for the weighted Euclidean model as

$$d_{ijk} = [(x_{ik} - x_{jk})(x_{ik} - x_{jk})']^{\frac{1}{2}}$$

Equation 7.26

where x_{ik} is the ith row of X_k. We see then that this is the same as the formula for Euclidean distance in individual k's personal space.

Rotation

It is very important to note that the dimensions of the WMDS joint space cannot be orthogonally rotated without violating the basic definition of the model (unlike the CMDS and RMDS dimensions, which can be rotated). This can be seen by defining the rotated stimulus space

$$X^* = XT$$

Equation 7.27

where T is an $r \times r$ orthogonal rotation matrix such that $TT' = T'T = I$. It follows that the distances between points in the rotated space are

$$d_{ijk} = [(x^*_{ik} - x^*_{jk})W_k(x^*_{ik} - x^*_{jk})']^{\frac{1}{2}}$$
$$d_{ijk} = [(x_{ik} - x_{jk})TW_kT'(x_{ik} - x_{jk})']^{\frac{1}{2}}$$
$$d_{ijk} = [(x_{ik} - x_{jk})W^*_k(x_{ik} - x_{jk})']^{\frac{1}{2}}$$

Equation 7.28

While it appears that the distances defined by the last equation satisfy the definition of the weighted Euclidean model, the matrix W^*_k in the last equation is not diagonal, thus violating the definition of the model. Therefore, orthogonal rotation is not allowed.

Details of WMDS

In this section we discuss the distinction between metric and nonmetric WMDS, the measures of fit in WMDS, and the fundamental WMDS equation.

Metric and Nonmetric WMDS

WMDS is appropriate for the same type of data as RMDS. However, RMDS generates a single distance matrix D, while WMDS generates m unique distance matrices D_k, one for each data matrix S_k. Just as in RMDS, the data can be symmetric or asymmetric, matrix or row conditional, have missing values, and be at the ordinal, interval, or ratio levels of measurement. Thus, we can have metric or nonmetric WMDS, depending on the measurement level.

The distances D_k are calculated so that they are all as much like their corresponding data matrices S_k as possible. For metric WMDS (when the data are quantitative), the least-squares problem is

$$l_k\{S_k\} = D_k^2 + E_k$$

Equation 7.29

and for nonmetric WMDS (qualitative data), the least-squares problem is

$$m_k\{S_k\} = D_k^2 + E_k$$

Equation 7.30

Thus, for WMDS, SPSS solves for the $n \times r$ matrix of coordinates X, for the m diagonal $r \times r$ matrices W_k, and also for the m transformations m_k or l_k. It does this so that the sum of squared elements in all error matrices E_k is minimal when summed over all matrices and when subject to normalization constraints on X and W_k. The scaling algorithm used by SPSS (ALSCAL) was the first to incorporate both nonmetric and metric WMDS, as well as the other types of MDS discussed above, and is considered to be the third breakthrough in multidimensional scaling (Takane et al., 1977).

Measures of Fit

The measures of fit (s-stress, stress, and RSQ) are all defined in the same way as RMDS, except that the weighted Euclidean distances D_k are used in the measures instead of the unweighted distances.

The Fundamental WMDS Equation

We can now summarize, in a single equation, the WMDS data analysis problem being solved by the MDS procedure. The fundamental equation is

$$S_k \stackrel{\underline{\ell}}{} T_k = D_k^2 + E_k$$

Equation 7.31

This equation parallels the fundamental CMDS and RMDS equations and is to be understood in a similar fashion.

Example: Perceived Body-Part Structure

We return to the Jacobowitz data (Young, 1974) concerning how children and adults understand the relationship between various parts of the body. The data are the same as those discussed for RMDS (see Table 7.1).

The WMDS results are shown in Figure 7.30 and Figure 7.31. These are the results of applying the WMDS model to the data for both the children and adults simultaneously. Figure 7.30 displays a three-dimensional stimulus space X (with the origin, which is not shown, at the center), and Figure 7.31 shows the positive portion of the three-dimensional weight space W (the origin is where the sides all intersect).

We can see in Figure 7.30 that the stimulus space displays the overall hierarchical structure that was hypothesized by Jacobowitz to exist in this data. We can also see in Figure 7.31 that the weights for adults and children occupy different portions of the space, implying that adults and children have different perceptions/cognitions concerning the body parts.

Figure 7.30   Three-dimensional stimulus space

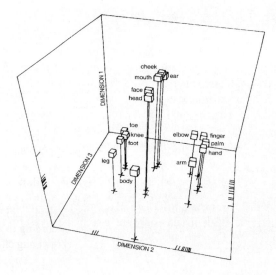

Figure 7.31   Positive portion of the three-dimensional weight space

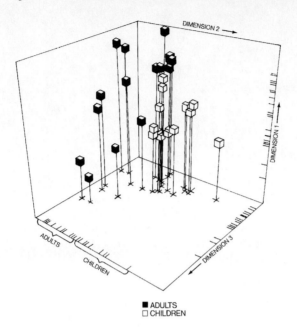

The weight space shows that the adults generally have a relatively small weight on dimension 2 (they are all on the left side of the space), whereas the children generally have a relatively small weight on dimension 3 (they are at the back of the space). This gives us a way to look at individual differences between adults and children. We can construct a hypothetical adult who has no weight on dimension 2 and a hypothetical child who has no weight on dimension 3 and investigate what structures such people would have.

A hypothetical child who has no weight on dimension 3 is one who collapses the three-dimensional space into a two-dimensional space consisting only of dimensions 1 and 2. Such a space is presented in Figure 7.32. We see that this space presents a very simple version of the hierarchical structure, showing only that this hypothetical child differentiates "body" from the other body parts, which in turn are clustered according to whether they are arm parts, leg parts, or head parts. This is a structure for a very young child (in fact, it is rather like the structure derived from the data of the youngest age group, data we do not analyze in this chapter).

Figure 7.32   Hypothetical child—no weight for dimension 3

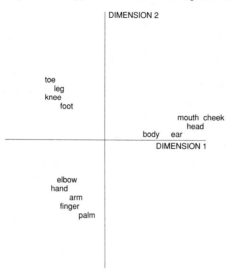

A hypothetical adult who has no weight on dimension 2 is one who collapses the three-dimensional space into a two-dimensional space consisting only of dimensions 1 and 3. This space is presented in Figure 7.33. We see that this space displays both the hierarchy and the classification. Thus, this space represents the structure of a hypothetical individual who has the most developed understanding of the relationships among body parts.

Figure 7.33   Hypothetical adult—no weight for dimension 2

The results shown in Figure 7.30 through Figure 7.33 are based on a three-dimensional WMDS analysis. The data are the same as those shown for the RMDS analysis. We have specified a three-dimensional solution because the RMDS analyses suggested that a three-dimensional solution is appropriate. We have also requested the weighted Euclidean (INDSCAL) model.

Figure 7.34 shows the iteration history for the three-dimensional solution. The initial iteration has an s-stress value of 0.29931. After seven iterations the value has improved modestly to 0.26620. At this point iterations stop because the s-stress improvement is less than 0.001. As with the RMDS analysis, for this amount of data the fit is good, but not excellent.

Figure 7.34   Iteration history for the three-dimensional solution

```
Iteration history for the 3 dimensional solution(in squared distances)

          Young's S-stress formula 1 is used.

       Iteration      S-stress      Improvement

           0           .29931
           1           .29413
           2           .27834        .01579
           3           .27264        .00570
           4           .26981        .00283
           5           .26812        .00169
           6           .26700        .00112
           7           .26620        .00080
                  Iterations stopped because
          S-stress improvement less than   .001000
```

SPSS then generates 450 stress and RSQ indexes (not shown), one for each of the 15 rows of the 30 matrices of data. In addition, there are 30 stress and RSQ indexes for each matrix of data. Then the RSQ (but not the stress) is calculated for each stimulus, averaged over matrices (this only appears for asymmetric, row conditional data). Finally, the RSQ and stress indexes averaged over all of the data are calculated. This last stress measure is 0.222, which does not equal the s-stress of 0.26620 because these formulas are defined differently, as discussed above.

The RSQ values for each matrix (not shown) vary between 0.398 and 0.969, indicating that there are no judges who are being fit very poorly, which in turn indicates that none of the judges are giving purely random judgments. There is some suggestion that the adults fit better than the children, as the adult RSQ's are higher (ranging from 0.604 to 0.969) than the children's (0.398 to 0.936).

The RSQ values for each stimulus vary between 0.704 and 0.810, except for the term "body," which fits noticeably better at 0.868. There seems to be a bit less error, or a bit more agreement, in the placement of "body" in the overall structure. There are no extremely low RSQ's for any given row of any given matrix (suggesting that none of the judged rank orders are reversed, a not uncommon problem).

Figure 7.35 shows the stimulus coordinates (*X*), and Figure 7.36 shows the subject

Figure 7.35   Stimulus coordinates

```
              Configuration derived in 3 dimensions

                      Stimulus Coordinates

                             Dimension

Stimulus    Stimulus      1         2         3
Number        Name

    1       CHEEK      -1.3626    -.4342    -.8806
    2       FACE       -1.3837    -.5132     .4784
    3       MOUTH      -1.2937    -.5574    -.8330
    4       HEAD       -1.3275    -.4392     .7624
    5       EAR        -1.2867    -.4263   -1.0778
    6       BODY        -.1832    -.1308    2.8438
    7       ARM          .5066    1.2065     .9686
    8       ELBOW        .6170    1.1554    -.6873
    9       HAND         .4571    1.4549     .0230
   10       PALM         .3128    1.5980    -.3819
   11       FINGER       .5306    1.3534    -.7872
   12       LEG         1.0279   -1.0707     .7948
   13       KNEE        1.1488   -1.0833    -.3341
   14       FOOT        1.1118   -1.0604    -.1647
   15       TOE         1.1249   -1.0529    -.7242
```

Figure 7.36   Subject weights and weirdness index

```
Subject weights measure the importance of each dimension to each subject.
Squared weights sum to RSQ.

A subject with weights proportional to the average weights has a weirdness of
zero, the minimum value.
A subject with one large weight and many low weights has a weirdness near one.
A subject with exactly one positive weight has a weirdness of one,
the maximum value for nonnegative weights.
```

```
                      Subject Weights

                               Dimension
Subject    Weird-       1          2          3
Number      ness

    1       .2723      .7010      .5758      .2109
    2       .2305      .4320      .4569      .2207
    3       .1694      .4460      .4177      .3114
    4       .3341      .6441      .6722      .2208
    5       .2281      .4977      .5516      .2903
    6       .1493      .7486      .5133      .2652
    7       .2020      .3946      .4223      .2566
    8       .1990      .4487      .4524      .2367
    9       .3247      .6780      .6681      .2195
   10       .1815      .4326      .4368      .2791
   11       .3660      .6361      .6961      .2101
   12       .1330      .5224      .3696      .3339
   13       .4692      .8585      .3704      .1026
   14       .1503      .5041      .4608      .3294
   15       .3859      .5750      .5913      .1592
   16       .2659      .8186      .4254      .2000
   17       .7846      .3841      .0928      .8281
   18       .1971      .7665      .4877      .2321
   19       .4360      .4316      .3532      .5428
   20       .2459      .7663      .3992      .1984
   21       .4257      .7679      .4145      .1051
   22       .4724      .9040      .1454      .2856
   23       .4150      .8484      .4743      .1219
   24       .4116      .9019      .1958      .2759
   25       .7125      .9105      .3052      .0000
   26       .0436      .7525      .5285      .3491
   27       .6492      .2883      .2988      .7115
   28       .2313      .7800      .3310      .4266
   29       .5126      .6724      .2157      .6323
   30       .4585      .7017      .2432      .5964
Overall importance
of each dimension:     .4418      .1974      .1268
```

weights (*W*). Displayed with the subject weights is the weirdness index, whose interpretation is briefly noted on the output and is explained extensively in the next section. It is useful to look over the values of the weirdness index for values near 1.0, as these values indicate the associated subject's weights w_k are unusual. We see that some of the weirdness values for the children (first 15 values) range up to 0.48, whereas these values range up to 0.79 for adults (subjects 16 through 30), since there are five adults with values higher than the children's values. This suggests that there are more adults than children who have at least one very low weight, indicating that more of the adults tend to have nearly two-dimensional solutions.

Figure 7.37 shows an SPSS plot of the stimulus coordinates used to create the display in Figure 7.30.

Figure 7.37   Plot of stimulus coordinates

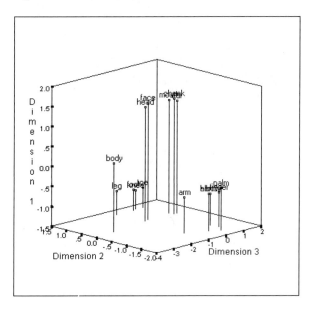

Figure 7.38, Figure 7.39, and Figure 7.40 show the plots of derived subject weights. Individuals are identified in these plots by the subject numbers shown in Figure 7.36. The correct interpretation of the three plots shown here is that the points plotted for each individual represent the ends of vectors drawn from the origin of the space. We interpret both the direction and the length of each vector. If two vectors point in the same direction, they represent subjects who have equivalent weighting schemes (the ratios of one subject's weights on the various dimensions are the same as the ratios of the other subject's weights) and, therefore, the same stimulus structure in their personal stimulus spaces. This is true even if the vectors are of different lengths, since the length simply indicates goodness of fit (the squared length of a vector—that is, the sum of the squared weights—equals RSQ).

Figure 7.38   Plot of derived subject weights, dimension 1 vs. dimension 2

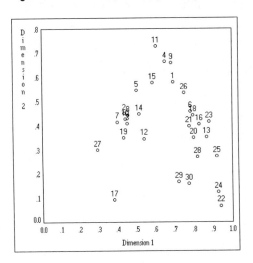

Figure 7.39   Plot of derived subject weights, dimension 1 vs. dimension 3

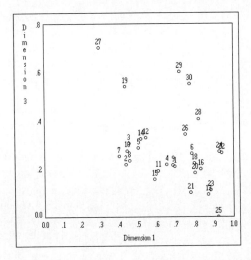

Figure 7.40   Plot of derived subject weights, dimension 2 vs. dimension 3

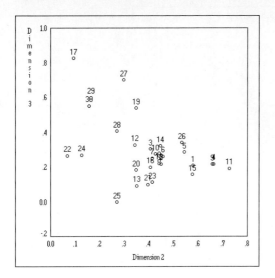

With this in mind, let's look at the three weight space plots. In Figure 7.38, we note that if we draw a line from the origin through the subject whose plot symbol is 12 (in the middle of the plot), then all the subjects below the line are adults (with two exceptions) and all the subjects above the line are children (with four exceptions). Thus, essentially all adults weight dimension 1 (horizontal axis) more heavily relative to dimension 2 (vertical axis) than is the case for children. More simply stated, adults find dimension 1 more salient than children do.

In Figure 7.39, which displays dimensions 1 and 3, we can draw a similar line from the origin to just below the subject whose plot symbol is 30. The subjects above this line are adults. Thus, some of the adults, but none of the children, find dimension 1 more important than dimension 3. Furthermore, the adults who are below this line are all further from the origin than the children, suggesting that children find neither dimension 1 nor dimension 3 as salient as adults do.

Looking at Figure 7.40, which displays dimensions 2 and 3, we conclude that some adults find dimension 3 more salient than 2, whereas all children find dimension 2 more salient than 3. Putting all of these observations together, we arrive at the interpretation presented in the results section above.

Figure 7.41 shows the scatterplot of linear fit, which presents the plot of all of the $15 \times 14 = 210$ transformed dissimilarities for each of the 30 matrices T_k (6300 elements in total) versus their corresponding elements in the matrices D. We see that this plot shows fairly little scatter, particularly when one considers all the points along the diagonal of the plot. However, there is a definite suggestion of greater scatter for the small distances than for the large distances, an artifact explained above.

Figure 7.41   Scatterplot of linear fit

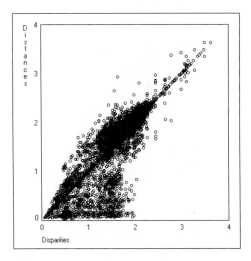

The matrix and plot of flattened subject weights appear in Figure 7.42 and Figure 7.43. In Figure 7.43, individuals are identified by the subject numbers shown in Figure 7.42. The meaning of the flattened weights, and their interpretation, is discussed below.

Figure 7.42   Flattened subject weights

```
                   Flattened Subject Weights

                              Variable
    Subject    Plot      1           2
    Number    Symbol
       1        1      -.1297      .8410
       2        2      -.6954      .9916
       3        3      -.7491      .4906
       4        4      -.4628     1.2118
       5        5      -.8391      .9984
       6        6       .2769      .0991
       7        7      -.8516      .8268
       8        8      -.6386      .8442
       9        9      -.3526     1.1184
      10        A      -.7638      .6933
      11        B      -.6837     1.5942
      12        C      -.3132     -.0803
      13        D      1.3614     -.2204
      14        E      -.6579      .4742
      15        F      -.3131     1.2373
      16        G       .7149     -.0892
      17        H     -1.4864    -1.9314
      18        I       .4634      .0791
      19        J     -1.2175     -.2589
      20        K       .8828     -.2651
      21        L       .9643      .1527
      22        M      1.9543    -2.0927
      23        N      1.0794      .0168
      24        O      1.6680    -1.7280
      25        P      2.2208     -.5667
      26        Q      -.1867      .3062
      27        R     -1.9968     -.5461
      28        S       .4794     -.9846
      29        T      -.0034    -1.5860
      30        U       .2756    -1.6262
```

Figure 7.43   Plot of flattened subject weights

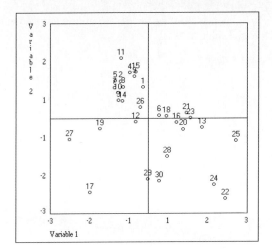

The Weirdness Index

It has been pointed out by Takane et al. (1977) and especially by MacCallum (1977) that the weights used to represent individual differences in the INDSCAL model are commonly misinterpreted. The correct interpretation of the weights is that they represent the end of a vector directed from the origin of the weight space. Thus, the angle of each subject's vector, relative to the dimensions of the space (and relative to other subjects' vectors), is interpretable. A common mistake is to treat the weights as a point and interpret the distances between points, when instead the weights should be treated as a vector and the angles between vectors should be interpreted. Thus, a common misinterpretation is that subject weight points that are "near each other" in the subject weight space are "similar," when in fact the correct interpretation is that subject weight vectors which are oriented in "roughly the same direction" are "similar."

The **weirdness index** is designed to help interpret subject weights. The index indicates how unusual or weird each subject's weights are relative to the weights of the typical subject being analyzed. The index varies from 0.00 to 1.00. A subject with a weirdness of 0.00 has weights that are proportional to the average subject's weights (to the mean weights). Such a subject is a totally typical subject. As the weight ratios become more and more extreme, the weirdness index approaches 1.00. Finally, when a subject has only one positive weight and all the remaining weights are 0, the weirdness index is 1.00. Such a subject is very weird, using only one of the dimensions of the analysis.

Consider the hypothetical subject weight space presented in Figure 7.44. In this figure we present the weight vector for just one subject. It is shown as a vector directed from the origin of the weight space. The endpoint of the vector, when projected onto dimensions 1 and 2, has Cartesian coordinates w_{k1} and w_{k2}, respectively. In the usual interpretation of individual differences, the subject is said to have weight w_{k1} on dimension 1 and weight w_{k2} on dimension 2, the weights representing the degree of importance (salience or relevance) of the dimensions to the subject.

Figure 7.44   Hypothetical subject weight space

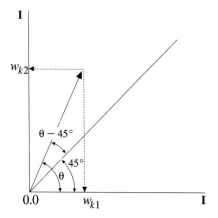

The Cartesian coordinates can be converted into polar coordinates without loss of information. The polar coordinates of vector w_k are the length of the vector and its angle relative to dimension 1. We can represent the length as r_k (not labeled in Figure 7.44) and the angle as θ_k (labeled as θ in the figure). The length r_k is set equal to the square root of the RSQ value displayed for each subject. Thus, the usual representation of individual differences, namely w_{k1} and w_{k2}, can be changed to the wholly equivalent representation r_k and θ_k. When there are more than two dimensions, we still have r_k but several θ_{ka}, one for each dimension a except the last.

The reference axis for the angle is of course arbitrary. We could have chosen dimension 2 instead of dimension 1. In fact, we could have chosen any other direction through the subject space. The 45° line through Figure 7.44, for example, could serve as the reference for a new angle $\theta - 45°$, and we could express the location of the subject's vector by its length and the angle between it and the 45° line.

Consider the 45° line. It has the simple interpretation that it represents equal weighting of both dimensions. Furthermore, as a subject's weight vector departs from this line, the subject has a more and more extreme pattern of weights. In the extreme, if the subject's vector lies along one of the dimensions, the subject is using that dimension to the complete exclusion of the other dimension.

This interpretation of the 45° line is, however, entirely dependent on a particular way of arbitrarily normalizing the subject weights. As is shown in the left-hand portion of Figure 7.45, SPSS normalizes the subject weights so that on average dimension 1 gets the heaviest weighting, dimension 2 the next heaviest, and so forth. As mentioned above, this normalization is arbitrary. If instead we were to normalize so that the 45° line represented the typical subject's weights (instead of equal weights), then the line would correspond to the average subject. This modification, which is shown in the right-hand portion of Figure 7.45, is done by simply defining a new set of weights:

$$w'_{ka} = w_{ka} \Big/ \left(\sum_{k}^{n} w_{ka} \right)$$

Equation 7.32

When there are more than two dimensions, this normalization orients the typical subject's weight vector along the line that is at a 45° angle to all dimensions.

Figure 7.45   Normalized subject weights

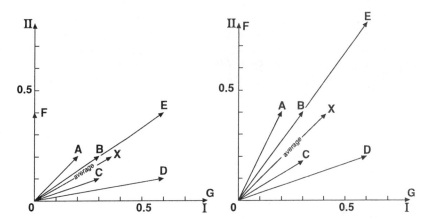

If we make this modification in the normalization of the weights, then departures from the 45° line have a very nice interpretation. First, a subject whose vector is on the 45° line is one who weights the dimensions just as the typical subject does. Second, as a subject's vector departs farther and farther from the line, the subject becomes less and less like the typical subject.

While this normalization has desirable aspects, it is used only in the definition of the weirdness index. In particular, SPSS does not normalize the weights in this fashion because it seems to be more desirable to continue with the normalization conventions adopted in other MDS programs. However, this normalization is involved in calculating the weirdness index.

The final steps in defining a convenient index of a subject's "weirdness" (that is, how far the subject's weight vector is from the average subject's vector) are first to determine the angle between the subject's normalized weight vector and the 45° line, and second to define a function of this angle that varies from 0.00 to 1.00. We do this by defining standardized vectors v_k which are unit-length and collinear with the weight vectors w_k:

$$v_{ka} = w'_{ka} / \left[\sum_a^r (w'_{ka})^2 \right]^{\frac{1}{2}}$$

Equation 7.33

The angle between a subject's weight vector and the $45°$ line can now be defined, in radians, as:

$$cos^{-1} \left[r^{-\frac{1}{2}} \left(\sum_a^r v_{ka} \right) \right]$$

Equation 7.34

This angle varies from a minimum that occurs when the subject's vector coincides with the $45°$ line (that is, when the subject's weights are proportional to the average weights) to a maximum value that occurs when the subject's vector coincides with one of the edges of the subject weight space (that is, when the subject has only one positive weight). A little investigation shows that the maximum angle, in radians, is $cos^{-1} r^{-1/2}$. Thus, if we divide by this maximum value we obtain an index that varies from 0.00 to 1.00. Finally, we divide the previous formula by this maximum value to obtain the complete formula for the weirdness index:

$$\left(cos^{-1} \left[r^{-\frac{1}{2}} \left(\sum_a^r v_{ka} \right) \right] \right) / \left(cos^{-1} r^{-\frac{1}{2}} \right)$$

Equation 7.35

Flattened Weights

As pointed out above, the subject weights in WMDS are often misinterpreted. A common mistake is to interpret the distance between subject points instead of interpreting the angle between subject vectors. In addition, standard statistical procedures are inappropriate for interpreting these weights because the weights present angular information, not linear information.

Because of these characteristics of the weights, SPSS calculates and displays information called **flattened weights**. The weight vectors, when flattened, become weight points. The angles between the vectors, when flattened, become distances between the points. Thus, the flattened weight variables are ordinary linear variables that can be used in ordinary statistical procedures. However, because of lack of independence between the weights, hypothesis testing is inappropriate. The statistical procedure should be used in a descriptive fashion only.

Flattened weights are calculated by normalizing each subject's weights so that their sum is 1.00, as illustrated by the two matrices at the bottom left of Figure 7.46. This defines a set of r normalized weight vectors. The rth one is dropped (because it is a linear combination of the others) and the remaining ones are centered and normalized, as illustrated by the matrix at bottom right in the figure. This is the complete definition of the flattening transformation used in the SPSS multidimensional scaling procedure. The rank of the flattened weights matrix is $r - 1$. Thus, any one of its variables is a linear combination of the remaining variables. Therefore, one of the variables can be dropped.

Figure 7.46   Flattened transformation

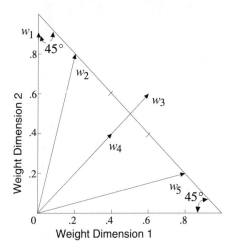

	Matrix Weights W				Normalized Matrix Weights W*			Flattened Weights
	I	II	Length		I	II	Sum	I
w_1	0	0.9	0.90	w_1*	0	1.0	1.0	−0.4
w_2	0.2	0.8	0.82	w_2*	0.2	0.8	1.0	−0.2
w_3	0.6	0.6	0.85	w_3*	0.5	0.5	1.0	0.1
w_4	0.4	0.4	0.56	w_4*	0.5	0.5	1.0	0.1
w_5	0.8	0.2	0.82	w_5*	0.8	0.2	1.0	0.4

The geometry underlying the idea of flattened weights, as implemented in SPSS, is also illustrated in Figure 7.46. The flattening transformation directly projects the weight vectors (labeled w_1 through w_5 in the figure) onto a space having one less dimension than the weight space, and which is at a 45° angle to all dimensions. In the figure, the weight space (whose dimensions are the horizontal and vertical sides of the triangle) is two-dimensional, whereas the flattened weight space (which is the hypotenuse of the triangle) is one dimensional. Note that the weight vector w_3 extends beyond the hypotenuse before flattening, so its projection onto the flattened space is shorter than the original vector. However, the weight vectors w_1 and w_2 are lengthened in their projection onto the flattened space. Finally, we look at the points in the flattened space defined by the projections from the original weight space.

Notice that this flattening transformation does not map the angles in the weight space onto distances in the flattened space in a one-to-one fashion. (In fact, there is no one-to-one flattening transformation.) An angle that is at the edge of the weight space is represented by a distance which is larger than the distance for an equal angle in the middle of the weight space. That is, subjects who are peripheral in the weight space appear to be even more peripheral in the flattened space.

How to Obtain a Multidimensional Scaling Analysis

The Multidimensional Scaling procedure uses Euclidean and weighted Euclidean models to derive stimulus coordinates or weights in multidimensional space. The Multidimensional Scaling procedure operates on distance matrices. The procedure can read an existing distance matrix as input or compute a distance matrix from raw data. Plots are available for stimulus coordinates, weights, and transformations.

The minimum specifications are:

- For an existing distance matrix (the default) or for computation of a distance matrix between variables, four or more numeric variables.

- For computation of a distance matrix between cases, at least one numeric variable.

To get a multidimensional scaling (MDS) analysis, from the menus choose:

Statistics
  Scale ▶
    Multidimensional Scaling...

This opens the Multidimensional Scaling dialog box, as shown in Figure 7.47.

Figure 7.47   Multidimensional Scaling dialog box

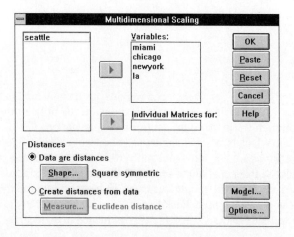

The variables in your data file appear in the source list. If data are an existing matrix, select four or more numeric variables that define the columns of the matrix and click on OK to get the default, nonmetric Euclidean solution in two dimensions. By default, the matrix is assumed to be square and symmetric. If you want SPSS to compute a distance matrix from raw data, select four or more variables for a matrix of distances between variables, or select at least one variable for a matrix of distances between cases (at least four cases are needed for a casewise analysis).

Distances. SPSS can read existing matrices or compute a distance matrix from raw data. You can choose one of the following alternatives:

❍ **Data are distances**. Data are one or more dissimilarities matrices. This is the default. Individual elements of a matrix should indicate the degree of dissimilarity between pairs represented by the rows and columns of the matrix. The currently selected matrix shape is displayed.

❍ **Create distances from data.** SPSS creates a square, symmetric matrix. The currently selected distance measure is displayed. By default, SPSS computes distances between variables.

By default, if you create distances from data, SPSS produces a single matrix. Optionally, you can get separate matrices for cases having different values of a variable. Select a variable for Individual Matrices. This option is not available if your data are already in distance matrix form.

MDS: Shape of Data

To define characteristics of existing dissimilarities matrices, choose Data are distances in the Multidimensional Scaling dialog box and click on Shape... to open the Multidimensional Scaling Shape of Data dialog box, as shown in Figure 7.48.

Figure 7.48   Multidimensional Scaling Shape of Data dialog box

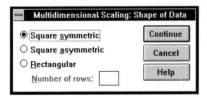

You can choose one of the following data matrix shapes:

❍ **Square symmetric**. Rows and columns represent the same items, and corresponding values in the upper and lower triangles are equal. This is the default. Optionally, you can omit values on or above the diagonal.

○ **Square asymmetric.** Rows and columns represent the same items, and corresponding values in the upper and lower triangles are not equal. Optionally, you can omit diagonal values.

○ **Rectangular.** Rows and columns represent different sets of items. By default, SPSS treats the syntax file as a single rectangular matrix. If your file contains two or more rectangular matrices, you must define the number of rows per matrix. The number of rows must be 4 or greater (since SPSS requires at least a 4×4 input matrix) and must divide evenly into the total number of rows in the data set.

Number of Matrices

SPSS calculates the number of input matrices by dividing the total number of observations in the file by the number of observations in each matrix. For square matrices, SPSS sets the number of observations in each matrix to the number of variables. For rectangular matrices, SPSS sets the number of column stimuli equal to the number of variables; the number of row stimuli is set to the value of Number of rows (if you do not define the number of rows, SPSS treats the file as a single matrix). All matrices must contain the same number of observations.

MDS: Create Measure from Data

To compute distances for use in your MDS analysis, choose Create distances from data in the Multidimensional Scaling dialog box and click on Measure... to open the Multidimensional Scaling Create Measure from Data dialog box, as shown in Figure 7.49.

Figure 7.49   Multidimensional Scaling Create Measure from Data dialog box

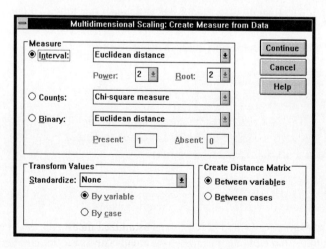

Measure. Measure selection controls the computation of dissimilarities. There are three types of measures available—interval, frequency-count, and binary. You can choose one of the following alternatives:

○ **Interval.** Dissimilarity measures for interval data. This is the default. You can choose one of the following alternatives:

⬇ **Euclidean distance.** This is the default for interval data. The distance between two items, X and Y, is the square root of the sum of the squared differences between the values for the items:

$$\text{Distance } (X, Y) = \sqrt{\sum_i (X_i - Y_i)^2}$$

Squared Euclidean distance. The distance between two items is the sum of the squared differences between the values for the items:

$$\text{Distance } (X, Y) = \sum_i (X_i - Y_i)^2$$

Chebychev. Chebychev distance metric. The distance between two items is the maximum absolute difference between the values for the items:

$$\text{Distance } (X, Y) = MAX_i |X_i - Y_i|$$

Block. City-block, or Manhattan, distance. The distance between two items is the sum of the absolute differences between the values for the items:

$$\text{Distance } (X, Y) = \sum_i |X_i - Y_i|$$

Minkowski. Distance in an absolute Minkowski power metric. The distance between two items is the pth root of the sum of the absolute differences to the pth power between the values for the items:

$$\text{Distance } (X, Y) = \left(\sum_i |X_i - Y_i|^p\right)^{\frac{1}{p}}$$

Customized. Distance in an absolute power metric. The distance between two items is the rth root of the sum of the absolute differences to the pth power between the values for the items:

$$\text{Distance } (X, Y) = \left(\sum_i |X_i - Y_i|^p\right)^{\frac{1}{r}}$$

⬇ **Power and Root.** For the Minkowski and customized measures, you can override the default power value of 2. Optionally, you can choose 1, 3, or 4. For customized measures, you can also override the default root value. Choose 1, 3, or 4. For both methods, the default values yield Euclidean distances. Appropriate selection of p and r yields squared Euclidean, Minkowski, city-block, and many other distance metrics.

○ **Counts**. Dissimilarity measures for frequency-count data. You can choose one of the following alternatives:

⬇ **Chi-square measure**. Based on the chi-square test of equality for two sets of frequencies. This is the default for counts. The magnitude of this measure depends on the total frequencies of the two items whose distance is computed. Expected values are from the model of independence of items X and Y.

$$\text{Distance}\,(X, Y)\ =\ \sqrt{\sum_i \frac{(X_i - E\,(X_i))^2}{E\,(X_i)} + \sum_i \frac{(Y_i - E\,(Y_i))^2}{E\,(Y_i)}}$$

Phi-square measure. This is the chi-square dissimilarity measure normalized by the square root of the combined frequency.

$$\text{Distance}\,(X, Y)\ =\ \sqrt{\frac{\sum_i \dfrac{(X_i - E\,(X_i))^2}{E\,(X_i)} + \sum_i \dfrac{(Y_i - E\,(Y_i))^2}{E\,(Y_i)}}{N}}$$

○ **Binary**. Dissimilarity measures for binary data. SPSS constructs a 2×2 contingency table for each pair of items. It uses this table to compute a distance measure for the pair. SPSS computes all binary measures from the values of the four cells in the table (a, b, c, and d). These values are tallies across variables (when the items are cases) or tallies across cases (when the items are variables).

		Item 2	
		Present	**Absent**
Item 1	**Present**	a	b
	Absent	c	d

You can choose one of the following binary measures:

⬇ **Euclidean distance**. Binary Euclidean distance. It has a minimum value of 0 and no upper limit. This is the default for binary data.

$$\text{Distance}\,(X, Y)\ =\ \sqrt{b + c}$$

Squared Euclidean distance. Binary squared Euclidean distance. It has a minimum value of 0 and no upper limit.

$$\text{Distance}\,(X, Y)\ =\ b + c$$

Size difference. It has a minimum value of 0 and no upper limit.

$$\text{Distance}(X, Y) = \frac{(b-c)^2}{(a+b+c+d)^2}$$

Pattern difference. It has a range of 0 to 1.

$$\text{Distance}(X, Y) = \frac{bc}{(a+b+c+d)^2}$$

Variance. It has a minimum value of 0 and no upper limit.

$$\text{Distance}(X, Y) = \frac{b+c}{4(a+b+c+d)}$$

Lance and Williams. Binary Lance-and-Williams nonmetric dissimilarity measure (also known as the Bray-Curtis nonmetric coefficient). This measure has a range of 0 to 1.

$$\text{Distance}(X, Y) = \frac{b+c}{2a+b+c}$$

Present and Absent. By default, if you select a binary measure, the data value 1 indicates presence of a characteristic and the value 0 indicates absence (other values are ignored). Optionally, you can specify different values for Present and Absent.

Transform Values. You can standardize data values for either cases or variables to equalize the effect of variables measured on different scales.

⬇ **Standardize**. To control standardization of item values prior to computation of dissimilarities, you can choose one of the following alternatives. Available for frequency-counts and interval data only.

None. Does not standardize. This is the default.

Z Scores. Standardizes values to Z scores, with a mean of 0 and a standard deviation of 1. SPSS subtracts the mean from each value for the item being standardized and then divides by the standard deviation of the values. If a standard deviation is 0, all values are set to 0.

Range −1 to 1. Standardizes values to unit range. Each value for the item being standardized is divided by the range of the values. If the range is 0, all values are left unchanged.

Range 0 to 1. Standardizes values to a range of 0 to 1. SPSS subtracts the minimum value from each item being standardized and then divides by the range. If a range is 0, all values for the item are set to 0.50.

Maximum magnitude of 1. Standardizes values to a maximum magnitude of 1. SPSS divides each value for the item being standardized by the maximum of the values. If the maximum of a set of values is 0, SPSS divides by the absolute magnitude of the smallest value and adds 1.

Mean of 1. Standardizes values to unit mean. SPSS divides each value for the item being standardized by the mean of the values. If a mean is 0, SPSS adds 1 to all values for the case or variable to produce a mean of 1.

Standard deviation of 1. Standardizes values to unit standard deviation. SPSS divides each value for the variable or case being standardized by the standard deviation of the values. SPSS does not change the values if their standard deviation is 0.

If you request standardization, you can choose one of the following alternatives:

○ **By variable.** Standardizes the values for each variable. This is the default.

○ **By case.** Standardizes the values within each case.

Create Distance Matrix. You can choose one of the following:

○ **Between variables.** Computes dissimilarities between pairs of variables. This is the default. Select this item to use variables as stimuli in the scaling analysis.

○ **Between cases.** Computes dissimilarities between pairs of cases. Select this item to use cases as stimuli in the scaling analysis.

MDS: Model

To control model specifications, click on Model... in the Multidimensional Scaling dialog box. This opens the Multidimensional Scaling Model dialog box, as shown in Figure 7.50.

Figure 7.50   Multidimensional Scaling Model dialog box

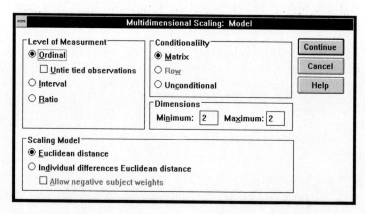

Level of Measurement. You can choose one of the following alternatives:

○ **Ordinal.** Treats data as ordinal, using Kruskal's (1964) least-squares monotonic transformation. This is the default. The analysis is nonmetric.

❑ **Untie tied observations.** By default, tied ranks remain tied throughout the analysis. Select this option to allow ties to be untied.

○ **Interval.** Data are at the interval level of measurement. Produces a metric analysis.

○ **Ratio.** Data are at the ratio level of measurement. Produces a metric analysis.

Conditionality. Conditionality concerns ways in which you can compare numbers in a data set. You can choose one of the following alternatives:

○ **Matrix.** The meaning of the numbers is conditional on the subject, or matrix. This is the default.

○ **Row.** Choose this option if you can make meaningful comparisons only among numbers within the rows of each matrix (see "Example: Perceived Body-Part Structure" on p. 181). This option is available only for asymmetric and rectangular matrices.

○ **Unconditional.** Choose this option if you can make meaningful comparisons among all values in the input matrix or matrices.

Dimensions. By default, SPSS produces a two-dimensional solution. To get solutions for other dimensions, enter minimum and maximum values between 1 and 6. To obtain a single solution, enter the same value twice. For weighted models, the minimum dimension should be at least 2.

Scaling Model. You can choose one of the following alternatives:

○ **Euclidean distance.** This is the default. The Euclidean model can be used with any type of matrix. If data are a single matrix, SPSS performs a classical multidimensional scaling (CMDS) analysis. If data are two or more matrices, a replicated multidimensional scaling (RMDS) analysis is produced.

○ **Individual differences Euclidean distance.** Scales the data using the weighted individual differences Euclidean distance (WMDS) model. This model requires two or more matrices.

❑ **Allow negative subject weights.** By default, SPSS does not permit subject weights to take negative values. To allow negative weights, select this item.

MDS: Options

To control display options, iteration criteria, or the handling of missing values, click on Options... in the Multidimensional Scaling dialog box. This opens the Multidimensional Scaling Options dialog box, as shown in Figure 7.51.

Figure 7.51   Multidimensional Scaling Options dialog box

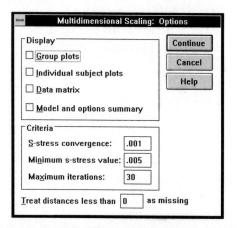

Display. You can choose one or more of the following display options:

❑ **Group plots**. Displays plots of stimulus coordinates and, for weighted models, matrix weights. Also displays a scatterplot of the linear fit between the data and the model and, where applicable, scatterplots of nonlinear fit and of the data transformation.

❑ **Individual subject plots**. Displays separate plots of each subject's data transformation for ordinal, matrix conditional data (for other types of data, only group plots are shown). Individual subject plots are not available for row conditional matrices.

❑ **Data matrix**. Displays input matrix and scaled data for each subject.

❑ **Model and options summary**. Displays data, model, output, and algorithmic options in effect for the analysis.

Criteria. SPSS uses an iterative algorithm designed to minimize the s-stress goodness-of-fit criterion. Iterations proceed until the improvement in s-stress is less than the convergence value, until s-stress reaches a minimum, or until the number of completed iterations reaches a maximum.

You can override the following settings:

S-stress convergence. By default, iteration stops when the improvement in s-stress from one iteration to the next is 0.001 or less. To increase the precision of your solution, enter a smaller number. To reduce processing time, enter a larger value. The convergence value must be non-negative. If you enter 0, SPSS performs 30 iterations.

Minimum s-stress value. By default, iteration stops when s-stress reaches 0.005 or less. If you want the iterations to continue beyond this point, enter a smaller value. Large values tend to reduce the number of iterations. The value must be greater than 0 and less than or equal to 1.

Maximum iterations. The default maximum iterations is 30. To specify a different maximum, enter a positive integer. A higher value may give you a more precise solution, but it may increase processing time substantially.

The following option is also available:

Treat distances less than n as missing. By default, dissimilarities less than 0 are treated as missing. Optionally, you can use a different cutoff for missing values. For example, if you enter 5 as a cutoff value, all distances less than 5 are treated as missing. User- and system-missing values are treated as missing regardless of the cutoff value.

Additional Features Available with Command Syntax

You can customize your multidimensional scaling analysis if you paste your selections to a syntax window and edit the resulting ALSCAL command syntax. Additional features include:

- Additional scaling models (with the MODEL subcommand).
- The ability to save coordinate and weight matrices (with the OUTFILE subcommand) and to use them as initial values in a subsequent analysis (with the FILE subcommand).
- Analysis of ordinal similarities and nominal data (with the LEVEL subcommand).
- Polynomial transformations for interval and ratio data (with the LEVEL subcommand).
- Constrained multidimensional unfolding (with the CRITERIA subcommand).
- Individual subject plots for row conditional data (with the PLOT subcommand).

See the Syntax Reference section of this manual for command syntax rules and for complete ALSCAL command syntax.

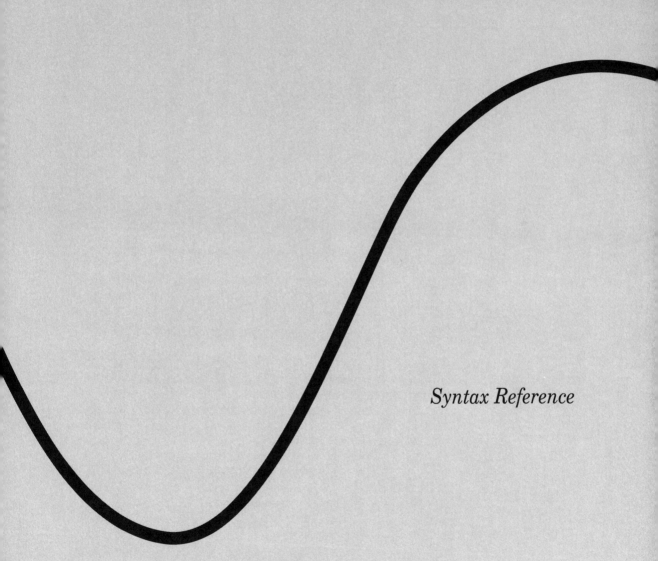

SPSS

Syntax Reference

Introduction

This syntax reference guide describes the SPSS command language underlying SPSS Professional Statistics. Most of the features of these commands are implemented in the dialog boxes; you can use those features directly from the dialog boxes or paste the syntax in a syntax window and edit it to include additional specifications or to build a command file that you can save and reuse. The features that are available only in command syntax are summarized at the end of each of the preceding chapters on statistical procedures, following the discussion of the dialog-box interface to the procedure. For more information about SPSS command syntax, see Universals in the *SPSS Base System Syntax Reference Guide*. For more information about running commands in SPSS for Windows, see Chapter 5 in the *SPSS for Windows Base System User's Guide*.

A Few Useful Terms

All terms in the SPSS command language fall into one or more of the following categories:

- **Keyword**. A word already defined by SPSS to identify a command, subcommand, or specification. Most keywords are, or resemble, common English words.
- **Command**. A specific instruction that controls the execution of SPSS.
- **Subcommand**. Additional instructions for SPSS commands. A command can contain more than one subcommand, each with its own specifications.
- **Specifications**. Instructions added to a command or subcommand. Specifications may include subcommands, keywords, numbers, arithmetic operators, variable names, special delimiters, and so forth.

Each command begins with a command keyword (which may contain more than one word). The command keyword is followed by at least one blank space and then any additional specifications. Each command ends with a command terminator, which is usually a period or a carriage return. For example:

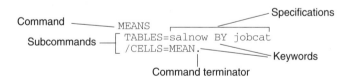

Syntax Diagrams

Each SPSS command described in this manual includes a syntax diagram that shows all the subcommands, keywords, and specifications allowed for that command. By remembering the following rules, you can use the syntax diagram as a quick reference for any command.

- Elements shown in all capital letters are keywords defined by SPSS to identify commands, subcommands, functions, operators, and other specifications.

- Elements in lower case describe specifications you supply.
- Elements in boldface type are defaults. A default indicated with ** is in effect when the keyword is not specified.
- Parentheses, apostrophes, and quotation marks are required where indicated.
- Elements enclosed in square brackets ([ ]) are optional.
- Braces ({ }) indicate a choice between elements. You can specify any one of the elements enclosed within the aligned braces.
- Ellipses indicate that an element can be repeated.
- Most abbreviations are obvious; for example, varname stands for variable name and varlist stands for a list of variables.
- The command terminator is not shown in the syntax diagrams.

Syntax Rules

Keep in mind the following simple rules when writing and editing commands in a syntax window:

- Each command must begin on a new line and end with a period (.).
- Subcommands are separated by slashes (/). The slash before the first subcommand in a command is optional in most commands.
- SPSS keywords are not case-sensitive, and three-letter abbreviations can be used for most keywords.
- Variable names must be spelled out in full.
- You can use as many lines as you want to specify a single command. However, text included within apostrophes or quotation marks must be contained on a single line.
- You can add space or break lines at almost any point where a single blank is allowed, such as around slashes, parentheses, arithmetic operators, or between variable names.
- Each line of syntax cannot exceed 80 characters.
- The period (.) must be used as the decimal indicator, regardless of your Windows international settings.

For example,

```
FREQUENCIES
 VARIABLES=JOBCAT SEXRACE
 /PERCENTILES=25 50 75
 /BARCHART.
```

and

```
freq var=jobcat sexrace /percent=25 50 75 /bar.
```

are both acceptable alternatives that generate the same results. The second example uses three-letter abbreviations and lower case, and the command is on one line.

Include Files

If your SPSS commands are contained in a command file that is specified on the SPSS IN-
CLUDE command, the syntax rules are slightly different:

- Each command must begin in the first column of a new line.
- Continuation lines within a command must be indented at least one space.
- The period at the end of the command is optional.

If you generate command syntax by pasting dialog box choices to a syntax window, the format of the commands is suitable for both INCLUDE files and commands run in a syntax window.

ALSCAL

```
ALSCAL   VARIABLES=varlist

[/FILE=file]   [CONFIG  [({INITIAL})]]   [ROWCONF  [({INITIAL})]]
                         {FIXED  }                 {FIXED  }

               [COLCONF  [({INITIAL})]]   [SUBJWGHT[({INITIAL})]]
                         {FIXED  }                 {FIXED  }

               [STIMWGHT[({INITIAL})]]
                        {FIXED  }

[/INPUT=ROWS  ({ALL**})]
              { n   }

[/SHAPE={SYMMETRIC**}]
        {ASYMMETRIC }
        {RECTANGULAR}

[/LEVEL={ORDINAL**   [([UNTIE] [SIMILAR])]}]
        {INTERVAL[({1})]                  }
        {         {n}                     }
        {RATIO[({1})]                     }
        {       {n}                       }
        {NOMINAL                          }

[/CONDITION={MATRIX       }]
            {ROW          }
            {UNCONDITIONAL}

[/{MODEL }={EUCLID**}]
  {METHOD} {INDSCAL }
           {ASCAL   }
           {AINDS   }
           {GEMSCAL }

[/CRITERIA=[NEGATIVE]  [CUTOFF({0**})]  [CONVERGE({.001})]
                              { n }              { n }

           [ITER({30})]  [STRESSMIN({.005})]  [NOULB]
                 {n }               { n }

           [DIMENS({2**      })]  [DIRECTIONS(n)]
                   {min[,max]}

           [CONSTRAIN]  [TIESTORE(n)]]

[/PRINT=[DATA] [HEADER]]     [/PLOT=[DEFAULT] [ALL]]

[/OUTFILE=file]

[/MATRIX=IN({file})]
            {*   }
```

**Default if the subcommand is omitted.

Example:

```
ALSCAL VARIABLES=ATLANTA TO TAMPA.
```

*ALSCAL was originally designed and programmed by Forrest W. Young, Yoshio Takane,
and Rostyslaw J. Lewyckyj of the Psychometric Laboratory, University of North Carolina.*

Overview

ALSCAL uses an alternating least-squares algorithm to perform multidimensional scaling (MDS) and multidimensional unfolding (MDU). You can select one of the five models to obtain stimulus coordinates and/or weights in multidimensional space.

Options

Data Input. You can read inline data matrices, including all types of two- or three-way data, such as a single matrix or a matrix for each of several subjects, using the INPUT subcommand. You can read square (symmetrical or asymmetrical) or rectangular matrices of proximities with the SHAPE subcommand and proximity matrices created by PROXIMITIES and CLUSTER with the MATRIX subcommand. You can also read a file of coordinates and/or weights to provide initial or fixed values for the scaling process with the FILE subcommand.

Methodological Assumptions. You can specify data as matrix-conditional, row-conditional, or unconditional on the CONDITION subcommand. You can treat data as nonmetric (nominal or ordinal) or as metric (interval or ratio) using the LEVEL subcommand. You can also use LEVEL to identify ordinal-level proximity data as measures of similarity or dissimilarity and can specify tied observations as untied (continuous) or leave them tied (discrete).

Model Selection. You can specify most commonly used multidimensional scaling models by selecting the correct combination of ALSCAL subcommands, keywords, and criteria. In addition to the default Euclidean distance model, the MODEL subcommand offers the individual differences (weighted) Euclidean distance model (INDSCAL), the asymmetric Euclidean distance model (ASCAL), the asymmetric individual differences Euclidean distance model (AINDS), and the generalized Euclidean metric individual differences model (GEMSCAL).

Output. You can produce output that includes raw and scaled input data, missing-value patterns, normalized data with means, squared data with additive constants, each subject's scalar product and individual weight space, plots of linear or nonlinear fit, and plots of the data transformations using the PRINT and PLOT subcommands.

Basic Specification

The basic specification is VARIABLES followed by a variable list. By default, ALSCAL produces a two-dimensional nonmetric Euclidean multidimensional scaling solution. Input is assumed to be one or more square symmetric matrices with data elements that are dissimilarities at the ordinal level of measurement. Ties are not untied, and conditionality is by subject. Values less than 0 are treated as missing. The default output includes the improvement in Young's s-stress for successive iterations, two measures of fit for each input matrix (Kruskal's stress and the squared correlation, RSQ), and the derived configurations for each of the dimensions.

Subcommand Order

Subcommands can be named in any order.

Operations

- ALSCAL calculates the number of input matrices by dividing the total number of observations in the data set by the number of rows in each matrix. All matrices must contain the same number of rows. This number is determined by the settings on SHAPE and INPUT (if used). For square matrix data, the number of rows in the matrix equals the number of variables. For rectangular matrix data, it equals the number of rows specified or implied. For additional information, see the INPUT and SHAPE subcommands on pp. 233–234.

- ALSCAL ignores user-missing specifications in all variables in the configuration/weights file (see the FILE subcommand on p. 235). The system-missing value is converted to 0.

- With split-file data, ALSCAL reads initial or fixed configurations from the configuration/weights file for each split-file group (see the FILE subcommand on p. 235). If there is only one initial configuration in the file, ALSCAL rereads these initial or fixed values for successive split-file groups.

- By default, ALSCAL estimates upper and lower bounds on missing values in the working data file in order to compute the initial configuration. To prevent this, specify CRITERIA=NOULB. Missing values are always ignored during the iterative process.

Limitations

- Maximum 100 variables on the VARIABLES subcommand.
- Maximum six dimensions can be scaled.
- ALSCAL does not recognize data weights created by the WEIGHT command.
- ALSCAL analyses can include no more than 32,767 values in each of the input matrices. Large analyses may require significant computing time.

Example

```
* Air distances among U.S. cities.
* Data are from Johnson and Wichern (1982), page 563.
DATA LIST
 /ATLANTA BOSTON CINCNATI COLUMBUS DALLAS INDNPLIS
   LITTROCK LOSANGEL MEMPHIS STLOUIS SPOKANE TAMPA 1-60.
BEGIN DATA
    0
 1068    0
  461  867    0
  549  769  107    0
  805 1819  943 1050    0
  508  941  108  172  882    0
  505 1494  618  725  325  562    0
 2197 3052 2186 2245 1403 2080 1701    0
  366 1355  502  586  464  436  137 1831    0
  558 1178  338  409  645  234  353 1848  294    0
 2467 2747 2067 2131 1891 1959 1988 1227 2042 1820    0
  467 1379  928  985 1077  975  912 2480  779 1016 2821    0
END DATA.
```

```
ALSCAL VARIABLES=ATLANTA TO TAMPA
  /PLOT.
```

- By default, ALSCAL assumes a symmetric matrix of dissimilarities for ordinal-level variables. Only values below the diagonal are used. The upper triangle can be left blank. The 12 cities form the rows and columns of the matrix.
- The result is a classical MDS analysis that reproduces a map of the United States when the output is rotated to a north-south by east-west orientation.

VARIABLES Subcommand

VARIABLES identifies the columns in the proximity matrix or matrices that ALSCAL reads.

- VARIABLES is required and can name only numeric variables.
- Each matrix must have at least four rows and four columns.

INPUT Subcommand

ALSCAL reads data row by row, with each case in the working data file representing a single row in the data matrix. (VARIABLES specifies the columns.) Use INPUT when reading rectangular data matrices to specify how many rows are in each matrix.

- The specification on INPUT is ROWS. If INPUT is not specified or is specified without ROWS, the default is ROWS(ALL). ALSCAL assumes that each case in the working data file represents one row of a single input matrix, and the result is a square matrix.
- You can specify the number of rows (n) in each matrix in parentheses after keyword ROWS. The number of matrices equals the number of observations divided by the number specified.
- The number specified on ROWS must be at least 4 and must divide evenly into the total number of rows in the data.
- With split-file data, n refers to the number of cases in each split-file group. All split-file groups must have the same number of rows.

Example

```
ALSCAL VARIABLES=V1 to V7 /INPUT=ROWS(8).
```

- INPUT indicates there are eight rows per matrix, with each case in the working data file representing one row.
- The total number of cases must be divisible by 8.

SHAPE Subcommand

Use SHAPE to specify the structure of the input data matrix or matrices.

- You can specify one of the three keywords listed below.
- Both SYMMETRIC and ASYMMETRIC refer to square matrix data.

SYMMETRIC *Symmetric data matrix or matrices.* For a symmetric matrix, ALSCAL looks only at the values below the diagonal. Values on and above the diagonal can be omitted. This is the default.

ASYMMETRIC *Asymmetric data matrix or matrices.* The corresponding values in the upper and lower triangles are not all equal. The diagonal is ignored.

RECTANGULAR *Rectangular data matrix or matrices.* The rows and columns represent different sets of items.

Example

```
ALSCAL VAR=V1 TO V8 /SHAPE=RECTANGULAR.
```

- ALSCAL performs a classical MDU analysis, treating the rows and columns as separate sets of items.

LEVEL Subcommand

LEVEL identifies the level of measurement for the values in the data matrix or matrices. You can specify one of the keywords defined below.

ORDINAL *Ordinal-level data.* This specification is the default. It treats the data as ordinal, using Kruskal's (1964) least-squares monotonic transformation. The analysis is nonmetric. By default, the data are treated as discrete dissimilarities. Ties in the data remain tied throughout the analysis. To change the default, specify UNTIE and/or SIMILAR in parentheses. UNTIE treats the data as continuous and resolves ties in an optimal fashion; SIMILAR treats the data as similarities. UNTIE and SIMILAR cannot be used with the other levels of measurement.

INTERVAL(n) *Interval-level data.* This specification produces a metric analysis of the data using classical regression techniques. You can specify any integer from 1 to 4 in parentheses for the degree of polynomial transformation to be fit to the data. The default is 1.

RATIO(n) *Ratio-level data.* This specification produces a metric analysis. You can specify an integer from 1 to 4 in parentheses for the degree of polynomial transformation. The default is 1.

NOMINAL *Nominal-level data.* This specification treats the data as nominal by using a least-squares categorical transformation (Takane et al, 1977). This option produces a nonmetric analysis of nominal data. It is useful when there are few observed categories, when there are many observations in each category, and when the order of the categories is not known.

Example

```
ALSCAL VAR=ATLANTA TO TAMPA /LEVEL=INTERVAL(2).
```

- This example identifies the distances between U.S. cities as interval-level data. The 2 in parentheses indicates a polynomial transformation with linear and quadratic terms.

CONDITION Subcommand

CONDITION specifies which numbers in a data set are comparable.

MATRIX   *Only numbers within each matrix are comparable.* If each matrix represents a different subject, this specification makes comparisons conditional by subject. This is the default.

ROW   *Only numbers within the same row are comparable.* This specification is appropriate only for asymmetric or rectangular data. They cannot be used when ASCAL or AINDS is specified on MODEL.

UNCONDITIONAL   *All numbers are comparable.* Comparisons can be made among any values in the input matrix or matrices.

Example

```
ALSCAL VAR=V1 TO V8 /SHAPE=RECTANGULAR /CONDITION=ROW.
```

- ALSCAL performs a Euclidean MDU analysis conditional on comparisons within rows.

FILE Subcommand

ALSCAL can read proximity data from the working data file or, with the MATRIX subcommand, from a matrix data file created by PROXIMITIES or CLUSTER. The FILE subcommand reads a file containing additional data: an initial or fixed configuration for the coordinates of the stimuli and/or weights for the matrices being scaled. This file can be created with the OUTFILE subcommand on ALSCAL or with an SPSS input program.

- The minimum specification is the file that contains the configurations and/or weights.

- FILE can include additional specifications that define the structure of the configuration/weights file.

- The variables in the configuration/weights file that correspond to successive ALSCAL dimensions must have the names *DIM1, DIM2. . . DIMr*, where *r* is the maximum number of ALSCAL dimensions. The file must also contain the short string variable *TYPE_* to identify the types of values in all rows.

- Values for the variable *TYPE_* can be CONFIG, ROWCONF, COLCONF, SUBJWGHT, and STIMWGHT, in that order. Each value can be truncated to the first three letters. Stimulus coordinate values are specified as CONFIG; row stimulus coordinates as ROWCONF; column stimulus coordinates as COLCONF; and subject and stimulus weights as SUBJWGHT and STIMWGHT, respectively. ALSCAL accepts CONFIG and ROWCONF interchangeably.

- ALSCAL skips unneeded types as long as they appear in the file in their proper order. Generalized weights (GEM) and flattened subject weights (FLA) cannot be initialized or fixed and will always be skipped. (These weights can be generated by ALSCAL but cannot be used as input.)

The following list summarizes the optional specifications that can be used on FILE to define the structure of the configuration/weights file.

- Each specification can be further identified with option INITIAL or FIXED in parentheses.

- INITIAL is the default. INITIAL indicates that the external configuration or weights are to be used as initial coordinates and are to be modified during each iteration.
- FIXED forces ALSCAL to use the externally defined structure without modification to calculate the best values for all unfixed portions of the structure.

CONFIG   *Read stimulus configuration.* The configuration/weights file contains initial stimulus coordinates. Input of this type is appropriate when SHAPE=SYMMETRIC or SHAPE=ASYMMETRIC, or when the number of variables in a matrix equals the number of variables on the ALSCAL command. The value of the *TYPE_* variable must be either CON or ROW for all stimulus coordinates for the configuration.

ROWCONF   *Read row stimulus configuration.* The configuration/weights file contains initial row stimulus coordinates. This specification is appropriate if SHAPE=RECTANGULAR and if the number of ROWCONF rows in the matrix equals the number of rows specified on the INPUT subcommand (or, if INPUT is omitted, the number of cases in the working data file). The value of *TYPE_* must be either ROW or CON for the set of coordinates for each row.

COLCONF   *Read column stimulus configuration.* The configuration/weights file contains initial column stimulus coordinates. This kind of file can be used only if SHAPE=RECTANGULAR and if the number of COLCONF rows in the matrix equals the number of variables on the ALSCAL command. The value of *TYPE_* must be COL for the set of coordinates for each column.

SUBJWGHT   *Read subject (matrix) weights.* The configuration/weights file contains subject weights. The number of observations in a subject-weights matrix must equal the number of matrices in the proximity file. Subject weights can be used only if the model is INDSCAL, AINDS, or GEMSCAL. The value of *TYPE_* for each set of weights must be SUB.

STIMWGHT   *Read stimulus weights.* The configuration/weights file contains stimulus weights. The number of observations in the configuration/weights file must equal the number of matrices in the proximity file. Stimulus weights can be used only if the model is AINDS or ASCAL. The value of *TYPE_* for each set of weights must be STI.

If the optional specifications for the configuration/weights file are not specified on FILE, ALSCAL sequentially reads the *TYPE_* values appropriate to the model and shape according to the defaults in Table 1.

Example

```
ALSCAL VAR=V1 TO V8 /FILE=ONE CON(FIXED) STI(INITIAL).
```

- ALSCAL reads the configuration/weights file *ONE*.
- The stimulus coordinates are read as fixed values, and the stimulus weights are read as initial values.

Table 1   Default specifications for the FILE subcommand

Shape	Model	Default specifications
SYMMETRIC	EUCLID	CONFIG (or ROWCONF)
	INDSCAL	CONFIG (or ROWCONF) SUBJWGHT
	GEMSCAL	CONFIG (or ROWCONF) SUBJWGHT
ASYMMETRIC	EUCLID	CONFIG (or ROWCONF)
	INDSCAL	CONFIG (or ROWCONF) SUBJWGHT
	GEMSCAL	CONFIG (or ROWCONF) SUBJWGHT
	ASCAL	CONFIG (or ROWCONF) STIMWGHT
	AINDS	CONFIG (or ROWCONF) SUBJWGHT STIMWGHT
RECTANGULAR	EUCLID	ROWCONF (or CONFIG) COLCONF
	INDSCAL	ROWCONF (or CONFIG) COLCONF SUBJWGHT
	GEMSCAL	ROWCONF (or CONFIG) COLCONF SUBJWGHT

MODEL Subcommand

MODEL (alias METHOD) defines the scaling model for the analysis. The only specification is MODEL (or METHOD) and any one of the five scaling and unfolding model types. EUCLID is the default.

EUCLID   *Euclidean distance model.* This model can be used with any type of proximity matrix and is the default.

INDSCAL   *Individual differences (weighted) Euclidean distance model.* ALSCAL scales the data using the weighted individual differences Euclidean distance model proposed by Carroll and Chang (1970). This type of analysis can be specified only if the analysis involves more than one data matrix and more than one dimension is specified on CRITERIA.

ASCAL   *Asymmetric Euclidean distance model.* This model (Young, 1975) can be used only if SHAPE=ASYMMETRIC and more than one dimension is requested on CRITERIA.

AINDS   *Asymmetric individual differences Euclidean distance model.* This option combines Young's (1975) asymmetric Euclidean model with the individual differences model proposed by Carroll and Chang (1970). This model can only be used when SHAPE=ASYMMETRIC, the analysis involves more than one data matrix, and more than one dimension is specified on CRITERIA.

GEMSCAL   *Generalized Euclidean metric individual differences model.* The number of directions for this model is set with the DIRECTIONS option on CRITERIA. The number of directions specified can be equal to but cannot exceed the group space dimensionality. By default, the number of directions equals the number of dimensions in the solution.

Example

```
ALSCAL VARIABLES = V1 TO V6
 /SHAPE = ASYMMETRIC
 /CONDITION = ROW
 /MODEL = GEMSCAL
 /CRITERIA = DIM(4) DIRECTIONS(4).
```

- In this example, the number of directions in the GEMSCAL model is set to 4.

CRITERIA Subcommand

Use CRITERIA to control features of the scaling model and to set convergence criteria for the solution. You can specify one or more of the following:

CONVERGE(n)   *Stop iterations if the change in s-stress is less than* n. S-stress is a goodness-of-fit index. By default, n=0.001. To increase the precision of a solution, specify a smaller value, for example 0.0001. To obtain a less precise solution (perhaps to reduce computing time), specify a larger value, for example 0.05. Negative values are not allowed. If n= 0, the algorithm will iterate 30 times unless a value is specified with the ITER option.

ITER(n)   *Set the maximum number of iterations to* n. The default value is 30. A higher value will give a more precise solution but will take longer to compute.

STRESSMIN(n)   *Set the minimum stress value to* n. By default, ALSCAL stops iterating when the value of s-stress is 0.005 or less. STRESSMIN can be assigned any value from 0 to 1.

NEGATIVE   *Allow negative weights in individual differences models.* By default, ALSCAL does not permit the weights to be negative. Weighted models include INDSCAL, ASCAL, AINDS, and GEMSCAL. The NEGATIVE option is ignored if the model is EUCLID.

CUTOFF(n)   *Set the cutoff value for treating distances as missing to* n. By default, ALSCAL treats all negative similarities (or dissimilarities) as missing, and 0 and positive similarities as nonmissing (n=0). Changing the CUTOFF value causes ALSCAL to treat similarities greater than or equal to that value as nonmissing. User- and system-missing values are considered missing regardless of the CUTOFF specification.

NOULB   *Do not estimate upper and lower bounds on missing values.* By default, ALSCAL estimates the upper and lower bounds on missing values in order to compute the initial configuration. This specification has no effect during the iterative process, when missing values are ignored.

DIMENS(min[,max])   *Set the minimum and maximum number of dimensions in the scaling solution.* By default, ALSCAL calculates a solution with two dimensions. To obtain solutions for more than two dimensions, specify the minimum and the maximum number of dimensions in parentheses after DIMENS. The minimum and maximum can be integers between 2 and 6. A single value represents both the minimum and the maximum. For example, DIMENS(3) is equivalent to DIMENS(3,3). The minimum number of dimensions can be set to 1 only if MODEL=EUCLID.

DIRECTIONS(n)   *Set the number of principal directions in the generalized Euclidean model to* n. This option has no effect for models other than GEMSCAL. The number of principal directions can be any positive integer between 1 and the number of dimensions specified on the DIMENS option. By default, the number of directions equals the number of dimensions.

TIESTORE(n)   *Set the amount of storage needed for ties to* n. This option estimates the amount of storage needed to deal with ties in ordinal data. By default, the amount of storage is set to 1000 or the number of cells in a matrix, whichever is smaller. Should this be insufficient, ALSCAL terminates and displays a message that more space is needed.

CONSTRAIN   *Constrain multidimensional unfolding solution.* This option can be used to keep the initial constraints throughout the analysis.

PRINT Subcommand

PRINT requests output not available by default. You can specify the following:

DATA   *Display input data.* The display includes both the initial data and the scaled data for each subject according to the structure specified on SHAPE.

HEADER   *Display a header page.* The header includes the model, output, algorithmic, and data options in effect for the analysis.

- Data options listed by PRINT=HEADER include the number of rows and columns, number of matrices, measurement level, shape of the data matrix, type of data (similarity or dissimilarity), whether ties are tied or untied, conditionality, and data cutoff value.

- Model options listed by PRINT=HEADER are the type of model specified (EUCLID, INDSCAL, ASCAL, AINDS, or GEMSCAL), minimum and maximum dimensionality, and whether or not negative weights are permitted.

- Output options listed by PRINT=HEADER indicate whether the output includes the header page and input data, whether ALSCAL plotted configurations and transformations, whether an output data set was created, and whether initial stimulus coordinates, initial column stimulus coordinates, initial subject weights, and initial stimulus weights were computed.

- Algorithmic options listed by PRINT=HEADER include the maximum number of iterations permitted, the convergence criterion, the maximum s-stress value, whether or not missing data are estimated by upper and lower bounds, and the amount of storage allotted for ties in ordinal data.

Example

```
ALSCAL VAR=ATLANTA TO TAMPA /PRINT=DATA.
```

- In addition to scaled data, ALSCAL will display initial data.

PLOT Subcommand

PLOT controls the display of plots. The minimum specification is simply PLOT to produce the defaults.

DEFAULT   *Default plots.* Default plots include plots of stimulus coordinates, matrix weights (if the model is INDSCAL, AINDS, or GEMSCAL), and stimulus weights (if the model is AINDS or ASCAL). The default also includes a scatterplot of the linear fit between the data and the model and, for certain types of data, scatterplots of the nonlinear fit and the data transformation. If the SET command specifies HIGHRES=ON, ALSCAL sends all stimulus dimensions to the graphic editor and shows a 3-D plot with the first three dimensions if the solution has three or more dimensions. If HIGHRES=OFF, ALSCAL generates $d*(d-1)/2$ pages of plots for the stimulus space, where d is the number of dimensions in the solution. When appropriate, the same is true for the weight space.

ALL   *Transformation plots in addition to the default plots.* SPSS produces a separate plot for each subject if CONDITION=MATRIX and a separate plot for each row if CONDITION=ROW. For interval and ratio data, PLOT=ALL has the same effect as PLOT=DEFAULT. This option can generate voluminous output, particularly when CONDITION=ROW.

Example

```
ALSCAL VAR=V1 TO V8 /INPUT=ROWS(8) /PLOT=ALL.
```

- This command produces all the default plots (the number may be different depending on the setting of HIGHRES). It also produces a separate plot for each subject's data transformation and a plot of *V1* through *V8* in a two-dimensional space for each subject.

OUTFILE Subcommand

OUTFILE saves coordinate and weight matrices to an SPSS data file. The only specification is a name for the output file.

- The output data file has an alphanumeric (short string) variable named *TYPE_* that identifies the kind of values in each row, a numeric variable *DIMENS* that specifies the number of dimensions, a numeric variable *MATNUM* that indicates the subject (matrix) to which each set of coordinates corresponds, and variables *DIM1, DIM2...DIMn* that correspond to the *n* dimensions in the model.
- The values of any split-file variables are also included in the output file.
- The file created by OUTFILE can be used by subsequent ALSCAL commands as initial data.

The following are the types of configurations and weights that can be included in the output file:

CONFIG   *Stimulus configuration coordinates.*

ROWCONF   *Row stimulus configuration coordinates.*

COLCONF   *Column stimulus configuration coordinates.*

SUBJWGHT   *Subject (matrix) weights.*

FLATWGHT   *Flattened subject (matrix) weights.*

GEMWGHT   *Generalized weights.*

STIMWGHT   *Stimulus weights.*

Only the first three characters of each identifier are written to variable *TYPE_* in the file. For example, CONFIG becomes CON. The structure of the file is determined by the SHAPE and MODEL subcommands, as shown in Table 2 (p. 242).

Example

```
ALSCAL VAR=ATLANTA TO TAMPA /OUTFILE=ONE.
```

- OUTFILE creates the SPSS configuration/weights file *ONE* from the example of air distances between cities.

MATRIX Subcommand

MATRIX reads SPSS matrix data files. It can read a matrix written by either PROXIMITIES or CLUSTER.

- Generally, data read by ALSCAL are already in matrix form. If the matrix materials are in the working data file, you do not need to use MATRIX to read them. Simply use the VARIABLES subcommand to indicate the variables (or columns) to be used. However, if the matrix materials are not in the working data file, MATRIX must be used to specify the matrix data file that contains the matrix.
- The proximity matrices ALSCAL reads have *ROWTYPE_* values of PROX. No additional statistics should be included with these matrix materials.
- ALSCAL ignores unrecognized *ROWTYPE_* values in the matrix file. In addition, it ignores variables present in the matrix file that are not specified on the VARIABLES subcommand in ALSCAL. The order of rows and columns in the matrix is unimportant.

Table 2   Types of configurations and/or weights in output files

Shape	Model	TYPE_
SYMMETRIC	EUCLID	CON
	INDSCAL	CON SUB FLA
	GEMSCAL	CON SUB FLA GEM
ASYMMETRIC	EUCLID	CON
	INDSCAL	CON SUB FLA
	GEMSCAL	CON SUB FLA GEM
	ASCAL	CON STI
	AINDS	CON SUB FLA STI
RECTANGULAR	EUCLID	ROW COL
	INDSCAL	ROW COL SUB FLA
	GEMSCAL	ROW COL SUB FLA GEM

- Since ALSCAL does not support case labeling, it ignores values for the *ID* variable (if present) in a CLUSTER or PROXIMITIES matrix.
- If split-file processing was in effect when the matrix was written, the same split file must be in effect when ALSCAL reads that matrix.
- The specification on MATRIX is keyword IN and the matrix file in parentheses.

- MATRIX=IN cannot be used unless a working data file has already been defined. To read an existing matrix data file at the beginning of a session, first use GET to retrieve the matrix file and then specify IN(*) on MATRIX.

IN (filename)   *Read a matrix data file.* If the matrix data file is the working data file, specify an asterisk in parentheses (*). If the matrix data file is another file, specify the filename in parentheses. A matrix file read from an external file does not replace the working data file.

Example

```
PROXIMITIES V1 TO V8 /ID=NAMEVAR /MATRIX=OUT(*).
ALSCAL VAR=CASE1 TO CASE10 /MATRIX=IN(*).
```

- PROXIMITIES uses *V1* through *V8* in the working data file to generate a matrix file of Euclidean distances between each pair of cases based on the eight variables. The number of rows and columns in the resulting matrix equals the number of cases. MATRIX=OUT then replaces the working data file with this new matrix data file.
- MATRIX=IN on ALSCAL reads the matrix data file, which is the new working data file. In this instance, MATRIX is optional because the matrix materials are in the working file.
- If there were ten cases in the original working data file, ALSCAL performs a multidimensional scaling analysis in two dimensions on *CASE1* through *CASE10*.

Example

```
GET FILE PROXMTX.
ALSCAL VAR=CASE1 TO CASE10 /MATRIX=IN(*).
```

- GET retrieves the matrix data file *PROXMTX*.
- MATRIX=IN specifies an asterisk because the working data file is the matrix. MATRIX is optional, however, since the matrix materials are in the working file.

Example

```
GET FILE PRSNNL.
FREQUENCIES VARIABLE=AGE.
ALSCAL VAR=CASE1 TO CASE10 /MATRIX=IN(PROXMTX).
```

- This example performs a frequencies analysis on file *PRSNNL* and then uses a different file containing matrix data for ALSCAL. The file is an existing matrix data file.
- MATRIX=IN is required because the matrix data file, *PROXMTX*, is not the working file. *PROXMTX* does not replace *PRSNNL* as the working data file.

Specification of Analyses

Table 3 summarizes the analyses that can be performed for the major types of proximity matrices you can use with ALSCAL. Table 4 lists the specifications needed to produce these analyses for nonmetric models, and Table 5 lists the specifications for metric models. You can include additional specifications to control the precision of your analysis with CRITERIA.

Table 3   Models for types of matrix input

Matrix mode	Matrix form	Model class	Single matrix	Replications of single matrix	Two or more individual matrices
Object by object	Symmetric	Multi-dimensional scaling	CMDS Classical multi-dimensional scaling	RMDS Replicated multi-dimensional scaling	WMDS(INDSCAL) Weighted multi-dimensional scaling
	Asymmetric single process	Multi-dimensional scaling	CMDS(row conditional) Classical row conditional multi-dimensional scaling	RMDS(row conditional) Replicated row conditional multi-dimensional scaling	WMDS(row conditional) Weighted row conditional multi-dimensional scaling
	Asymmetric multiple process	Internal asymmetric multi-dimensional scaling	CAMDS Classical asymmetric multidimensional scaling	RAMDS Replicated asymmetric multidimensional scaling	WAMDS Weighted asymmetric multidimensional scaling
		External asymmetric multi-dimensional scaling	CAMDS(external) Classical external asymmetric multidimensional scaling	RAMDS(external) Replicated external asymmetric multi-dimensional scaling	WAMDS(external) Weighted external asymmetric multi-dimensional scaling
Object by attribute	Rectangular	Internal unfolding	CMDU Classical internal multidimensional unfolding	RMDU Replicated internal multidimensional unfolding	WMDU Weighted internal multi-dimensional unfolding
		External unfolding	CMDU(external) Classical external multidimensional unfolding	RMDU(external) Replicated external multidimensional unfolding	WMDU(external) Weighted external multi-dimensional unfolding

Table 4   ALSCAL specifications for nonmetric models

Matrix mode	Matrix form	Model class	Single matrix	Replications of single matrix	Two or more individual matrices
Object by object	Symmetric	Multi-dimensional scaling	ALSCAL VAR= varlist.	ALSCAL VAR= varlist.	ALSCAL VAR= varlist /MODEL=INDSCAL.
	Asymmetric single process	Multi-dimensional scaling	ALSCAL VAR= varlist /SHAPE= ASYMMETRIC /CONDITION=ROW.	ALSCAL VAR= varlist /SHAPE= ASYMMETRIC /CONDITION=ROW.	ALSCAL VAR= varlist /SHAPE=ASYMMETRIC /CONDITION=ROW /MODEL=INDSCAL.
	Asymmetric multiple process	Internal asymmetric multi-dimensional scaling	ALSCAL VAR= varlist /SHAPE= ASYMMETRIC /MODEL=ASCAL.	ALSCAL VAR= varlist /SHAPE= ASYMMETRIC /MODEL=ASCAL.	ALSCAL VAR= varlist /SHAPE= ASYMMETRIC /MODEL=AINDS.
		External asymmetric multi-dimensional scaling	ALSCAL VAR= varlist /SHAPE=ASYMMETRIC /MODEL=ASCAL /FILE=file COLCONF(FIX).	ALSCAL VAR= varlist /SHAPE= ASYMMETRIC /MODEL=ASCAL /FILE=file COLCONF(FIX).	ALSCAL VAR= varlist /SHAPE= ASYMMETRIC /MODEL=AINDS /FILE=file COLCONF(FIX).
Object by attribute	Rectangular	Internal unfolding	ALSCAL VAR= varlist /SHAPE=REC /INP=ROWS /CONDITION=ROW.	ALSCAL VAR= varlist /SHAPE=REC /INP=ROWS /CONDITION(ROW).	ALSCAL VAR= varlist /SHAPE=REC /INP=ROWS /CONDITION=ROW /MODEL=INDSCAL.
		External unfolding	ALSCAL VAR= varlist /SHAPE=REC /INP=ROWS /CONDITION=ROW /FILE=file ROWCONF(FIX).	ALSCAL VAR= varlist /SHAPE=REC /INP=ROWS /CONDITION=ROW /FILE=file ROWCONF(FIX).	ALSCAL VAR= varlist /SHAPE=REC /INP=ROWS /CONDITION=ROW /FILE=file ROWCONF(FIX) /MODEL=INDSCAL.

Table 5   ALSCAL specifications for metric models

Matrix mode	Matrix form	Model class	Single matrix	Replications of single matrix	Two or more individual matrices
Object by object	Symmetric	Multi-dimensional scaling	ALSCAL VAR= varlist /LEVEL=INT.	ALSCAL VAR= varlist /LEVEL=INT.	ALSCAL VAR= varlist /LEVEL=INT /MODEL=INDSCAL.
	Asymmetric single process	Multi-dimensional scaling	ALSCAL VAR= varlist /SHAPE=ASYMMETRIC /CONDITION=ROW /LEVEL=INT.	ALSCAL VAR= varlist /SHAPE= ASYMMETRIC /CONDITION=ROW /LEVEL=INT.	ALSCAL VAR= varlist /SHAPE= ASYMMETRIC /CONDITION=ROW /LEVEL=INT /MODEL=INDSCAL.
	Asymmetric multiple process	Internal asymmetric multi-dimensional scaling	ALSCAL VAR= varlist /SHAPE=ASYMMETRIC /LEVEL=INT /MODEL=ASCAL.	ALSCAL VAR= varlist /SHAPE= ASYMMETRIC /LEVEL=INT /MODEL=ASCAL.	ALSCAL VAR= varlist /SHAPE=ASYMMETRIC /LEVEL=INT /MODEL=AINDS.
		External asymmetric multi-dimensional scaling	ALSCAL VAR= varlist /SHAPE=ASYMMETRIC /LEVEL=INT /MODEL=ASCAL /FILE=file COLCONF(FIX).	ALSCAL VAR= varlist /SHAPE= ASYMMETRIC /LEVEL=INT /MODEL=ASCAL /FILE=file COLCONF(FIX).	ALSCAL VAR= varlist /SHAPE= ASYMMETRIC /LEVEL=INT /MODEL=AINDS /FILE=file COLCONF(FIX).
Object by attribute	Rectangular	Internal unfolding	ALSCAL VAR= varlist /SHAPE=REC /INP=ROWS /CONDITION=ROW /LEVEL=INT.	ALSCAL VAR= varlist /SHAPE=REC /INP=ROWS /CONDITION=ROW /LEVEL=INT.	ALSCAL VAR= varlist /SHAPE=REC /INP=ROWS /CONDITION=ROW /LEVEL=INT /MODEL=INDSCAL.
		External unfolding	ALSCAL VAR= varlist /SHAPE=REC /INP=ROWS /CONDITION=ROW /LEVEL=INT /FILE=file ROWCONF(FIX).	ALSCAL VAR= varlist /SHAPE=REC /INP=ROWS /CONDITION=ROW /LEVEL=INT /FILE=file ROWCONF(FIX).	ALSCAL VAR= varlist /SHAPE=REC /INP=ROWS /CONDITION=ROW /LEVEL=INT /FILE=file ROWCONF(FIX) /MODEL=INDSCAL.

CLUSTER

```
CLUSTER varlist [/MISSING=LISTWISE**] [INCLUDE]

[/MEASURE={SEUCLID** }] [/METHOD={BAVERAGE**}[(rootname)] [...]]
           {EUCLID    }          {WAVERAGE  }
           {COSINE    }          {SINGLE    }
           {POWER(p,r)}          {COMPLETE  }
           {BLOCK     }          {CENTROID  }
           {CHEBYCHEV }          {MEDIAN    }
           {DEFAULT** }          {WARD      }
                                 {DEFAULT** }

[/SAVE=CLUSTER({level  })]   [/ID=varname]
              {min,max}

[/PRINT=[CLUSTER({level  })] [DISTANCE] [SCHEDULE**] [NONE]]
                {min,max}

[/PLOT=[VICICLE**[(min[,max[,inc]])]]] [DENDROGRAM] [NONE]]
       [HICICLE[(min[,max[,inc]])]]]

[/MATRIX=[IN({file})] [OUT({file})]]
            {*   }        {*   }
```

** Default if the subcommand is omitted.

Example:
```
CLUSTER V1 TO V4
 /PLOT=DENDROGRAM
 /PRINT=CLUSTER (2,4).
```

Overview

CLUSTER produces hierarchical clusters of items based on distance measures of dissimilarity or similarity. The items being clustered are usually cases from the working data file, and the distance measures are computed from their values for one or more variables. You can also cluster variables if you read in a matrix measuring distances between variables. Cluster analysis is discussed in Anderberg (1973).

Options

Cluster Measures and Methods. You can specify one of six similarity or distance measures on the MEASURE subcommand, and you can cluster items using any one of seven methods using the METHOD subcommand: single linkage, complete linkage, between- and within-groups average linkage, and median, centroid, and Ward's methods. You can request more than one clustering method on a single CLUSTER command.

New Variables. You can save cluster membership for specified solutions as new variables in the working data file using the SAVE subcommand.

Display and Plots. You can display cluster membership, the distance or similarity matrix used to cluster variables or cases, and the agglomeration schedule for the cluster solution

247

with the PRINT subcommand. You can request either a horizontal or vertical icicle plot or a dendrogram of the cluster solution, and you can control the cluster levels displayed on the icicle plot with the PLOT subcommand. You can also specify a variable to be used as a case identifier in the display on ID.

Matrix Input and Output. You can write out the distance matrix and use it in subsequent CLUSTER, PROXIMITIES, or ALSCAL analyses with the MATRIX subcommand. You can also read in matrices produced by other CLUSTER or PROXIMITIES procedures.

Basic Specification

The basic specification is a variable list. CLUSTER assumes the items being clustered are cases and uses the squared Euclidean distances between cases on the variables in the analysis as the measure of distance.

Subcommand Order

- The variable list must be specified first.
- The remaining subcommands can be specified in any order.

Syntax Rules

- The variable list and subcommands can each be specified once.
- More than one clustering method can be specified.

Operations

The CLUSTER procedure involves four steps:

- First, CLUSTER obtains distance measures of similarities between or distances separating initial clusters (individual cases or individual variables if the input is a matrix measuring distances between variables).
- Second, it combines the two nearest clusters to form a new cluster.
- Third, it recomputes similarities or distances of existing clusters to the new cluster.
- It then returns to the second step until all items are combined in one cluster.

This process yields a hierarchy of cluster solutions, ranging from one overall cluster to as many clusters as there are items being clustered. Clusters at a higher level can contain several lower-level clusters. Within each level, the clusters are disjoint (each item belongs to only one cluster).

- CLUSTER identifies clusters in solutions by sequential integers (1, 2, 3, and so on).
- When a narrow width is defined on the SET command, plots exceeding the defined width are broken into two sections and are displayed one after the other.
- The BOX specification on the SET command controls the character used in dendrograms.

Limitations

- CLUSTER stores cases and a lower-triangular matrix of proximities in memory. Storage requirements increase rapidly with the number of cases. You should be able to cluster 100 cases using a small number of variables in an 80K workspace.
- CLUSTER does not honor weights.

Example

```
CLUSTER V1 TO V4
  /PLOT=DENDROGRAM
  /PRINT=CLUSTER (2 4).
```

- This example clusters cases based on their values for all variables between and including *V1* and *V4* on the SPSS working data file.
- The analysis uses the default measure of distance (squared Euclidean) and the default clustering method (average linkage between groups).
- PLOT requests a dendrogram.
- PRINT displays a table of the cluster membership of each case for the two-, three-, and four-cluster solutions.

Variable List

The variable list identifies the variables used to compute similarities or distances between cases.

- The variable list is required except when matrix input is used. It must be specified before the optional subcommands.
- If matrix input is used, the variable list can be omitted. The names for the items in the matrix are used to compute similarities or distances.
- You can specify a variable list to override the names for the items in the matrix. This allows you to read in a subset of cases for analysis. Specifying a variable that does not exist in the matrix results in an error.

MEASURE Subcommand

MEASURE specifies the distance or similarity measure used to cluster cases.

- If the MEASURE subcommand is omitted or included without specifications, squared Euclidean distances are used.
- Only one measure can be specified.

SEUCLID   *Squared Euclidean distances.* The distance between two cases is the sum of the squared differences in their values for each variable. SEUCLID is the measure commonly used with centroid, median, and Ward's methods of clustering. SEUCLID is the default and can also be requested with keyword DEFAULT.

EUCLID   *Euclidean distances.* The distance between two cases is the square root of the sum of the squared differences in their values for each variable.

COSINE   *Cosine of vectors of variables.* This is a pattern similarity measure.

BLOCK   *City-block or Manhattan distances.* The distance between two cases is the sum of the absolute differences in their values for each variable.

CHEBYCHEV *Chebychev distance metric.* The distance between two cases is the maximum absolute difference in their values for any variable.

POWER(p,r) *Distances in an absolute power metric.* The distance between two cases is the rth root of the sum of the absolute differences to the pth power of their values for each variable. Appropriate selection of integer parameters p and r yields Euclidean, squared Euclidean, Minkowski, city-block, and many other distance metrics.

METHOD Subcommand

METHOD specifies one or more clustering methods.

- If the METHOD subcommand is omitted or included without specifications, the method of average linkage between groups is used.
- Only one METHOD subcommand can be used, but more than one method can be specified on it.
- When the number of items is large, CENTROID and MEDIAN require significantly more CPU time than other methods.

BAVERAGE   *Average linkage between groups (UPGMA).* BAVERAGE is the default and can also be requested with keyword DEFAULT.

WAVERAGE   *Average linkage within groups.*

SINGLE   *Single linkage or nearest neighbor.*

COMPLETE   *Complete linkage or furthest neighbor.*

CENTROID   *Centroid clustering (UPGMC).* Squared Euclidean distances are commonly used with this method.

MEDIAN   *Median clustering (WPGMC).* Squared Euclidean distances are commonly used with this method.

WARD   *Ward's method.* Squared Euclidean distances are commonly used with this method.

Example

```
CLUSTER V1 V2 V3
 /METHOD=SINGLE COMPLETE WARDS.
```

- This example clusters cases based on their values for variables *V1*, *V2*, and *V3*, and uses three clustering methods: single linkage, complete linkage, and Ward's method.

SAVE Subcommand

SAVE allows you to save cluster membership at specified solution levels as new variables in the SPSS working data file.

- The specification on SAVE is the CLUSTER keyword, followed by either a single number indicating the level (number of clusters) of the cluster solution or a range separated by a comma indicating the minimum and maximum numbers of clusters when membership of more than one solution is to be saved. The number or range must be enclosed in parentheses and applies to all methods specified on METHOD.

- You can specify a rootname in parentheses after each method specification on the METHOD subcommand. CLUSTER forms new variable names by appending the number of the cluster solution to the rootname.

- If no rootname is specified, CLUSTER forms variable names using the formula $CLUn\_m$, where m increments to create a unique rootname for the set of variables saved for a method and n is the number of the cluster solution.

- As n and m increase, the prefix CLU is truncated to keep names within eight characters.

- CLUSTER generates a table listing the new variables added to the working data file.

- You cannot use the SAVE subcommand if you are replacing the working data file with matrix materials (see "Matrix Output" on p. 254).

Example

```
CLUSTER A B C
 /METHOD=BAVERAGE SINGLE (SINMEM) WARD
 /SAVE=CLUSTERS(3,5).
```

- This command creates nine new variables: $CLU5\_1$, $CLU4\_1$, and $CLU3\_1$ for BAVERAGE, $SINMEM5$, $SINMEM4$, and $SINMEM3$ for SINGLE, and $CLU5\_2$, $CLU4\_2$, and $CLU3\_2$ for WARD. The variables contain the cluster membership for each case at the five-, four-, and three-cluster solutions using the three clustering methods. Ward's method is the third specification on METHOD but uses the second set of default names since it is the second method specified without a rootname.

- The order of the new variables in the working data file is the same as listed above, since the solutions are obtained in the order from 5 to 3.

- The following table is generated to describe the new variables:

```
CLU5_1 to CLU3_1     for Average Linkage (Between Groups)
SINMEM5 to SINMEN3   for Single Linkage
CLU5_2  to CLU3_2    for Ward Method
```

ID Subcommand

ID names a string variable to be used as the case identifier in cluster membership tables, icicle plots, and dendrograms. If the ID subcommand is omitted, cases are identified by case number.

PRINT Subcommand

PRINT controls the display of cluster output (except plots, which are controlled by the PLOT subcommand).

- If the PRINT subcommand is omitted or included without specifications, an agglomeration schedule is displayed. If any keywords are specified on PRINT, the agglomeration schedule is displayed only if explicitly requested.

- CLUSTER automatically displays summary information (the method and measure used, the number of cases) for each method named on the METHOD subcommand. This summary is displayed regardless of specifications on PRINT.

You can specify any or all of the following on the PRINT subcommand:

SCHEDULE

Agglomeration schedule. The agglomeration schedule shows the order and distances at which items and clusters combine to form new clusters. It also shows the cluster level at which an item joins a cluster. SCHEDULE is the default and can also be requested with keyword DEFAULT.

CLUSTER(min,max)

Cluster membership. For each item, the display includes the value of the case identifier (or the variable name if matrix input is used), the case sequence number, and a value (1, 2, 3, etc.) identifying the cluster to which that case belongs in a given cluster solution. Specify either a single integer value in parentheses indicating the level of a single solution or a minimum and a maximum value indicating a range of solutions for which display is desired. If the number of clusters specified exceeds the number produced, the largest number of clusters is used (the number of items minus 1). If CLUSTER is specified more than once, the last specification is used.

DISTANCE

Matrix of distances or similarities between items. DISTANCE displays either the matrix computed by CLUSTER or the input matrix if one is specified on MATRIX. The type of matrix produced (similarities or dissimilarities) depends upon the measure selected. DISTANCE produces a large volume of output and uses significant CPU time when the number of cases is large.

NONE

None of the above. NONE overrides any other keywords specified on PRINT.

Example

```
CLUSTER V1 V2 V3 /PRINT=CLUSTER(3,5).
```

- This example displays cluster membership for each case for the three-, four-, and five-cluster solutions.

PLOT Subcommand

PLOT controls the plots produced for each method specified on the METHOD subcommand. For icicle plots, PLOT allows you to control the cluster solution at which the plot begins and ends and the increment for displaying intermediate cluster solutions.

- If the PLOT subcommand is omitted or included without specifications, a vertical icicle plot is produced.
- If any keywords are specified on PLOT, only those plots requested are produced.
- If there is not enough memory for a dendrogram or an icicle plot, the plot is skipped and a warning is issued.
- The size of an icicle plot can be controlled by specifying range values or an increment for VICICLE or HICICLE. Smaller plots require significantly less workspace and time.

VICICLE(min,max,inc)   *Vertical icicle plot.* This is the default. The range specifications are optional. If used, they must be integer and must be enclosed in parentheses. *min* is the cluster solution at which to start the display (the default is 1), and *max* is the cluster solution at which to end the display (the default is the number of cases minus 1). If *max* is greater than the number of cases minus 1, the default is used. *inc* is the increment to use between cluster solutions (the default is 1). If *max* is specified, *min* must be specified, and if *inc* is specified, both *min* and *max* must be specified. If VICICLE is specified more than once, only the last range specification is used.

HICICLE(min,max,inc)   *Horizontal icicle plot.* The range specifications are the same as for VICICLE. If both VICICLE and HICICLE are specified, the last range specified is used for both. If a range is not specified on the last instance of VICICLE or HICICLE, the defaults are used even if a range is specified earlier.

DENDROGRAM   *Tree diagram.* The dendrogram is scaled by the joining distances of the clusters.

NONE   *No plots.*

Example

```
CLUSTER V1 V2 V3 /PLOT=VICICLE(1,20).
```

- This example produces a vertical icicle plot for the one-cluster through the twenty-cluster solution.

Example

```
CLUSTER V1 V2 V3 /PLOT=VICICLE(1,151,5).
```

- This example produces a vertical icicle plot for every fifth cluster solution starting with 1 and ending with 151 (1 cluster, 6 clusters, 11 clusters, and so on).

MISSING Subcommand

MISSING controls the treatment of cases with missing values. By default, a case that has a missing value for any variable in the variable list is omitted from the analysis.

LISTWISE   *Delete cases with missing values listwise.* Only cases with nonmissing values for all variables in the variable list are used. LISTWISE is the default and can also be requested with keyword DEFAULT.

INCLUDE   *Include cases with user-missing values.* Only cases with system-missing values are excluded.

MATRIX Subcommand

MATRIX reads and writes SPSS matrix data files.

- Either IN or OUT and a matrix file in parentheses are required. When both IN and OUT are used on the same CLUSTER procedure, they can be specified on separate MATRIX subcommands or on the same subcommand.

OUT (filename)   *Write a matrix data file.* Specify either a filename or an asterisk, enclosed in parentheses. If you specify a filename, the file is stored on disk and can be retrieved at any time. If you specify an asterisk (*), the matrix data file replaces the working data file but is not stored on disk unless you use SAVE or XSAVE.

IN (filename)   *Read a matrix data file.* If the matrix data file is the current working data file, specify an asterisk (*) in parentheses. If the matrix data file is another file, specify the filename in parentheses. A matrix file read from an external file does not replace the working data file.

Matrix Output

- CLUSTER writes proximity-type matrices with *ROWTYPE_* values of PROX. CLUSTER neither reads nor writes additional statistics with its matrix materials. See "Format of the Matrix Data File" on p. 255 for a description of the file.

- The matrices produced by CLUSTER can be used by subsequent CLUSTER procedures or by procedures PROXIMITIES and ALSCAL. For more information, see Universals in the *SPSS Base System Syntax Reference Guide.*

- Any documents contained in the working data file are not transferred to the matrix file.

Matrix Input

- CLUSTER can read matrices written by a previous CLUSTER command or by PROXIMITIES, or created by MATRIX DATA. When the input matrix contains distances between variables, CLUSTER clusters all or a subset of the variables.

- The order among rows and cases in the input matrix file is unimportant, as long as values for split-file variables precede values for *ROWTYPE_*.

- CLUSTER ignores unrecognized *ROWTYPE_* values.
- When you are reading a matrix created with MATRIX DATA, you should supply a value label for PROX of either *SIMILARITY* or *DISSIMILARITY* so the matrix is correctly identified. If you do not supply a label, CLUSTER assumes *DISSIMILARITY*. (See "Format of the Matrix Data File" below.)
- SPSS reads variable names, variable and value labels, and print and write formats from the dictionary of the matrix data file.
- With a large number of cases, the matrix will wrap when it is displayed (such as with the LIST command) and will be difficult to read. Nonetheless, the matrix values are accurate and can be used as input.
- MATRIX=IN cannot be specified unless a working data file has already been defined. To read an existing matrix data file at the beginning of a session, use GET to retrieve the matrix file and then specify IN(*) on MATRIX.
- The variable list on CLUSTER can be omitted when a matrix data file is used as input. By default, all cases or variables in the matrix data file are used in the analysis. Specify a variable list only when you want to read in a subset of items for analysis.

Format of the Matrix Data File

- The matrix data file can include three special variables created by SPSS: *ROWTYPE_*, *ID* and *VARNAME_*.
- Variable *ROWTYPE_* is a string variable with value PROX (for proximity measure). PROX is assigned value labels containing the distance measure used to create the matrix and either *SIMILARITY* or *DISSIMILARITY* as an identifier.
- *ID* is included only when an identifying variable is not specified on the ID subcommand. *ID* is a short string and takes the value CASE *m*, where *m* is the actual number of each case. Note that *m* may not be consecutive if cases have been selected.
- If an identifying variable is specified on the ID subcommand, it takes the place of *ID* between *ROWTYPE_* and *VARNAME_*. Up to 20 characters can be displayed for the identifying variable.
- *VARNAME_* is a string variable which takes the values VAR1, VAR2 ...VAR*n*, to correspond to the names of the distance variables in the matrix (*VAR1, VAR2 ... VARn*, where *n* is the number of cases in the largest split file). The numeric suffix for the variable names is consecutive and may not be the same as the actual case number.
- The remaining variables in the matrix file are the distance variables used to form the matrix. The distance variables are assigned variable labels in the form of CASE *m* to identify the actual number of each case.

Split Files

- When split-file processing is in effect, the first variables in the matrix data file are the split variables, followed by *ROWTYPE_*, the case-identifier variable or *ID*, *VARNAME_*, and the distance variables.

- A full set of matrix materials is written for each split-file group defined by the split variables.
- A split variable cannot have the same name as any other variable written to the matrix data file.
- If split-file processing is in effect when a matrix is written, the same split file must be in effect when that matrix is read by any procedure.

Missing Values

Missing-value treatment affects the values written to a matrix data file. When reading a matrix data file, be sure to specify a missing-value treatment on CLUSTER that is compatible with the treatment that was in effect when the matrix materials were generated.

Example

```
DATA LIST FILE=ALMANAC1 RECORDS=3
  /1 CITY 6-18(A) POP80 53-60
  /2 CHURCHES 10-13 PARKS 14-17 PHONES 18-25 TVS 26-32
     RADIOST 33-35 TVST 36-38 TAXRATE 52-57(2).
N OF CASES 8.

CLUSTER CHURCHES TO TAXRATE
  /ID=CITY
  /MEASURE=EUCLID
  /MATRIX=OUT(CLUSMTX).
```

- CLUSTER reads raw data from file *ALMANAC1* and writes one set of matrix materials to file *CLUSMTX.*
- The working data file is still the *ALMANAC1* file defined on DATA LIST. Subsequent commands are executed on *ALMANAC1.*

Example

```
DATA LIST FILE=ALMANAC1 RECORDS=3
  /1 CITY 6-18(A) POP80 53-60
  /2 CHURCHES 10-13 PARKS 14-17 PHONES 18-25 TVS 26-32
     RADIOST 33-35 TVST 36-38 TAXRATE 52-57(2).
N OF CASES 8.

CLUSTER CHURCHES TO TAXRATE
  /ID=CITY
  /MEASURE=EUCLID
  /MATRIX=OUT(*).
LIST.
```

- CLUSTER writes the same matrix as in the previous example. However, the matrix data file replaces the working data file. The LIST command is executed on the matrix file, not on *ALMANAC1.*

Example

```
GET FILE=CLUSMTX.
CLUSTER
  /ID=CITY
  /MATRIX=IN(*).
```

- This example starts a new session and reads an existing matrix data file. GET retrieves the matrix data file *CLUSMTX*.
- MATRIX=IN specifies an asterisk because the matrix data file is the working data file. If MATRIX=IN(CLUSMTX) is specified, SPSS issues an error message.
- If the GET command is omitted, SPSS issues an error message.

Example

```
GET FILE=PRSNNL.
FREQUENCIES VARIABLE=AGE.

CLUSTER
  /ID=CITY
  /MATRIX=IN(CLUSMTX).
```

- This example performs a frequencies analysis on file *PRSNNL* and then uses a different file for CLUSTER. The file is an existing matrix data file.
- The variable list is omitted on the CLUSTER command. By default, all cases in the matrix file are used in the analysis.
- MATRIX=IN specifies the matrix data file *CLUSMTX*.
- *CLUSMTX* does not replace *PRSNNL* as the working data file.

Example

```
GET FILE=CRIME.
PROXIMITIES MURDER TO MOTOR
  /VIEW=VARIABLE
  /MEASURE=PH2
  /MATRIX=OUT(*).
CLUSTER
  /MATRIX=IN(*).
```

- GET retrieves an SPSS data file.
- PROXIMITIES uses the data from the *CRIME* file, which is now the working data file. The VIEW subcommand specifies computation of proximity values between variables. The MATRIX subcommand writes the matrix to the working data file.
- MATRIX=IN(*) on the CLUSTER command reads the matrix materials from the working data file. Since the matrix contains distances between variables, CLUSTER clusters variables based on distance measures in the input. The variable list is omitted on the CLUSTER command, so all variables are used in the analysis. The slash preceding the MATRIX subcommand is required because there is an implied variable list. Without the slash,

CLUSTER would attempt to interpret MATRIX as a variable name rather than a subcommand name.

DISCRIMINANT

```
DISCRIMINANT GROUPS=varname(min,max)  /VARIABLES=varlist

 [/SELECT=varname(value)]

 [/ANALYSIS=varlist[(level)] [varlist...]]

 [/METHOD={DIRECT**}]  [/TOLERANCE={0.001}]
         {WILKS    }              {  n  }
         {MAHAL    }
         {MAXMINF  }
         {MINRESID }
         {RAO      }

 [/MAXSTEPS={n}]

 [/FIN={3.84**}]  [/FOUT={2.71**}]  [/PIN={n}]
       { n    }         { n    }

 [/POUT={n}]  [/VIN={0**}]
                    { n  }

 [/FUNCTIONS={g-1,100.0,1.0**}]  [/PRIORS={EQUAL**    }]
             {n_1 , n_2 ,n_3  }           {SIZE       }
                                          {value list }
 [/SAVE=[CLASS[=varname]] [PROBS[=rootname]]

        [SCORES[=rootname]]]

 [/ANALYSIS=...]

 [/MISSING={EXCLUDE**}]
           {INCLUDE  }

 [/MATRIX=[OUT({*   })] [IN({*   })]]
              {file}      {file}

 [/HISTORY={STEP** } {END**  }]
           {NOSTEP}  {NOEND  }

 [/ROTATE={NONE**   }]
          {COEFF    }
          {STRUCTURE}

 [/CLASSIFY={NONMISSING  } {POOLED  }  [MEANSUB]]
            {UNSELECTED  } {SEPARATE}
            {UNCLASSIFIED}

 [/STATISTICS=[MEAN  ]  [COV ]  [FPAIR]  [RAW  ]  [ALL]]
              [STDDEV]  [GCOV]  [UNIVF]  [COEFF]
              [CORR  ]  [TCOV]  [BOXM ]  [TABLE]

 [/PLOT=[MAP]  [SEPARATE]  [COMBINED]  [CASES]  [ALL]]
```

**Default if the subcommand is omitted.

Example:

```
DISCRIMINANT GROUPS=OUTCOME (1,4)
  /VARIABLES=V1 TO V7
  /SAVE CLASS=PREDOUT.
```

Overview

DISCRIMINANT performs linear discriminant analysis for two or more groups. The goal of discriminant analysis is to classify cases into one of several mutually exclusive groups based on their values for a set of predictor variables. In the analysis phase, a classification rule is developed using cases for which group membership is known. In the classification phase, the rule is used to classify cases for which group membership is not known. The grouping variable must be categorical, and the independent (predictor) variables must be interval or dichotomous, since they will be used in a regression-type equation.

Options

Variable Selection Method. In addition to the direct-entry method, you can specify any of several stepwise methods for entering variables into the discriminant analysis using the METHOD subcommand. You can set the values for the statistical criteria used to enter variables into the equation using the TOLERANCE, FIN, PIN, FOUT, POUT, and VIN subcommands, and you can specify inclusion levels on the ANALYSIS subcommand. You can also specify the maximum number of steps in a stepwise analysis using the MAXSTEPS subcommand.

Case Selection. You can select a subset of cases for the analysis phase using the SELECT subcommand.

Prior Probabilities. You can specify prior probabilities for membership in a group using the PRIORS subcommand. Prior probabilities are used in classifying cases.

New Variables. You can add new variables to the working data file containing the predicted group membership, the probability of membership in each group, and discriminant function scores using the SAVE subcommand.

Classification Options. With the CLASSIFY subcommand you can classify only those cases that were not selected for inclusion in the discriminant analysis, or only those cases whose value for the grouping variable was missing or fell outside the range analyzed. In addition, you can classify cases based on the separate-group covariance matrices of the functions instead of the pooled within-groups covariance matrix.

Statistical Display. You can request any of a variety of statistics on the STATISTICS subcommand. You can rotate the pattern or structure matrices using the ROTATE subcommand. You can compare actual with predicted group membership using a classification results table (the STATISTICS subcommand) or any of several types of plots or histograms using the PLOT subcommand. With PLOT you can also display discriminant scores and actual and predicted group membership for each case.

Basic Specification

The basic specification requires two subcommands:
- GROUPS specifies the variable used to group cases.
- VARIABLES specifies the predictor variables.

By default, DISCRIMINANT enters all variables simultaneously into the discriminant equation (the DIRECT method) provided that they are not so highly correlated that multicollinearity problems arise. Default output includes counts of cases in the groups, the method used and associated criteria, and a summary of results including eigenvalues, standardized discriminant function coefficients, and within-groups correlations between the discriminant functions and the predictor variables.

Subcommand Order

- The GROUPS, VARIABLES, and SELECT subcommands must precede all other subcommands and may be entered in any order.
- The analysis block follows, which may include ANALYSIS, METHOD, TOLERANCE, MAXSTEPS, FIN, FOUT, PIN, POUT, VIN, FUNCTIONS, PRIORS, and SAVE. Each analysis block performs a single analysis. To do multiple analyses, specify multiple analysis blocks.
- The keyword ANALYSIS is optional for the first analysis block. Each new analysis block must begin with an ANALYSIS subcommand. Remaining subcommands in the block may be used in any order and apply only to the analysis defined within the same block.
- No analysis block subcommands can be specified after any of the global subcommands, which apply to all analysis blocks. The global subcommands are MISSING, MATRIX, HISTORY, ROTATE, CLASSIFY, STATISTICS, and PLOT. If an analysis block subcommand appears after a global subcommand, SPSS displays a warning and ignores it.

Syntax Rules

- Only one GROUPS, one SELECT, and one VARIABLES subcommand can be specified per DISCRIMINANT command.

Operations

- DISCRIMINANT first estimates one or more discriminant functions that best distinguish among the groups.
- Using these functions, DISCRIMINANT then classifies cases into groups (if classification output is requested).
- If more than one analysis block is specified, the above steps are repeated for each block.

Limitations

- Pairwise deletion of missing data is not available.

Example

```
DISCRIMINANT GROUPS=OUTCOME (1,4)
  /VARIABLES=V1 TO V7
  /SAVE CLASS=PREDOUT
  /STATISTICS=COV GCOV TCOV.
```

- Only cases with values 1, 2, 3, or 4 for the grouping variable GROUPS will be used in computing the discriminant functions.
- The variables in the working data file between and including *V1* and *V7* will be used to compute the discriminant functions and to classify cases.
- Predicted group membership will be saved in variable *PREDOUT*.
- In addition to the default output, the STATISTICS subcommand requests the pooled within-in-groups covariance matrix and the group and total covariance matrices.

GROUPS Subcommand

GROUPS specifies the name of the grouping variable, which defines the categories or groups, and a range of categories.

- GROUPS is required and can be specified only once.
- The specification consists of a variable name followed by a range of values in parentheses.
- Only one grouping variable may be specified; its values must be integers. To use a string variable as the grouping variable, first use AUTORECODE to convert the string values to integers and then specify the recoded variable as the grouping variable.
- Empty groups are ignored and do not affect calculations. For example, if there are no cases in group 2, the value range (1,5) will define only four groups.
- Cases with values outside the value range or missing are ignored during the analysis phase but are classified during the classification phase.

VARIABLES Subcommand

VARIABLES identifies the predictor variables, which are used to classify cases into the groups defined on the GROUPS subcommand. The list of variables follows the usual SPSS conventions for variable lists.

- VARIABLES is required and can be specified only once. Use the ANALYSIS subcommand to obtain multiple analyses.
- Only numeric variables can be used.
- Variables should be suitable for use in a regression-type equation, either measured at the interval level or dichotomous.

SELECT Subcommand

SELECT limits cases used in the analysis phase to those with a specified value for any one variable.

- Only one SELECT subcommand is allowed. It can follow the GROUPS and VARIABLES subcommands but must precede all other subcommands.
- The specification is a variable name and a single integer value in parentheses. Multiple variables or values are not permitted.
- The selection variable does not have to be specified on the VARIABLES subcommand.
- Only cases with the specified value for the selection variable are used in the analysis phase.
- All cases, whether selected or not, are classified by default. Use CLASSIFY=UNSELECTED to classify only the unselected cases.
- When SELECT is used, classification statistics are reported separately for selected and unselected cases, unless CLASSIFY=UNSELECTED is used to restrict classification.

Example

```
DISCRIMINANT GROUPS=APPROVAL(1,5)
  /VARS=Q1 TO Q10
  /SELECT=COMPLETE(1)
  /CLASSIFY=UNSELECTED.
```

- Using only cases with value 1 for variable *COMPLETE*, DISCRIMINANT estimates a function of *Q1* to *Q10* that discriminates between the categories 1 to 5 of the grouping variable *APPROVAL*.
- Because CLASSIFY=UNSELECTED is specified, the discriminant function will be used to classify only the unselected cases (cases for which *COMPLETE* does not equal 1).

ANALYSIS Subcommand

ANALYSIS is used to request several different discriminant analyses using the same grouping variable, or to control the order in which variables are entered into a stepwise analysis.

- ANALYSIS is optional for the first analysis block. By default all variables specified on the VARIABLES subcommand are included in the analysis.
- The variables named on ANALYSIS must first be specified on the VARIABLES subcommand.
- Keyword ALL includes all variables on the VARIABLES subcommand.
- If keyword TO is used to specify a list of variables on an ANALYSIS subcommand, it refers to the order of variables on the VARIABLES subcommand, which is not necessarily the order of variables in the working data file.

Example

```
DISCRIMINANT GROUPS=SUCCESS(0,1)
  /VARIABLES=V10 TO V15, AGE, V5
  /ANALYSIS=V15 TO V5
  /ANALYSIS=ALL.
```

- The first analysis will use variables *V15*, *AGE*, and *V5* to discriminate between cases where *SUCCESS* equals 0 and *SUCCESS* equals 1.
- The second analysis will use all variables named on the VARIABLES subcommand.

Inclusion Levels

When you specify a stepwise method on the METHOD subcommand (any method other than the default direct-entry method), you can control the order in which variables are considered for entry or removal by specifying *inclusion levels* on the ANALYSIS subcommand. By default, all variables in the analysis are entered according to the criterion requested on the METHOD subcommand.

- An inclusion level is an integer between 0 and 99, specified in parentheses after a variable or list of variables on the ANALYSIS subcommand.
- The default inclusion level is 1.
- Variables with higher inclusion levels are considered for entry before variables with lower inclusion levels.
- Variables with even inclusion levels are entered as a group.
- Variables with odd inclusion levels are entered individually, according to the stepwise method specified on the METHOD subcommand.
- Only variables with an inclusion level of 1 are considered for removal. To make a variable with a higher inclusion level eligible for removal, name it twice on the ANALYSIS subcommand, first specifying the desired inclusion level and then an inclusion level of 1.
- Variables with an inclusion level of 0 are never entered. However, the statistical criterion for entry is computed and displayed.
- Variables that fail the TOLERANCE criterion are not entered regardless of their inclusion level.

The following are some common methods of entering variables and the inclusion levels that could be used to achieve them. These examples assume that one of the stepwise methods is specified on the METHOD subcommand (otherwise inclusion levels have no effect).

Direct. ANALYSIS=ALL(2) forces all variables into the equation. (This is the default and can be requested with METHOD=DIRECT or simply by omitting the METHOD subcommand.)

Stepwise. ANALYSIS=ALL(1) yields a stepwise solution in which variables are entered and removed in stepwise fashion. (This is the default when anything other than DIRECT is specified on the METHOD subcommand.)

Forward. ANALYSIS=ALL(3) enters variables into the equation stepwise but does not remove variables.

Backward. ANALYSIS=ALL(2) ALL(1) forces all variables into the equation and then allows them to be removed stepwise if they satisfy the criterion for removal.

Example

```
DISCRIMINANT GROUPS=SUCCESS(0,1)
  /VARIABLES=A, B, C, D, E
  /ANALYSIS=A TO C (2) D, E (1)
  /METHOD=WILKS.
```

- *A*, *B*, and *C* are entered into the analysis first, assuming that they pass the tolerance criterion. Since their inclusion level is even, they are entered together.
- *D* and *E* are then entered stepwise. The one that minimizes the overall value of Wilks' lambda is entered first.
- After entering *D* and *E*, SPSS checks whether the partial *F* for either one justifies removal from the equation (see the FOUT and POUT subcommands on p. 266 and 267).

Example

```
DISCRIMINANT GROUPS=SUCCESS(0,1)
  /VARIABLES=A, B, C, D, E
  /ANALYSIS=A TO C (2) D, E (1).
```

- Since no stepwise method is specified, inclusion levels have no effect and all variables are entered into the model at once.

METHOD Subcommand

METHOD is used to select a method for entering variables into an analysis.

- A variable will never be entered into the analysis if it does not pass the tolerance criterion specified on the TOLERANCE subcommand (or the default).
- A METHOD subcommand applies only to the *preceding* ANALYSIS subcommand, or to an analysis using all predictor variables if no ANALYSIS subcommand has been specified before it.
- If more than one METHOD subcommand is specified within one analysis block, the last is used.

Any one of the following methods can be specified on the METHOD subcommand:

DIRECT *All variables passing the tolerance criteria are entered simultaneously.* This is the default method.

WILKS *At each step, the variable that minimizes the overall Wilks' lambda is entered.*

MAHAL *At each step, the variable that maximizes the Mahalanobis distance between the two closest groups is entered.*

MAXMINF *At each step, the variable that maximizes the smallest F ratio between pairs of groups is entered.*

MINRESID   *At each step, the variable that minimizes the sum of the unexplained varia-tion for all pairs of groups is entered.*

RAO   *At each step, the variable that produces the largest increase in Rao's V is entered.*

TOLERANCE Subcommand

TOLERANCE specifies the minimum tolerance a variable can have and still be entered into the analysis. The tolerance of a variable that is a candidate for inclusion in the analysis is the proportion of its within-group variance not accounted for by other variables in the analysis. A variable with very low tolerance is nearly a linear function of the other variables; its inclusion in the analysis would make the calculations unstable.

- The default tolerance is 0.001.
- You can specify any decimal value between 0 and 1 as the minimum tolerance.

FIN Subcommand

FIN specifies the minimum partial F value a variable must have to enter the analysis.

- If neither FIN nor PIN is specified, the default for FIN (3.84) is used.
- You can set FIN to any nonnegative number.
- FIN is ignored if PIN is specified.
- FIN applies only to the stepwise methods and is ignored if the METHOD subcommand is omitted or if METHOD specifies DIRECT.

PIN Subcommand

PIN specifies the maximum probability of F a variable can have to enter the analysis.

- If PIN is omitted, FIN is used by default.
- You can set PIN to any decimal value between 0 and 1.
- PIN overrides FIN if both are specified.
- PIN applies only to the stepwise methods and is ignored if the METHOD subcommand is omitted or if METHOD specifies DIRECT.

FOUT Subcommand

As additional variables are entered into the analysis, the partial F for variables already in the equation changes. FOUT specifies the smallest partial F a variable can have and not be re-moved from the model.

- If neither FOUT nor POUT is specified, the default for FOUT (2.71) is used.
- You can set FOUT to any nonnegative number. However, FOUT should be less than FIN if FIN is also specified.

- FOUT is ignored if POUT is specified.
- FOUT applies only to the stepwise methods and is ignored if the METHOD subcommand is omitted or if METHOD specifies DIRECT.

POUT Subcommand

POUT is the maximum probability of F a variable can have and not be removed from the model.

- If POUT is omitted, FOUT is used by default.
- You can set POUT to any decimal value between 0 and 1. However, POUT should be greater than PIN if PIN is also specified.
- POUT overrides FOUT if both are specified.
- POUT applies only to the stepwise methods and is ignored if the METHOD subcommand is omitted or if METHOD specifies DIRECT.

VIN Subcommand

VIN specifies the minimum Rao's V a variable must have to enter the analysis. When you use METHOD=RAO, variables satisfying one of the other criteria for entering the equation may actually cause a decrease in Rao's V for the equation. The default VIN prevents this but does not prevent the addition of variables that provide no additional separation between groups.

- You can specify any value for VIN. The default is 0.
- VIN should be used only when you have specified METHOD=RAO. Otherwise, it is ignored.

MAXSTEPS Subcommand

MAXSTEPS is used to decrease the maximum number of steps allowed. By default, the maximum number of steps allowed in a stepwise analysis is the number of variables with inclusion levels greater than 1 plus twice the number of variables with inclusion levels equal to 1. This is the maximum number of steps possible without producing a loop in which a variable is repeatedly cycled in and out.

- MAXSTEPS applies only to the stepwise methods (all except DIRECT).
- MAXSTEPS applies only to the preceding METHOD subcommand.
- The format is MAX=n, where n is the maximum number of steps desired.
- If multiple MAXSTEPS subcommands are specified, the last is used.

FUNCTIONS Subcommand

By default, DISCRIMINANT computes all possible functions. This is either the number of groups minus 1 or the number of predictor variables, whichever is less. Use FUNCTIONS to set more restrictive criteria for the extraction of functions.

FUNCTIONS has three parameters:

n_1 *Maximum number of functions.* The default is the number of groups minus 1 or the number of predictor variables, whichever is less.

n_2 *Cumulative percentage of the sum of the eigenvalues.* The default is 100%.

n_3 *Significance level of function.* The default is 1.0.

- The parameters must always be specified in sequential order (n_1, n_2, n_3). To specify n_2, you must explicitly specify the default for n_1. Similarly, to specify n_3, you must specify the defaults for n_1 and n_2.
- If more than one restriction is specified, SPSS stops extracting functions when any one of the restrictions is met.
- When multiple FUNCTIONS subcommands are specified, SPSS uses the last; however, if n_2 or n_3 are omitted on the last FUNCTIONS subcommand, the corresponding specifications on the previous FUNCTIONS subcommands will remain in effect.

Example

```
DISCRIMINANT  GROUPS=CLASS(1,5)
  /VARIABLES = SCORE1 TO SCORE20
  /FUNCTIONS=4,100,.80.
```

- The first two parameters on the FUNCTIONS subcommand are defaults: the default for n_1 is 4 (the number of groups minus 1), and the default for n_2 is 100.
- The third parameter tells DISCRIMINANT to use fewer than four discriminant functions if the significance level of a function is greater than 0.80.

PRIORS Subcommand

By default, DISCRIMINANT assumes equal prior probabilities for groups when classifying cases. You can provide different prior probabilities with the PRIORS subcommand.

- Prior probabilities are used only during classification.
- If you provide unequal prior probabilities, DISCRIMINANT adjusts the classification coefficients to reflect this.
- If adjacent groups have the same prior probability, you can use the notation $n*c$ in the value list to indicate that n adjacent groups have the same prior probability c.
- You can specify a prior probability of 0. No cases are classified into such a group.
- If the sum of the prior probabilities is not 1, SPSS rescales the probabilities to sum to 1 and issues a warning.

EQUAL   *Equal prior probabilities.* This is the default.

SIZE   *Proportion of the cases analyzed that fall into each group.* If 50% of the cases included in the analysis fall into the first group, 25% in the second, and 25% in the third, the prior probabilities are 0.5, 0.25, and 0.25, respectively. Group size is determined after cases with missing values for the predictor variables are deleted.

Value list   *User-specified prior probabilities.* The list of probabilities must sum to 1.0. The number of prior probabilities named or implied must equal the number of groups.

Example

```
DISCRIMINANT  GROUPS=TYPE(1,5)
  /VARIABLES=A TO H
  /PRIORS = 4*.15,.4.
```

- The PRIORS subcommand establishes prior probabilities of 0.15 for the first four groups and 0.4 for the fifth group.

SAVE Subcommand

SAVE allows you to save casewise information as new variables in the working data file.

- SAVE applies only to the current analysis block. To save casewise results from more than one analysis, specify a SAVE subcommand in each analysis block.
- You can specify a variable name for CLASS and rootnames for SCORES and PROBS to obtain descriptive names for the new variables.
- If you do not specify a variable name for CLASS, SPSS forms variable names using the formula *DSC_m*, where *m* increments to distinguish group membership variables saved on different SAVE subcommands for different analysis blocks.
- If you do not specify a rootname for SCORES or PROBS, SPSS forms new variable names using the formula *DSCn_m*, where *m* increments to create unique rootnames and *n* increments to create unique variable names. For example, the first set of default names assigned to discriminant scores or probabilities are *DSC1_1, DSC2_1, DSC3_1*, and so forth. The next set of default names assigned will be *DSC1_2, DSC2_2, DSC3_2*, and so forth, regardless of whether discriminant scores or probabilities are being saved or whether they are saved by the same SAVE subcommand.
- As *m* and/or *n* increase, the prefix *DSC* is truncated to keep variable names within eight characters. For example, *DS999_12* increases to *D1000_12*. The initial character *D* is required.
- Keywords CLASS, SCORES, and PROBS can be used in any order, but the new variables are always added to the end of the working file in the following order: first the predicted group, then the discriminant scores, and finally probabilities of group membership.
- Appropriate variable labels are automatically generated. The labels describe whether the variables contain predictor group membership, discriminant scores, or probabilities, and for which analysis they are generated.
- The CLASS variable will use the value labels (if any) from the grouping variable specified for the analysis.
- You cannot use the SAVE subcommand if you are replacing the working data file with matrix materials (see "Matrix Output" on p. 274).

CLASS [(varname)]   *Predicted group membership.*

SCORES [(varname)]   *Discriminant scores.* One score is saved for each discriminant function derived. If a rootname is specified, DISCRIMINANT will append a sequential number to the name to form new variable names for the discriminant scores.

PROBS [(varname)]   *For each case, the probabilities of membership in each group.* As many variables are added to each case as there are groups. If a rootname is specified, DISCRIMINANT will append a sequential number to the name to form new variable names.

Example

```
DISCRIMINANT GROUPS=WORLD(1,3)
 /VARIABLES=FOOD TO FSALES
 /SAVE CLASS=PRDCLASS SCORES=SCORE PROBS=PRB
 /ANALYSIS=FOOD SERVICE COOK MANAGER FSALES
 /SAVE CLASS SCORES PROBS.
```

- Two analyses are specified. The first uses all variables named on the VARIABLES subcommand and the second narrows down to five variables. For each analysis, a SAVE subcommand is specified.

- On the first SAVE subcommand, a variable name and two rootnames are provided. With three groups, the following variables are added to each case:

Name	Variable label	Description
PRDCLASS	Predicted group for analysis 1	Predicted group membership
SCORE1	Function 1 for analysis 1	Discriminant score for function 1
SCORE2	Function 2 for analysis 1	Discriminant score for function 2
PRB1	Probability 1 for analysis 1	Probability of being in group 1
PRB2	Probability 2 for analysis 1	Probability of being in group 2
PRB3	Probability 3 for analysis 1	Probability of being in group 3

- Since no variable name or rootnames are provided on the second SAVE subcommand, DISCRIMINANT uses default names. Note that *m* serves only to distinguish variables saved as a set and does not correspond to the sequential number of an analysis. To find out what information a new variable holds, read the variable label, as shown in the following table:

Name	Variable label	Description
DSC_1	Predicted group for analysis 2	Predicted group membership
DSC1_1	Function 1 for analysis 2	Discriminant score for function 1
DSC2_1	Function 2 for analysis 2	Discriminant score for function 2
DSC1_2	Probability 1 for analysis 2	Probability of being in group 1
DSC2_2	Probability 2 for analysis 2	Probability of being in group 2
DSC3_2	Probability 3 for analysis 2	Probability of being in group 3

STATISTICS Subcommand

By default, DISCRIMINANT produces the following statistics for each analysis:

- *Summary statistics.* Eigenvalues, percent of variance, cumulative percent of variance, canonical correlations, Wilks' lambda, chi-square, degrees of freedom, and significance of chi-square are reported for the functions.

- *Summary table.* A table showing the action taken at every step. This table is displayed for stepwise methods only.

- *Step statistics.* Wilks' lambda, equivalent F, degrees of freedom, and significance of F are reported for each step. Tolerance, F-to-remove, and the value of the statistic used for variable selection are reported for each variable in the equation. Tolerance, minimum tolerance, F-to-enter, and the value of the statistic used for variable selection are reported for each variable not in the equation. (These statistics can be suppressed with HISTORY=NOSTEP.)

- *Final statistics.* Standardized canonical discriminant function coefficients, the structure matrix of discriminant functions and all variables named in the analysis (whether they were entered into the equation or not), and functions evaluated at group means are reported following the last step.

In addition, you can request optional statistics on the STATISTICS subcommand. STATISTICS can be specified by itself or with one or more keywords.

- STATISTICS without keywords displays MEAN, STDDEV, and UNIVF. If you include a keyword or keywords on STATISTICS, only the statistics you request are displayed.

MEAN   *Means.* Total and group means for all variables named on the ANALYSIS subcommand are displayed.

STDDEV   *Standard deviations.* Total and group standard deviations for all variables named on the ANALYSIS subcommand are displayed.

UNIVF   *Univariate* F *ratios.* The analysis of variance F statistic for equality of group means for each predictor variable is displayed. This is a one-way analysis of variance test for equality of group means on a single discriminating variable.

COV   *Pooled within-groups covariance matrix.*

CORR   *Pooled within-groups correlation matrix.*

FPAIR   *Matrix of pairwise* F *ratios.* The F ratio for each pair of groups is displayed. This F is the significance test for the Mahalanobis distance between groups. This statistic is available only with stepwise methods.

BOXM   *Box's* M *test.* This is a test for equality of group covariance matrices.

GCOV   *Group covariance matrices.*

TCOV   *Total covariance matrix.*

RAW   *Unstandardized canonical discriminant functions.*

COEFF   *Classification function coefficients.* Although DISCRIMINANT does not directly use these coefficients to classify cases, you can use them to classify other samples (see the CLASSIFY subcommand on p. 272).

TABLE   *Classification results table.* If both selected and unselected cases are classified, two tables are produced, one for selected cases and one for unselected cases.

ALL   *All optional statistics.*

ROTATE Subcommand

The coefficient and correlation matrices can be rotated to facilitate interpretation of results. To control varimax rotation, use the ROTATE subcommand.

• Neither COEFF nor STRUCTURE affects the classification of cases.

COEFF   *Rotate pattern matrix.*

STRUCTURE   *Rotate structure matrix.*

NONE   *Do not rotate.* This is the default.

HISTORY Subcommand

HISTORY controls the display of stepwise and summary output.

• By default, HISTORY displays both the step-by-step output and the summary table (keywords STEP and END).

STEP   *Display step-by-step output.*

NOSTEP   *Suppress step-by-step output.*

END   *Display the summary table.*

NOEND   *Suppress the summary table.*

CLASSIFY Subcommand

CLASSIFY determines how cases are handled during classification.

• By default, all cases with nonmissing values for all predictors are classified, and the pooled within-groups covariance matrix is used to classify cases.

• The default keywords for CLASSIFY are NONMISSING and POOLED.

NONMISSING   *Classify all cases that do not have missing values on any predictor variables.* Two sets of classification results are produced, one for selected cases (those specified on the SELECT subcommand) and one for unselected cases. This is the default.

UNSELECTED   *Classify only unselected cases.* The classification phase is suppressed for cases selected via the SELECT subcommand.

UNCLASSIFIED   *Classify only unclassified cases.* The classification phase is suppressed for cases that fall within the range specified on the GROUPS subcommand.

POOLED   *Use the pooled within-groups covariance matrix to classify cases.* This is the default.

SEPARATE   *Use separate-groups covariance matrices of the discriminant functions for classification.* Since classification is based on the discriminant functions and not the original variables, this option is not necessarily equivalent to quadratic discrimination.

MEANSUB   *Substitute means for missing predictor values during classification.* During classification, means are substituted for missing values and cases with missing values are classified. Cases with missing values are not used during analysis.

PLOT Subcommand

PLOT requests additional output to help you examine the effectiveness of the discriminant analysis.

- If PLOT is specified without keywords, the default is COMBINED and CASES.
- If any keywords are requested on PLOT, only the requested plots are displayed.

COMBINED   *All-groups plot.* For each case, the first two function values are plotted. A histogram is displayed if only one function is used.

CASES   *Discriminant scores and classification information for each case.*

MAP   *Territorial map.* A plot of group centroids and boundaries used for classifying groups. The map is not displayed if only one function is used or if SET HIGHRES=ON (see SET in the *SPSS Base System Syntax Reference Guide*).

SEPARATE   *Separate-groups plots.* These are the same types of plots produced by keyword COMBINED, except that separate plots are produced for each group.

ALL   *All available plots.*

MISSING Subcommand

MISSING controls the treatment of cases with missing values in the analysis phase. By default, cases with missing values for any variable named on the VARIABLES subcommand and cases with values out of range or missing for the grouping variable are not used in the analysis phase but are used in classification.

- Keyword INCLUDE includes cases with user-missing values in analysis phase.

EXCLUDE   *Exclude all cases with missing values.* Cases with user- or system-missing values are excluded from the analysis. This is the default.

INCLUDE   *Include cases with user-missing values.* User-missing values are treated as valid values. Only the system-missing value is treated as missing.

MATRIX Subcommand

MATRIX reads and writes SPSS matrix data files.

- Either IN or OUT and the matrix file in parentheses are required. When both IN and OUT are used on the same DISCRIMINANT procedure, they can be specified on separate MATRIX subcommands or on the same subcommand.

OUT (filename)   *Write a matrix data file.* Specify either a filename or an asterisk (*), enclosed in parentheses. If you specify a filename, the file is stored on disk and can be retrieved at any time. If you specify an asterisk (*), the matrix data file replaces the working data file but is not stored on disk unless you use SAVE or XSAVE.

IN (filename)   *Read a matrix data file.* If the matrix data file is the working data file, specify an asterisk (*) in parentheses. If the matrix file is another file, specify the filename in parentheses. A matrix file read from an external file does not replace the working data file.

Matrix Output

- In addition to Pearson correlation coefficients, the matrix materials written by DISCRIMINANT include weighted and unweighted numbers of cases, means, and standard deviations. (See "Format of the Matrix Data File" on p. 275 for a description of the file.) These materials can be used in subsequent DISCRIMINANT procedures.
- Any documents contained in the working data file are not transferred to the matrix file.
- If BOXM or GCOV is specified on the STATISTICS subcommand or SEPARATE is specified on the CLASSIFY subcommand when a matrix file is written, the STDDEV and CORR records in the matrix materials represent within-cell data, and separate covariance matrices are written to the file. When the matrix file is used as input for a subsequent DISCRIMINANT procedure, at least one of these specifications must be used on that DISCRIMINANT command.

Matrix Input

- DISCRIMINANT can read correlation matrices written by a previous DISCRIMINANT command or by other procedures. Matrix materials read by DISCRIMINANT must contain records with *ROWTYPE_* values MEAN, N or COUNT (or both), STDDEV, and CORR.
- If the data do not include records with *ROWTYPE_* value COUNT (unweighted number of cases), DISCRIMINANT uses information from records with *ROWTYPE_* value N (weighted number of cases). Conversely, if the data do not have N values, DISCRIMINANT uses the COUNT values. These records can appear in any order in the matrix input file with the following exceptions: the order of split-file groups cannot be violated and all CORR vectors must appear consecutively within each split-file group.
- If you want to use a covariance-type matrix as input to DISCRIMINANT, you must first use the MCONVERT command to change the covariance matrix to a correlation matrix.

- DISCRIMINANT can use a matrix from a previous data set to classify data in the working data file. SPSS checks to make sure that the grouping variable (specified on GROUPS) and the predictor variables (specified on VARIABLES) are the same in the working file as in the matrix file. If they are not, SPSS displays an error message and the classification will not be executed.
- MATRIX=IN cannot be used unless a working data file has already been defined. To read an existing matrix data file at the beginning of a session, first use GET to retrieve the matrix file and then specify IN(*) on MATRIX.

Format of the Matrix Data File

- The matrix data file has two special variables created by SPSS: *ROWTYPE_* and *VARNAME_*. Variable *ROWTYPE_* is a short string variable having values N, COUNT, MEAN, STDDEV, and CORR (for Pearson correlation coefficient). Variable *VARNAME_* is a short string variable whose values are the names of the variables used to form the correlation matrix.
- When *ROWTYPE_* is CORR, *VARNAME_* gives the variable associated with that row of the correlation matrix.
- Between *ROWTYPE_* and *VARNAME_* is the group variable, which is specified on the GROUPS subcommand of DISCRIMINANT.
- The remaining variables are the variables used to form the correlation matrix.

Split Files

- When split-file processing is in effect, the first variables in the matrix data file will be split variables, followed by *ROWTYPE_*, the group variable, *VARNAME_*, and then the variables used to form the correlation matrix.
- A full set of matrix materials is written for each subgroup defined by the split variables.
- A split variable cannot have the same variable name as any other variable written to the matrix data file.
- If split-file processing is in effect when a matrix is written, the same split file must be in effect when that matrix is read by another procedure.

STDDEV and CORR Records

Records written with *ROWTYPE_* values STDDEV and CORR are influenced by specifications on the STATISTICS and CLASSIFY subcommands.

- If BOXM or GCOV is specified on STATISTICS or SEPARATE is specified on CLASSIFY, the STDDEV and CORR records represent within-cell data and receive values for the grouping variable.
- If none of the above specifications is in effect, the STDDEV and CORR records represent pooled values. The STDDEV vector contains the square root of the mean square error for

each variable, and STDDEV and CORR records receive the system-missing value for the grouping variable.

Missing Values

Missing-value treatment affects the values written to a matrix data file. When reading a matrix data file, be sure to specify a missing-value treatment on DISCRIMINANT that is compatible with the treatment that was in effect when the matrix materials were generated.

Example

```
GET FILE=UNIONBK /KEEP WORLD FOOD SERVICE BUS MECHANIC
                 CONSTRUC COOK MANAGER FSALES APPL RENT.
DISCRIMINANT  GROUPS=WORLD(1,3)
 /VARIABLES=FOOD SERVICE BUS MECHANIC CONSTRUC COOK MANAGER FSALES
 /METHOD=WILKS
 /PRIORS=SIZE
 /MATRIX=OUT(DISCMTX).
```

- DISCRIMINANT reads data from the SPSS data file *UNIONBK* and writes one set of matrix materials to the file *DISCMTX*.
- The working data file is still *UNIONBK*. Subsequent commands are executed on this file.

Example

```
* Use matrix output to classify data in a different file.

GET FILE=UB2 /KEEP WORLD FOOD SERVICE BUS MECHANIC
             CONSTRUC COOK MANAGER FSALES APPL RENT.
DISCRIMINANT  GROUPS=WORLD(1,3)
 /VARIABLES=FOOD SERVICE BUS MECHANIC CONSTRUC COOK MANAGER FSALES
 /METHOD=WILKS
 /PRIORS=SIZE
 /MATRIX=IN(DISCMTX).
```

- The matrix data file created in the previous example is used to classify data from file *UB2*.

Example

```
GET FILE=UNIONBK /KEEP WORLD FOOD SERVICE BUS MECHANIC
                 CONSTRUC COOK MANAGER FSALES APPL RENT.
DISCRIMINANT  GROUPS=WORLD(1,3)
 /VARIABLES=FOOD SERVICE BUS MECHANIC CONSTRUC COOK MANAGER FSALES
 /METHOD=WILKS
 /PRIORS=SIZE
 /MATRIX=OUT(*).
LIST.
```

- DISCRIMINANT writes the same matrix as in the first example. However, the matrix data file replaces the working data file.

- The LIST command is executed on the matrix file, not on the *UNIONBK* file.

Example

```
GET FILE=DISCMTX.
DISCRIMINANT  GROUPS=WORLD(1,3)
 /VARIABLES=FOOD SERVICE BUS MECHANIC CONSTRUC COOK MANAGER FSALES
 /METHOD=RAO
 /MATRIX=IN(*).
```

- This example assumes you are starting a new session and want to read an existing matrix data file. GET retrieves the matrix data file *DISCMTX.*
- MATRIX=IN specifies an asterisk because the matrix data file is the working data file. If MATRIX=IN(DISCMTX) is specified, SPSS issues an error message.
- If the GET command is omitted, SPSS issues an error message.

Example

```
GET FILE=UNIONBK /KEEP WORLD FOOD SERVICE BUS MECHANIC
                  CONSTRUC COOK MANAGER FSALES APPL RENT.
DISCRIMINANT  GROUPS=WORLD(1,3)
 /VARIABLES=FOOD SERVICE BUS MECHANIC CONSTRUC COOK MANAGER FSALES
 /CLASSIFY=SEPARATE
 /MATRIX=OUT(*).
DISCRIMINANT  GROUPS=WORLD(1,3)
 /VARIABLES=FOOD SERVICE BUS MECHANIC CONSTRUC COOK MANAGER FSALES
 /STATISTICS=BOXM
 /MATRIX=IN(*).
```

- The first DISCRIMINANT command creates a matrix with CLASSIFY=SEPARATE in effect. To read this matrix, the second DISCRIMINANT command must specify either BOXM or GCOV on STATISTICS or SEPARATE on CLASSIFY. STATISTICS=BOXM is used.

FACTOR

```
FACTOR VARIABLES=varlist† [/MISSING=[{LISTWISE**}] [INCLUDE]]
                                      {PAIRWISE }
                                      {MEANSUB  }
                                      {DEFAULT**}

    [/WIDTH={132    }]
            {n      }
            {DEFAULT}

    [/MATRIX=[IN({COR=file})]   [OUT({COR=file})]]
                 {COR=*   }          {COR=*   }
                 {FAC=file}          {FAC=file}
                 {FAC=*   }          {FAC=*   }

    [/ANALYSIS=varlist...]

    [/PRINT=[DEFAULT**] [INITIAL**] [EXTRACTION**] [ROTATION**]
            [UNIVARIATE] [CORRELATION] [DET] [INV] [REPR] [AIC]
            [KMO] [FSCORE] [SIG] [ALL]]

    [/PLOT=[EIGEN] [ROTATION [(n1,n2)]]]

    [/DIAGONAL={value list}]
               {DEFAULT**  }

    [/FORMAT=[SORT] [BLANK(n)] [DEFAULT**]]

    [/CRITERIA=[FACTORS(n)] [MINEIGEN({1.0**})] [ITERATE({25**})]
                                      {n    }            {n   }

               [RCONVERGE({0.0001**})] [DELTA({0**})] [{KAISER**}]
                         {n       }          {n }     {NOKAISER}

               [ECONVERGE({0.001**})]] [DEFAULT**]
                         {n      }

    [/EXTRACTION={PC**     }] [/ROTATION={VARIMAX**}]
                 {PA1**    }             {EQUAMAX  }
                 {PAF      }             {QUARTIMAX}
                 {ALPHA    }             {OBLIMIN  }
                 {IMAGE    }             {NOROTATE }
                 {ULS      }             {DEFAULT**}
                 {GLS      }
                 {ML       }
                 {DEFAULT**}

    [/SAVE=[{REG    } ({ALL}[rootname])]]
            {BART   }  {n }
            {AR     }
            {DEFAULT}

    [/ANALYSIS...]

    [/CRITERIA...]    [/EXTRACTION...]

    [/ROTATION...]    [/SAVE...]
```

† Omit VARIABLES with matrix input.
**Default if the subcommand is omitted.

Example:

```
FACTOR VARIABLES=V1 TO V12.
```

Overview

FACTOR performs factor analysis using one of the seven extraction methods. FACTOR accepts matrix input in the form of correlation matrices or factor loading matrices and can also write the matrix materials to matrix data file.

Options

Analysis Block Display. You can tailor the statistical display for an analysis block to include correlation matrices, reproduced correlation matrices, and other statistics using the PRINT subcommand. You can sort the output in the factor pattern and structure matrices with the FORMAT subcommand. You can also request scree plots and plots of the variables in factor space for all analyses within an analysis block on the PLOT subcommand.

Extraction Phase Options. With the EXTRACTION subcommand you can specify one of six extraction methods in addition to the default principal components extraction: principal axis factoring, alpha factoring, image factoring, unweighted least squares, generalized least squares, and maximum likelihood. You can supply initial diagonal values for principal axis factoring on the DIAGONAL subcommand. On the CRITERIA subcommand you can select the statistical criteria used in the extraction.

Rotation Phase Options. You can control the criteria for factor rotation with the CRITERIA subcommand. On the ROTATION subcommand you can choose among three rotation methods (equamax, quartimax, and oblimin) in addition to the default varimax rotation, or you can specify no rotation.

Factor Scores. You can save factor scores as new variables in the working data file using any of the three methods available on the SAVE subcommand.

Display Format. You can control the width of the display within FACTOR using the WIDTH subcommand.

Matrix Input and Output. With the MATRIX subcommand you can write a correlation matrix or a factor loading matrix. You can also read matrix materials written either by a previous FACTOR procedure or by a procedure that writes matrices with Pearson correlation coefficients.

Basic Specification

The basic specification is the VARIABLES subcommand with a variable list. FACTOR performs principal components analysis with a varimax rotation on all variables in the analysis using default criteria.

- When matrix materials are used as input, VARIABLES cannot be specified.

Subcommand Order

The standard subcommand order is illustrated in Figure 8.

Figure 8   Subcommand order

```
FACTOR VARIABLES=...
    / MISSING=...
    / WIDTH=...
    / MATRIX=...
```

┌───┐
│   **Analysis Block(s)**   │
│   / **ANALYSIS**=...   │
│   / PRINT=...   │
│   / PLOT=...   │
│   / DIAGONAL=...   │
│   / FORMAT=...   │
│   ┌──┐ │
│   │   **Extraction Block(s)**   │ │
│   │   / CRITERIA=(extraction criteria)   │ │
│   │   / **EXTRACTION**=...   │ │
│   │   ┌───┐   │ │
│   │   │   **Rotation Block(s)**   │   │ │
│   │   │   / CRITERIA=(rotation criteria)   │   │ │
│   │   │   / **ROTATION**=...   │   │ │
│   │   │   / SAVE=...   │   │ │
│   │   └───┘   │ │
│   └──┘ │
└───┘

- Subcommands listed in the analysis block apply to all extraction and rotation blocks within that analysis block. Subcommands listed in the extraction block apply to all rotation blocks within that extraction block.

- Each analysis block can contain multiple extraction blocks, and each extraction block can contain multiple rotation blocks.

- The CRITERIA and FORMAT subcommands remain in effect until explicitly overridden. Other subcommands affect only the block in which they are contained.

- The order of subcommands can be different from the order shown in Figure 8. However, any analysis that can be performed with procedure FACTOR can be performed using this order, repeating analysis, rotation, and extraction blocks as needed. (If MATRIX=IN is specified, VARIABLES should be omitted.) Specifying commands out of order can produce unexpected results.

- If you enter any subcommand other than the global subcommands (VARIABLES, MISSING, WIDTH, and MATRIX) before the first ANALYSIS subcommand, an implicit analysis block including all variables on the VARIABLES subcommand is activated. Factors are extracted and rotated for this implicit block before any explicitly requested analysis block is activated.

- If you enter a SAVE or ROTATION subcommand before the first EXTRACTION in any analysis block, an implicit extraction block using the default method (principal components) is activated. Factors are extracted and rotated for this implicit block before any explicitly requested extraction block is activated.

- If you enter CRITERIA *after* an EXTRACTION or ROTATION subcommand, the criteria do not affect that extraction or rotation.

Example

```
FACTOR VAR=V1 TO V12
  /ANALYSIS=V1 TO V8
  /CRITERIA=FACTORS(3)
  /EXTRACTION=PAF
  /ROTATION=QUARTIMAX.
```

- **FACTOR** extracts three factors using the principal axis method and quartimax rotation.

Example

```
* Unexpected results in FACTOR.

FACTOR VAR=V1 TO V12
  /CRITERIA=FACTORS(3)
  /ANALYSIS=V1 TO V8
  /EXTRACTION=PAF
  /ROTATION=QUARTIMAX.
```

- The **CRITERIA** subcommand activates an analysis block of all twelve variables. **FACTOR** extracts three factors using the default extraction method (principal components) and rotation (varimax) before activating the analysis block with *V1* to *V8*, where different extraction and rotation methods are requested.

Example

```
* Unexpected results in FACTOR.

FACTOR VARIABLES=V1 TO V12
  /SAVE DEFAULT (ALL,FAC)
  /EXTRACTION=PAF
  /ROTATION=OBLIMIN.
```

- The **SAVE** subcommand activates an extraction block using the default extraction method (principal components) and rotation (varimax). These factors are saved in the working data file as *FAC1*, *FAC2*, and so on.
- The next extraction block uses principal axis factoring and oblimin rotation but does not contain a **SAVE** subcommand, so no factor scores for this extraction block are saved in the working data file.

Example

```
* Unexpected results in FACTOR.

FACTOR V1 TO V12
  /EXTRACTION PAF
  /CRITERIA FACTORS(5).
```

- Since no **CRITERIA** subcommand precedes EXTRACTION, default criteria are used, and the specified **CRITERIA** subcommand is ignored.

Syntax Rules

- The global subcommands **VARIABLES** or **MATRIX=IN** can be specified only once and are in effect for the entire FACTOR procedure. Multiple specifications of MISSING and WIDTH are allowed, but only the last specified is in effect for the entire procedure.

- VARIABLES (or MATRIX=IN) and MISSING must precede any of the other subcommands. WIDTH can be specified anywhere.

- Subcommands ANALYSIS, PRINT, PLOT, DIAGONAL, and FORMAT are **analysis block** subcommands. ANALYSIS initiates an analysis block and specifies a subset of variables; the other subcommands apply to analyses performed on those variables.

- The PRINT, PLOT, and DIAGONAL subcommands are in effect only for the current analysis block. Defaults are restored when another analysis block is specified. The FORMAT subcommand remains in effect until a new FORMAT subcommand is specified. Defaults are *not* restored when a new analysis block is specified.

- Only one PRINT, PLOT, DIAGONAL, and FORMAT subcommand can be in effect for each ANALYSIS subcommand. If any of these is specified more than once in a given analysis block, the last one specified for that block is in effect.

- You can request more than one analysis block within a FACTOR procedure.

- Subcommands CRITERIA and EXTRACTION are **extraction block** subcommands. EXTRACTION triggers the extraction of factors according to a specified method.

- CRITERIA can be used one or more times in an extraction block to set parameters governing any *subsequent* EXTRACTION and ROTATION subcommands. Specifications on the CRITERIA subcommand carry over from analysis to analysis until explicitly overridden by another CRITERIA subcommand. Defaults are *not* restored when a new analysis block is specified.

- You can request more than one extraction block within an analysis block.

- Subcommands SAVE and ROTATION are **rotation block** subcommands. ROTATION triggers a rotation of the factors in the current extraction block, and SAVE adds factor scores for the following rotation to the working data file.

- You can specify SAVE more than once within a rotation block.

- You can request more than one rotation block within an extraction block.

Operations

- VARIABLES calculates a correlation matrix, which is the basis for all further analyses.

- The width specified on the WIDTH subcommand, if any, overrides the width defined on SET.

Example

```
FACTOR VARIABLES=V1 TO V12.
```

- This example produces the default principal components analysis of twelve variables. Those with eigenvalues greater than 1 (the default criterion for extraction) are rotated using varimax rotation (the default).

VARIABLES Subcommand

VARIABLES names all the variables to be used in the FACTOR procedure. FACTOR computes a correlation matrix that includes all the variables named. This matrix is used by all analysis blocks that follow.

* VARIABLES is required except when matrix input is used. When FACTOR reads a matrix data file, the VARIABLES subcommand cannot be used.
* The specification on VARIABLES is a list of numeric variables.
* Keyword ALL on VARIABLES refers to all variables in the working data file.
* All variables named on subsequent subcommands must first be named on the VARIABLES subcommand.
* Only one VARIABLES subcommand can be specified, and it must precede any analysis or rotation block subcommands. Only the MISSING and WIDTH subcommands can precede it.

MISSING Subcommand

MISSING controls the treatment of cases with missing values.

* If MISSING is omitted or included without specifications, listwise deletion is in effect.
* MISSING must precede any analysis block subcommands.
* The MISSING specification controls all analyses requested on FACTOR.
* The LISTWISE, PAIRWISE, and MEANSUB keywords are alternatives, but any one of them can be used with INCLUDE.

LISTWISE *Delete cases with missing values listwise.* Only cases with nonmissing values for all variables named on the VARIABLES subcommand are used. Listwise deletion can also be requested with keyword DEFAULT.

PAIRWISE *Delete cases with missing values pairwise.* All cases with nonmissing values for each pair of variables correlated are used to compute that correlation, regardless of whether the cases have missing values for any other variable.

MEANSUB *Replace missing values with the variable mean.* All cases are used after the substitution is made. If INCLUDE is also specified, user-missing values are included in the computation of the means, and means are substituted only for the system-missing value.

INCLUDE *Include user-missing values.* Cases with user-missing values are treated as valid.

WIDTH Subcommand

WIDTH controls the width of the output.

* WIDTH can be specified anywhere and affects all FACTOR output. If more than one width is specified, the last is in effect.

- The specification on WIDTH is an integer ranging from 72 to 132.
- If WIDTH is omitted or if WIDTH specifies DEFAULT, the width specified on the SET command is used.
- If WIDTH is entered without specifications, a width of 132 is used.

ANALYSIS Subcommand

The ANALYSIS subcommand specifies a subset of the variables named on VARIABLES for use in an analysis block.

- The specification on ANALYSIS is a list of variables, all of which must have been named on the VARIABLES subcommand. For matrix input, ANALYSIS can specify a subset of the variables in the matrix.
- Each ANALYSIS subcommand initiates an analysis block. The analysis block ends when another ANALYSIS subcommand is specified or the FACTOR procedure ends.
- Within an analysis block, only those variables named on the ANALYSIS subcommand are available.
- If ANALYSIS is omitted, all variables named on the VARIABLES subcommand (or included in the matrix input file) are used in all extractions.
- Keyword TO in a variable list on ANALYSIS refers to the order in which variables are named on the VARIABLES subcommand, not to their order in the working data file.
- Keyword ALL refers to all variables named on the VARIABLES subcommand.

Example

```
FACTOR VARIABLES=V1 V2 V3 V4 V5 V6
   /ANALYSIS=V1 TO V4
   /ANALYSIS=V4 TO V6.
```

- This example specifies two analysis blocks. Variables *V1*, *V2*, *V3*, and *V4* are included in the first analysis block. Variables *V4*, *V5*, and *V6* are in the second analysis block.
- Keyword TO on ANALYSIS refers to the order of variables on VARIABLES, not the order in the working data file.
- A default principal components analysis with a varimax rotation will be performed for each analysis block.

FORMAT Subcommand

FORMAT modifies the format of factor pattern and structure matrices.

- FORMAT can be specified once in each analysis block. If more than one FORMAT is encountered in an analysis block, the last is in effect.
- If FORMAT is omitted or included without specifications, variables appear in the order in which they are named and all matrix entries are displayed.
- Once specified, FORMAT stays in effect until it is overridden. Defaults are not automatically restored when a new analysis block is specified.

SORT	*Order the factor loadings in descending order by the magnitude of the first factor.*
BLANK(n)	*Suppress coefficients lower in absolute value than* n.
DEFAULT	*Turn off keywords SORT and BLANK.*

Example

```
FACTOR VARIABLES=V1 TO V12
  /MISSING=MEANSUB
  /FORMAT=SORT BLANK(.3)
  /EXTRACTION=ULS
  /ROTATION=NOROTATE.
```

- This example specifies a single analysis block. All variables between and including *V1* and *V12* in the working data file are included.
- The MISSING subcommand substitutes variable means for missing values.
- The FORMAT subcommand orders variables in factor pattern matrices by descending value of loadings. Factor loadings with an absolute value less than 0.3 are omitted.
- Factors are extracted using unweighted least squares and are not rotated.

PRINT Subcommand

PRINT controls the statistical output for an analysis block and all extraction and rotation blocks within it.

- Keywords INITIAL, EXTRACTION, and ROTATION are the defaults if PRINT is omitted or specified without keywords.
- If any keywords are specified, only the output specifically requested is produced for the current analysis block.
- The defaults are reinstated when a new ANALYSIS subcommand is encountered.
- The requested statistics are displayed only for variables in the analysis block.
- PRINT can be specified anywhere within the analysis block. If more than one PRINT subcommand is specified, only the last is in effect.

INITIAL	*Initial communalities for each variable, eigenvalues of the unreduced correlation matrix and percentage of variance for each factor.*
EXTRACTION	*Factor pattern matrix, revised communalities, the eigenvalue of each factor retained, and the percentage of variance each eigenvalue represents.*
ROTATION	*Rotated factor pattern matrix, factor transformation matrix, and factor correlation matrix.*
UNIVARIATE	*Valid number of cases, means, and standard deviations.* (Not available with matrix input.)
CORRELATION	*Correlation matrix.*
SIG	*Matrix of significance levels of correlations.*

DET   *Determinant of the correlation matrix.*

INV   *Inverse of the correlation matrix.*

AIC   *Anti-image covariance and correlation matrices* (Kaiser, 1970). The measure of sampling adequacy for the individual variable is displayed on the diagonal of the anti-image correlation matrix.

KMO   *Kaiser-Meyer-Olkin measure of sampling adequacy and Bartlett's test of sphericity.* Tests of significance are not computed for an input matrix when it does not contain N values.

REPR   *Reproduced correlations and residual correlations.*

FSCORE *Factor score coefficient matrix.* Factor score coefficients are calculated using the method requested on the SAVE subcommand. The default is the regression method.

ALL   *All available statistics.*

DEFAULT *INITIAL, EXTRACTION, and ROTATION.*

Example

```
FACTOR VARS=V1 TO V12
  /MISS=MEANS
  /PRINT=DEF AIC KMO REPR
  /EXTRACT=ULS
  /ROTATE=VARIMAX.
```

- This example specifies a single analysis block that includes all variables between and including *V1* and *V12* in the working data file.
- Variable means are substituted for missing values.
- The output includes the anti-image correlation and covariance matrices, the Kaiser-Meyer-Olkin measure of sampling adequacy, the reproduced correlation and residual matrix, as well as the default statistics.
- Factors are extracted using unweighted least squares.
- The factor pattern matrix is rotated using the varimax rotation.

PLOT Subcommand

Use PLOT to request scree plots or plots of variables in rotated factor space.

- If PLOT is omitted, no plots are produced. If PLOT is used without specifications, it is ignored.
- PLOT is in effect only for the current analysis block. The default (no plots) is reinstated when a new ANALYSIS subcommand is encountered.
- PLOT can be specified anywhere within the analysis block. If more than one PLOT subcommand is specified, only the last one is in effect.

EIGEN   *Scree plot* (Cattell, 1966). The eigenvalues from each extraction are plotted in descending order.

ROTATION   *Plots of variables in factor space.* When used without any additional speci-fications, ROTATION can produce only high-resolution graphics. If three or more factors are extracted, a 3-D plot is produced with the factor space defined by the first three factors. You can request two-dimensional plots by specifying pairs of factor numbers in parentheses; for example, PLOT RO-TATION(1,2)(1,3)(2,3) requests three plots, each defined by two factors. When SET HIGHRES is OFF, ROTATION can only produce two-dimensional plots, and they must be explicitly requested; otherwise, SPSS issues an error message. The ROTATION subcommand must be explicitly specified when you enter the keyword ROTATION on the PLOT subcommand.

DIAGONAL Subcommand

DIAGONAL specifies values for the diagonal in conjunction with principal axis factoring.

- If DIAGONAL is omitted or included without specifications, FACTOR uses the default method for specifying the diagonal.
- DIAGONAL is in effect for all PAF extractions within the analysis block. It is ignored with extraction methods other than PAF.
- The default method for specifying the diagonal is reinstated when a new ANALYSIS subcommand is encountered. DIAGONAL can be specified anywhere within the analysis block. If more than one DIAGONAL subcommand is specified, only the last one is in effect. Default communality estimates for PAF are squared multiple correlations. If these cannot be computed, the maximum absolute correlation between the variable and any other variable in the analysis is used.

valuelist   *Diagonal values.* The number of values supplied must equal the number of variables in the analysis block. Use the notation n* before a value to indicate the value is repeated *n* times.

DEFAULT   *Initial communality estimates.*

Example

```
FACTOR VARIABLES=V1 TO V12
  /DIAGONAL=.56 .55 .74 2*.56 .70 3*.65 .76 .64 .63
  /EXTRACTION=PAF
  /ROTATION=VARIMAX.
```

- A single analysis block includes all variables between and including *V1* and *V12* in the working data file.
- DIAGONAL specifies 12 values to use as initial estimates of communalities in principal axis factoring.
- The factor pattern matrix is rotated using varimax rotation.

CRITERIA Subcommand

CRITERIA controls extraction and rotation criteria.

- CRITERIA can be specified before any implicit or explicit request for an extraction or rotation.
- Only defaults specifically altered are changed.
- Any criterion that is altered remains in effect for *all* subsequent analysis blocks until it is explicitly overridden.

The following keywords on CRITERIA apply to extractions:

FACTORS(n)   *Number of factors extracted.* The default is the number of eigenvalues greater than MINEIGEN. When specified, FACTORS overrides MINEIGEN.

MINEIGEN(n)   *Minimum eigenvalue used to control the number of factors extracted.* The default is 1.

ECONVERGE(n)   *Convergence criterion for extraction.* The default is 0.001.

The following keywords on CRITERIA apply to rotations:

RCONVERGE(n)   *Convergence criterion for rotation.* The default is 0.0001.

KAISER   *Kaiser normalization in the rotation phase.* This is the default. The alternative is NOKAISER.

NOKAISER   *No Kaiser normalization.*

DELTA(n)   *Delta for direct oblimin rotation.* DELTA affects the ROTATION subcommand only when OBLIMIN rotation is requested. The default is 0. The maximum acceptable value is 0.8. If you specify a value greater than 0.8, SPSS displays a warning and resets the value to the default.

The following keywords on CRITERIA apply to both extractions and rotations:

ITERATE(n)   *Maximum number of iterations for solutions in the extraction or rotation phases.* The default is 25.

DEFAULT   *Reestablish default values for all criteria.*

Example

```
FACTOR VARIABLES=V1 TO V12
  /CRITERIA=FACTORS(6)
  /EXTRACTION=PC
  /ROTATION=NOROTATE
  /CRITERIA=DEFAULT
  /EXTRACTION=ML
  /ROTATION=VARIMAX
  /PLOT=ROTATION.
```

- This example initiates a single analysis block that analyzes all variables between and including *V1* and *V12* in the working data file.
- Six factors are extracted in the first extraction. The extraction uses the default principal components method, and the factor pattern matrix is not rotated.

- The default criteria are reinstated for the second extraction, which uses the maximum-likelihood method. The second factor pattern matrix is rotated using the varimax rotation.
- PLOT sends all extracted factors to the graphics editor and shows a 3-D plot of the first three factors. If HIGHRES is set to OFF, SPSS displays an error message.
- PLOT applies to both extractions, since there is only one analysis block.

EXTRACTION Subcommand

EXTRACTION specifies the factor extraction technique.

- Multiple EXTRACTION subcommands can be specified within an analysis block.
- If EXTRACTION is not specified or is included without specifications, principal components extraction is used.
- If you specify criteria for EXTRACTION, the CRITERIA subcommand must precede the EXTRACTION subcommand.
- When you specify EXTRACTION, you should always explicitly specify the ROTATION subcommand. If ROTATION is not specified, the factors are not rotated.

PC   *Principal components analysis* (Harman, 1967). This is the default. PC can also be requested with keyword PA1 or DEFAULT.

PAF   *Principal axis factoring.* PAF can also be requested with keyword PA2.

ALPHA   *Alpha factoring* (Kaiser & Caffry, 1965).

IMAGE   *Image factoring* (Kaiser, 1963).

ULS   *Unweighted least squares* (Harman & Jones, 1966).

GLS   *Generalized least squares.*

ML   *Maximum likelihood* (Jöreskog & Lawley, 1968).

Example

```
FACTOR VARIABLES=V1 TO V12
  /EXTRACTION=ULS
  /ROTATE=NOROTATE
  /ANALYSIS=V1 TO V6
  /EXTRACTION=ULS
  /ROTATE=NOROTATE
  /EXTRACTION=ML
  /ROTATE=NOROTATE.
```

- This example specifies two analysis blocks. In the first analysis block, variables *V1* through *V12* are analyzed using unweighted least-squares extraction. The factor pattern matrix is not rotated.
- In the second analysis block, variables *V1* through *V6* are analyzed first with an unweighted least-squares extraction and then with a maximum-likelihood extraction. No rotation is performed for either extraction.

ROTATION Subcommand

ROTATION specifies the factor rotation method. It can also be used to suppress the rotation phase entirely.

- You can specify multiple ROTATION subcommands after each extraction.
- Rotations are performed on the matrix resulting from the previous extraction.
- If you specify the ROTATION subcommand without specifications or omit both the EXTRACTION and ROTATION subcommands, varimax rotation is used.
- If you include an EXTRACTION subcommand but omit the ROTATION subcommand, factors are not rotated.
- Keyword NOROTATE on the ROTATION subcommand produces a plot of variables in unrotated factor space if the PLOT subcommand is also included in the analysis block.

VARIMAX   *Varimax rotation.* This is the default if ROTATION is entered without specifications or if EXTRACTION and ROTATION are both omitted. Varimax rotation can also be requested with keyword DEFAULT.

EQUAMAX   *Equamax rotation.*

QUARTIMAX   *Quartimax rotation.*

OBLIMIN   *Direct oblimin rotation.* This is a nonorthogonal rotation; thus, a factor correlation matrix will also be displayed. For this method, specify DELTA on the CRITERIA subcommand.

NOROTATE   *No rotation.*

Example

```
FACTOR VARIABLES=V1 TO V12
  /EXTRACTION=ULS
  /ROTATION
  /ROTATION=OBLIMIN.
```

- The first ROTATION subcommand specifies the default varimax rotation.
- The second ROTATION subcommand specifies an oblimin rotation based on the same extraction of factors.

SAVE Subcommand

SAVE allows you to save factor scores from any rotated or unrotated extraction as new variables in the working data file. You can use any of the three methods for computing the factor scores.

- SAVE must follow the ROTATE subcommand specifying the rotation for which factor scores are to be saved. If no ROTATE subcommand precedes SAVE, a varimax rotation is used and factor scores are saved for varimax-rotated factors.
- You cannot use the SAVE subcommand if you are replacing the working data file with matrix materials (see "Matrix Output" on p. 292).

- You can specify SAVE more than once in a rotation block. Thus, you can calculate and save factor scores using different methods for a single rotation.
- Each specification applies to the previous rotation.
- The new variables are added to the end of the working data file.

Keywords to specify the method of computing factor scores are:

REG   *Regression method.* This is the default.

BART   *Bartlett method.*

AR   *Anderson-Rubin method.*

DEFAULT   *The same as REG.*

- After one of the above keywords, specify in parentheses the number of scores to save and a rootname to use in naming the variables.
- You can specify either an integer or the keyword ALL. The maximum number of scores you can specify is the number of factors in the solution.
- FACTOR forms variable names by appending sequential numbers to the rootname you specify. The rootname must begin with a letter and conform to the rules for SPSS variable names. It must be short enough that the variable names formed will not exceed eight characters.
- If you do not specify a rootname, FACTOR forms unique variable names using the formula *FACn_m*, where *m* increments to create a new rootname and *n* increments to create variable names. For example, the scores for the first SAVE subcommand without a specified rootname will be named *FAC1_1, FAC2_1, FAC3_1*, and so forth. The next set of scores will be saved as *FAC1_2, FAC2_2, FAC3_2*, and so forth. As *m* and *n* increase, the prefix *FAC* is truncated to keep the variable names within eight characters. For example, *FA999_12* is increased to *F1000_12*. The initial *F* is required.
- FACTOR automatically generates variable labels for the new variables. Each label contains information about the method of computing the factor score, its sequential number, and the sequential number of the analysis.

Example

```
FACTOR VARIABLES=V1 TO V12
  /CRITERIA FACTORS(4)
  /ROTATION
  /SAVE REG (4,PCOMP)
  /CRITERIA DEFAULT
  /EXTRACTION PAF
  /ROTATION
  /SAVE DEF (ALL).
```

- Since there is no EXTRACTION subcommand before the first ROTATION, the first extraction will be the default principal components.
- The first CRITERIA subcommand specifies that four principal components should be extracted.
- The first ROTATION subcommand requests the default varimax rotation for the principal components.

- The first SAVE subcommand calculates scores using the regression method. Four scores will be added to the file: *PCOMP1*, *PCOMP2*, *PCOMP3*, and *PCOMP4*.
- The next CRITERIA subcommand restores default criteria. Here it implies that subsequent extractions should extract all factors with eigenvalues greater than 1.
- The second EXTRACTION subcommand specifies principal axis factoring.
- The second ROTATION subcommand requests the default varimax rotation for PAF factors so that varimax-rotated factor scores are saved. If this subcommand had been omitted, the rotation phase would have been skipped, and scores for unrotated factors would be added to the file.
- The second SAVE subcommand calculates scores using the regression method (the default). The number of scores added to the file is the number extracted and their names will be *FAC1_1*, *FAC2_1*, and so on. The first set of default names is used because this is the first SAVE subcommand without a specified rootname.

MATRIX Subcommand

MATRIX reads and writes SPSS matrix data files.

- MATRIX must always be specified before the analysis block.
- Only one IN and one OUT keyword can be specified on the MATRIX subcommand. If either IN or OUT is specified more than once, the FACTOR procedure is not executed.
- The matrix type must be indicated on IN or OUT. The types are COR for correlation matrix and FAC for factor loading matrix. Indicate the matrix type within parentheses immediately before you identify the matrix file.
- If you use both IN and OUT on MATRIX, you can specify them in either order.

OUT (filename) *Write a matrix data file.* Specify the matrix type (COR or FAC) and the matrix file in parentheses. Use COR for a correlation matrix or FAC for a factor loading matrix. For the matrix data file, specify a filename to store the matrix materials on disk or an asterisk to replace the working data file. If you specify an asterisk, the matrix data file is not stored on disk unless you use SAVE or XSAVE.

IN (filename) *Read a matrix data file.* Specify the matrix type (COR or FAC) and the matrix file in parentheses. For the matrix data file, specify an asterisk if the matrix data file is the working data file. If the matrix file is another file, specify the filename in parentheses. A matrix file read from an external file does not replace the working data file.

Matrix Output

- FACTOR can write matrix materials in the form of a correlation matrix or a factor loading matrix. The correlation matrix materials include counts, means, and standard deviations in addition to Pearson correlation coefficients. The factor loading matrix materials contain only factor values and no additional statistics. See "Format of the Matrix Data File" on p. 293 for a description of the file.

- FACTOR generates matrix output from the first analysis block and writes one matrix per split file. You cannot write a matrix from subsequent analysis blocks on the same FACTOR subcommand.
- Any documents contained in the working data file are not transferred to the matrix file.

Matrix Input

- FACTOR can read matrix materials written either by a previous FACTOR procedure or by a procedure that writes matrices with Pearson correlation coefficients. For more information, see Universals in the *SPSS Base System Syntax Reference Guide*.
- MATRIX=IN cannot be used unless a working data file has already been defined. To read an existing matrix data file at the beginning of a session, first use GET to retrieve the matrix file and then specify IN(COR=*) or IN(FAC=*) on MATRIX.
- The VARIABLES subcommand cannot be used with matrix input.
- FACTOR cannot read split-file matrices.
- For correlation matrix input, the ANALYSIS subcommand can specify a subset of the variables in the matrix. You cannot specify a subset of variables for factor matrix input. For either type of matrix input, the ANALYSIS subcommand uses all variables in the matrix by default.

Format of the Matrix Data File

- For correlation matrices, the matrix data file has two special variables created by SPSS: *ROWTYPE_* and *VARNAME_*. Variable *ROWTYPE_* is a short string variable with the value CORR (for Pearson correlation coefficient) for each matrix row. Variable *VARNAME_* is a short string variable whose values are the names of the variables used to form the correlation matrix.
- For factor loading matrices, SPSS generates two special variables named *ROWTYPE_* and *FACTOR_*. The value for *ROWTYPE_* is always FACTOR. The values for *FACTOR_* are the ordinal numbers of the factors.
- The remaining variables are the variables used to form the matrix.

Split Files

- FACTOR can write split-file matrices that can be read by other procedures. However, FACTOR cannot read split-file matrices, even if the matrices were generated by a previous FACTOR command.
- When split-file processing is in effect, the first variables in the matrix data file are the split variables, followed by *ROWTYPE_*, *VARNAME_* (or *FACTOR_*), and then the variables used to form the matrix.
- A full set of matrix materials is written for each split-file group defined by the split variables.

- A split variable cannot have the same variable name as any other variable written to the matrix data file.
- If split-file processing is in effect when a matrix is written, the same split file must be in effect when that matrix is read by any other procedure. FACTOR itself cannot read split-file matrices.

Example

```
GET FILE=GSS80 /KEEP ABDEFECT TO ABSINGLE.
FACTOR VARIABLES=ABDEFECT TO ABSINGLE
  /MATRIX OUT(COR=CORMTX).
```

- FACTOR retrieves the *GSS80* file and writes a factor correlation matrix to the file *CORMTX*.
- The working data file is still *GSS80*. Subsequent commands will be executed on this file.

Example

```
GET FILE=GSS80 /KEEP ABDEFECT TO ABSINGLE.
FACTOR VARIABLES=ABDEFECT TO ABSINGLE
  /MATRIX OUT(COR=*).
LIST.
```

- FACTOR writes the same matrix as in the previous example.
- The working data file is replaced with the correlation matrix. The LIST command is executed on the matrix file, not on *GSS80*.

Example

```
GET FILE=GSS80 /KEEP ABDEFECT TO ABSINGLE.
FACTOR VARIABLES=ABDEFECT TO ABSINGLE
  /MATRIX OUT(FAC=*).
```

- FACTOR generates a factor loading matrix that replaces the working data file.

Example

```
GET FILE=COUNTRY /KEEP SAVINGS POP15 POP75 INCOME GROWTH.
REGRESSION MATRIX OUT(*)
  /VARS=SAVINGS TO GROWTH
  /MISS=PAIRWISE
  /DEP=SAVINGS /ENTER.
FACTOR MATRIX IN(COR=*) /MISSING=PAIRWISE.
```

- The GET command retrieves the *COUNTRY* file and selects the variables needed for the analysis.
- The REGRESSION command computes correlations among five variables with pairwise deletion. MATRIX=OUT writes a matrix data file, which replaces the working file.

- MATRIX IN(COR=*) on FACTOR reads the matrix materials REGRESSION has written to the working file. An asterisk is specified because the matrix materials are in the working file. FACTOR uses pairwise deletion, since this is what was in effect when the matrix was built.

Example

```
GET FILE=COUNTRY /KEEP SAVINGS POP15 POP75 INCOME GROWTH.
REGRESSION
  /VARS=SAVINGS TO GROWTH
  /MISS=PAIRWISE
  /DEP=SAVINGS /ENTER.
FACTOR MATRIX IN(COR=CORMTX).
```

- This example performs a regression analysis on file *COUNTRY* and then uses a different file for FACTOR. The file is an existing matrix data file.
- MATRIX=IN specifies the matrix data file *CORMTX*.
- *CORMTX* does not replace *COUNTRY* as the working data file.

Example

```
GET FILE=CORMTX.
FACTOR MATRIX IN(COR=*).
```

- This example starts a new session and reads an existing matrix data file. GET retrieves the matrix data file *CORMTX*.
- MATRIX=IN specifies an asterisk because the matrix data file is the working data file. If MATRIX=IN(CORMTX) is specified, SPSS issues an error message.
- If the GET command is omitted, SPSS issues an error message.
References

PROXIMITIES

```
PROXIMITIES  varlist  [/VIEW={CASE**  }]
                            {VARIABLE}

[/STANDARDIZE=[{VARIABLE}]  [{NONE**  }]]
               {CASE    }    {Z      }
                             {SD     }
                             {RANGE  }
                             {MAX    }
                             {MEAN   }
                             {RESCALE}

[/MEASURE=[{EUCLID**            }]  [ABSOLUTE]  [REVERSE]  [RESCALE]
           {SEUCLID            }
           {COSINE             }
           {CORRELATION        }
           {BLOCK              }
           {CHEBYCHEV          }
           {POWER(p,r)         }
           {MINKOWSKI(p)       }
           {CHISQ              }
           {PH2                }
           {RR[(p[,np])]       }
           {SM[(p[,np])]       }
           {JACCARD[(p[,np])]  }
           {DICE[(p[,np])]     }
           {SS1[(p[,np])]      }
           {RT[(p[,np])]       }
           {SS2[(p[,np])]      }
           {K1[(p[,np])]       }
           {SS3[(p[,np])]      }
           {K2[(p[,np])]       }
           {SS4[(p[,np])]      }
           {HAMANN[(p[,np])]   }
           {OCHIAI[(p[,np])]   }
           {SS5[(p[,np])]      }
           {PHI[(p[,np])]      }
           {LAMBDA[(p[,np])]   }
           {D[(p[,np])]        }
           {Y[(p[,np])]        }
           {Q[(p[,np])]        }
           {BEUCLID[(p[,np])]  }
           {SIZE[(p[,np])]     }
           {PATTERN[(p[,np])]  }
           {BSEUCLID[(p[,np])] }
           {BSHAPE[(p[,np])]   }
           {DISPER[(p[,np])]   }
           {VARIANCE[(p[,np])] }
           {BLWMN[(p[,np])]    }
           {NONE               }
[/PRINT=[{PROXIMITIES**}]]   [/ID=varname]
         {NONE         }

[/MISSING=[LISTWISE**]   [INCLUDE]

[/MATRIX=[IN({file})]  OUT({file})]]
             {*   }        {*   }
```

**Default if the subcommand is omitted.

Example:

```
PROXIMITIES A B C.
```

Overview

PROXIMITIES computes a variety of measures of similarity, dissimilarity, or distance be-tween pairs of cases or pairs of variables for moderate-sized data sets (see "Limitations" be-low). PROXIMITIES matrix output can be used as input to procedures ALSCAL, CLUSTER, and FACTOR. To learn more about proximity matrices and their uses, consult Anderberg (1973) and Romesburg (1984).

Options

Standardizing Data. With the STANDARDIZE subcommand you can standardize the values for each variable or for each case by any of several different methods.

Proximity Measures. You can compute a variety of similarity, dissimilarity, and distance measures using the MEASURE subcommand. (Similarity measures increase with greater similarity; dissimilarity and distance measures decrease.) MEASURE can compute measures for continuous data, frequency count data, and binary data. Only one measure can be request-ed in any one PROXIMITIES procedure. With the VIEW subcommand, you can control whether proximities are computed between variables or between cases.

Output. You can display a computed matrix using the PRINT subcommand. By default, PROXIMITIES identifies cases by case number. Optionally you can specify a string variable that contains an identifier for each case on the ID subcommand.

Matrix Input and Output. You can write a computed distance matrix to an SPSS data file using the MATRIX subcommand. This matrix can be used as input to procedures CLUSTER, ALSCAL, and FACTOR. You can also use MATRIX to read a similarity, dissimilarity, or dis-tance matrix. This option lets you rescale or transform existing proximity matrices.

Basic Specification

The basic specification is a variable list, which obtains Euclidean distances between cases based on the values of each specified variable.

Subcommand Order

- The variable list must be first.
- Subcommands can be named in any order.

Operations

- PROXIMITIES ignores case weights when computing coefficients

Limitations

- PROXIMITIES keeps the raw data for the current split-file group in memory. Storage requirements increase rapidly with the number of cases and the number of items (cases or variables) for which PROXIMITIES computes coefficients.

Example

```
PROXIMITIES A B C.
```

- PROXIMITIES computes Euclidean distances between cases based on the values of variables *A*, *B*, and *C*.

Variable Specification

- The variable list must be specified first.
- The variable list can be omitted when an input matrix data file is specified. A slash must then be specified before the first subcommand to indicate that the variable list is omitted.

STANDARDIZE Subcommand

Use STANDARDIZE to standardize data values for either cases or variables before computing proximities. One of two options can be specified to control the direction of standardization:

VARIABLE   *Standardize the values for each variable*. This is the default.

CASE   *Standardize the values within each case*.

Several standardization methods are available. These allow you to equalize selected properties of the values. All methods can be used with either VARIABLE or CASE. Only one standardization method can be specified.

- If STANDARDIZE is omitted, proximities are computed using the original values (keyword NONE).
- If STANDARDIZE is used without specifications, proximities are computed using *Z* scores (keyword Z).
- STANDARDIZE cannot be used with binary measures.

NONE   *Do not standardize*. Proximities are computed using the original values. This is the default if STANDARDIZE is omitted.

Z   *Standardize values to Z scores, with a mean of 0 and a standard deviation of 1*. PROXIMITIES subtracts the mean value for the variable or case from each value being standardized and then divides by the standard deviation. If the standard deviation is 0, PROXIMITIES sets all values for the case or variable to 0. This is the default if STANDARDIZE is used without specifications.

RANGE   *Standardize values to have a range of 1*. PROXIMITIES divides each value being standardized by the range of values for the variable or case. If the range is 0, PROXIMITIES leaves all values unchanged.

RESCALE   *Standardize values to have a range from 0 to 1.* From each value being standardized, PROXIMITIES subtracts the minimum value and then divides by the range for the variable or case. If a range is 0, PROXIMITIES sets all values for the case or variable to 0.50.

MAX   *Standardize values to a maximum magnitude of 1.* PROXIMITIES divides each value being standardized by the maximum value for the variable or case. If the maximum of the values is 0, PROXIMITIES divides each value by the absolute magnitude of the smallest value and adds 1.

MEAN   *Standardize values to a mean of 1.* PROXIMITIES divides each value being standardized by the mean of the values for the variable or case. If the mean is 0, PROXIMITIES adds 1 to all values for the case or variable to produce a mean of 1.

SD   *Standardize values to unit standard deviation.* PROXIMITIES divides each value being standardized by the standard deviation of the values for the variable or case. PROXIMITIES does not change the values if their standard deviation is 0.

Example

```
PROXIMITIES A B C
  /STANDARDIZE=CASE RANGE.
```

- Within each case, values are standardized to have ranges of 1.

VIEW Subcommand

VIEW indicates whether proximities are computed between cases or between variables.

CASE   *Compute proximity values between cases.* This is the default.

VARIABLE   *Compute proximity values between variables.*

MEASURE Subcommand

MEASURE specifies the similarity, dissimilarity, or distance measure that PROXIMITIES computes. Three transformations are available with any of these measures:

ABSOLUTE   *Take the absolute values of the proximities.* Use ABSOLUTE when the sign of the values indicates the direction of the relationship (as with correlation coefficients) but only the magnitude of the relationship is of interest.

REVERSE   *Transform similarity values into dissimilarities, or vice versa.* Use this specification to reverse the ordering of the proximities by negating the values.

RESCALE   *Rescale the proximity values to a range of 0 to 1.* RESCALE standardizes the proximities by first subtracting the value of the smallest and then dividing by the range. You would not usually use RESCALE with measures that are already standardized on meaningful scales, as are correlations, cosines, and many binary coefficients.

PROXIMITIES can compute any one of a number of measures between items. You can choose among measures for continuous data, frequency count data, or binary data. Available keywords for each of these types of measures are defined in the following sections.

- Only one measure can be specified. However, each measure can be specified with any of the transformations ABSOLUTE, REVERSE, or RESCALE. To apply a transformation to an existing matrix of proximity values without computing any measures, use keyword NONE (see p. 307).

- If more than one transformation is specified, PROXIMITIES does them in the order listed above: first ABSOLUTE, then REVERSE, and then RESCALE.

- Each entry in the resulting proximity matrix represents a pair of items. The items can be either cases or variables, whichever is specified on the VIEW subcommand.

- When the items are cases, the computation for each pair of cases involves pairs of values for the specified variables.

- When the items are variables, the computation for each pair of variables involves pairs of values for the variables across all cases.

Example

```
PROXIMITIES A B C
   /MEASURE=EUCLID REVERSE.
```

- MEASURE specifies a EUCLID measure and a REVERSE transformation.

Measures for Continuous Data

To obtain proximities for continuous data, use any one of the following keywords on MEASURE:

EUCLID   *Euclidean distance.* This is the default specification for MEASURE. The distance between two items, x and y, is the square root of the sum of the squared differences between the values for the items.

$$\text{EUCLID}\,(x, y) \ = \ \sqrt{\Sigma_i\,(x_i - y_i)^2}$$

SEUCLID   *Squared Euclidean distance.* The distance between two items is the sum of the squared differences between the values for the items.

$$\text{SEUCLID}\,(x, y) \ = \ \Sigma_i\,(x_i - y_i)^2$$

CORRELATION   *Correlation between vectors of values.* This is a pattern similarity measure.

$$\text{CORRELATION}\,(x, y) \ = \ \frac{\Sigma_i\,(Z_{xi}Z_{yi})}{N - 1}$$

where Z_{xi} is the Z-score (standardized) value of x for the ith case or variable, and N is the number of cases or variables.

COSINE   *Cosine of vectors of values.* This is a pattern similarity measure.

$$\text{COSINE}\ (x, y)\ =\ \frac{\Sigma_i\,(x_i y_i)}{\sqrt{(\Sigma_i x_i^2)\ (\Sigma_i y_i^2)}}$$

CHEBYCHEV   *Chebychev distance metric.* The distance between two items is the maximum absolute difference between the values for the items.

$$\text{CHEBYCHEV}\ (x, y)\ =\ \max_i |x_i - y_i|$$

BLOCK   *City-block or Manhattan distance.* The distance between two items is the sum of the absolute differences between the values for the items.

$$\text{BLOCK}\ (x, y)\ =\ \Sigma_i |x_i - y_i|$$

MINKOWSKI(p)   *Distance in an absolute Minkowski power metric.* The distance between two items is the pth root of the sum of the absolute differences to the pth power between the values for the items. Appropriate selection of the integer parameter p yields Euclidean and many other distance metrics.

$$\text{MINKOWSKI}\ (x, y)\ =\ \left(\Sigma_i |x_i - y_i|^p\right)^{1/p}$$

POWER(p,r)   *Distance in an absolute power metric.* The distance between two items is the rth root of the sum of the absolute differences to the pth power between the values for the items. Appropriate selection of the integer parameters p and r yields Euclidean, squared Euclidean, Minkowski, city-block, and many other distance metrics.

$$\text{POWER}\ (x, y)\ =\ \left(\Sigma_i |x_i - y_i|^p\right)^{1/r}$$

Measures for Frequency Count Data

To obtain proximities for frequency count data, use either of the following keywords on MEASURE:

CHISQ   *Based on the chi-square test of equality for two sets of frequencies.* The magnitude of this dissimilarity measure depends on the total frequencies of the two cases or variables whose dissimilarity is computed. Expected values are from the model of independence of cases or variables x and y.

$$\text{CHISQ}\ (x, y)\ =\ \sqrt{\frac{\Sigma_i\,(x_i - E\,(x_i))^2}{E\,(x_i)} + \frac{\Sigma_i\,(y_i - E\,(y_i))^2}{E\,(y_i)}}$$

PH2   *Phi-square between sets of frequencies.* This is the CHISQ measure normalized by the square root of the combined frequency. Therefore, its value does not depend on the total frequencies of the two cases or variables whose dissimilarity is computed.

$$PH2\ (x, y)\ =\ \sqrt{\dfrac{\dfrac{\Sigma_i\,(x_i - E\,(x_i))^2}{E\,(x_i)} + \dfrac{\Sigma_i\,(y_i - E\,(y_i))^2}{E\,(y_i)}}{N}}$$

Measures for Binary Data

Different binary measures emphasize different aspects of the relationship between sets of binary values. However, all the measures are specified in the same way. Each measure has two optional integer-valued parameters, p (present) and np (not present).

- If both parameters are specified, PROXIMITIES uses the value of the first as an indicator that a characteristic is present and the value of the second as an indicator that a characteristic is absent. PROXIMITIES skips all other values.

- If only the first parameter is specified, PROXIMITIES uses that value to indicate presence and all other values to indicate absence.

- If no parameters are specified, PROXIMITIES assumes that 1 indicates presence and 0 indicates absence.

Using the indicators for presence and absence within each item (case or variable), PROXIMITIES constructs a 2×2 contingency table for each pair of items in turn. It uses this table to compute a proximity measure for the pair.

	Item 2 characteristics	
	Present	**Absent**
Item 1 characteristics		
Present	a	b
Absent	c	d

PROXIMITIES computes all binary measures from the values of a, b, c, and d. These values are tallied across variables (when the items are cases) or cases (when the items are variables). For example, if variables V, W, X, Y, Z have values 0, 1, 1, 0, 1 for case 1 and values 0, 1, 1, 0, 0 for case 2 (where 1 indicates presence and 0 indicates absence), the contingency table is as follows:

	Case 2 characteristics	
	Present	**Absent**
Case 1 characteristics		
Present	2	1
Absent	0	2

The contingency table indicates that both cases are present for two variables (W and X), both cases are absent for two variables (V and Y), and case 1 is present and case 2 is absent for one variable (Z). There are no variables for which case 1 is absent and case 2 is present.

The available binary measures include matching coefficients, conditional probabilities, predictability measures, and others.

Matching Coefficients. Table 6 shows a classification scheme for PROXIMITIES matching coefficients. In this scheme, *matches* are joint presences (value *a* in the contingency table) or joint absences (value *d*). *Nonmatches* are equal in number to value *b* plus value *c*. Matches and nonmatches may be weighted equally or not. The three coefficients JACCARD, DICE, and SS2 are related monotonically, as are SM, SS1, and RT. All coefficients in Table 6 are similarity measures, and all except two (K1 and SS3) range from 0 to 1. K1 and SS3 have a minimum value of 0 and no upper limit.

Table 6   Binary matching coefficients in PROXIMITIES

	Joint absences excluded from numerator	Joint absences included in numerator
All matches included in denominator		
Equal weight for matches and nonmatches	RR	SM
Double weight for matches		SS1
Double weight for nonmatches		RT
Joint absences excluded from denominator		
Equal weight for matches and nonmatches	JACCARD	
Double weight for matches	DICE	
Double weight for nonmatches	SS2	
All matches excluded from denominator		
Equal weight for matches and nonmatches	K1	SS3

RR[(p[,np])]   *Russell and Rao similarity measure.* This is the binary dot product.

$$RR\,(x, y)\ =\ \frac{a}{a + b + c + d}$$

SM[(p[,np])]   *Simple matching similarity measure.* This is the ratio of the number of matches to the total number of characteristics.

$$SM\,(x, y)\ =\ \frac{a + d}{a + b + c + d}$$

JACCARD[(p[,np])]   *Jaccard similarity measure.* This is also known as the *similarity ratio.*

$$\text{JACCARD } (x, y) \; = \; \frac{a}{a+b+c}$$

DICE[(p[,np])]

Dice (or Czekanowski or Sorenson) similarity measure.

$$\text{DICE } (x, y) \; = \; \frac{2a}{2a+b+c}$$

SS1[(p[,np])]

Sokal and Sneath similarity measure 1.

$$\text{SS1 } (x, y) \; = \; \frac{2\,(a+d)}{2\,(a+d)+b+c}$$

RT[(p[,np])]

Rogers and Tanimoto similarity measure.

$$\text{RT } (x, y) \; = \; \frac{a+d}{a+d+2\,(b+c)}$$

SS2[(p[,np])]

Sokal and Sneath similarity measure 2.

$$\text{SS2 } (x, y) \; = \; \frac{a}{a+2\,(b+c)}$$

K1[(p[,np])]

Kulczynski similarity measure 1. This measure has a minimum value of 0 and no upper limit. It is undefined when there are no nonmatches ($b=0$ and $c=0$). PROXIMITIES assigns an artificial upper limit of 10,000 to K1 when it is undefined or exceeds this value.

$$\text{K1 } (x, y) \; = \; \frac{a}{b+c}$$

SS3[(p[,np])]

Sokal and Sneath similarity measure 3. This measure has a minimum value of 0 and no upper limit. It is undefined when there are no nonmatches ($b=0$ and $c=0$). PROXIMITIES assigns an artificial upper limit of 10,000 to SS3 when it is undefined or exceeds this value.

$$\text{SS3 } (x, y) \; = \; \frac{a+d}{b+c}$$

Conditional Probabilities. The following binary measures yield values that can be interpreted in terms of conditional probability.m All three are similarity measures.

K2[(p[,np])]

Kulczynski similarity measure 2. This yields the average conditional probability that a characteristic is present in one item given that the characteristic is present in the other item. The measure is an average over both items acting as predictors. It has a range of 0 to 1.

$$\text{K2 } (x, y) \; = \; \frac{a/\,(a+b)+a/\,(a+c)}{2}$$

SS4[(p[,np])]

Sokal and Sneath similarity measure 4. This yields the conditional probability that a characteristic of one item is in the same state (presence or absence) as the characteristic of the other item. The measure is an average over both items acting as predictors. It has a range of 0 to 1.

$$SS4\ (\dot{x}, y)\ =\ \frac{a/(a+b) + a/(a+c) + d/(b+d) + d/(c+d)}{4}$$

HAMANN[(p[,np])]   *Hamann similarity measure.* This measure gives the probability that a characteristic has the same state in both items (present in both or absent from both) minus the probability that a characteristic has different states in the two items (present in one and absent from the other). HAMANN has a range of −1 to +1 and is monotonically related to SM, SS1, and RT.

$$HAMANN\ (x, y)\ =\ \frac{(a+d) - (b+c)}{a+b+c+d}$$

Predictability Measures. The following four binary measures assess the association between items as the predictability of one given the other. All four measures yield similarities.

LAMBDA[(p[,np])]   *Goodman and Kruskal's lambda (similarity).* This coefficient assesses the predictability of the state of a characteristic on one item (present or absent) given the state on the other item. Specifically, LAMBDA measures the proportional reduction in error using one item to predict the other when the directions of prediction are of equal importance. LAMBDA has a range of 0 to 1.

$$LAMBDA\ (x, y)\ =\ \frac{t_1 - t_2}{2(a+b+c+d) - t_2}$$

where
$t_1 = \max(a,b) + \max(c,d) + \max(a,c) + \max(b,d)$
$t_2 = \max(a+c, b+d) + \max(a+d, c+d).$

D[(p[,np])]   *Anderberg's D (similarity).* This coefficient assesses the predictability of the state of a characteristic on one item (present or absent) given the state on the other. D measures the actual reduction in the error probability when one item is used to predict the other. The range of D is 0 to 1.

$$D\ (x, y)\ =\ \frac{t_1 - t_2}{2(a+b+c+d)}$$

where
$t_1 = \max(a,b) + \max(c,d) + \max(a,c) + \max(b,d)$
$t_2 = \max(a+c, b+d) + \max(a+d, c+d)$

Y[(p[,np])]   *Yule's Y coefficient of colligation (similarity).* This is a function of the cross ratio for a 2×2 table. It has a range of −1 to +1.

$$Y\ (x, y)\ =\ \frac{\sqrt{ad} - \sqrt{bc}}{\sqrt{ad} + \sqrt{bc}}$$

Q[(p[,np])]
Yule's Q *(similarity)*. This is the 2×2 version of Goodman and Kruskal's ordinal measure *gamma*. Like Yule's Y, Q is a function of the cross ratio for a 2×2 table and has a range of −1 to +1.

$$Q(x, y) = \frac{ad - bc}{ad + bc}$$

Other Binary Measures. The remaining binary measures available in PROXIMITIES are either binary equivalents of association measures for continuous variables or measures of special properties of the relationship between items.

OCHIAI[(p[,np])]
Ochiai similarity measure. This is the binary form of the cosine. It has a range of 0 to 1.

$$OCHIAI(x, y) = \sqrt{\frac{a}{a + b} \cdot \frac{a}{a + c}}$$

SS5[(p[,np])]
Sokal and Sneath similarity measure 5. The range is 0 to 1.

$$SS5(x, y) = \frac{ad}{\sqrt{(a + b)(a + c)(b + d)(c + d)}}$$

PHI[(p[,np])]
Fourfold point correlation (similarity). This is the binary form of the Pearson product-moment correlation coefficient.

$$PHI(x, y) = \frac{ad - bc}{\sqrt{(a + b)(a + c)(b + d)(c + d)}}$$

BEUCLID[(p[,np])]
Binary Euclidean distance. This is a distance measure. Its minimum value is 0, and it has no upper limit.

$$BEUCLID(x, y) = \sqrt{b + c}$$

BSEUCLID[(p[,np])]
Binary squared Euclidean distance. This is a distance measure. Its minimum value is 0, and it has no upper limit.

$$BSEUCLID(x, y) = b + c$$

SIZE[(p[,np])]
Size difference. This is a dissimilarity measure with a minimum value of 0 and no upper limit.

$$SIZE(x, y) = \frac{(b - c)^2}{(a + b + c + d)^2}$$

PATTERN[(p[,np])]
Pattern difference. This is a dissimilarity measure. The range is 0 to 1.

$$PATTERN(x, y) = \frac{bc}{(a + b + c + d)^2}$$

BSHAPE[(p[,np])]   *Binary shape difference.* This dissimilarity measure has no upper or lower limit.

$$\text{BSHAPE}\ (x, y)\ =\ \frac{(a + b + c + d)\ (b + c)\ -\ (b - c)^2}{(a + b + c + d)^2}$$

DISPER[(p[,np])]   *Dispersion similarity measure.* The range is −1 to +1.

$$\text{DISPER}\ (x, y)\ =\ \frac{ad - bc}{(a + b + c + d)^2}$$

VARIANCE[(p[,np])]   *Variance dissimilarity measure.* This measure has a minimum value of 0 and no upper limit.

$$\text{VARIANCE}\ (x, y)\ =\ \frac{b + c}{4\ (a + b + c + d)}$$

BLWMN[(p[,np])]   *Binary Lance-and-Williams nonmetric dissimilarity measure.* This measure is also known as the Bray-Curtis nonmetric coefficient. The range is 0 to 1.

$$\text{BLWMN}\ (x, y)\ =\ \frac{b + c}{2a + b + c}$$

Example

```
PROXIMITIES A B C
  /MEASURE=RR(1,2).
```

- **MEASURE** computes Russell and Rao coefficients from data in which 1 indicates the presence of a characteristic and 2 indicates the absence. Other values are ignored.

Example

```
PROXIMITIES A B C
  /MEASURE=SM(2).
```

- **MEASURE** computes simple matching coefficients from data in which 2 indicates presence and all other values indicate absence.

Transforming Measures in Proximity Matrix

Use keyword NONE to apply the ABSOLUTE, REVERSE, and/or RESCALE transformations to an existing matrix of proximity values without computing any proximity measures.

NONE   *Do not compute proximity measures.* Use NONE only if you have specified an existing proximity matrix on keyword IN on the MATRIX subcommand.

PRINT Subcommand

PROXIMITIES always prints the name of the measure it computes and the number of cases. Use PRINT to control printing of the proximity matrix.

PROXIMITIES   *Print the matrix of the proximities between items.* This is the default. The matrix may have been either read or computed. When the number of cases or variables is large, this specification produces a large volume of output and uses significant CPU time.

NONE   *Do not print the matrix of proximities.*

ID Subcommand

By default, PROXIMITIES identifies cases by case number alone. Use ID to specify an identifying string variable for cases.

- Any string variable in the working data file can be named as the identifier. PROXIMITIES uses the first eight characters of this variable to identify cases in the output.

MISSING Subcommand

MISSING controls the treatment of cases with missing values.

- By default, PROXIMITIES deletes cases with missing values listwise and excludes user-missing values from the analysis.

LISTWISE   *Delete cases with missing values listwise.* This is the default.

INCLUDE   *Include cases with user-missing values.* Only cases with system-missing values are deleted.

MATRIX Subcommand

MATRIX reads and writes SPSS matrix data files.

- Either IN or OUT and the matrix file in parentheses are required. When both IN and OUT are used on the same PROXIMITIES command, they can be specified on separate MATRIX subcommands or on the same subcommand.

OUT (filename)   *Write a matrix data file.* Specify either a filename or an asterisk, enclosed in parentheses. If you specify a filename, the file is stored on disk and can be retrieved at any time. If you specify an asterisk (*), the matrix data file replaces the working data file but is not stored on disk unless you use SAVE or XSAVE.

IN (filename)   *Read a matrix data file.* If the matrix data file is the working data file, specify an asterisk (*) in parentheses. If the matrix data file is another file, specify the filename in parentheses. A matrix file read from an external file does not replace the working data file.

Matrix Output

- PROXIMITIES writes a variety of proximity matrices, each with *ROWTYPE_* values of PROX. PROXIMITIES neither reads nor writes additional statistics with its matrix materials. See "Format of the Matrix Data File" on p. 310 for a description of the file.
- The matrices PROXIMITIES writes can be used by PROXIMITIES or other procedures. Procedures CLUSTER and ALSCAL can read a proximity matrix directly. Procedure FACTOR can read a correlation matrix written by PROXIMITIES, but RECODE must first be used to change the *ROWTYPE_* value PROX to *ROWTYPE_* value CORR. Also, the ID subcommand cannot be used on PROXIMITIES if the matrix will be used in FACTOR. For more information, see Universals in the *SPSS Base System Syntax Reference Guide.*
- If VIEW=VARIABLE, the variables in the matrix file will have the names and labels of the original variables.
- If VIEW=CASE (the default), the variables in the matrix file will be named *VAR1, VAR2, ...VARn*, where *n* is the sequential number of the variable in the new file. The numeric suffix *n* is consecutive and does not necessarily match the number of the actual case. If there are no split files, the case number appears in the variable label in the form *CASE m*. The numeric suffix *m* is the actual case number and may not be consecutive (for example, if cases were selected before PROXIMITIES was executed).
- The new file preserves the names and values of any split-file variables in effect. When split-file processing is in effect, no labels are generated for variables in the new file. The actual case number is retained by the variable *ID*.
- Any documents contained in the working data file are not transferred to the matrix file.

Matrix Input

- PROXIMITIES can read a matrix written to the working data file by a previous PROXIMITIES procedure.
- The order among rows and variables in the input matrix file is unimportant as long as values for split-file variables precede values for *ROWTYPE_*.
- PROXIMITIES ignores unrecognized *ROWTYPE_* values. In addition, it ignores variables present in the matrix file that are not specified (or used by default) on the PROXIMITIES variable list.
- SPSS reads variable names, variable and value labels, and print and write formats from the dictionary of the matrix data file.
- MATRIX=IN cannot be used unless a working data file has already been defined. To read an existing matrix data file at the beginning of a session, first use GET to retrieve the matrix file and then specify IN(*) on MATRIX.
- When you read a matrix created with MATRIX DATA, you should supply a value label for PROX of either *SIMILARITY* or *DISSIMILARITY* so the matrix is correctly identified. If you do not supply a label, PROXIMITIES assumes *DISSIMILARITY*. (See "Format of the Matrix Data File" on p. 310.)
- The variable list on PROXIMITIES can be omitted when a matrix file is used as input. When the variable list is omitted, all variables in the matrix data file are used in the anal-

ysis. If a variable list is specified, the specified variables can be a subset of the variables in the matrix file.

- With a large number of variables, the matrix data file will wrap when it is displayed (as with LIST) and will be difficult to read. Nonetheless, the matrix values are accurate and can be used as matrix input.

Format of the Matrix Data File

- The matrix data file includes two special variables created by SPSS: *ROWTYPE_* and *VARNAME_*. Variable *ROWTYPE_* is a short string variable with values PROX (for proximity measure). PROX is assigned value labels containing the distance measure used to create the matrix and either *SIMILARITY* or *DISSIMILARITY* as an identifier. Variable *VARNAME_* is a short string variable whose values are the names of the new variables.

- The matrix file includes the string variable named on the ID subcommand. This variable is used to identify cases. Up to 20 characters can be displayed for the identifier variable; longer values are truncated. The identifier variable is present only when VIEW=CASE (the default) and the ID subcommand is used.

- The remaining variables in the matrix file are the variables used to form the matrix.

Split Files

- When split-file processing is in effect, the first variables in the matrix system file are the split variables, followed by *ROWTYPE_*, the case-identifier variable (if VIEW=CASE and ID are used), *VARNAME_*, and the variables that make up the matrix.

- A full set of matrix materials is written for each split-file group defined by the split variables.

- A split variable cannot have the same name as any other variable written to the matrix data file.

- If split-file processing is in effect when a matrix is written, the same split file must be in effect when that matrix is read by any procedure.

Example

```
PROXIMITIES  V1 TO V20
  /MATRIX=OUT(DISTOUT).
```

- PROXIMITIES produces a default Euclidean distance matrix for cases using variables *V1* through *V20* and saves the matrix in the SPSS file *DISTOUT*.
- The names of the variables on the matrix file will be *VAR1, VAR2...VARn*.

Example

```
GET FILE=CRIME.
PROXIMITIES MURDER TO MOTOR
  /ID=CITY
  /MEASURE=EUCLID
  /MATRIX=OUT(PROXMTX).
```

- PROXIMITIES reads data from the SPSS data file *CRIME* and writes one set of matrix materials to file *PROXMTX*.
- The working data file is still *CRIME*. Subsequent commands are executed on this file.

Example

```
GET FILE=CRIME.
PROXIMITIES MURDER TO MOTOR
  /ID=CITY
  /MEASURE=EUCLID
  /MATRIX=OUT(*).
LIST.
```

- PROXIMITIES writes the same matrix as in the example above. However, the matrix data file replaces the working data file. The LIST command is executed on the matrix file, not on the *CRIME* file.

Example

```
GET FILE PRSNNL.
FREQUENCIES VARIABLE=AGE.

PROXIMITIES CASE1 TO CASE8
  /ID=CITY
  /MATRIX=IN(PROXMTX).
```

- This example performs a frequencies analysis on file *PRSNNL* and then uses a different file containing matrix data for PROXIMITIES.
- MATRIX=IN specifies the matrix data file *PROXMTX*. *PROXMTX* does not replace *PRSNNL* as the working data file.

Example

```
GET FILE PROXMTX.
PROXIMITIES CASE1 TO CASE8
  /ID=CITY
  /MATRIX=IN(*).
```

- This example assumes that you are starting a new session and want to read an existing matrix data file. GET retrieves the matrix file *PROXMTX*.
- MATRIX=IN specifies an asterisk because the matrix data file is the working data file. If MATRIX=IN(PROXMTX) is specified, SPSS issues an error message.
- If the GET command is omitted, SPSS issues an error message.

Example

```
GET FILE=CRIME.
PROXIMITIES MURDER TO MOTOR
  /ID=CITY
  /MATRIX=OUT(*).
PROXIMITIES
  /MATRIX=IN(*)
  /STANDARDIZE.
```

- GET retrieves the SPSS data file *CRIME*.

- The first PROXIMITIES command specifies variables for the analysis and reads data from file *CRIME*. ID specifies *CITY* as the case identifier. MATRIX writes the resulting matrix to the working data file.

- The second PROXIMITIES command uses the matrix file written by the first PROXIMITIES command as input. The asterisk indicates that the matrix file is the working data file. The variable list is omitted, indicating that all variables in the matrix are to be used.

- The slash preceding the MATRIX subcommand on the second PROXIMITIES is required. Without the slash, PROXIMITIES would attempt to interpret MATRIX as a variable name rather than as a subcommand.

Example

In this example, PROXIMITIES and FACTOR are used for a *Q*-factor analysis, in which factors account for variance shared among observations rather than among variables. Procedure FACTOR does not perform *Q*-factor analysis without some preliminary transformation such as that provided by PROXIMITIES. Because the number of cases exceeds the number of variables, the model is not of full rank and FACTOR will print a warning. This is a common occurrence when case-by-case matrices from PROXIMITIES are used as input to FACTOR.

```
* Recoding a PROXIMITIES matrix for procedure FACTOR.

GET FILE=CRIME.
PROXIMITIES    MURDER TO MOTOR
  /MEASURE=CORR
  /MATRIX=OUT(*).

RECODE ROWTYPE_ ('PROX' = 'CORR').

FACTOR MATRIX IN(COR=*).
```

- The MATRIX subcommand on PROXIMITIES writes the correlation matrix to the working data file. Because the matrix materials will be used in procedure FACTOR, the ID subcommand is not specified.

- RECODE recodes *ROWTYPE_* values PROX to CORR so procedure FACTOR can read the matrix.

- When FACTOR reads matrix materials, it reads all the variables in the file. The MATRIX subcommand on FACTOR indicates that the matrix is a correlation matrix and data are in the working data file.

QUICK CLUSTER

```
QUICK CLUSTER {varlist}
             {ALL    }

[/MISSING=[{LISTWISE**}] [INCLUDE]]
          {PAIRWISE  }
          {DEFAULT   }

[/FILE=file]

[/INITIAL=(value list)]

[/CRITERIA=[CLUSTER({2**})][NOINITIAL][MXITER({10**})]  [CONVERGE({0.02**})]]
                    {n  }                {n  }                   {n     }

[/METHOD=[{KMEANS[(NOUPDATE)]**}]
          {KMEANS(UPDATE) }    }
          {CLASSIFY       }    }

[/PRINT=[INITIAL**]  [CLUSTER]  [ID(varname)]  [DISTANCE]  [ANOVA]  [NONE]]

[/OUTFILE=file]

[/SAVE=[CLUSTER[(varname)]]  [DISTANCE[(varname)]]]
```

**Default if the subcommand is omitted.

Example:

```
QUICK CLUSTER V1 TO V4
  /CRITERIA=CLUSTER(4)
  /SAVE=CLUSTER(GROUP) .
```

Overview

When the desired number of clusters is known, QUICK CLUSTER groups cases efficiently into clusters. It is not as flexible as CLUSTER, but it uses considerably less processing time and memory, especially when the number of cases is large.

Options

Algorithm Specifications. You can specify the number of clusters to form with the CRITE-RIA subcommand. You can also use CRITERIA to control initial cluster selection and the criteria for iterating the clustering algorithm. With the METHOD subcommand you can specify how to update cluster centers, and you can request classification only when working with very large data files (see "Operations" on p. 314).

Initial Cluster Centers. By default, QUICK CLUSTER chooses the initial cluster centers. Alternatively, you can provide initial centers on the INITIAL subcommand. You can also read initial cluster centers from an SPSS data file using the FILE subcommand.

Optional Output. With the PRINT subcommand you can display the cluster membership of each case and the distance of each case from its cluster center. You can also display the distances between the final cluster centers and a univariate analysis of variance between clusters for each clustering variable.

Saving Results. You can write the final cluster centers to an SPSS data file using the OUTFILE subcommand. In addition, you can save the cluster membership of each case and the distance from each case to its classification cluster center as new variables in the working data file using the SAVE subcommand.

Basic Specification

The basic specification is a list of variables. By default, QUICK CLUSTER produces two clusters. The two cases that are farthest apart based on the values of the clustering variables are selected as initial cluster centers and the rest of the cases are assigned to the nearer center. The new cluster centers are calculated as the means of all cases in each cluster, and if neither the minimum change or the maximum iteration criterion is met, all cases are assigned to the new cluster centers again. When one of the criteria is met, iteration stops, the final cluster centers are updated, and the distance of each case is computed.

Subcommand Order

- The variable list must be specified first.
- Subcommands can be named in any order.

Operations

The procedure generally involves four steps:

- First, initial cluster centers are selected, either by choosing one case for each cluster requested or by using the specified values.
- Second, each case is assigned to the nearest cluster center and the mean of each cluster is calculated to obtain the new cluster centers.
- Third, the maximum change between the new cluster centers and the initial cluster centers is computed. If the maximum change is not less than the minimum change value and the maximum iteration number is not reached, the second step is repeated and the cluster centers are updated. The process stops when either the minimum change or maximum iteration criterion is met. The resulting clustering centers are used as classification centers in the last step.
- In the last step, all cases are assigned to the nearest classification center. The final cluster centers are updated and the distance for each case is computed.

When the number of cases is large, directly clustering all cases may be impractical. As an alternative you can cluster a sample of cases and then use the cluster solution for the sample to classify the entire group. This can be done in two phases:

- The first phase obtains a cluster solution for the sample. This involves all four steps of the QUICK CLUSTER algorithm. OUTFILE then saves the final cluster centers to an SPSS data file.

- The second phase requires only one pass through the data. First, the FILE subcommand specifies the file containing the final cluster centers from the first analysis. These final cluster centers are used as the initial cluster centers for the second analysis. CLASSIFY is specified on the METHOD subcommand to skip the second and third steps of the clustering algorithm, and cases are classified using the initial cluster centers. When all cases are assigned, the cluster centers are updated and the distance of each case is computed. This phase can be repeated until final cluster centers are stable.

Example

```
QUICK CLUSTER V1 TO V4
  /CRITERIA=CLUSTERS(4)
  /SAVE=CLUSTER(GROUP).
```

- This example clusters cases based on their values for all variables between and including *V1* and *V4* on the working data file.
- Four clusters, rather than the default two, will be formed.
- Initial cluster centers are chosen by finding four widely spaced cases. This is the default.
- The cluster membership of each case is saved in variable *GROUP* in the working data file. *GROUP* has integer values from 1 to 4, indicating the cluster to which each case belongs.

Variable List

The variable list identifies the clustering variables.
- The variable list is required and must be the first specification on QUICK CLUSTER.
- You can use keyword ALL to refer to all user-defined variables on the working data file.
- QUICK CLUSTER uses squared Euclidean distances, which equally weight all clustering variables. If the variables are measured in units that are not comparable, the procedure will give more weight to variables with large variances. Therefore, you should standardize variables measured on different scales before clustering by using procedure DESCRIPTIVES.

CRITERIA Subcommand

CRITERIA specifies the number of clusters to form, and it controls options for the clustering algorithm. You can use any or all of the keywords below.
- The NOINITIAL option followed by the remaining steps of the default QUICK CLUSTER algorithm makes QUICK CLUSTER equivalent to MacQueen's *n*-means clustering method.

CLUSTER(n)   *Number of clusters.* QUICK CLUSTER assigns cases to *n* clusters. The default is 2.

NOINITIAL   *No initial cluster center selection.* By default, initial cluster centers are formed by choosing one case (with valid data for the clustering variables) for each cluster requested. The initial selection requires a pass through the data to ensure that the centers are well separated from one another. If NOINITIAL is specified, QUICK CLUSTER selects the first *n* cases without missing values as initial cluster centers.

MXITER(n) *Maximum number of iterations for updating cluster centers.* The default is 10. Iteration stops when maximum number of iterations has been reached. MXITER is ignored when METHOD=CLASSIFY.

CONVERGE(n) *Convergence criterion controlling minimum change in cluster centers.* The default value for *n* is 0.02. The minimum change value equals the convergence value (*n*) times the minimum distance between initial centers. Iteration stops when the largest change of any cluster center is less than or equal to the minimum change value. CONVERGE is ignored when METHOD=CLASSIFY.

METHOD Subcommand

By default, QUICK CLUSTER recalculates cluster centers after assigning all the cases and repeats the process until one of the criteria is met. You can use the METHOD subcommand to recalculate cluster centers after each case is assigned or to suppress recalculation until after classification is complete.

KMEANS (NOUPDATE) *Recalculate cluster centers after all cases are assigned for each iteration.* This is the default.

KMEANS(UPDATE) *Recalculate a cluster center each time a case is assigned.* QUICK CLUSTER calculates the mean of cases currently in the cluster and uses this new cluster center in subsequent case assignment.

CLASSIFY *Do not recalculate cluster centers.* QUICK CLUSTER uses the initial cluster centers for classification and computes the final cluster centers as the means of all the cases assigned to the same cluster. When CLASSIFY is specified, the CONVERGE or MXITER specifications on CRITERIA are ignored.

INITIAL Subcommand

INITIAL specifies the initial cluster centers. Initial cluster centers can also be read from an SPSS data file (see the FILE subcommand on p. 317).

- One value for each clustering variable must be included for each cluster requested. Values are specified in parentheses cluster by cluster.

Example

```
QUICK CLUSTER  A B C D
  /CRITERIA = CLUSTER(3)
  /INITIAL = (13 24  1  8
               7 12  5  9
              10 18 17 16).
```

- This example specifies four clustering variables and requests three clusters. Thus, twelve values are supplied on INITIAL.
- The initial center of the first cluster has a value of 13 for variable *A*, 24 for variable *B*, 1 for *C*, and 8 for *D*.

FILE Subcommand

Use FILE to obtain initial cluster centers from an SPSS data file.

- The only specification is the name of the file.

Example

```
QUICK CLUSTER  A B C D
  /FILE=INIT
  /CRITERIA = CLUSTER(3).
```

- In this example, the initial cluster centers are read from file *INIT*. The file must contain cluster centers for the same four clustering variables specified (*A*, *B*, *C*, and *D*).

PRINT Subcommand

QUICK CLUSTER always displays the centers used to classify cases (classification cluster centers), the mean values of the cases in each cluster (final cluster centers), and the number of cases in each cluster. Use PRINT to request other types of output.

- If PRINT is not specified or is specified without keywords, the default is INITIAL.

INITIAL   *Initial cluster centers.* When SPLIT FILES is in effect, the initial cluster center for each split file is displayed. This is the default.

CLUSTER   *Cluster membership for each case.* Each case displays an identifying number or value, the number of the cluster to which it was assigned, and its distance from the center of that cluster. This output is extensive when the number of cases is large.

ID(varname)   *Case identification.* The value of the specified variable is used to identify cases in output. If ID is not specified, the number of each case is used as an identifier. This number may not be sequential if cases have been selected.

DISTANCE   *Pairwise distances between all final cluster centers.* This output can consume a great deal of processing time when the number of clusters requested is large.

ANOVA   *Descriptive univariate* F *tests for the clustering variables.* Since cases are systematically assigned to clusters to maximize differences on the clustering variables, these tests are descriptive only and should not be used to test the null hypothesis that there are no differences between clusters. Statistics after clustering are also available through procedure DISCRIMINANT or MANO-VA (MANOVA is available in the SPSS Advanced Statistics option).

NONE   *No additional output.* Only the default output is displayed. NONE overrides any other specifications on PRINT.

Example

```
QUICK CLUSTER A B C D E
  /CRITERIA=CLUSTERS(6)
  /PRINT=CLUSTER ID(CASEID) DISTANCE.
```

- Six clusters are formed on the basis of the five variables *A*, *B*, *C*, *D*, and *E*.
- For each case in the file, cluster membership and distance from cluster center are displayed. Cases are identified by the values of the variable *CASEID*.
- Distances between all cluster centers are printed.

OUTFILE Subcommand

OUTFILE saves the final cluster centers in an SPSS data file. You can later use these final cluster centers as initial cluster centers for a different sample of cases that use the same variables. You can also cluster the final cluster centers themselves to obtain clusters of clusters.

- The only specification is a filename for the file.

Example

```
QUICK CLUSTER A B C D
  /CRITERIA = CLUSTER(3)
  /OUTFILE = QC1.
```

- QUICK CLUSTER writes the final cluster centers to file *QC1*.

SAVE Subcommand

Use SAVE to save results of cluster analysis as new variables in the working data file.

- You can specify a variable name in parentheses following either keyword. If no variable name is specified, QUICK CLUSTER forms unique variable names by appending an underscore and a sequential number to the rootname *QCL*. The number increments with each new variable saved.
- SPSS displays a message listing each new variable and a description.

CLUSTER[(varname)]   *The cluster number of each case.* The value of the new variable is set to an integer from 1 to the number of clusters.

DISTANCE[(varname)]   *The distance of each case from its classification cluster center.*

Example

```
QUICK CLUSTER A B C D
  /CRITERIA=CLUSTERS(6)
  /SAVE=CLUSTER DISTANCE.
```

- Six clusters of cases are formed on the basis of variables *A*, *B*, *C*, and *D*.

- A new variable *QCL_1* is created and set to an integer between 1 and 6 to indicate cluster membership for each case.
- Another new variable *QCL_2* is created and set to the Euclidean distance between a case and the center of the cluster to which it is assigned.

MISSING Subcommand

MISSING controls the treatment of cases with missing values.

- LISTWISE, PAIRWISE, and DEFAULT are alternatives. However, each can be used with INCLUDE.

LISTWISE   *Delete cases with missing values listwise.* A case with a missing value for any of the clustering variables is deleted from the analysis and will not be assigned to a cluster. This is the default.

PAIRWISE   *Assign each case to the nearest cluster on the basis of the clustering variables for which the case has nonmissing values.* Only cases with missing values for *all* clustering variables are deleted.

INCLUDE   *Treat user-missing values as valid.*

DEFAULT   *Same as LISTWISE.*

RELIABILITY

```
RELIABILITY VARIABLES={varlist}
                      {ALL    }

[/SCALE(scalename)=varlist [/SCALE... ]]

[/MODEL={ALPHA         }] [/VARIABLES...]
        {SPLIT[(n)]    }
        {GUTTMAN       }
        {PARALLEL      }
        {STRICTPARALLEL}

[/STATISTICS=[DESCRIPTIVE]  [SCALE]     [{ANOVA          }] [ALL]]
             [COVARIANCES]  [TUKEY]     {ANOVA FRIEDMAN }
             [CORRELATIONS] [HOTELLING] {ANOVA COCHRAN  }

[/SUMMARY=[MEANS] [VARIANCE] [COV] [CORR] [TOTAL] [ALL]]


[/METHOD=COVARIANCE]

[/FORMAT={NOLABELS**}]
         {LABELS    }

[/MISSING={EXCLUDE**}]
          {INCLUDE  }

[/MATRIX =[IN({*   })] [OUT({*   })] [NOPRINT]]
             {file}        {file}
```

**Default if the subcommand is omitted.

Example:
```
RELIABILITY  VARIABLES=SCORE1 TO SCORE10
  /SCALE (OVERALL) = ALL
  /MODEL = ALPHA
  /SUMMARY = MEANS TOTAL.
```

Overview

RELIABILITY estimates reliability statistics for the components of multiple-item additive scales. It uses any one of five models for reliability analysis and offers a variety of statistical displays. RELIABILITY can also be used to perform a repeated measures analysis of variance, a two-way factorial analysis of variance with one observation per cell, Tukey's test for additivity, Hotelling's T-square test for equality of means in repeated measures designs, and Friedman's two-way analysis of variance on ranks. For more complex repeated measures designs, use the MANOVA procedure (available in the SPSS Advanced Statistics option).

Options

Model Type. You can specify any one of five models on the MODEL subcommand.

Statistical Display. Statistics available on the STATISTICS subcommand include descriptive statistics, correlation and covariance matrices, a repeated measures analysis of variance table, Hotelling's T-square, Tukey's test for additivity, Friedman's chi-square for the analysis of ranked data, and Cochran's Q.

Computational Method. You can force RELIABILITY to use the covariance method, even when you are not requesting any output that requires it, by using the METHOD subcommand.

Matrix Input and Output. You can read data in the form of correlation matrices and you can write correlation-type matrix materials to a data file using the MATRIX subcommand.

Basic Specification

The basic specification is VARIABLES and a variable list. By default, RELIABILITY displays the number of cases, number of items, and Cronbach's alpha. Whenever possible, it uses an algorithm that does not require the calculation of the covariance matrix.

Subcommand Order

- VARIABLES must be specified first.
- The remaining subcommands can be named in any order.

Operations

- STATISTICS and SUMMARY are cumulative. If you enter them more than once, all requested statistics are produced for each scale.
- If you request output that is not available for your model or for your data, RELIABILITY ignores the request.
- RELIABILITY uses an economical algorithm whenever possible but calculates a covariance matrix when necessary (see the METHOD subcommand on p. 324).

Limitations

- Maximum 10 VARIABLES subcommands.
- Maximum 50 SCALE subcommands.
- Maximum 500 variables on the combined VARIABLES subcommands. Each occurrence of a variable counts as 1 toward this limit.
- Maximum 500 variables on one SCALE subcommand.
- Maximum 1,000 variables on all SCALE subcommands combined. Each mention of a variable counts one toward this limit.
- If the available workspace is insufficient to handle multiple VARIABLES subcommands, RELIABILITY deletes them in the reverse order of specification until the workspace is sufficient.

Example

```
RELIABILITY  VARIABLES=SCORE1 TO SCORE10
  /SCALE (OVERALL) = ALL
  /SCALE (ODD) = SCORE1 SCORE3 SCORE5 SCORE7 SCORE9
  /SUMMARY = MEANS TOTAL.
```

- This example analyzes two additive scales.
- One scale (labeled *OVERALL* in the output) includes all ten items. Another (labeled *ODD*) includes every other item.
- Summary statistics are displayed for each scale, showing item means and the relationship of each item to the total scale.

Example

```
RELIABILITY  VARIABLES=SCORE1 TO SCORE10.
```

- This example analyzes one scale (labeled *ALL* in the display output) that includes all ten items.
- Because there is no SUMMARY subcommand, no summary statistics are displayed.

VARIABLES Subcommand

VARIABLES specifies the variables to be used in the analysis. Only numeric variables can be used.

- VARIABLES is required and must be specified first.
- You can use keyword ALL to refer to all user-defined variables in the working data file.
- You can specify VARIABLES more than once on a single RELIABILITY command. A reliability analysis is performed on each set of variables.

SCALE Subcommand

SCALE defines a scale for analysis, providing a label for the scale and specifying its component variables. If SCALE is omitted, all variables named on VARIABLES are used, and the label for the scale is *ALL*.

- The label is specified in parentheses after SCALE. It can have a maximum of eight characters and can use only the letters A to Z and the numerals 0 to 9.
- RELIABILITY does not add any new variables to the working data file. The label is used only to identify the output. If the analysis is satisfactory, use COMPUTE to create a new variable containing the sum of the component items.
- Variables named on SCALE must have been named on the previous VARIABLES subcommand. Use keyword ALL to refer to all variables named on the preceding VARIABLES subcommand.
- To analyze different groups of component variables, specify SCALE more than once following a VARIABLES subcommand.

Example

```
RELIABILITY VARIABLES = ITEM1 TO ITEM20
  /SCALE (A) = ITEM1 TO ITEM10
  /SCALE (B) = ITEM1 ITEM3 ITEM5 ITEM16 TO ITEM20
  /SCALE (C) = ALL.
```

- This command analyzes three different scales: scale A has 10 items, scale B has 8 items, and scale C has 20 items.

MODEL Subcommand

MODEL specifies the type of reliability analysis for the scale named on the preceding SCALE subcommand.

ALPHA   *Cronbach's* α. Standardized item α is displayed. This is the default.

SPLIT [(n)]   *Split-half coefficients.* You can specify a number in parentheses to indicate how many items should be in the second half. For example, MODEL SPLIT (6) uses the last six variables for the second half and all others for the first. By default, each half has an equal number of items, with the odd item, if any, going to the first half.

GUTTMAN   *Guttman's lower bounds for true reliability.*

PARALLEL   *Maximum-likelihood reliability estimate under parallel assumptions.* This model assumes that items have the same variance but not necessarily the same mean.

STRICTPARALLEL   *Maximum-likelihood reliability estimate under strictly parallel assumptions.* This model assumes that items have the same means, the same true score variances over a set of objects being measured, and the same error variance over replications.

STATISTICS Subcommand

STATISTICS displays optional statistics. There are no default statistics.

- STATISTICS is cumulative. If you enter it more than once, all requested statistics are produced for each scale.

DESCRIPTIVES *Item means and standard deviations.*

COVARIANCES *Inter-item variance-covariance matrix.*

CORRELATIONS *Inter-item correlation matrix.*

SCALE   *Scale means and scale variances.*

TUKEY   *Tukey's test for additivity.* This helps determine whether a transformation of the items is needed to reduce nonadditivity. The test displays an estimate of the power to which the items should be raised in order to be additive.

HOTELLING   *Hotelling's T-square.* This is a test for equality of means among the items.

ANOVA   *Repeated measures analysis of variance table.*

FRIEDMAN   *Friedman's chi-square and Kendall's coefficient of concordance.* These apply to ranked data. You must request ANOVA in addition to FRIEDMAN; Friedman's chi-square appears in place of the usual *F* test.

COCHRAN   *Cochran's* Q. This applies when all items are dichotomies. You must request ANOVA in addition to COCHRAN; the *Q* statistic appears in place of the usual *F* test.

ALL   *All applicable statistics.*

SUMMARY Subcommand

SUMMARY displays summary statistics for each individual item in the scale.

- SUMMARY is cumulative. If you enter it more than once, all requested statistics are produced for each scale.
- You can specify one or more of the following:

MEANS   *Statistics on item means.* The average, minimum, maximum, range, ratio of maximum to minimum, and variance of the item means.

VARIANCE   *Statistics on item variances.* This displays the same statistics as for MEANS.

COVARIANCES   *Statistics on item covariances.* This displays the same statistics as for MEANS.

CORRELATIONS   *Statistics on item correlations.* This displays the same statistics as for MEANS.

TOTAL   *Statistics comparing each individual item to the scale composed of the other items.* The output includes the scale mean, variance, and Cronbach's α without the item, and the correlation between the item and the scale without it.

ALL   *All applicable summary statistics.*

METHOD Subcommand

By default, RELIABILITY uses a computational method that does not require the calculation of a covariance matrix wherever possible. METHOD forces RELIABILITY to calculate the covariance matrix. Only a single specification applies to METHOD:

COVARIANCE   *Calculate and use the covariance matrix, even if it is not needed.*

If METHOD is not specified, RELIABILITY computes the covariance matrix for all variables on each VARIABLES subcommand only if any of the following is true:

- You specify a model other than ALPHA or SPLIT.

- You request COV, CORR, FRIEDMAN, or HOTELLING on the STATISTICS subcommand.
- You request anything other than TOTAL on the SUMMARY subcommand.
- You write the matrix to a matrix data file, using the MATRIX subcommand.

FORMAT Subcommand

FORMAT controls the initial display of variable names and labels before the analysis.

NOLABELS   *Do not display names and labels before the analysis.* This is the default.

LABELS   *Display names and labels for all items before the analysis.*

MISSING Subcommand

MISSING controls the deletion of cases with user-missing data.

- RELIABILITY deletes cases from analysis if they have a missing value for any variable named on the current VARIABLES subcommand. By default, both system-missing and user-missing values are excluded.

EXCLUDE *Exclude user- and system-missing values.* This is the default.

INCLUDE *Treat user-missing values as valid.* Only system-missing values are excluded.

MATRIX Subcommand

MATRIX reads and writes SPSS matrix data files.

- Either IN or OUT and the matrix file in parentheses are required. When both IN and OUT are used on the same RELIABILITY procedure, they can be specified on separate MATRIX subcommands or on the same subcommand.
- If both IN and OUT are used on the same RELIABILITY command and there are grouping variables, these variables are treated as if they were split variables. Values of the grouping variables in the input matrix are passed on to the output matrix (see "Split Files" on p. 326).

OUT (filename)   *Write a matrix data file.* Specify either a filename or an asterisk (*), enclosed in parentheses. If you specify a filename, the file is stored on disk and can be retrieved at any time. If you specify an asterisk, the matrix file replaces the working data file but is not stored on disk unless you use SAVE or XSAVE.

IN (filename)   *Read a matrix data file.* If the matrix data file is the working data file, specify an asterisk (*) in parentheses. If it is another file, specify the filename in parentheses. A matrix file read from an external file does not replace the working data file.

Matrix Output

- RELIABILITY writes correlation-type matrices that include the number of cases, means, and standard deviations with the matrix materials (see "Format of the Matrix Data File" below for a description of the file). These matrix materials can be used as input to RELIABILITY or other procedures.

- Any documents contained in the working data file are not transferred to the matrix file.

- RELIABILITY displays the scale analyses when it writes matrix materials. To suppress the display of scale analyses, specify keyword NOPRINT on MATRIX.

Matrix Input

- RELIABILITY can read a matrix data file created by a previous RELIABILITY command or by another SPSS procedure. The matrix input file must have records of type N, MEAN, STDDEV, and CORR for each split-file group. For more information, see Universals in the *SPSS Base System Syntax Reference Guide*.

- SPSS reads variable names, variable and value labels, and print and write formats from the dictionary of the matrix data file.

- MATRIX=IN cannot be used unless a working data file has already been defined. To read an existing matrix data file at the beginning of a session, use GET to retrieve the matrix file and then specify IN(*) on MATRIX.

Format of the Matrix Data File

- The matrix data file includes two special variables created by SPSS: *ROWTYPE_* and *VARNAME_*. Variable *ROWTYPE_* is a short string variable having values N, MEAN, STDDEV, and CORR. Variable *VARNAME_* is a short string variable whose values are the names of the variables used to form the correlation matrix.

- When *ROWTYPE_* is CORR, *VARNAME_* gives the variable associated with that row of the correlation matrix.

- The remaining variables in the matrix file are the variables used to form the correlation matrix.

Split Files

- When split-file processing is in effect, the first variables in the matrix data file will be the split variables, followed by *ROWTYPE_*, *VARNAME_*, and the dependent variable(s).

- If grouping variables are in the matrix input file, their values are between *ROWTYPE_* and *VARNAME_*. The grouping variables are treated like split-file variables.

- A full set of matrix materials is written for each split-file group defined by the split variables.

- A split variable cannot have the same variable name as any other variable written to the matrix data file.

- If split-file processing is in effect when a matrix is written, the same split file must be in effect when that matrix is read by any procedure.

Missing Values

Missing-value treatment affects the values written to a matrix data file. When reading a matrix data file, be sure to specify a missing-value treatment on RELIABILITY that is compatible with the treatment that was in effect when the matrix materials were generated.

Example

```
DATA LIST / TIME1 TO TIME5 1-10.
BEGIN DATA
 0 0 0 0 0
 0 0 1 1 0
 0 0 1 1 1
 0 1 1 1 1
 0 0 0 0 1
 0 1 0 1 1
 0 0 1 1 1
 1 0 0 1 1
 1 1 1 1 1
 1 1 1 1 1
END DATA.
RELIABILITY  VARIABLES=TIME1 TO TIME5
  /MATRIX=OUT(RELMTX).
LIST.
```

- RELIABILITY reads data from the working data file and writes one set of matrix materials to file *RELMTX*.
- The working data file is still the file defined by DATA LIST. Subsequent commands are executed on this file.

Example

```
DATA LIST  / TIME1 TO TIME5 1-10.
BEGIN DATA
 0 0 0 0 0
 0 0 1 1 0
 0 0 1 1 1
 0 1 1 1 1
 0 0 0 0 1
 0 1 0 1 1
 0 0 1 1 1
 1 0 0 1 1
 1 1 1 1 1
 1 1 1 1 1
END DATA.
RELIABILITY  VARIABLES=TIME1 TO TIME5
  /MATRIX=OUT(*) NOPRINT.
LIST.
```

- RELIABILITY writes the same matrix as in the previous example. However, the matrix data file replaces the working data file. The LIST command is executed on the matrix file, not on the file defined by DATA LIST.
- Because NOPRINT is specified on MATRIX, scale analyses are not displayed.

Example

```
GET FILE=RELMTX.
RELIABILITY VARIABLES=ALL
  /MATRIX=IN(*).
```

- This example assumes that you are starting a new session and want to read an existing matrix data file. GET retrieves the matrix data file *RELMTX*.
- MATRIX=IN specifies an asterisk because the matrix data file is the working data file. If MATRIX=IN(RELMTX) is specified, SPSS issues an error message.
- If the GET command is omitted, SPSS issues an error message.

Example

```
GET FILE=PRSNNL.
FREQUENCIES VARIABLE=AGE.

RELIABILITY VARIABLES=ALL
  /MATRIX=IN(RELMTX).
```

- This example performs a frequencies analysis on file *PRSNNL* and then uses a different file containing matrix data for RELIABILITY. The file is an existing matrix data file. In order for this to work, the analysis variables named in *RELMTX* must also exist in *PRSNNL*.
- *RELMTX* must have records of type N, MEAN, STDDEV, and CORR for each split-file group.
- *RELMTX* does not replace *PRSNNL* as the working data file.

Example

```
GET FILE=PRSNNL.
CORRELATIONS VARIABLES=V1 TO V5
  /MATRIX=OUT(*).
RELIABILITY VARIABLES=V1 TO V5
  /MATRIX=IN(*).
```

- RELIABILITY uses matrix input from procedure CORRELATIONS. An asterisk is used to specify the working file for both the matrix output from CORRELATIONS and the matrix input for RELIABILITY.

Bibliography

Anderberg, M. R. 1973. *Cluster analysis for applications*. New York: Academic Press.

Andrews, D. F., R. Gnanadesikan, and J. L. Warner. 1973. Methods for assessing multivariate normality. In *Multivariate analysis III*, ed. P. R. Krishnaiah. New York: Academic Press.

Carroll, J.D., and J.J. Chang. 1970. Analysis of individual differences in multidimensional scaling via an *n*-way generalization of "Eckart-Young" decomposition. *Psychometrika*, 35: 238–319.

Cattell, R. B. 1966. The meaning and strategic use of factor analysis. In *Handbook of multivariate experimental psychology*, ed. R. B. Cattell. Chicago: Rand McNally.

Churchill, G. A., Jr. 1979. *Marketing research: Methodological foundations*. Hinsdale, Ill.: Dryden Press.

Consumer Reports. 1983. Beer. *Consumer reports*, July, 342–348.

Everitt, B. S. 1980. *Cluster analysis*. 2nd ed. London: Heineman Educational Books Ltd.

Gilbert, E. S. 1968. On discrimination using qualitative variables. *Journal of the american statistical association*, 63: 1399–1412.

Goldstein, M., and W. R. Dillon. 1978. *Discrete discriminant analysis*. New York: John Wiley and Sons.

Green, B.F. 1979. The two kinds of linear discriminant functions and their relationship. *Journal of educational statistics*, 4:3, 247-263

Hand, D. J. 1981. *Discrimination and classification*. New York: John Wiley and Sons.

Harman, H. H. 1967. *Modern factor analysis*. 2nd ed. Chicago: University of Chicago Press.

Harman, H. H., and W. H. Jones. 1966. Factor analysis by minimizing residuals (Minres). *Psychometrika* 31: 351-368.

Johnson, R., and D. W. Wichern. 1982. *Applied multivariate statistical analysis*. Englewood Cliffs, N.J.: Prentice-Hall.

Jonassen, C. T., and S. H. Peres. 1960. *Interrelationships of dimensions of community systems*. Columbus: Ohio State University Press.

Jöreskog, K. G., and D. N. Lawley. 1968. New methods in maximum likelihood factor analysis. *British journal of mathematical and statistical psychology*, 21: 85-96.

Kaiser, H. F. 1963. Image analysis. In *Problems in measuring change*, ed. C. W. Harris. Madison: University of Wisconsin Press.

Kaiser, H. F. 1970. A second-generation Little Jiffy. *Psychometrika*, 35: 401-415.

Kaiser, H. F. 1974. An index of factorial simplicity. *Psychometrika*, 39: 31–36.

Kaiser, H. F., and J. Caffry. 1965. Alpha factor analysis. *Psychometrika*, 30: 1-14.

Kim, J. O., and C. W. Mueller. 1978. *Introduction to factor analysis*. Beverly Hills, Calif.: Sage Press.

Kruskal, J.B. 1964. Nonmetric multidimensional scaling. *Psychometrika*, 29: 1–27, 115–129.

Kshirsager, A.M., and E. Arseven. 1975. A note on the equivalency of two discrimination procedures. *The american statistician*, 29: 38-39.

Lachenbruch, P. A. 1975. *Discriminant analysis*. New York: Hafner Press.

Lord, F. M., and M. R. Novick. 1968. *Statistical theories of mental test scores*. Reading, Mass.: Addison-Wesley.

MacCallum, R.C. 1977. Effects of conditionality on INDSCAL and ALSCAL weights. *Psychometrika*, 42: 297–305.

McGee, V.C. 1968. Multidimensional scaling of n sets of similarity measures: A nonmetric individual differences approach. *Multivariate behavioral research*, 3: 233–248.

Milligan, G. W. 1980. An examination of the effect of six types of error perturbation on fifteen clustering algorithms. *Psychometrika*, 45: 325–342.

Moore, D.H. 1973. Evaluation of five discrimination procedures for binary variables. *Journal of the american statistical association*, 68: 399.

Morrison, D. F. 1967. *Multivariate statistical methods*. New York: McGraw-Hill.

Nunnally, J. 1978. *Psychometric theory*. 2nd ed. New York: McGraw-Hill.

Romesburg, H. C. 1984. *Cluster analysis for researchers*. Belmont, Calif.: Lifetime Learning Publications.

Shepard, R. N. 1962. The analysis of proximities: Multidimensional scaling with an unknown distance function, I and II. *Psychometrika*, 27: 125–140.

Sneath, P. H. A., and R. R. Sokal. 1973. *Numerical taxonomy*. San Francisco: W.H. Freeman and Co.

Stoetzel, J. 1960. A factor analysis of liquor preference of French consumers. *Journal of advertising research*, 1:1, 7–11.

Takane, Y., F. W. Young, and J. de Leeuw. 1977. Nonmetric individual differences multidimensional scaling: An alternating least squares method with optimal scaling features. *Psychometrika*, 42: 7–67.

Tatsuoka, M. M. 1971. *Multivariate analysis*. New York: John Wiley and Sons.

Torgerson, W. S. 1952. Multidimensional scaling: I. Theory and method. *Psychometrika*, 17: 401–419.

Tucker, L. R. 1971. Relations of factor score estimates to their use. *Psychometrika*, 36: 427–436.

Tucker, R. F., R. F. Koopman, and R. L. Linn. 1969. Evaluation of factor analytic research procedures by means of simulated correlation matrices. *Psychometrika*, 34: 421–459.

Van Vliet, P. K. J., and J. M. Gupta. 1973. THAM v. sodium bicarbonate in idiopathic respiratory distress syndrome. *Archives of disease in childhood*, 48: 249–255.

Wahl, P.W. and R. A. Kronmal. 1977. Discriminant functions when covariances are unequal and sample sizes are moderate. *Biometrics*, 33: 479–484.

Young, F.W. 1974. Scaling replicated conditional rank order data. In *Sociological methodology*, ed. D. Heise. American Sociological Association, 129–170.

Young, F.W. 1975. An asymmetric Euclidean model for multiprocess asymmetric data. *Proceedings of US–Japan Seminar on Multidimensional Scaling*.

Young, F.W. 1981. Quantitative analysis of qualitative data. *Psychometrika*, 40: 357-387.

Young, F.W. 1987. *Multidimensional scaling: history, theory, and applications*. Edited by R. M. Hamer. Hillside, N.J.: Lawrence Erlbaum Associates.

Young, F.W., and R.M. Hamer. 1979. *Multi-dimensional scaling: history, theory & applications*. Hillsdale, N.J.: Erlbaum.

Young, F.W., and R. Lewyckyj. 1979. *ALSCAL–4 user's guide*. Carrboro, N.C.: Data Analysis and Theory Associate.

Subject Index

Syntax Index